AMERICAN Headway

Proven success beyond the classroom

THIRD EDITION

5

Liz and John Soars
Paul Hancock

OXFORD
UNIVERSITY PRESS

Scope and Sequence   LANGUAGE INPUT

SKILLS DEVELOPMENT

Scope and Sequence LANGUAGE INPUT

SKILLS DEVELOPMENT

VIDEOS
A video to accompany each unit can be found on iTools and Online.

 1 What makes us human?
The similarities and differences between human and primate intelligence.

 2 Behind the scenes
A look at the role of the backstage team at one of the most prestigious regional theaters in the UK.

 3 Information is beautiful
A visit to the Information is Beautiful Studio, showcasing the current trend for data visualization.

 4 Eyewitness
Eyewitness behavior and the impact of forensic psychology on criminal investigation procedures.

 5 Across cultures
Reflections on migration from those who have returned home, and those who never return to their homeland.

 6 Bletchley Park
The work of Bletchley Park's Government Code and Cypher School during World War II and its lasting legacy.

 7 Graffiti life
A collective of artists who are changing lives through graffiti.

 8 Ruth Shackleton – a life less ordinary
Ruth Shackleton, team manager of the world's most famous aerobatic display team, the Red Arrows.

 9 Silent film music
World-renowned silent film accompanist, John Sweeney, talks about film music in the era of the silent film.

 10 The science of sport
A look at the importance of well-funded scientific research in creating today's sporting elite.

 11 Survival skills
The life-changing experience of wilderness survival training in a technology-driven world.

 12 The Human Genome Project
The completion of the Human Genome Project and its impact on medicine.

1 What makes us human?

Tense review • Reflexive pronouns • The ages of man • Getting emotional

VIDEO What makes us human?

STARTER

1 These questions cover some very common human situations. Which have you experienced? Discuss with a partner. Give examples from your life if you can.

2 Can you think of other situations? Share ideas with the class.

3 **CD1 2** Listen to Bridget and Mark. Where has Bridget been? Which of the situations has she experienced?

Have you ever ...?

1 felt dismayed when somebody, in response to, *Hi, how are you?*, doesn't answer, *Fine, thanks,* but actually starts to tell you about their health?

2 had a tricky conversation with someone whose name you've forgotten when they clearly know who *you* are? Should you ask their name?

3 discovered to your embarrassment that you've been walking along, talking to yourself because your friend stopped a while ago to look in a store window?

4 said that you're happy with your hair in a hair salon, despite knowing you hate it and can't wait to leave the salon and comb it out?

5 spent a meal debating with yourself whether to tell the person you're eating with that there is some food on their face?

6 felt distressed when someone who got in line after you got served before you?

7 asked someone in a supermarket where something is, only to learn that the person is another customer like yourself? Or worse, have you had the reverse happen to you?

8 wished that you'd bought some of the things in the grocery cart of the person ahead of you in line in the supermarket?

9 worried that you've been too rude to a cold caller when you've said *No, thank you* and slammed the phone down?

10 found it difficult to keep your smile and patience after a third failed attempt when someone is taking a group photograph?

11 felt awkward because after saying a long and affectionate goodbye to someone, you both set off in the same direction?

12 said, *We should get together again sometime* when you really meant *Not a chance*?

READING AND SPEAKING
What makes us human?

1 Look at the photographs. Read the introduction to the text and the ten headings. What information do you expect to find under each one? Which do you think are most important? Why? Discuss as a class.

2 Read the full article. The last phrase or sentence in each section is missing. Which one below completes them?
   a a capacity for music evolved early in our history
   b they are among the oldest visual images discovered so far
   c from telephones to toothbrushes; from cars to computers
   d each new generation would be forced to reinvent the wheel
   e developed rules for linking them into sentences
   f we do have to learn such things as reading, writing, and sharing with others
   g It gave us the works of Einstein, Mozart, and many other geniuses
   h thus contributing to bigger brains and a reduction in tooth and gut size
   i long after they themselves can have children
   j A century ago, childbirth was a leading cause of death for women

In your own words

3 Read the article again. Then work with a partner and use the prompts below to tell each other what makes us human in your own words.

   1 **Our brains** – set us apart / other animals and birds / amazing achievements
   2 **Walking upright** – other primates / hands / tools / childbirth
   3 **Long childhoods** – puzzling paradox / helpless infants / long time to grow and learn
   4 **Language** – special form of communication because … / clues as to how developed / chimpanzees / rules
   5 **Music** – not known when / functions / everywhere
   6 **Art** – why art? / when? / cave paintings
   7 **Tools and technology** – first stone tools / 2.5 million years ago / amazing variety
   8 **Learning from each other** – importance of culture / sharing ideas / past, present, future / the wheel
   9 **Life after children** – humans and animals different / role of grandparents
   10 **Clothing and fire** – not really naked / colder parts of the world / cooking

Ten things that make us human

All species on Earth, including humans, are unique. Yet our intelligence and creativity go well beyond those of any other animal. Humans have long communicated through language, created and appreciated art and music, and invented ever more complex tools that have enabled our species to survive and thrive.

We owe our creative success to the human brain and its capacity to use symbols to re-create the world mentally. This symbolic thought has also opened our minds to spirituality and a sense of empathy and morality.

Vocabulary

4 Match the words below with their synonyms highlighted in the text.

characteristic	little evidence	uses
forebears	live in	main
flourish	perplexing	ties
desire	achievements with	

What do you think?

- "Our intelligence and creativity go well beyond those of any other animal." In what ways? Why has this happened?
- Which animals have abilities closest to us? What can/can't they do?
- Give examples of instinctive and learned activities for both humans and animals.
- What is meant by "symbolic thought"? Give examples.
- Work in small groups. What else would you like to add to the list of ten things that make us human? Discuss as a class.

1 Our brains

Without doubt, the human trait that sets us apart the most from the animal kingdom is our extraordinary brain. Humans don't have the largest brains in the world – those belong to sperm whales. We don't even have the largest brains relative to body size – many birds have brains that make up more than 8 percent of their body weight, compared to only 2.5 percent for humans. Yet the human brain, which weighs about three pounds when fully grown, gives us the ability to reason and think on our feet beyond the capabilities of the rest of the animal kingdom. (1) ___ .

2 Walking upright

Humans are unique among the primates in how walking fully upright is our chief mode of locomotion. This frees our hands up for using tools. Unfortunately, it also results in changes to the pelvis which, in combination with the large brains of our babies, makes human childbirth unusually dangerous compared with the rest of the animal kingdom. (2) ___ .

3 Long childhoods

It seems a puzzling paradox that for all our brilliance, human babies come into the world so useless and helpless. However, our large heads plus our upright posture mean that a later birth would be even more difficult. Therefore, humans remain in the care of their parents for much longer than other living primates because we require a long time to grow and learn. We have more learned behaviors and skills. Flies don't have to "learn" how to fly. We don't have to "learn" how to walk and talk, but (3) ___ .

4 Language

Many species communicate with vocal sounds. But language is a special form of communication. Full language, with rules for combining sounds into words, and words into sentences, probably originated at some point about 50,000 years ago. But we will probably never know precisely when and where language originated. Fossils, DNA evidence, comparisons with other animals, and studies of how languages change over time all provide clues, but spoken language itself leaves few traces. It most likely evolved from a simpler form of communication. Chimpanzees use both gestures and vocal calls to communicate status and other complex social information. It is possible that our ancestors also expressed themselves first with gestures or simple words, and then (4) ___ .

5 Music

No one knows if music was invented before language, after language, or at the same time. Music might have served many functions for early humans. It could have been used for courtship, territorial claims, and uniting social groups, much as calls and songs are used by whales, birds, and apes. Whatever its original uses, music is now present in every human culture, implying that (5) ___ .

6 Art

We create art to communicate, depict the material world, and stir emotions. Where did this urge to create come from, and when did it strike for the first time? European cave paintings of astonishing beauty date back as far as 35,000 years, and (6) ___ .

7 Tools and technology

Life is hard to imagine without tools. We use them every day, and we have for a very long time. Our ancestors made the first stone tools at least 2.5 million years ago – long before modern humans evolved. Since then, our ability to invent has taken us far beyond our basic need for food and shelter: (7) ___ .

8 Learning from each other

Our unique brains and the dexterity of our hands make amazing feats of tool use possible, but we also rely on the cultural transmission of ideas. Culture is at the heart of being human. We put our heads together, we share ideas, and we learn from each other, recognizing a past, a present, and a future. We learn from the past, build on this in the present, and anticipate the future. Without culture, (8) ___ .

9 Life after children

Most animals reproduce until they die, but human females survive long after ceasing reproduction. This might be due to the social bonds seen in humans – grandparents can help ensure the success of their families (9) ___ .

10 Clothing and fire

Humans are sometimes called "naked apes" because we look naked compared to our hairier ape cousins. Surprisingly, however, a square inch of human skin on average possesses as many hair-producing follicles as other primates. We just have thinner, shorter, lighter hairs, and we use clothing and fire to keep warm. The development of clothing and our ability to control fire enabled humans to inhabit colder parts of the world. Fire also gave us cooking, which some scientists suggest influenced human evolution because cooked foods are easier to chew and digest, (10) ___ .

LANGUAGE FOCUS
Tense review

1 Work with a partner. What tenses are the verb forms in *italics*? Write them in the correct place in the charts. Complete any gaps in the chart with examples of your own.

1 The family of great apes *is made up of* gorillas, orangutans, chimpanzees, bonobos, and humans.
2 The largest brains *belong* to sperm whales.
3 You*'re blushing*. *Have* you *been embarrassed* by something?
4 No one knows when music *was invented*, but cave paintings *were being created* as long as 35,000 years ago.
5 This room *is being used* for a conference. The anthropologist Alice Roberts *will be giving* a talk.
6 I *haven't seen* you in a long time. What *have* you *been doing*?
7 I wish I*'d realized* that she*'d been lying* to me all along.
8 He *didn't recognize* his hometown. It *had been rebuilt* since his childhood.
9 We*'ll have been living* here three years this November.

Simple and/or continuous

2 Where possible, change the verb forms in these sentences from simple to continuous and vice versa. What is the change in meaning? Why is a change sometimes not possible?

1 What do you do?
2 I see him every Wednesday.
3 Everyone's being very nice to me. I don't know why.
4 I'll take a taxi to the airport.
5 I've cut my finger. It's really hurting.
6 Dave always gives Pam expensive presents.
7 When I stopped by to see her, she baked a cake.
8 I've been checking my emails. I've received a lot of them.
9 The train leaves in five minutes.
10 She said they'd been staying at the Ritz.
11 The winner is interviewed by CNN.

Perfect and non-perfect

3 Compare the use of tenses in these pairs of sentences.

1 Did you ever meet my grandfather?
  Have you ever met my grandfather?
2 I come from Canada.
  I've come from Canada.
3 When I've talked to him, I'll tell you.
  When I talk to him, I'll tell you.
4 The arrangements will be finalized on Friday.
  The arrangements will have been finalized by Friday.
5 I wish I knew the way.
  I wish I'd known the way.

GRAMMAR SPOT

ACTIVE	Simple	Continuous
NON-PERFECT	Simple Present **belong**	Present Continuous **are blushing**
	Simple Past	Past Continuous
	Simple Future	Future Continuous
PERFECT	Simple Present Perfect	Present Perfect Continuous
	Simple Past Perfect	Past Perfect Continuous
	Simple Future Perfect	Future Perfect Continuous

PASSIVE	Simple	Continuous
NON-PERFECT	Simple Present **is made up of**	Present Continuous
	Simple Past	Past Continuous
	Simple Future	
PERFECT	Simple Present Perfect	
	Simple Past Perfect	
	Simple Future Perfect	

▶▶ **Grammar Reference p. 141**

I've had a perfectly wonderful evening, but this wasn't it.

Active and passive

4 Correct these sentences.

1 The lecture can't give in the main hall, it's decorating.
2 A large number of tickets have bought.
3 I was thrilled to introduce to Professor Roberts.
4 The children enjoyed taking to the zoo.
5 They had warned not to frighten the animals.
6 English speaks itself here.

Reflexive pronouns

1 Look at these examples of reflexive pronouns. Why are they used?

> **GRAMMAR SPOT**
>
> He was walking along, talking to **himself**.
>
> She spent the meal debating with **herself** whether to tell him the truth.
>
> The person I asked was another customer like **myself**.
>
> We learn from **each other**.
>
> Grandmothers help their families long after they **themselves** can have children.
>
> ▶▶ Grammar Reference p. 142

2 Compare the use or absence of reflexives in these sentences.

1 My wife was talking to her.
  My wife was talking to herself.

2 She got dressed quickly and went to work.
  She's growing up fast. She can now get herself dressed.

3 I burned my finger badly.
  I burned myself badly.

4 I spoke to the senator.
  I spoke to the senator himself.
  I spoke to the senator myself.

5 They hurt themselves playing basketball.
  They hurt each other fencing.

6 Look, Mommy, I painted it all by myself.
  I choose to live by myself.

3 Why is this cartoon funny? Correct the sentence.

When the bell rang, the boxers started hitting themselves.

> **SPOKEN ENGLISH Expressions with reflexives**
>
> There are many expressions with reflexives used in everyday English.
>
> **1** Work with a partner. Match an expression in **A** with a sentence in **B**.
>
> | A | B |
> |---|---|
> | 1 He really thinks highly of himself. | a You never stop whining! |
> | 2 Honestly, just listen to yourself! | b You've been looking a little tired lately. |
> | 3 Don't put yourself down. | c Believe in yourself. |
> | 4 Take care of yourself. | d He thinks his own work on the project is the best. |
> | 5 I could kick myself. | e I didn't get her phone number. |
> | 6 Think for yourself. | f You don't have to agree with everything he says. |
> | 7 Suit yourself! | g You didn't win because you're the best. Your opponent was terrible! |
> | 8 Just be yourself. | h You never listen to my advice anyway. |
> | 9 Think of yourself sometimes. | i You're always putting others first. |
> | 10 Don't flatter yourself! | j Don't try to be something that you're not. |
>
> **2** **CD1 3** Listen and check. With your partner, think of a suitable response to each one. Compare ideas as a class.
>
> **3** **CD1 4** Listen to the conversations. Identify the situations and note all the expressions with reflexives.

▶▶ **WRITING Introducing yourself – A personal profile** *p. 103*

VOCABULARY AND LISTENING
The seven ages of man

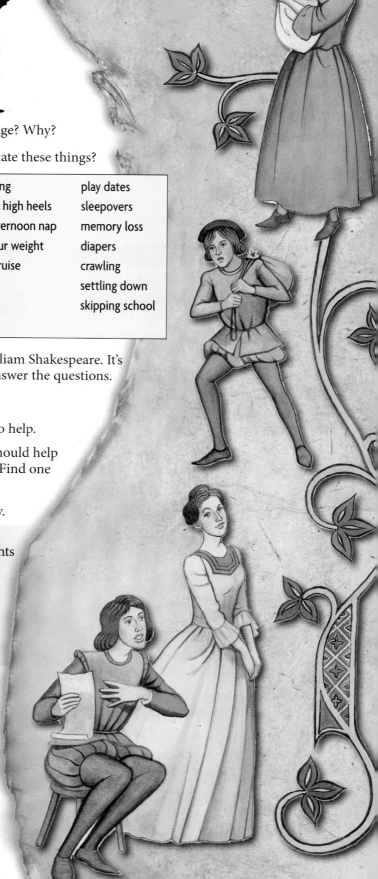

1 Are you happy with the age you are? What is your perfect age? Why?

2 Work with a partner. With which stage of life do you associate these things?

scraping your knee	aches and pains	going clubbing	play dates
getting a mortgage	coloring with crayons	teetering on high heels	sleepovers
riding in a carriage	sleeping in late	taking an afternoon nap	memory loss
Internet dating	getting divorced	watching your weight	diapers
getting promoted	having a tantrum	going on a cruise	crawling
wearing sensible shoes	having a pot belly	insomnia	settling down
needing reading glasses	going gray/bald	a book bag	skipping school
working out	cramming for a test		

3 This is a famous speech from the play *As You Like It* by William Shakespeare. It's known as *The Seven Ages of Man*. Read the first part and answer the questions.

  1 What metaphor is used to describe the world?
  2 Explain the words *players*, *exits* and *entrances*, and *parts*.
  3 What do you think the seven ages are? Use the pictures to help.

4 **CD1 5** Read and listen to the whole extract. The glossary should help with unfamiliar words. What are Shakespeare's seven ages? Find one thing that goes with each age.

5 Read again. Each of the seven people is described negatively.

Who …?
1 would die just to be famous and likes to swear and pick fights
2 writes rather ridiculous and mournful poetry
3 is rather portly and full of boring advice
4 is sulky and complaining
5 has lost weight and needs to get new clothes
6 is loud and smelly
7 isn't aware of anything very much

What do you think?

• In what ways are Shakespeare's descriptions of people true today? Give some modern examples of negative behavior for each age.
• What could you say to describe each age more positively?

Listening

6 **CD1 6** Listen to some people. What age do you think they are? Are they positive or negative about their lives? In what ways?

The Seven Ages of Man
by William Shakespeare

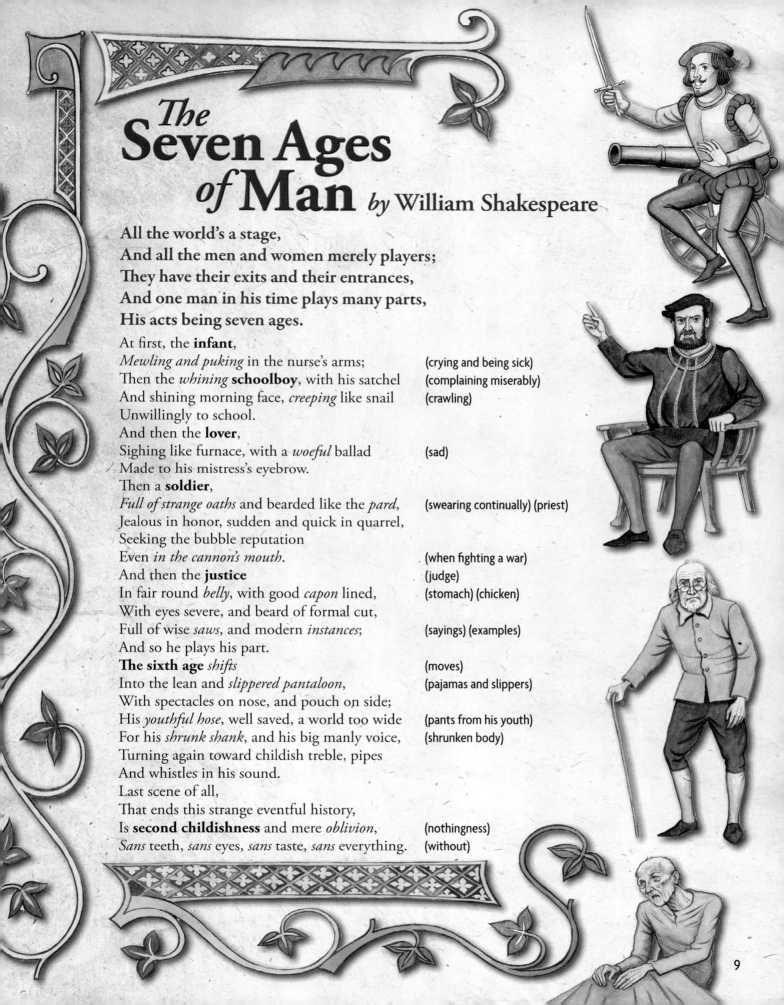

All the world's a stage,
And all the men and women merely players;
They have their exits and their entrances,
And one man in his time plays many parts,
His acts being seven ages.

At first, the **infant**,
Mewling and puking in the nurse's arms;   (crying and being sick)
Then the *whining* **schoolboy**, with his satchel   (complaining miserably)
And shining morning face, *creeping* like snail   (crawling)
Unwillingly to school.
And then the **lover**,
Sighing like furnace, with a *woeful* ballad   (sad)
Made to his mistress's eyebrow.
Then a **soldier**,
Full of strange oaths and bearded like the *pard*,   (swearing continually) (priest)
Jealous in honor, sudden and quick in quarrel,
Seeking the bubble reputation
Even *in the cannon's mouth*.   (when fighting a war)
And then the **justice**   (judge)
In fair round *belly*, with good *capon* lined,   (stomach) (chicken)
With eyes severe, and beard of formal cut,
Full of wise *saws*, and modern *instances*;   (sayings) (examples)
And so he plays his part.
The sixth age *shifts*   (moves)
Into the lean and *slippered pantaloon*,   (pajamas and slippers)
With spectacles on nose, and pouch on side;
His *youthful hose*, well saved, a world too wide   (pants from his youth)
For his *shrunk shank*, and his big manly voice,   (shrunken body)
Turning again toward childish treble, pipes
And whistles in his sound.
Last scene of all,
That ends this strange eventful history,
Is **second childishness** and mere *oblivion*,   (nothingness)
Sans teeth, *sans* eyes, *sans* taste, *sans* everything.   (without)

THE LAST WORD

We all get emotional!

1 **CD1 7** Read and listen to the statements. Discuss with a partner. Who could be speaking? What might the situation be? Share ideas as a class.

1 I'm absolutely heartbroken. They were winning 2–0 at halftime, and then they went on to lose 3–2!

2 You mean the world to me. More than words could ever say.

3 Wow! I'm completely blown away! I've never gotten such an expensive present.

4 I'll have to consult my calendar. Life's just so hectic right now – I'm always so busy.

5 Come on, you can tell me. I'm dying to know. I won't breathe a word to anyone.

6 Could you *not* keep picking on me in front of your friends? It looks so awful.

7 Oh, yeah? So you run the company now after just a week on the job? Tell me another one!

8 Thank goodness you're here! When we couldn't get through to you, we thought you'd had an accident.

9 He came in the top 2 percent in the country, so his father and I are thrilled to pieces.

10 It was nothing, really. Anybody would have done the same.

11 Well, I think you did very well to come in third. Keep up the good work, and you'll win next time.

12 Oh, come on now. Don't make such a fuss. You'll be fine. It's only a scrape. It's hardly bleeding at all.

13 I'm out of here right now! I don't like the looks of those people standing on the corner.

14 What do you mean I'm a couch potato? I go to the gym twice a week.

15 I totally lost it with that poor guy, but it was the sixth call today. How do they get our numbers?

2 Try to figure out the meaning of the highlighted words and phrases from the contexts.

3 Which of these emotions are expressed by the statements in exercise 1? Sometimes more than one is suitable.

adoration	anxiety	pride	boastfulness	curiosity	disappointment
encouragement	fear	fury	gratitude	indignation	sarcasm
irritation	relief	modesty	astonishment	reassurance	delight

4 **CD1 7** Say the statements to your partner according to the emotion. Listen again and compare the stress and intonation.

5 **CD1 8** Listen to people saying the sentence *"Oh, look at that!"* in several different ways. Try to identify the emotion. What could the contexts be?

Oxford Online Skills Program
Log in for additional online learning

2 In so many words

Adverbs and adjectives • Expressions with *word* • Breaking the rules of English

▶ VIDEO Behind the scenes

1 Work with a partner. What have you read recently? What is your favorite type of book?

2 Read the opening lines of seven different books. Match them to their literary genres and their covers. What helped you identify them?

a horror story	a children's book	a biography	a modern romance
a classic romantic novel	a psychological thriller	a historical novel	*(Also known as "chick lit" — literature for "chicks"/modern young women.)*

3 Choose two of the extracts. What could the next line be? Share ideas with the class.

4 Which, if any, of these books would you like to continue reading? Have you read any books in English? Which ones? Discuss reasons for doing this.

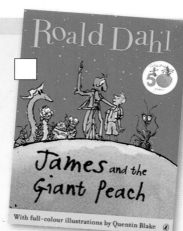

⌐ Opening lines ⌐

(1) She was born with a sense of theater, of carefully choreographed exits and entrances, an eagerly awaited baby, who arrived an improbable six weeks late in Southampton Hospital, Long Island, on July 28, 1929.

(2) Until he was four years old, James Henry Trotter had a happy life. He lived peacefully with his mother and father in a beautiful house beside the sea.

(3) Norman Bates heard the noise and a shock went through him. It sounded as though somebody was tapping on the windowpane.

(4) It is a truth universally acknowledged that a single man in possession of a good fortune must be in want of a wife.

(5) The bedroom is strange. Unfamiliar. I don't know where I am, how I came to be here. I don't know how I'm going to get home.

(6) I could hear a roll of muffled drums. But I could see nothing but the lacing on the bodice of the lady standing in front of me, blocking my view of the scaffold.

(7) I wish I were thin. I wish I were thin, gorgeous, and could get any man I want. You probably think I'm crazy. I mean here I am, sitting at work on my own with a massive double-decker club sandwich, but I'm allowed to dream, aren't I?

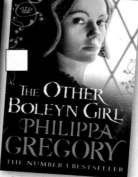

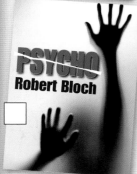

11

READING AND LISTENING
Pygmalion

1 **CD1 10** Read a short biography of George Bernard Shaw, a famous 20th-century playwright. Listen and correct the nine mistakes in it.

George Bernard Shaw (1856–1950) was an English playwright. He won the Nobel Prize in Literature in 1935. Shaw's instincts were to refuse this honor, but his editor persuaded him to accept it as a tribute to his publisher. He also won an Academy Award in 1939 for the movie version of his play *The Apple Cart*. He is one of only two writers to win both awards. He wrote over 60 plays, but *Pygmalion* is probably his most famous work because, in 1946, he adapted it into the highly successful musical for stage and screen, *My Fair Lady*. He died at the age of 94 after falling down the stairs.

2 Read about the **setting** and **characters** for **Act II** of *Pygmalion*. What job does each character have? Why would Higgins want to transcribe the speech of a flower girl? What is a "Cockney"?

ACT II SETTING	CHARACTERS
Higgins's house in London. In Act I, the night before, he had been transcribing the speech of a Cockney flower girl that he and Pickering had heard in Covent Garden. Now they are in Higgins's laboratory talking about phonetics.	**Professor Higgins** *A professor of phonology* **Colonel Pickering** *Higgins's friend, a language expert* **Mrs. Pearce** *Higgins's housekeeper* **Eliza Doolittle** *A Cockney flower girl*

3 **CD1 11** Read and listen to the opening scene from **Act II**. Answer the questions.

1 Why was Pickering so impressed by Professor Higgins?
2 Why didn't Mrs. Pearce send the young girl away?
3 What does she describe as "something dreadful"?
4 Why does Higgins agree to see the girl?
5 Why is Eliza confident that she's not asking for a favor?
6 How has she figured out how much to pay him?
7 "I shall make a duchess of this draggletailed guttersnipe." What is Higgins planning to do?
8 Which of these adjectives do you think describe Professor Higgins? Which describe Eliza? Which describe both/neither?

arrogant	condescending	apprehensive	haughty
underprivileged	articulate	cocky	straightforward
naive	humble	self-confident	compassionate
self-satisfied	bullying	heartless	insensitive

4 **CD1 12** Listen only to a later scene in **Act II**. Eliza is having a lesson. What is the difference between Higgins's and Colonel Pickering's approaches to teaching Eliza? You can draw on the adjectives in exercise 3.

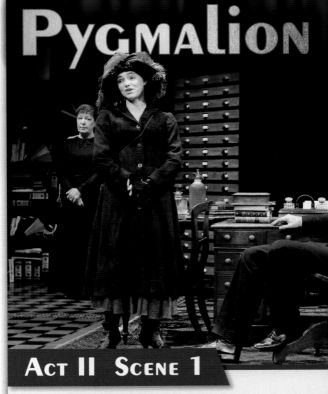

PYGMALION

ACT II SCENE 1

Higgins Well, I think that's the whole show.
Pickering It's really amazing. I haven't taken half of it in, you know.
Higgins Would you like to go over any of it again?
Pickering No, thank you; not now.
Higgins Tired of listening to sounds?
Pickering Yes, it's a fearful strain. I rather fancied myself because I can pronounce 24 distinct vowel sounds; but your 130 beat me. I can't hear a bit of difference between most of them.
Higgins Oh that comes with practice.

[Mrs. Pearce enters.]

What's the matter?
Mrs. Pearce A young woman wants to see you, sir.
Higgins A young woman! What does she want?
Mrs. Pearce Well, sir, she says you'll be glad to see her when you know what she's come about. She's quite a common girl, sir. Very common indeed. I should have sent her away, only I thought perhaps you wanted her to talk into your machines.
Higgins Oh, that's all right, Mrs. Pearce. Has she an interesting accent?
Mrs. Pearce Oh, something dreadful, sir, really, I don't know how you can take an interest in it.
Higgins Let's have her up. Show her up, Mrs. Pearce.
Mrs. Pearce Very well, sir. It's not for me to say.
Higgins This is rather a bit of luck. *[to Pickering]* I'll show you how I make records. We'll set her talking and then we'll get her onto the phonograph so that you can turn her on as often as you like with the written transcript before you.
Mrs. Pearce This is the young woman, sir.
Higgins Why, this is the girl I jotted down last night. She's no use. Be off with you. I don't want you.

Act III

Liza Don't you be so saucy! You ain't heard what I come for yet. Oh, we are proud! He ain't above giving lessons, not him: I heard him say so. Well, I ain't come here to ask for any compliment; and if my money's not good enough, I can go elsewhere. I'm come to have lessons, I am. And to pay for 'em, too: make no mistake.

Higgins WELL!

Pickering What is it you want, my girl?

Liza I want to be a lady in a flower shop, but they won't take me unless I can talk more genteel. He said he could teach me. Well, here I am ready to pay him – not asking any favor – and he treats me as if I was dirt.

Higgins What's your name?

Liza Eliza Doolittle.

Higgins How much do you propose to pay me for the lessons?

Liza Oh, I know what's right. A lady friend of mine gets French lessons for 18 pence an hour from a real French gentleman. Well, you wouldn't have the face to ask me the same for teaching me my own language as you would for French; so I won't give more than a shilling. Take it or leave it.

Higgins It's almost irresistible. She's so deliciously low – so horribly dirty.

Liza Ah-ah-ah-ah-ow-ow-ooo! I ain't dirty: I washed my face and hands afore I come, I did.

Pickering You're certainly not going to turn her head with flattery, Higgins.

Higgins I shall make a duchess of this draggletailed guttersnipe.

Liza Ah-ah-ah-ah-ow-ow-ooo!

Higgins Yes, in six months – in three if she has a good ear and a quick tongue – I'll take her anywhere and pass her off as anything. We'll start today: now! This moment! Take her away and clean her, Mrs. Pearce.

5 Read the **introduction** and list of **characters** in **Act III**. What do you think happens?

ACT III INTRODUCTION	CHARACTERS
In Act III, Higgins decides that Eliza is ready to make a first entry into society. She is dressed beautifully and taken to a tea party at his mother's house. Unfortunately, Eliza has only practiced pronunciation and has no idea what constitutes polite conversation.	**Mrs. Higgins** *Professor Higgins's kind and wise mother* **Mrs. Eynsford-Hill** *a high-society friend of Mrs. Higgins* **Freddy** *her impressionable, handsome son in his early 20s* **Clara** *her daughter* **Professor Higgins** **Colonel Pickering** **Eliza Doolittle**

6 **CD1 13** Listen to a scene from **Act III**. Answer the questions.

1 Who is impressed with Eliza?
2 What are her topics of conversation?
3 Why does her final comment shock everyone?

7 Work with a partner. Read what Eliza says about her aunt's health. Reword it in standard English.

> My aunt died of influenza: so they said. But it's my belief they done the old woman in. Lord love you! Why should she die of influenza? She come through diphtheria right enough the year before. Fairly blue with it, she was. They all thought she was dead; but my father, he kept ladling gin down her throat 'til she came to so sudden that she bit the bowl off the spoon.
>
> What call would a woman with that strength in her have to die of influenza? What become of her new straw hat that should have come to me? Somebody pinched it; and what I say is, them as pinched it done her in. Them she lived with would have killed her for a hatpin, let alone a hat.
>
> Here! What are you sniggering at?

What do you think?

- In Greek mythology, Pygmalion was a king who fell in love with a statue he had sculpted and brought to life with his prayers. Explain the connection with Shaw's play.
- How does the play end? Turn to page 168 and see if you were right.

VOCABULARY

Phrasal verbs

How are the sentences below expressed in the play? Which phrasal verbs are used?

1 I haven't *understood* the half of it.
2 Would you like to *examine* any of it again?
3 This is the girl I *made a note of* last night.
4 She *survived* diphtheria easily enough.
5 She *regained consciousness* so suddenly.
6 It's my belief they *killed* her.

LANGUAGE FOCUS
Adverbs and adjectives

Adverb collocations

> **GRAMMAR SPOT**
>
> Adverbs often go with certain verbs and adjectives.
> Look at these examples.
>
> | **verb + adverb** | **adverb + adjective** |
> |---|---|
> | speak **clearly** | **highly** successful |
> | move **slowly** | **horribly** dirty |
> | protest **vehemently** | **awfully** funny |
>
> ▶▶ **Grammar Reference pp. 142–143**

1 Complete the sentences with an adverb in the box.

severely	sorely	blindingly	eagerly	bitterly	desperately
highly	virtually	distinctly	shabbily	perfectly	fatally

1 Poor Eliza was _____ **dressed** in a tattered old coat and hat.
2 The return of the actor Bradley Cooper to the New York stage is _____ **awaited**.
3 She was _____ **disappointed** when she didn't get the part.
4 I work with a _____ **motivated** sales team. We all work hard.
5 It's _____ **impossible** to get seats for a Yankees game.
6 I _____ **need** a vacation. I haven't had a break for three years.
7 Bad weather has _____ **affected** the roads this weekend. Driving conditions are treacherous.
8 Don't you get it? It's _____ **obvious** that he's in love with you.
9 I hate this cold climate. I'm _____ **tempted** to move south.
10 I _____ **remember** telling you not to call me after ten o'clock.
11 Two people survived the crash with serious injuries, but unfortunately one man was _____ **injured**.
12 I've made my views on the subject of politicians _____ **clear**. I don't trust any of them.

CD1 14 Listen and check.

2 Match the verbs and adverbs. Then make sentences using the collocations.

> *She screamed hysterically when she saw the spider.*

VERBS	ADVERBS
~~scream~~	passionately
care	~~hysterically~~
work	profusely
break something	conscientiously
gaze	longingly
apologize	deliberately

Adverbs with two forms

> **GRAMMAR SPOT**
>
> Some adverbs have two forms, one with and one without -ly.
>
> | aiming **high** | **highly** successful |
> |---|---|
> | doing **fine** | **finely** chopped onions |
>
> ▶▶ **Grammar Reference p. 143**

3 Complete the sentences with the correct form of the adverb.

1 **hard / hardly**
   We all worked extremely _____.
   Some countries can _____ feed their own people.

2 **easy / easily**
   She hiked up the mountain _____.
   Relax! Take it _____!

3 **late / lately**
   I hate it when people arrive _____.
   What have you been doing _____?

4 **sure / surely**
   "Can you lend me some money?"
   "_____."
   _____ you can see that your plan just wouldn't work?

5 **wrong / wrongly**
   He was _____ accused of being a spy.
   At first everything was great, but then it all went _____.

6 **most / mostly**
   What do you like _____ about him?
   She worked wherever she could, _____ as a waitress.

7 **wide / widely**
   She has traveled _____ in Europe and the Far East.
   When I got to their house, the door was _____ open.

Adjective order

4 When several adjectives go before a noun, there is usually a more natural-sounding order.
Work with a partner. Write the adjectives in these sentences into the chart.

1 He was an arrogant, middle-aged English professor.
2 He lived in an imposing, four-story, modern row house.
3 He wore a beautiful, antique, Swiss, gold watch.
4 It was a huge, white, L-shaped living room.

Quality

Subjective evaluation	Size	Age	Color	Shape	Nationality	Material	Compound	Noun
								professor
								house
								watch
								room

5 Put the adjectives in parentheses into a natural-sounding order.

1 I had some bread for breakfast. (brown, whole-grain, delicious)
2 Thieves stole a painting. (Impressionist, priceless, 19th-century)
3 She was wearing some jeans. (white, cropped, divine, designer)
4 I like my Honda. (second-hand, old, little)
5 We went on a walk. (coastal, six-mile, exhausting)
6 He wears cologne. (cheap, French, revolting, smelly)
7 She's written a novel. (new, great, historical)
8 They bought a TV. (HD, massive, amazing)

CD1 15 Listen and compare. What are the contexts for the short conversations?

"Chick lit"

6 Read the opening of a modern romantic novel. Which adverbs or adjectives in **bold** are possible?

7 **CD1 16** Listen and compare. What is it about this extract that signifies it is "chick lit"? What is your opinion of this type of book?

Jemima J by Jane Green

From the bestselling author of **Life Swap**

Jemima J. **JANE GREEN**

'The kind of novel you'll gobble up at a single sitting' *Cosmopolitan*

I wish I were thin. I wish I were thin, gorgeous, and could get any man I want. You probably think I'm crazy, I mean here I am, sitting at work on my own with a massive double-decker club sandwich in front of me, but I'm allowed to dream, aren't I?

Half an hour to go of my lunch break. I finish my sandwich and look ¹**cautiously/furtively/privately** around the office to see whether anyone is looking. It's OK, the coast is ²**clear/fair**, so I can pull open my top drawer and sneak out the slab of chocolate.

Another day in my ³**humdrum/docile/dreary** life, but it shouldn't be ⁴**humdrum/docile/dreary**. I'm a journalist, for goodness sake. Surely that's a(n) ⁵**stunning/glamorous/exciting** existence. I love the English language, playing with words, but ⁶**alas/miserably/sadly** my talents are wasted here at the *Kilburn Herald*. I hate this job. When I meet new people and they ask what I do for a living, I hold my head up ⁷**tall/high/highly** and say, "I'm a journalist." I then try to change the subject, for the ⁸**inevitable/necessary** question after that is, "Who do

you work for?" I hang my head ⁹**lowly/low**, mumble the *Kilburn Herald*, and confess that I do the *Top Tips* column. Every week I'm flooded with mail from sad and ¹⁰**alone/lonely/derelict** people in Kilburn with nothing better to do than write in with questions like, "What's the best way to bleach a white marbled linoleum floor?" and "I have a pair of silver candlesticks. The silver is now ¹¹**tarnished/faded**, any suggestions?" And every week I sit for hours on the phone, calling linoleum manufacturers, silver-makers, and ask them for the answers. This is my form of journalism.

Ben Williams is the deputy news editor. ¹²**Tall/High** and handsome, he is also the office Lothario. Ben Williams is ¹³**secretly/slyly** sought after by every woman at the *Kilburn Herald*, not to mention the woman in the sandwich bar who follows his stride ¹⁴**thoughtfully/longingly** as he walks past every lunchtime. Ben Williams is gorgeous. His ¹⁵**fair/light** brown hair is ¹⁶**carelessly/casually/awkwardly** hanging over his left eye, his eyebrows ¹⁷**perfectly/utterly** arched, his dimples, when he smiles, in ¹⁸**exactly/accurately** the right place. He is the perfect combination of handsome hunk and ¹⁹**vulnerable/thin/helpless** little boy.

VOCABULARY AND DICTIONARIES
Just say the word!

Read the dictionary entry giving information about the word *word*. Answer the questions about it with a partner.

Oxford Advanced American Dictionary for learners of English

> **word** /wərd/ • *noun, verb, exclamation*
> ➤ **UNIT OF LANGUAGE 1** [C] a single unit of language that means something and can be spoken or written: *Do not write more than 200 words.* ◇ *Tell me what happened **in your own words**.* ➲ SEE ALSO BUZZWORD, FOUR-LETTER WORD, SWEAR WORD
> ➤ **SOMETHING YOU SAY 2** [C] a thing that you say; a remark or statement: *Could I have **a quick word with you** (= speak to you quickly)?* ◇ *She left **without a word** (= without saying anything).* ◇ *Remember—**not a word to** (= don't tell) Peter about any of this.*
> ➤ **PROMISE 3** [sing.] a promise or guarantee that you will do something or that something will happen or is true: *I **give you my word** that this won't happen again.* ◇ *to **keep your word** (= do what you promised)* ◇ *I can't prove it—you'll have to **take my word for it** (= believe me).*
> ➤ **INFORMATION/NEWS 4** [sing.] a piece of information or news: *She **sent word** that she would be late.* ◇ ***Word has it that** she's leaving.* ◇ *He likes to **spread the word** about the importance of healthy eating.*
> **IDM** **by word of mouth** because people tell each other and not because they read about it: *The news spread by word of mouth.* **(right) from the word go** (*informal*) from the very beginning **(not) get a word in edgewise** (*not*) to be able to say anything because someone else is speaking too much: *When Mary starts talking, no one else can get a word in edgewise.* **in other words** used to introduce an explanation of something: *They asked him to leave—in other words he was fired.* **the last/final word (on sth)** the last comment or decision about something: *He always has to have the last word in any argument.* **not to have a good word to say for sb/sth** (*informal*) to never say anything good about someone or something: *Nobody had a good word to say about him.* **put in a (good) word for sb** to praise someone to someone else in order to help them get a job, etc. **say/give the word** to give an order or make a request: *Just say the word, and I'll go.* **too funny, silly, ridiculous, etc. for words** extremely funny, silly, ridiculous, etc. **word for word** in exactly the same words or (when translated) exactly equivalent words: *She repeated their conversation word for word to me.* ◇ *a word-for-word translation*

1 What do the expressions in **1** after "➲ SEE ALSO …" mean? How can you find out?

2 Which is more casual and informal?

   Can I talk to you?   Can I have a word with you?

3 Why do **3** and **4** have "[sing.]" after them? What does it mean?

4 Which use of the word *word* – **1**, **2**, **3**, or **4** – are these sentences?

   a We only have **his word** that he didn't do it.
   b What's the Spanish **word** for *table*?
   c He's a man of **few words**.
   d If **word gets out** about the affair, he'll have to resign.

5 What does "**IDM**" mean? Reword the sentences below with an expression from the dictionary.

   a I knew I loved him **from the very beginning**.
   b I think the best way for a book to become successful is **when people tell each other about it**.
   c Your ideas are always **extremely stupid**.
   d She doesn't like her boss. She never **says anything nice about her**.
   e Just **tell me** and I'll be there to help you.
   f I really like your sister. Can you **tell her I'm a good guy**?

He had to eat his words.

There are many expressions using the word *word*. Complete these examples with a word from the box. Some of them are in the dictionary entry.

| breathe | last | few | buzz | edgewise |
| meaning | loss | funny | eat | mince |

1 We couldn't help laughing. It was **too _____** for words.
2 He may be **a man of _____ words**, but I think he's worth listening to.
3 Pam just rambles on and on about herself. You can't get **a word in _____**.
4 What? Trust you again? You're kidding. You don't know the **_____ of the word**.
5 I got the latest Apple iPad Air. It's **the _____ word** in tablets. I love it.
6 That's so kind of you. I'm at a **_____ for words**. I can't thank you enough.
7 Well! **Not to _____ words**, but I don't think you stand a chance of getting that job.
8 You said I had no chance. Well, you'll have to **_____ your words**! I got the job!
9 I think "selfie" is the latest **_____ word**. It's even in the *Oxford English Dictionary* now.
10 This is just between you and me. Don't **_____ a word** to anyone else.

CD1 17 Listen and check. What are the extra sentences in the conversations? Practice them with your partner.

SPEAKING

Creating a horror story

1 Work in small groups. Have you ever seen any horror movies or read any horror stories? Tell the others about them. Do you like or hate them?

2 Using your own ideas and any of the "ingredients" below, devise a horror story. Figure out a plot and appoint someone to take notes on your ideas. Aim for a dramatic end.

In your own words

3 Tell your story to the class. Whose is the most interesting and scary?

4 Using the same headings, change the "ingredients" to create a romantic novel. Share your ideas.

Period
- when there's a new moon
- the Middle Ages
- the 19th century
- the year 2099
- now
- when the clock struck 13

Characters
- psychic child
- a mad scientist
- ghostly figures
- hitchhiker
- giant rats, spiders, birds, bats
- identical twins

Location
- a medieval castle
- an abandoned factory
- a dark forest
- a graveyard
- a distant planet
- an uninhabited island

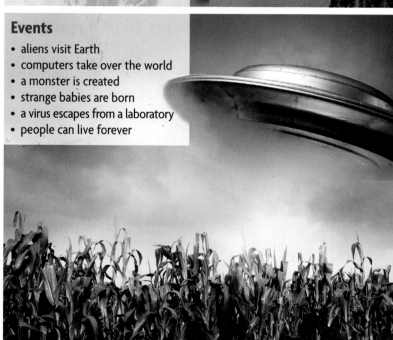

Events
- aliens visit Earth
- computers take over the world
- a monster is created
- strange babies are born
- a virus escapes from a laboratory
- people can live forever

▶▶ **WRITING Narrative writing – Different genres** *pp. 104–105*

THE LAST WORD
Breaking the rules of English

1 Read the two quotations on the subject of English grammar rules. What point is being made by both writers?

2 Work with a partner. There are some "rules" in English that linguistic pedants insist should be taught to children. Read these tips and say how the "rule" in each one is broken. Correct them pedantically where possible.

> Ending a sentence with a preposition is something up with which I will not put.
> *Winston Churchill*

> There is a busybody on your staff who devotes a lot of his time to chasing split infinitives. Every good literary craftsman splits his infinitives when the sense demands it. I call for the immediate dismissal of this pedant. It is of no consequence whether he decides "to go quickly" or "quickly to go" or "to quickly go." The important thing is that he should go at once.
>
> *George Bernard Shaw in a letter to* The Times *newspaper.*

20 tips for *proper* English ❧

1 A preposition is a terrible word to end a sentence with. Never do it.

2 Remember to never split an infinitive.

3 Don't use no double negatives.

4 Don't ever use contractions.

5 And never start a sentence with a conjunction.

6 Write *i* before *e* except after *c*. I'm relieved to receive this anciently weird rule.

7 Foreign words and phrases are not *chic*.

8 The passive voice is to be avoided wherever possible.

9 Who needs rhetorical questions?

10 Reserve the apostrophe for it's proper use and omit it when its not necessary.

11 Use *fewer* with number and *less* with quantity. Less and less people do.

12 Proofread carefully to see if you any words out.

13 Me and John are careful to use subject pronouns correctly.

14 Verbs has to agree with their subjects.

15 You've done good to use adverbs correctly.

16 If any word is incorrect at the end of a sentence, an auxiliary verb is.

17 Steer clear of incorrect verb forms that have creeped into the language.

18 Take the bull by the hand and avoid mixing your idioms.

19 Tell the rule about *whom* to who you like.

20 At the end of the day, avoid clichés like the plague.

I'm sorry, but shouldn't there be an apostrophe in that?

3 Which rules above do you think are "good" rules? Why?

4 Are there any other rules in the English language that you think are unnecessary or silly? How about in your own language?

3 Enough is enough?

Verb patterns • Describing trends • Phrasal verbs with *up* and *down* • Workplace jargon

VIDEO Information is beautiful

1 Which global problem does the picture illust...

2 Take the quiz in pairs. You may need to guess... paints an excessively negative
Discuss them as a class. ...so, why?

3 **CD1 18** Listen to the answers. Which ones sur... appier despite increased wealth?
What other facts did you learn? ...in your country on the issues in

*Also do
reporting
verbs &
patterns
(see my clock)*

Quiz W...

1 In 2000 there were two billion children (0–14...
the world. What number is estimated for 2100?
a 1 billion b 2 billion c 3 billion d 4 billion

2 50 years ago, 1 in 5 children died by the age of
five. Now it's …
a 1 in 10. b 1 in 15. c 1 in 20. d 1 in 25.

3 What is life expectancy in the world as a whole?
a 50 years b 60 years c 70 years d 80 years

4 What is the global adult literacy rate?
a 20% b 40% c 60% d 80%

5 In the last 30 years, the proportion of the world's
population living in extreme poverty has …
a increased significantly. c remained the same.
b increased slightly. d decreased.

6 Americans' median family incomes have
increased by 85% since 1957. Their assessment
of their own happiness has …
a increased by 20%. c remained the same.
b increased by 50%. d decreased by 5%.

7 Between 2000 and 2012, the global average
amount of debt per adult increased by …
a 25%. b 35%. c 45%. d 55%.

8 The richest 10% in the world owns … of
global wealth.
a 58% b 69% c 78% d 86%

LISTENING AND SPEAKING
Limits to growth

1 Work in pairs. Discuss the questions.

1 What is *economic growth*? Does any of the global progress featured in the quiz on page 19 depend on it?

2 Do you know the rate of economic growth in your country right now? Is it good news?

3 When economies grow, it's said that *a rising tide lifts all boats*, due to the *trickle-down effect*. What do these phrases mean?

4 Is economic growth necessary? Can it continue when global resources are limited?

2 **CD1 19** Listen to **Part 1** of a radio discussion between **Tony Adams** and **Helen Armitage**. Which statements are true? Correct the false ones.

Economic growth ....
1 occurs automatically as the population grows *F - needs to*
2 helps to mask inequality in society *true*
3 leaves everyone better off *F*
4 has reduced the wealth gap between countries *T*
5 makes everyone more content with life *F*
6 is something humans naturally aspire to *T*

3 Who do you think will say these things in **Part 2** of the discussion, Tony (**T**) or Helen (**H**)?

1 ☐ The idea of economic growth is a delusion.

2 ☐ We keep finding ways to use resources more efficiently.

3 ☐ The last year that the global economy was at a level the planet could support was 1983.

4 ☐ No growth means more unemployment and less social spending because of lower tax revenues.

5 ☐ The alternative is the "steady state economy."

6 ☐ Why are we hooked on producing and buying so much needless stuff?

CD1 20 Listen and check. Who do you agree with? Why?

In your own words

4 Work with a partner and use the prompts to talk about the points in your own words.

1 **Population growth** – increase / economy / grow / speed / jobs

2 **Wealth gap** – between and within countries / redistribution / trickle-down

3 **Income and happiness** – rise / level / connection

4 **Economic growth** – 2.5% / modest / double in 30 years

5 **Technology** – developments / efficiency / resources

6 **Resources** – limited / growth / planet / capacity

7 **Steady state economy** – standard of living / work less / non-economic activities

8 **Consumption** – reduce / debt / repair

What do you think?

• At what level of income do you think having more money *wouldn't* make you significantly happier?

• Do you mind paying tax? Is it acceptable to find ways to pay as little tax as possible?

• Is it OK to get into debt? Is your attitude about debt different from your parents' or grandparents'?

• With less income, what could you do without easily? What would be difficult to give up?

• If you had more free time, how could you enjoy it without spending money?

LANGUAGE FOCUS
Verb patterns

Infinitive, base form, or -ing

1 Complete the sentences with the verbs in the box.

> **GRAMMAR SPOT**
>
> | feel | improve | believe | avoid | increase | protect |
> |------|---------|---------|-------|----------|---------|
>
> | | |
> |---|---|
> | verb + infinitive | Inequality has **continued** _____ . |
> | verb + base form | People think buying more stuff will **make** them _____ happier. |
> | verb + -ing | We want to **keep** _____ living standards. |
> | verb + object + infinitive | It's what our society **encourages us** _____ . |
> | adjective + infinitive | People at the top are **eager** _____ income redistribution. |
> | preposition + -ing | No growth means less money to spend **on** _____ the environment. |
>
> Find other examples in **CD1 19** on p. 120.
>
> ▶▶ **Grammar Reference p. 143**

Verbs that can take both infinitive and -ing

2 *Start*, *begin*, and *continue* can take either infinitive or *-ing* with no change in meaning.

It **starts** to happen / happening at a surprisingly modest level of income.

Why was one particular pattern used in these examples?
a We have to **start looking** at the issue of income redistribution.
b We're **beginning to realize** that earning more doesn't always make us happier.

3 Some verbs change meaning with the infinitive or *-ing*. Discuss the different meanings of the verbs in these pairs.
1 a … so they keep *trying to make* the pie bigger.
　b *Try watching* a sunset one day this week.
2 a If we *stop to think* about what makes us happiest, …
　b He thought that our economies would *stop growing*.
3 a We never *meant to create* such a stressful way of life.
　b It *means getting* things repaired more, …
4 a We *need to give* everyone the chance to be better off.
　b If the environment *needs protecting*, …
5 a We've *seen* our economies *grow* 24 times bigger.
　b You *see* lots of well-off people *looking* for new ways to make more money.

4 Complete the sentences with one of the verbs in exercise 3 and the correct form of the verb in parentheses.
1 I don't think Anna _____ (be) rude – she just speaks before thinking sometimes.
2 He's such a good actor – I _____ him _____ (play) Hamlet on Broadway last year.
3 You should _____ (walk) to work – I bet you'd get there earlier when the traffic's bad!
4 These windows really _____ (clean). I can hardly see through this one!
5 I didn't _____ (chat) with Kirsty because I was late for my lecture.

5 Choose the verb that completes each sentence correctly. Change the verb patterns to make the sentences correct with the other verbs.

1	My boss	stopped let wanted	me to go to the meeting in New York.
2	I	expected you apologized for didn't mean	telling him.
3	Jack	can't stand is used would rather	work outdoors.
4	Alex	made me started couldn't help	to laugh.
5	We	are trying are thinking of had better	selling our house.
6	Did you	see him remind him remember	pick up the children from school?

6 Complete the sentences in your own words, using a verb in the correct pattern. Compare with a partner.
1 I'm thinking of …
2 Sometimes I can't help …
3 I don't mind people …, unless …
4 … always makes me …
5 People are always encouraging me …
6 I find it difficult …
7 I'm going to start …
8 I've never tried …
9 I never meant …
10 I'd rather …

The billionaire who wasn't

1 Discuss the questions.

1 What are the pros and cons of being very rich?
2 What are the positive and negative effects on children when their parents are very wealthy?
3 What is *philanthropy*? How many famous philanthropists can you name?

2 Work in pairs. Look at the section headings in the text about a philanthropist named Chuck Feeney. What do you think each section is about?

3 Read the text. Are the statements true (**T**), false (**F**), or not given (**NG**)? Correct the false ones.

1 People wouldn't guess that Chuck Feeney was anyone special.
2 He went straight from school to college.
3 He has never shown off his wealth.
4 He has three children.
5 Some of his children are grateful that he was strict with them.
6 He doesn't think money is at all important in life.
7 He doesn't like attending public functions.
8 His family will get the rest of his fortune when he dies.

4 Explain what Chuck meant by …

"Get out the door. Do things yourself."

"I set out to work hard, not to get rich."

"I felt there was an element of payback."

"People need it today, not tomorrow."

"You can only wear one pair of shoes at a time."

5 Look at the highlighted words and phrases in the text. Write them under the heading they are associated with.

Wealth	Poverty
(make) a fortune	careful with money

What do you think?

- What do you think of Chuck Feeney's attitude about money and possessions?
- In what ways would and wouldn't you support your children if you were a billionaire?
- If you had billions to give away, who/what would you give it to?

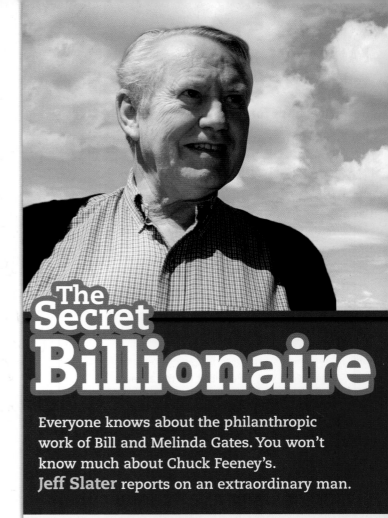

The Secret Billionaire

Everyone knows about the philanthropic work of Bill and Melinda Gates. You won't know much about Chuck Feeney's. **Jeff Slater** reports on an extraordinary man.

If you saw Chuck Feeney on the street, you wouldn't think there was anything remarkable about him. His clothes are nothing special, nor is his $15 watch – he's clearly careful with money. If you learned that his well-worn shoes are the only pair he owns, and that he owns neither house nor car, you might imagine that this elderly American has fallen on hard times. Well, if that were the case, it would have been a big fall because Chuck was worth billions of dollars and was once one of the wealthiest men on the planet. So maybe this is a tragic story of rags to riches and back again?

Making it big

Feeney's parents certainly weren't well-off. He was born in 1931, as the Great Depression was in full swing, and things were tough for the second of three children. As a teenager, Chuck did jobs for neighbors and sold greeting cards door-to-door. He got a free college education after serving in the US Air Force and supported himself through it by making and selling sandwiches on campus. But after making hundreds of millions of dollars opening duty-free shops at airports in the 1960s, Feeney's later return to a simple life was all his own choice. As his wealth continued to grow, he began to feel uncomfortable with the extravagant displays expected of the affluent and worried especially about the harmful effects it could all have on his children.

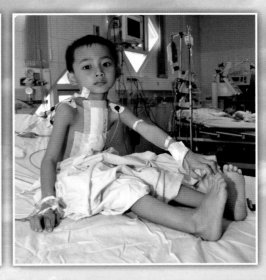

The
ATLANTIC
Philanthropies

Keeping it real

His daughter Caroleen remembers the wonderful house parties when she was a teenager, though she wasn't spoiled. Once she was 14, she says the message was "Get out the door. Do things yourself. Figure it out. More than anything, he wanted us to have goals and passions, and he thought, well, how could they – they're born with everything already? People have to fight and strive. So he made sure we did!" He made all his children take summer jobs as teenagers. When Caroleen's sister Leslie was a teenager, her father saw she was running up huge phone bills with a friend, calling boys in Europe. He disconnected the phone and put up maps showing all the pay phones in the area, along with a supply of coins. He then sent half of the phone bill to the other girl's father. "Now that was embarrassing," Leslie recalls. "It is eccentric," she admits, "but he sheltered us from people treating us differently because of the money. It made us normal people."

Giving it all away

Chuck clearly sees the danger of losing touch with normality ("I try to live a normal life, the way I grew up"), and says he never intended to make a fortune – "I set out to work hard, not to get rich." Eventually he saw the obvious solution – to give his money away. It seems dramatic, yet to Chuck, it was very straightforward: "I simply decided I had enough money." Enough makes you comfortable, he says, but after that, money doesn't add anything meaningful to your life. "It had a value if you wanted to buy something, but if you didn't want to buy something, you didn't need it."

Feeney had seen real hardship outside the prosperous areas he visited on business trips around the world. "I've always empathized with people who have it tough in life," he says. So he set up a charitable foundation, The Atlantic Philanthropies, in the 1980s, giving away an amount that averages $1 million every day.

Keeping it quiet

So why is Chuck Feeney not as well known a philanthropist as someone like Bill Gates? That's because Feeney chose to remain completely anonymous while giving his billions away. Education is his favorite beneficiary. "I had benefitted from education, and I felt there was an element of payback." He has helped to transform the higher education system in Ireland, has built a university, schools, and hospitals in Vietnam, and donated $500 million to fund medical research in Australia.

There are no plaques showing his name in the establishments he has funded. Some institutions that received funding began to make up names to put on plaques, "Golden Heart" being a popular one, but even these were later taken down when the foundation saw them. Feeney still prefers not to be recognized, in case he attracts people who are only interested in him for his money. His friend Hugh Lunn tells the story of when a photographer at a function went up to Chuck and asked, "Are you Chuck Feeney?" He said, "'No, that's him over there,' and pointed to me. The photographer came up and shook my hand and thanked me for everything I had done for science in Brisbane. It was very embarrassing. I didn't know what to say."

Giving while living

Feeney has only talked about his donations recently, and authorized a biography, because he wants to encourage other wealthy individuals to discover the joy of "Giving While Living." He can't understand why people wait till they die to leave money to good causes. "People need it today, not tomorrow." He also thinks the trade-offs in his life have been an easy choice. "You didn't wind up with a new boat, but you wound up helping someone, and that is a great feeling."

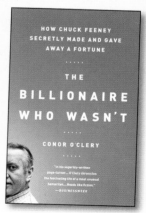

Chuck says he'll remain busy until he's given all his money away ("You'll never run out of people you can help"), having already given his family enough to live very comfortably. He has no plans to increase his own modest budget. "You can only wear one pair of shoes at a time. And if I can get a watch for $15 that keeps perfect time, what am I doing messing around with a Rolex?"

VOCABULARY AND SPEAKING
Describing trends

1 Look at the news headlines describing trends. Which trends go up? Which go down?

Inflation soars to 11%

Share prices plummet

Growth rate picks up again

Interest rates to fluctuate but remain broadly stable

House prices set to rocket again

Household debt shoots up by 45%

Consumer spending collapses

Applications to US colleges plunge

2 Describe the trends using the words in the boxes.

Inflation went up sharply to 11%.   *There was a dramatic rise in …*

Verb	Adverb
go down	slightly
fall	gradually
drop	steadily
decrease	sharply
go up	dramatically
rise	substantially
increase	

	Adjective	Noun
a	slight	fall
	gradual	
	steady	decrease
	sharp	rise
	dramatic	
	substantial	increase

3 Look at the graph showing **spending on new cars by age group**. Discuss the trends and try to explain them.

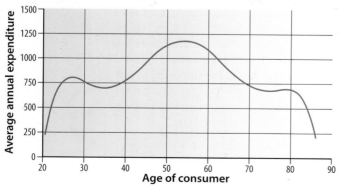

Spending on new cars rises sharply when people are in their 20s and presumably starting work. There's then a slight fall until …

CD1 21 Listen and compare.

4 Work in pairs. Tell each other about these life trends.

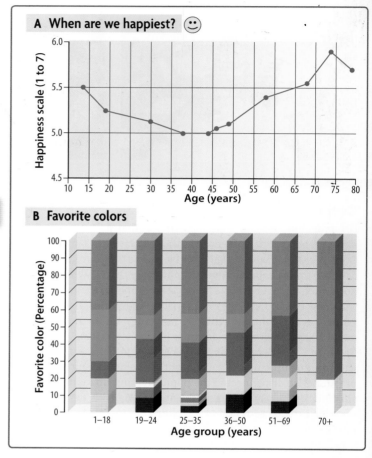

A When are we happiest? ☺

B Favorite colors

5 **CD1 22** Listen to someone describing the popularity of the name **Maria** in the US since 1880. Draw the line on the graph. What might explain the changes?

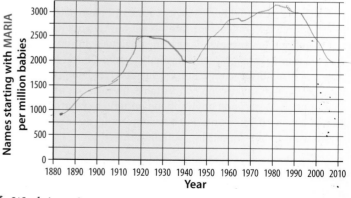

6 Work in pairs.

Student A Choose a name from page 164.
Student B Choose a name from page 166.

Give presentations to each other on the changes in the name's popularity and draw each other's graphs.

▶▶ WRITING Report writing – Using graphs *pp. 106–107*

VOCABULARY
Phrasal verbs with *up* and *down*

Particles in phrasal verbs *sometimes* help with understanding the meaning.

1 Movement is clear with literal uses of *up* ↑ and *down* ↓.

What's the situation *before* the movement in these examples?

1 Arsenal *moved up* to 4th place.
2 He *looked down* at the floor.
3 "*Sit up* straight!"
4 Please, *sit down*.
5 Her lip *curled up* in disgust.
6 I need to *lie down* for a bit.

2 Increase/decrease involve things going *up* or *down*.

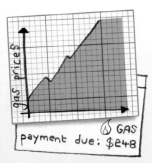

Gas prices continue to *go up*.

I'm so glad it's *cooled down*.

What is increasing and decreasing here?

1 *Turn it up* – I can't hear it!
2 Kids, *quiet down*!
3 I need to *save up* for a car.
4 They've *cut down* my hours.
5 *Speed up* – it's a 70-mph zone!
6 *Slow down* – my legs are tired!

CD1 23 Listen and check. What are the situations?

3 Better/worse are "higher *up*" and "lower *down*" on the value scale.

We just finished *fixing up* the house.

His colleagues' apathy gradually *wore* him *down*.

Discuss the questions.

1 When might you *brush up* on your language skills?
2 Is TV getting more and more *dumbed down*?
3 When do people *dress up*?
4 When might you *dress down*?

4 Start/end as, for example, of the day, when the sun comes *up* ☀ and goes *down*. ☀

Why might these things happen?

1 I'll *set up* my own business!
2 The president *stepped down*.
3 Let's *fire up* the barbecue!
4 My marriage *broke down*.
5 My laptop's so slow to *boot up*.
6 The drugstore's *shut down*.

CD1 24 Listen to the dialogues and compare. What caused the events?

5 Completion comes when *up/down* reach a limit.

I've *filled up* two cans with all your trash!

The police managed to *track* the thief *down*.

What has reached its limit in these examples?

1 You'll *wind up* in the hospital.
2 I finally *pinned* Harry *down*.
3 Who *bought up* all the tickets?
4 I've decided to *settle down*.
5 I've *used up* all my vacation.
6 I'll never *live* this *down*!

SPOKEN ENGLISH *up* and *down*

Complete the sentences with *up* or *down*. Which of the meanings 1–5 do they have?

1 Oh, grow _____ and stop acting like a child!
2 You need to wake _____ and smell the coffee!
3 You do look a little bit run _____ .
4 Speak _____! We can't hear in the back!
5 Oh lighten _____, will you! It's just a game!
6 Calm _____! I'll pay for the repair!
7 It's too difficult. I give _____! What's the answer?
8 I'm sorry. I've let you _____ .
9 Man _____, Tim, and stop being a wimp!
10 The management's playing it _____, but it's bad news.

CD1 25 Listen and check. What sentences prompt the responses?

💬 THE LAST WORD

Workplace jargon

1 Jargon and buzzwords have become increasingly common in workplaces. Why is that? Why do many people hate them?

2 **CD1 26** Listen to these examples of workplace jargon being used. How else could you express their meaning?

1 a going forward
   b grow the business
2 c to task somebody (with something)
   d to action
3 e mission-critical
   f best practice
4 g to impact something
   h a win-win situation

3 Match the following expressions with their meanings.

A	B
1 drill down	a have original and radical ideas about something
2 go the extra mile	b continually inform somebody of all developments
3 give people a heads-up	c make contact with somebody briefly to check that things are OK
4 keep somebody in the loop	d be aware of something that will need attention in the future
5 bring something to the table	e look at something in more depth and detail
6 hit the ground running	f contribute something of value to a project or discussion
7 think outside the box	g work harder than most people would to get a job done
8 touch base	h start work on something successfully and enthusiastically
9 bring somebody up to speed	i warn of a future development people need to be aware of
10 be on somebody's radar	j inform somebody of the latest developments on a project

I need an interpreter. Send in someone who speaks jargon.

Buzzword Bingo!

4 In meetings and presentations, workers have been known to play Buzzword Bingo. Try it. Fill in the Bingo card with some of the expressions in exercises 2 and 3.

   CD1 27 Listen to a presentation and cross out the expressions on your card as you hear them. The first person to get three in a row shouts, "**Bingo!**"

5 Are any of these expressions used in your language?

6 Which expressions in exercise 3 do you think were the most hated in a survey of workers? Which do you think people thought were actually OK and useful?

   CD1 28 Listen to **Sara** and **Danny** talking about workplace jargon and compare your ideas. Which expressions do they mention? What do they say about them? What do they think are the problems with using these expressions a lot?

7 Plan and give a short presentation using just *a few* of the expressions you think are useful. Remember, enough is enough!

Oxford Online Skills Program
Log in for additional online learning

4 Not all it seems

Modal auxiliaries, present, future, and past
Idiomatic adjective + noun collocations • Softening the message

VIDEO ◀ Eyewitness

1 Look at the photos. Discuss which you think are real / altered / real but staged. Check your answers on page 168.

Number 1 might be altered, but ...   *I think 2 is real. I've seen ...*   *3 can't be real, it's ...*

2 What are the different reasons for altering photos? Which ones do you think are justified?

1 Rubber duck in harbor

2 New York construction workers' lunch

3 Big jump

4 Rainbow landscape

5 Jet over beach

6 The Cottingley Fairies

7 Shark attack during ocean rescue

8 Pope resigns from Vatican

9 Unusual wolf

10 Victory Day kiss

11 Vacation selfie

12 Tennis match

LANGUAGE FOCUS 1
Modal auxiliary verbs

1 It's 10:30 a.m. Look at the picture of a scene in a jeweler's. Who do you think the people are? What do you think they're doing? Use modal verbs to speculate.

The woman in the coat must be a customer. She could be looking for a present. The man outside might be ...

2 **CD1 29** Look at the pictures on page 29, and listen to Karen telling a friend what happened in the jeweler's. Who were the two men? Why are they returning later?

In the Jeweler's

10:30 A.M.

Karen

3 It's 3:30 p.m. The police officers haven't returned to the jewelry store. What do you think has happened?

The police officers might have been called away to deal with another crime. They must have ...

GRAMMAR SPOT

Modal verbs for speculation – past

Modals expressing probability all form their past in the same way.

Verb + perfect base-form verb

She	**will**	
It	**might**	**have arrived** by now.
They	**should**, etc.	

▶▶ **Grammar Reference p. 145**

---

4 The police officers never returned. When the jewelry-store workers called the police station, they knew nothing about the incident. What do you think must have happened?

5 **CD1 30** Listen to Karen giving her friend an update on the story and check.

- Where did the police badges come from?
- Do you think the jewelry-store workers behaved stupidly?
- Why do the police need detailed witness statements?

💬 **SPEAKING Test your memory!**

6 Work in pairs. You were in the jeweler's at the time of the incident and have been asked to give a witness statement.

Student A Turn to page 164.
Student B Turn to page 166.

7 Complete the sentences with a modal verb and the correct form of the verb in parentheses.

1 Anyone _____ (fool) by scams and hoaxes if they're done convincingly enough.
2 Luckily I realized it was a fake website and logged off. Someone _____ (try) to get all my bank information.
3 I guess it _____ (be) your brother in that car. I didn't get a very close look.
4 Nick and Maria are in Rio de Janeiro. I'm sure they _____ (have) a wonderful time.
5 Pedro would never ignore you deliberately – he _____ (see) you.
6 There's no point going to the drugstore now – it _____ (close).

LANGUAGE FOCUS 2
Modal verbs: other meanings

1 Can people be convicted of crimes purely on the basis of eyewitness statements? Do you think they should be? Why/Why not?

2 **CD1 31** Listen to an account of **Professor Elizabeth Loftus's** work on the reliability of eyewitness statements. Answer the questions.

1 What was the court's attitude about eyewitnesses in the past?
2 How do we typically think our memory works? How is it different in reality?
3 What are leading questions? What examples are given?
4 What effect has Professor Loftus's work had on the criminal justice system?

Can we trust our memory?

GRAMMAR SPOT

1 Which of these meanings do the modals in sentences 1–7 have? Write them in the table.

Ability	
Permission	
Obligation	
Habit	*would*
Refusal	
Advice	

1 In the past, juries *would* usually *believe* eyewitnesses.
2 Witnesses *wouldn't accept* that they might be mistaken.
3 We *shouldn't think* of memory as an accurate record.
4 We *will* often *change* our memories by adding new details.
5 Professor Loftus *was able to show* how memories *can* be influenced by leading questions.
6 Suspects have the right to ask if they *can speak* to a lawyer before being interviewed.
7 Police interviewers *have to follow* strict guidelines and *must not ask* leading questions.

2 Which of the meanings can these modals be used for? Write them in the table and give examples.

must	may	could	won't	might
don't have to		can't		ought to

▶▶ **Grammar Reference p. 145**

3 Discuss why different modals are used in these pairs.

1 He *could swim* when he was six.
   When the boat sank, he *was able to swim* to shore.
2 I *must buy* a new suit. This one looks old and worn.
   I *have to buy* a suit for my new job.
3 You *should say* thank you.
   You *could* at least *say* thank you!
4 My dad *would* often *make up* stories for us.
   My dad *used to be* thin when he was young.
5 He *can't be* married.
   We *can't be* married.
6 There *could/may be* a train strike tomorrow.
   There *may not be* a train strike tomorrow now.
7 She *may be* in her 90s.
   She *may be* 92, but she's very sharp.
8 I bet that app *will be* expensive.
   This app *won't open*.

"Hey, I'll get to the meeting on time. It's those creative types you ought to be checking on."

4 Complete the second sentences using the past forms of the phrases in *italics* in the first sentences.

1 I *must lose some weight*.

I <u>had to lose some weight</u> because my clothes didn't fit me!

2 Walcott *should score* here – he only has the goalkeeper to beat.

Rooney crosses to Mata, who hits it, and … Ooh! _____ !

3 There's the phone. It*'ll be* Paul.

Did he have a deep voice? It _____ Paul.

4 My niece *can't read* very well because she's dyslexic.

My niece _____ until she was twelve.

5 David's phone is busy – he *might be talking* to Carolina.

David _____ to Carolina when you called.

6 Chris *won't help me*! He says I need to figure it out myself.

Heli _____ because she had her own work to do.

5 Which modal can complete *both* sentences in each pair? Which sentences express probability? What are the uses in the other sentences?

1 a He		have a very demanding job. He's always stressed.
b You		come sailing with us next time – you'd love it.
2 a I		say how likely it is right now; it's too early to tell.
b They		be coming. They'd have been here by now.
3 a It		snow here in May.
b You		borrow the car if you like. I don't need it.
4 a We		possibly stay over at Claire's if the party ends late.
b No, you		not use my photographs on your website.
5 a You		have no trouble passing your driver's test.
b You		be practicing the piano for your concert next week.
6 a Jim		spend hours playing computer games.
b Sara		know the answer – she's good at these kinds of quizzes.

▶▶ **WRITING** Writing a formal email – An apology *p. 108*

SPOKEN ENGLISH Modal auxiliaries

1 Look at the sentences. What do you think the situation might be in each one?

1 Oh, thanks, that's very thoughtful of you, but you really shouldn't have!

2 I could have sworn I left the car here!

3 I got all dressed up, but I really didn't have to.

4 Jenny will keep going on about my age!

5 You might want to check that your shirt's buttoned up correctly.

6 **A** "Oh, you can be so insensitive sometimes!"
   B "Me, insensitive! You should talk!"

7 Do you have to whistle all the time?

8 And who might you be?

9 I should think so!

10 Well, he would say that, wouldn't he?

CD1 32 Listen and compare your ideas.

2 Read the conversations aloud in pairs.

HYPOCHONDRIACS ANONYMOUS

First step is the hardest. You have to admit that you don't have a problem.

READING AND SPEAKING
The mystic and the skeptic

1 **Sir Arthur Conan Doyle** and **Harry Houdini** were two of the most famous celebrities of the 20th century. What were they famous for?

Look at the pictures. Which person do you think must have been …?

• very rational and questioning
• convinced of the existence of supernatural powers

2 Read about the two men in groups and answer the questions.

Group A Read about **Sir Arthur Conan Doyle**.

Group B Read about **Harry Houdini**.

1 What changes did he make to his name?
2 What was problematic about his father?
3 Who was a formative influence on him in his youth? How?
4 What brought career success after a difficult start?
5 How good a sportsman was he?
6 Why did he take an interest in mediums? Did he believe in them?
7 Was he ever deceived by people faking supernatural phenomena?
8 Why shouldn't he have continued with his final tour?
9 When did he die? What were his last words?
10 What attempts were made to communicate with him after his death?

3 Work with a partner from the other group. Compare your answers to the questions in exercise 2 and discuss the two men. What is paradoxical about both of them?

Look at the quote from Sherlock Holmes:

> **66**
>
> **When you have eliminated the impossible, whatever remains, no matter how improbable, must be the truth.**
>
> **99**

How would this apply to Conan Doyle and Houdini?

Sir Arthur Conan Doyle

Sir Arthur Conan Doyle was born on May 22, 1859, in Edinburgh, as Arthur Doyle (he later used his middle name, Conan, as part of his last name). His father, a civil servant and frustrated artist, became an alcoholic, and Arthur was sent to boarding school to escape the chaos at home.

He went on to study medicine at Edinburgh University, where one teacher, Dr. Joseph Bell, made a big impression on him. An eccentric character in his long coat and deerstalker hat, Bell had an uncanny ability to diagnose patients purely by making logical deductions from their appearance.

Arthur Conan Doyle
The Memoirs of
Sherlock Holmes
OXFORD WORLD'S CLASSICS

HARRY HOUDINI

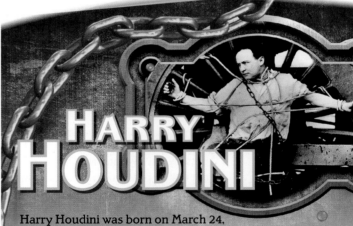

Harry Houdini was born on March 24, 1874, in Budapest, Hungary, as Erik Weisz. His family moved to Wisconsin in the US when he was four, and for some unknown reason Houdini later claimed he'd been born there on April 6. It's said this may have been because his father had to escape Budapest after killing a prince in a duel and Harry wanted to disguise his roots.

Houdini became fascinated by magic as a young boy, and when he read the autobiography of the great French magician, Robert-Houdin, he was hooked. At 17, he began performing tricks, using Houdin's name to create his own stage name.

Harry had little success as a magician at first, and was ready to give it up, but his career took off when he made escapology the focus of his act. He had long been an avid amateur athlete, boxer, swimmer, and cyclist (he was even considered for the US Olympic team). Combining his

Conan Doyle's first medical practice was slow to take off, and while waiting for patients, he wrote fiction. It was many years before his first novel was published, introducing the detective Sherlock Holmes, who was clearly based on Dr. Bell. A series of Sherlock Holmes stories followed.

Doyle grew tired of writing them, but when he killed Sherlock off in one story, there was a huge public outcry (people wore black armbands), and Doyle had to bring him back to life.

Doyle combined writing with an avid interest in sports; he played first-class cricket and was goalkeeper for Portsmouth AFC. More surprising, given the ultra-rational character of Sherlock Holmes, was Doyle's fascination with the supernatural.

In 1893, Doyle's father died in a psychiatric hospital, and his wife Louisa was given months to live. His resulting depression led Doyle to investigate spiritualism and communication with the dead. Later, during World War I, he lost several family members, and he became especially desperate to make contact with his dead son.

Doyle remarried after Louisa's death. His second wife, Jean, became a medium, and Doyle devoted all his time to giving lectures and writing about supernatural phenomena. In his book, *The Coming of the Fairies*, he insisted that the photographs of the "Cottingley fairies," taken by two young girls, could not have been faked.

The women finally admitted their hoax in 1983: "He had lost his son recently in the war," explained 81-year-old Elsie Wright, "and I think the poor man was trying to comfort himself in these things."

Despite heart problems, Conan Doyle went on a lecture tour of Europe in 1929. He returned in pain and was bedridden until his death on July 7, 1930 (though shortly before he died he was found lying in the garden, clutching his heart with one hand and holding a flower in the other). His last words to his wife were, "You are wonderful."

Six days after his death, a seance was held at the Royal Albert Hall, attended by 6,000 people. Jean was alone in claiming that she had heard a message from Arthur.

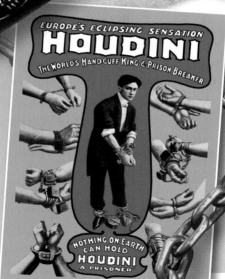

athleticism with an extraordinary ability to contort his body, he was able to escape from handcuffs in seemingly impossible situations, including locked crates that had been dropped into rivers. Ads for Houdini's shows claimed he could escape through solid barriers by dematerializing, but Houdini himself always denied he had any supernatural powers.

After the death of his beloved mother in 1913, Houdini investigated the popular interest in mediums who claimed to contact the dead. He said he never dismissed the possibility of communicating with spirits, but had never found anyone who could actually do it for real. It may seem paradoxical that a magician and illusionist should be so skeptical about the supernatural, but magicians know what fakery is, and Harry spent much of his life exposing the tricks that so-called mediums used in their seances.

In 1926, despite having broken his ankle, Houdini wouldn't cancel a US tour. After one of the shows, an enthusiastic fan decided to test Harry's famous ability to withstand any punch to the stomach, but without first warning him. Harry was clearly injured by the blow, and performed with severe stomach pains for two days. When he finally saw a doctor, he was diagnosed with acute appendicitis. He tried to go on with his next show with a fever of 104°F. He collapsed on stage, and died in a hospital on the somewhat inauspicious date of October 31 (Halloween). His last words were, "I'm tired of fighting."

Houdini had arranged that his wife, Bess, would hold seances after his own death, in which he would communicate a secret message if it proved possible. The seances continued for ten years, before Bess finally ended them saying, "Ten years is long enough to wait for any man."

Vocabulary

4 Check the meanings of the highlighted words in your text and then explain them to someone who read the other text.

What do you think?

- Which of the two men would you most like to have met? Why?
- What's the best magical trick you've seen performed? Do you have any idea how it was done?
- How did Conan Doyle's and Houdini's families directly impact the two men's lives? Has a family member directly impacted your life? How?

LISTENING AND SPEAKING
When Arthur met Harry: an unlikely friendship

1 Sir Arthur Conan Doyle and Harry Houdini did in fact meet on several occasions and were friends for a while.

Why do you think ...?
- they became friends
- Houdini performed a long and elaborate trick for Doyle in private
- Doyle held a seance for Houdini
- their friendship ended

2 **CD1 33** Listen to an extract from a radio program about unexpected friendships. Check your answers in exercise 1.

- What happened in Houdini's trick?
- What was Conan Doyle's reaction?
- What happened in the seance?
- What was Houdini's reaction?

3 Answer the questions with **CD (Conan Doyle)**, **H (Houdini)**, or **B (Both)**.

Who ...?
1 wanted to spend time with other writers _____
2 was interested in finding a true medium _____
3 tried to embrace the other person's attitude to spiritualism _____
4 tried to convince the other that their beliefs were wrong _____
5 thought the other was being dishonest in his arguments about the supernatural _____
6 wasn't able to be open about his work _____
7 made public his anger with the other _____

CD1 33 Listen again and check.

4 Match the words in **A** with words with similar meanings in **B**.

A			B		
to encounter	sham	to offend	anxious	to hurt	to delude
to expose	eager	to deceive	fake	to reveal	to meet

What do you think?
- Who was being the most honest in their relationship, Doyle or Houdini?
- Why couldn't Doyle take Houdini's advice about supernatural phenomena?
- What did Doyle mean when he talked about what he *knew* to be true?
- Are fake mediums harmless entertainers? Why/Why not?

VOCABULARY
Idiomatic collocations

1 Look at the sentences. What do the collocations in *italics* mean? What word class are the two words?

> Houdini tried to convince Doyle that mediums used tricks, but it was a *lost cause*.
>
> When Doyle wrote newspaper articles about the seance, it was the *final straw* for Houdini.

2 There are many common idiomatic collocations with an **adjective + noun**.

Work in groups, **A** and **B**. Match the adjectives and nouns for your group to make *idiomatic* collocations.

GROUP A		GROUP B	
Adjective	**Noun**	**Adjective**	**Noun**
gray	line	sore	thought
level	shot	wishful	blessing
slippery	feet	foregone	grace
wake-up	slope	last	spot
fine	area	second	feet
itchy	deal	saving	resort
long	call	mixed	conclusion
raw	playing field	cold	thinking

3 **Group A** Turn to page 165. **Group B** Turn to page 167. Read the dictionary extracts to check the meanings of your collocations and make notes. Write an example sentence of your own.

lost cause: *something that will never succeed e.g., I've given up trying to get him to exercise more – it's a lost cause.*

In your own words

4 Work with a partner from the other group. Explain the collocations to your partner *in your own words*, and tell them your example sentence.

5 Complete the sentences with one of the collocations from exercise 2.

1 Scientists have discovered there really is a _____ _____ between genius and insanity, as the same gene is involved in both.

2 I can't believe Adam called the wedding off. I guess he got _____ _____!

3 We're not asking for special advantages in bidding for this contract, we just want a _____ _____.

4 Steve realized that the diagnosis of heart problems was a _____ _____ and decided to get in shape.

5 The hotel was dirty, and the view was disappointing, but the food was the _____ _____ – it was delicious.

6 It's a _____ _____ that Sylvia Jones will win this marathon; she's won every race she's been in this year.

7 It's a _____ _____, but you might find the document with the work you lost in your temporary folder.

8 It was a _____ _____ getting to know another hypochondriac. It's nice to discuss our problems, but I have lots of new ones now!

6 **CD2 2** Listen to the statements. Which of the collocations could you use to respond? Think of a response. Then listen and compare.

> I don't think she left him just because he forgot their anniversary.

> No, but I think it might have been the final straw.

SPEAKING AND LISTENING

1 Read the description of a radio program. What do the contestants need to do to make their talk successful?

The Unbelievable Truth

The Unbelievable Truth is a radio panel show on BBC Radio where contestants take turns giving a short talk on a topic. Most of what the speaker says is completely, and often amusingly, untrue. However, five statements in the talk *are*, unbelievably, true and the other contestants have to spot them. The speaker gets a point for every truth they manage to "smuggle" past the other contestants.

In the clip you will hear:

The host:
- **David Mitchell**, comedian

The contestants:
- **Graeme Garden**, comedian and author
- **Henning Wehn**, comedian ("German Comedy Ambassador in London")
- **Jeremy Hardy**, comedian
- **Victoria Coren Mitchell**, writer and TV host, married to David Mitchell

2 **CD2 3** Listen to the clip. In which order are the things in the pictures mentioned? What is said about them?

hand grenade ☐

specimen beaker ☐

bishop ☐

straitjacket ☐

hospital trolley ☐

clown ☐

3 In this extract, the contestants spotted two of the truths. What do you think the other truth was?

4 Play *The Unbelievable Truth*.
Work in pairs. Each student prepares a short (2–3-minute) talk.

Student A Look at the topic on page 165 and follow the instructions.
Student B Look at the topic on page 167 and follow the instructions.

THE LAST WORD
Softening the message

1 Look at the picture. What do you think it is? Where might it be?

2 Read the conversation between Ted and Margaret. Where are they? Choose the correct words.

T That one's incredible, isn't it, Margaret? She looks so real!

M Yes. I was wondering if it ¹*could / might* be possible to take a photo of it. Do you think it would be ²*right / alright*?

T You ³*might / will* want to ask that attendant first.

M Oh, I thought he was one of the exhibits! Excuse me, ⁴*could / can* I possibly take a photo of that statue?

A Oh, we don't allow flash photography.

M I ⁵*think / thought* I might take it without flash. ⁶*Would / Could* that be OK?

A Yes, that's fine.

M Thank you. Ted, you ⁷*wouldn't / couldn't* take one of me next to it, could you?

T Yes, of course … Just move a little bit to the left, ⁸*would / may* you?

CD2 4 Listen and check.

Ron Mueck, Seated Woman, 1999

3 Look at the polite ways of speaking. Find more examples in exercise 2. Which category do they belong to? Which are the *most* polite expressions? Why is a past tense used in some of them?

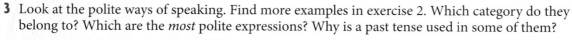

Polite ways of …	asking someone to do something	asking permission	suggesting something
	Could you (possibly) …?	Do you think I could/might …?	I was thinking I might …
	I wonder if you could (possibly) …?	Would it be/Is it alright if I …?	I thought you could …
	Would you mind …-ing?	Would you mind if I …?	It might be a good idea to …
	I don't suppose you could …, could you?	Is there any chance I could …?	I was wondering whether …

4 You are in a café. You want to look at someone's tablet. In pairs, use the instructions and prompts to act out the conversation.

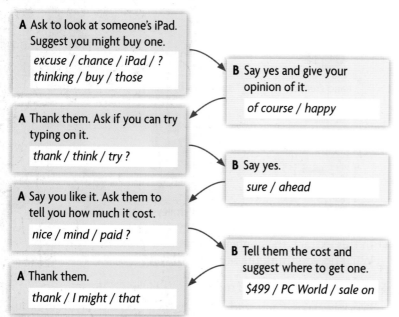

A Ask to look at someone's iPad. Suggest you might buy one.
excuse / chance / iPad / ?
thinking / buy / those

B Say yes and give your opinion of it.
of course / happy

A Thank them. Ask if you can try typing on it.
thank / think / try ?

B Say yes.
sure / ahead

A Say you like it. Ask them to tell you how much it cost.
nice / mind / paid ?

B Tell them the cost and suggest where to get one.
$499 / PC World / sale on

A Thank them.
thank / I might / that

CD2 5 Listen and compare. Act out the conversation again, using different ways of being polite.

5 How polite are these expressions?

Would you mind not …?	Do me a favor and …
Do you think you could …?	Do you mind …?

CD2 6 Listen and repeat some examples. What makes the polite forms not all they seem?

6 Say these sentences to a partner, politely or rudely. The partner should then say them in the opposite way.

1 Excuse me, would you mind speaking more quietly?
2 Perhaps you would like to explain this?
3 I'm afraid this isn't good enough.
4 Close the door, will you?
5 Could you possibly move your car?
6 Would you mind not making that noise?

CD2 7 Listen and repeat the sentences. What do you think the situations might be?

7 Write two conversations, one polite and one rude. Read them to the class.

Oxford Online Skills Program
Log in for additional online learning

5 Culture clashes

Avoiding repetition • Nationalities and stereotypes • American vs. British English

VIDEO Across cultures

STARTER

1 Signs in other countries can seem strange and surprising. What do you think these signs mean? Do you have any ideas which countries they could be from?

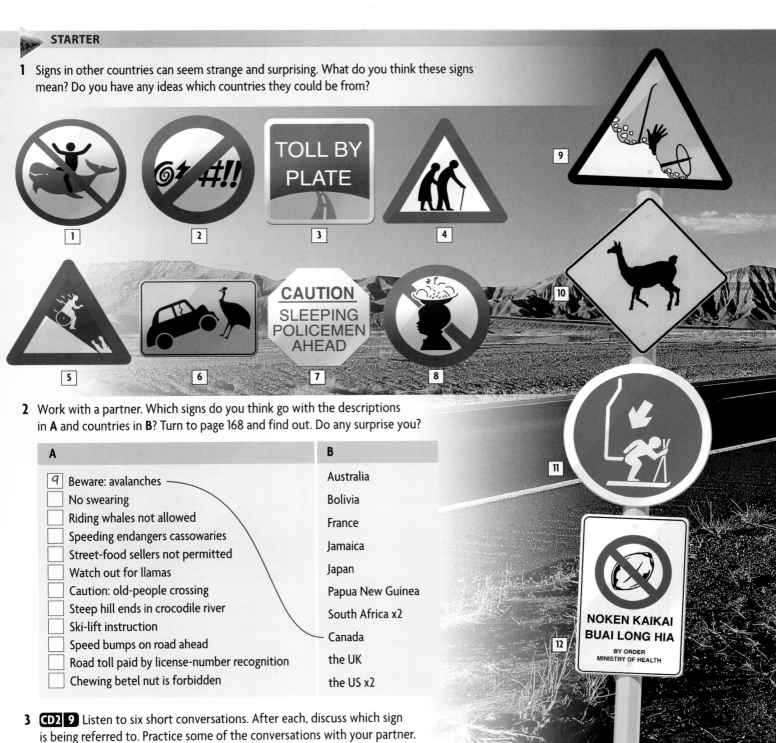

2 Work with a partner. Which signs do you think go with the descriptions in **A** and countries in **B**? Turn to page 168 and find out. Do any surprise you?

A	B
9 Beware: avalanches	Australia
No swearing	Bolivia
Riding whales not allowed	France
Speeding endangers cassowaries	Jamaica
Street-food sellers not permitted	Japan
Watch out for llamas	Papua New Guinea
Caution: old-people crossing	South Africa x2
Steep hill ends in crocodile river	Canada
Ski-lift instruction	the UK
Speed bumps on road ahead	the US x2
Road toll paid by license-number recognition	
Chewing betel nut is forbidden	

3 **CD2 9** Listen to six short conversations. After each, discuss which sign is being referred to. Practice some of the conversations with your partner.

READING AND SPEAKING
Worlds of difference

1 Look at the map of Papua New Guinea. Where is it? Do you know anything about it? Discuss as a class which facts you think are true.

Papua New Guinea
1 It has a population of over *1 million / 4 million / 7 million*.
2 There are about *100 / 200 / 700* different tribes.
3 More than *20 / 200 / 800* languages are spoken in the country.
4 Only *6% / 18% / 23%* of the population lives and works in urban areas.
5 Cannibalism was widely practiced until the *1920s / 1950s / 1990s*.
6 Its currency is the "kina," but *seashells / coconuts / cocoa beans* are still used in some transactions.
7 It was administered by Australia until *1945 / 1975 / 2005*.
8 The head of state is *a tribal chief / an elected president / the Queen of England*.

CD2 10 Listen and check. What extra information do you learn?

2 Read the **introduction** to the article by the investigative journalist Donal MacIntyre. Where are the people? Who are they? Who spluttered? Who almost choked? Why? How does the situation fit the title?

In your own words

3 Read **Part 1** of the article. Use the prompts to talk to a partner about it in your own words.

1 Donal MacIntyre was traveling the world in order to ... when he ...
2 He admired many things about the tribe's way of life, for example ...
3 They were able to speak English because ...
4 They were particularly interested to hear about ...
5 And despite never having traveled far before ...
6 Donal described the group of travelers as ...

4 Before you read **Part 2**, work as a class to make a list of six questions you'd most like answered about the Swagup Six's trip to London. Then read and see which of your questions are answered.

5 Are these statements true or false? Correct the false ones.

1 After some initial misgivings, the Swagup Six became bold.
2 Their visit to Britain was in September.
3 Samuel and Christina disapproved of Ameera wearing pants.
4 They embraced new experiences with enthusiasm and open minds.
5 They were surprised at how small St. Paul's Cathedral was.
6 James came up with his own theory about the construction of the Underground.
7 Donal didn't ask for an audience with the Queen. He knew it would be futile.
8 The visit would undoubtedly lead to the tribespeople modifying their lifestyles.

Vocabulary from context

6 Figure out the meaning of the highlighted words from their contexts.

THE ULTIMATE CULTURE CLASH ...

by Donal MacIntyre

We were entertaining our new house guests over tea and biscuits. Their conversational gambits were proving to be somewhat unusual. "How much did you pay for your wife?" Samuel coolly asked me. "I, uh ... I ... well ...," I spluttered. "Do you mind if your husband have baby with another woman?" Samuel's spouse Christina asked my pregnant wife Ameera, who almost choked on her tea. "Who is the boss?" asked Samuel, casting a knowing glance towards Ameera.

I think it's fair to say that crocodile-hunting polygamists from Papua New Guinea would add a certain frisson to any polite London soirée. Samuel and Christina, who is one of his two wives, are members of the 250-strong Insect tribe – hunter-gatherers. They hunt crocodiles with spears and stalk wild boar with bows and arrows. They speak their own language, Ngala, and practice polygamy, paying for wives' dowries with seashells. One tribesman has 12 wives. Another is said to have 112 children.

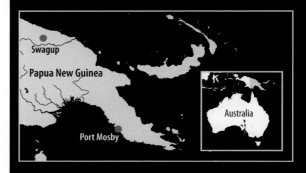

What do you think?

- Which of the Swagup Six's experiences do you think were most surprising or difficult for them?
- What can we learn about life from the lives and attitudes of these tribespeople?
- What does Samuel mean when he says, "We all come from the same pot"?
- Do you believe that the tribe really will hang on to its own culture?

PART 1

I first met them last year as I traveled the world to observe how ancient cultures and tribes were engaging with the ever-encroaching modern world. I lived in their remote village, Swagup, ate their food, shared their shelters, and mined their intimate family secrets.

The tribe had everything they wanted. The village's witch doctor serviced all medical and spiritual requirements. Everything else – fish, boar, fruit, building, and hunting materials – was gathered from the jungle. The tribespeople thought of their home as a land of plenty – a paradise that has provided their livelihood for thousands of years. They had robustly defended their culture against all-comers. Their one concession was allowing missionaries to school them in basic English. The village school still teaches them the language today.

The tribespeople revealed themselves to be as curious about my world as I was about theirs. They bombarded me with questions about Britain and our "chief" – or the Queen, as we call her. The tribe's own chief, a rather colorful character called Joseph, is elected by majority every five years and carries supreme authority.

Sitting in his wooden, three-story palace, the chief and I got to talking and, to return the overwhelming hospitality that they had shown me, I invited him and his kin to undertake the 12,000-mile journey to my home in Wimbledon, southwest London. The tribespeople have never before traveled beyond their local stomping ground. Making the journey were Joseph, Samuel, Christina, Steven and one of his three wives, Delma, and James. Together they made up the Swagup Six, a party of Stone-Age travelers coming to a microchip world. "I don't know what magic they have in Britain, but I'm about to find out," the chief declared.

I don't know what magic they have in Britain, but I'm about to find out.

PART 2

At Heathrow airport, every escalator was met with terror and every elevator with suspicion until one of them, usually Steven, an expert crocodile hunter, ventured forth, followed by the rest of the tribe. From Terminal 4, with spears on their backs and bows over their shoulders, the Swagup Six bravely ventured into our world.

My guests were fascinated by everyday scenes and situations. They believed the barren winter trees were dead. The battery-powered cries of my daughter's doll drew shrieks from the women. Samuel and Christina were interested in how Ameera and I related to each other. They seemed to suspect it was Ameera who wore the pants – unthinkable in their world. But whatever Samuel and Christina secretly thought, they maintained a public front of broad-mindedness. The chief's guiding principle was: "When in London … ."

Nonetheless, some of the capital's tourist spots proved a challenge. At the London Eye, the tribe held congress in the shadow of the huge wheel. "It not meant for humans," was the consensus. Eventually the chief decided that they should try to enjoy the bird's-eye view of London. When their capsule reached the summit, the chief asked for our "spirit house" to be pointed out. He found the great dome of St. Paul's Cathedral remarkable – not for its grandeur but for its diminutive stature. "In our village, no building can be bigger than the spirit house," he said.

However, the London Underground inspired awe. Astounded by the enormity of the network, James was convinced the Underground was built first, with the rest of London built on top later.

Spirits were also raised by the prospect of a visit to Buckingham Palace. As a tribal leader in a Commonwealth country, Joseph regards himself as the Queen's representative. We dutifully put in a request for a meeting, but unfortunately it was declined. In his part of the world, he is a king. Here, sadly, he is just another tourist.

After our trip to London, we spent some time in Wales, where the group encountered snow for the first time. "This is strange sand that falls from the sky," the chief said. "When will it stop?" However, they were soon throwing snowballs with pinpoint accuracy.

Their attitude and enthusiasm highlighted for me how jaded we have become, and how indifferent we are to wonderful sights on our own doorstep. The Swagup Six embraced our culture but without renouncing an ounce of their own. The goodbyes at Heathrow were emotional. "We come from the same pot," Samuel said, standing beside Christina. What do you most miss from home? I asked. "My second wife," he said without a blink.

In our village, no building can be bigger than the spirit house.

LANGUAGE FOCUS
Ways to avoid repetition

There are several ways to avoid repeating words or phrases.

1 Leaving words out

*They wanted us to answer their questions, but we **couldn't** (answer their questions).*

What words have been omitted in these sentences?

*They revealed themselves to be as curious about my world as I **was** about theirs.*

*I thought they would enjoy the view of London and they **did**.*

*A present for me? How nice. You **shouldn't have**.*

Notice that they end with an **auxiliary** or **modal**.

2 Reduced infinitives

Just *to* can be used instead of the whole infinitive when the meaning is clear from the context.

Which words are omitted after *to* in these sentences?

*"Does the chief advise them?" "Yes, they **expect him to**."*

*"Did the Queen meet them?" "No, she didn't. She **refused to**."*

*"Can you come for dinner?" "Yes, I'**d love to**."*

3 Synonyms in context

*They **hunt** crocodiles with spears and **stalk** wild boar with bows and arrows.*

*The battery-powered **cries** of my daughter's doll drew **shrieks** from the women.*

*"Were they **worried** about going?" "Well, they were a little bit **anxious**."*

Can you think of synonyms for these words?

| big | love (v) | afraid | happy | friend |

▶▶ **Grammar Reference p. 146**

1 Complete the sentences with an auxiliary or a modal verb. Sometimes you will need to make the verb form negative.

1 I tried to fix my car, but I __couldn't__ . It needs a mechanic.

2 "You look awful. Why don't you see a doctor?" "I _____. He just gave me some pills and told me to take it easy."

3 "Did you read this report?" "No, I _____, but I _____."

4 My car's being serviced right now. If it _____, I'd give you ride. Sorry.

5 I'm so glad you told Sue exactly what you thought of her, because if you _____, I certainly _____ _____!

6 "I think I'll call Rob." "You _____. You haven't been in touch with him for a long time."

7 I went to a party last night, but I wish I _____. It was awful.

8 My boyfriend insists on doing all the cooking, but I wish he _____ – it's inedible!

9 "Aren't you going to the beach for your vacation?" "Well, we _____, but we're still not sure."

10 "Andy got lost on his way to Anne's party and didn't show up until midnight." "He _____! That's so typical of him."

CD2 11 Listen and check.

2 **CD2 12** Listen to five more short conversations. Complete each response with an auxiliary verb.

A You met my sister last night!

B Yes, I did. She thought we'd met before, but we …. .

> hadn't

3 Work with a partner. Take turns reading **A**'s remarks and respond as **B**, using the verbs in parentheses and a reduced infinitive.

1 **A** Can you come over for dinner tonight?
  B _Thanks. I'd love to!_ (love)

2 **A** Did you mail my letter?
  B _____. (forget)

3 **A** I can't take you to the airport after all. Sorry.
  B _____. (promise)

4 **A** Was John surprised when he won?
  B _____. (not expect)

5 **A** Why did you slam the door in my face?
  B _____. (not mean)

6 **A** You'll be able to enjoy yourself when exams are over.
  B _____. (intend)

CD2 13 Listen and compare. Practice again.

Synonyms

Sometimes, from time to time, now and again, occasionally, at times I wish I'd never been given this Thesaurus.

4 Complete the sentences with a word that has a similar meaning to the word in *italics*. Sometimes the word class changes, e.g., from noun to verb, as in question 1.

1 I don't *trust* this government. I have no __faith__ in it whatsoever.

2 She is not only a *skilled* painter, she is also a(n) _____ piano player.

3 Advertisements are not allowed to *lie*, but they _____ us in many subtle ways.

4 Chess is a game of *tactics*. You have to plan your _____ well in advance.

5 The doctor looked at my notes *carefully*. Then he gave me a _____ examination.

6 He has an *annoying* habit of always being late. It really _____ me.

7 It's *very important* that you don't tell anyone. In fact, it's _____ .

8 Skiing can be *dangerous*, but I like to take a few _____ .

9 She wasn't *scared* at all by the dog, but I was _____ .

10 You've managed to *persuade* me. Your argument is most _____ .

5 Read the thesaurus explanations of these four near synonyms for *leader*.

> ## leader – chief, head, captain, boss
> A **chief** – a leader or ruler of people. A person of highest rank: army, industry, police.
> The **head** – the person in charge of a group of people or an organization, e.g., head of state.
> A **captain** – the person in charge of a ship. Leader of a sports team. A **boss** – the person in charge of others at work. (*Informal*) *Who's the boss in your marriage?*

Find synonyms or near synonyms for these words.
Put them into sentences to illustrate their differences in meaning.

> beautiful   laugh   hate   argument   enemy

SPOKEN ENGLISH   Finding things in common

1 **CD2 14** Listen and read the sentences. Notice all the ways of expressing things that *are* or *are not* in common.

Things in common	Things different
Ted's been to Mexico, and **so have I**.	He's tried windsurfing, but **I haven't**.
He likes traveling, and **I do, too**.	He comes from a big family, but **I don't**.
He doesn't speak Chinese, and **neither do I**.	He didn't see the soccer game, but **I did**.
He isn't married, and **neither am I**.	He hasn't been to Australia. **I have, though**.
He can't drive, and **I can't, either**.	

2 Work with a partner. Ask questions and make notes of things that you *do* or *don't* have in common.

> Do you like … ?
> How many … ?
> What kind of … ?

> Have you ever been to … ?
> Who are your favorite … ?
> Where do you usually go … ?

> Which social media sites … ?
> Did you see … (movie) ?
> Have you read … ?

3 Report back to the class about each other.
  Mia has never been to Peru, and neither have I.

Found in translation

1 Read about Alan Dein. How does he get the real-life stories for his program? Why do you think it is called *Don't Log Off*? Who features in this program? How did they meet?

Don't Log Off

Alan Dein is an oral historian and broadcaster. On his BBC Radio program *Don't Log Off*, he discovers the real-life stories behind online profiles on Facebook. Starting with nothing but the profile, he contacts the people on the Internet. The results are intriguing, funny, and often very moving. On this program, Alan hears the story of Bryan from Boise, Idaho, in the US and Anna from Russia, who met online. Anna decides to move to the US with her children. Will things work out?

2 **CD2 15** Listen to **Part 1** of the program. When Alan talks to Bryan, he makes comments aside to his radio audience. Read some of his asides and answer the questions.

1 *But this was more than a typical online romance.*
Why is it not typical? How do Bryan and Anna solve their particular problem?

2 *The next time he'd been to visit Anna in Russia.*
How does Bryan describe the visit?

3 *Six months later. Bryan had some big news for me.*
What was the news? What is the deadline connected with this news?

4 *I spoke to Bryan at the airport.*
Why is Bryan at the airport? What are his emotions? Why do they stop the phone call?

5 *It was then I had an idea.*
What was Alan's idea?

6 *Then I received a rather worrying message. Really big news.*
What do you think the news is? Give reasons for your ideas and how it might affect Alan's plan.

3 **CD2 16** Listen to **Part 2**.

1 What has happened? Were your ideas correct?

2 What reasons does Bryan give for the "big news"?

3 *"The clock is ticking, Bryan."* What does Alan mean by this?

4 What does Alan decide to do?

5 What does he learn from Bryan about Anna's life in the US?

What do you think?

- What was Anna's daily life in the US like? Why didn't she go out much?
- How did Bryan treat her?
- Will Bryan and Anna marry?
- Will Anna and her children return to Russia?

4 **CD2 17** Listen to **Part 3**. Say what happens. What is Alan's surprise? Tell it in your own words.

Discussion

- Explain the title *Found in translation*.
- Are you optimistic or pessimistic about Bryan and Anna's futures? What about Anna's children?
- What are the pros and cons of marrying someone with a different language and culture?

A quiz

5 Turn to page 168 and take the quiz.

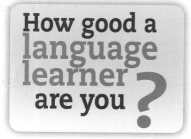

How good a language learner are you?

VOCABULARY AND LISTENING
Nationalities and stereotypes

1 Complete the chart of nationality words. Use your dictionary if necessary.

COUNTRY	ADJECTIVE	PERSON	PEOPLE	LANGUAGE(S)
the United States	American	an American	the Americans	English
Brazil				
Thailand				
Mexico				
China				
Sweden				
Ecuador				
Japan				
South Korea				
Australia				
Spain				
Turkey				
New Zealand				
Afghanistan				
Argentina				
Peru				

Listening

2 **CD2 18** Listen to four people talking about their experiences living in another country.

	What nationality are they?	Where are they?	What cultural differences do they mention?
1			
2			
3			
4			

Talking about stereotypes

3 Work in small groups. Choose a few nationalities that you know. First describe them in stereotypical fashion, and then discuss how much your experience with them fits the stereotype.

> Americans have a reputation for being loud and rude.

> Actually, most of my American friends are pretty low-key. They ...

> And Americans always dress down in athletic shorts and T-shirts. And the food is disgusting.

> That's a myth. Some wear very fashionable clothes ... and the food ...

4 What is your nationality's stereotype? Are you like that?

▶▶ **WRITING** Describing similarities and differences – Comparing two countries *p. 109*

43

THE LAST WORD
American and British English

1 Read two conversations. Which is **American English**? Which is **British English**? Work with a partner. Note all the differences you can find.

A	B
A Who's the parcel for? **B** Nancy – it's her birthday at the weekend. **A** Yeah, I know. What have you got her? **B** A beautiful, brown, leather handbag. **A** Fabulous! She'll love it. I've got her a lovely cashmere jumper. **B** She's a lucky girl. I want to post it to her. Have you got her address? **A** I have, but I haven't got the postcode.	**A** Who's the package for? **B** Nancy – it's her birthday this weekend. **A** Yeah, I know. What did you get her? **B** A beautiful, brown, leather purse. **A** Awesome! She'll love it. I got her a gorgeous cashmere sweater. **B** She's a lucky girl. I want to mail it to her. Do you have her address? **A** I do, but I don't have the zip code.

2 **CD2 19** Listen and check. Compare the differences in pronunciation.

3 **CD2 20** Listen and read the following conversations in **British English**. Try to convert them into **American English**.

1
A Have you got the time?
B Yeah, it's five past four.
A Did you say five to?
B No, five *past* four.

2
A What are you going to do at the weekend?
B Oh, you know, the usual. Play football with my kids and do a bit of gardening.

3
A Did you have a good holiday?
B Yeah, really good.
A How long were you away?
B Five days altogether. From Monday to Friday.

4
A Where do you live?
B We've got a small flat on the ground floor of a block of flats in the city centre.
A Have you got a garden?
B No, we haven't – just a car park at the rear.

5
A Have you seen Meryl Streep's new film yet?
B I have. She was terrific in it. She played this plain, old woman who drifted around in her dressing gown all day.
A Yeah, she's a great actor.

6
A Have they brought the bill yet?
B Yeah. They just have. But I can't read a thing. The lighting is so bad in here. You need a torch.

7
A Do we need to stop for petrol?
B Yeah, why not? Anyway, I need to go to the loo.

8
A Did you enjoy the match?
B Yeah, it was great, but we had to queue for half an hour to get tickets.

4 **CD2 21** Listen and compare your ideas.

5 What is the **American English** for these words? Use your dictionary to help.

motorway	rubbish	biscuit	chemist's	cupboard *can be larger closet too*	crisps
trousers	tap *faucet*	pavement	windscreen	lift	autumn

Do you know any more **British English** words or expressions?

[handwritten notes:] roundabout, petrol, maths, garden = yard, jumper, lorry, trainers, nappy, in hospital, trolley - shopping cart, zebra crossing, loo, wardrobe

6 Fruits of war

Ways of adding emphasis • Tense review
Nouns from phrasal verbs • Keeping the peace

VIDEO Bletchley Park

STARTER

1 Look back in history. How many wars can you name? Who was fighting who?

2 Work in groups. Read the quotations and discuss what you think they mean.
Try to match them with their sources. Compare ideas as a class.

1 "I came, I saw, I conquered."

2 "Happiness lies in conquering one's enemies, in driving them in front of oneself, in taking their property, in savoring their despair, in outraging their wives and daughters."

3 "The supreme art of war is to subdue the enemy without fighting."

4 "It is not enough to say we must not wage war. It is necessary to love peace and sacrifice for it."

5 "War does not determine who is right, only who is left."

6 "The tragedy of modern war is that the young men die fighting each other, instead of their real enemies back home in the capitals."

7 "No one is born hating another person because of the color of his skin, or his background, or his religion. People must learn to hate, and if they can learn to hate, they can be taught to love...."

8 "I know not with what weapons World War III will be fought, but World War IV will be fought with sticks and stones."

9 "In war, truth is the first casualty."

10 "Mankind must put an end to war before war puts an end to Mankind."

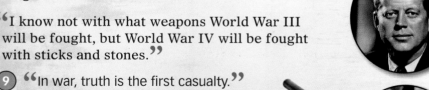

SOURCES

a **Sun Tzu,** Chinese military general (544 BC–496 BC)

b **Aeschylus,** Greek tragic dramatist (525 BC–456 BC)

c **Julius Caesar,** Roman general (100 BC–44 BC)

d **Genghis Khan,** Mongol Emperor (1162–1227)

e **Bertrand Russell,** philosopher and pacifist (1872–1970)

f **Albert Einstein,** physicist (1879–1955)

g **John F. Kennedy,** US President (1917–1963)

h **Nelson Mandela,** South African President (1918–2013)

i **Edward Abbey,** American writer and anarchist (1927–1989)

j **Martin Luther King, Jr.,** US activist (1929–1968)

3 **CD2 22** Listen and check your answers. What extra information do you hear for each one?

4 What do you know about any conflicts in the world right now? Why do you think human beings continue to wage wars against each other? Can violence ever solve conflicts?

READING AND SPEAKING
When good comes from bad

1 War may be violent and destructive, but it can also generate some things that are worthwhile. Work in groups. Look at the four headings below.

Technology	Medicine	Politics	Society

Use them to list some possible good things that have come out of war. Discuss ideas with the class.

2 Read through the texts quickly. Did you think of any of the things mentioned? Make a note of *one* important or interesting fact from each topic. Compare your ideas with your group.

3 Read the texts again. Look at the words below. Which heading do they go with and what is said about them?

refrigerators	the horse	grafts
a draft	twitches	dress codes

4 Answer the questions.

1 What did Adam Hochschild get right and Douglas Haig get wrong?
2 What differences are there between the medical understanding of "shell shock" then and now?
3 Which two breakthroughs led to blood banks? Why was the death rate still high?
4 What were the two main things that impacted the lives of the upper classes?
5 How did women's lives change after World War I? Why is there still debate about this?
6 What part did the trenches in World War I play in the development of plastic surgery?

In your own words

5 What do these numbers refer to?

6,500,000	30 and 1944	1,000s
1901	80,000	1980

What do you think?

- Which of the six "lasting legacies" do you believe are most important? Why?
- Which would have come about without war? What difference did the war make?
- Why does war often lead to rapid progress?

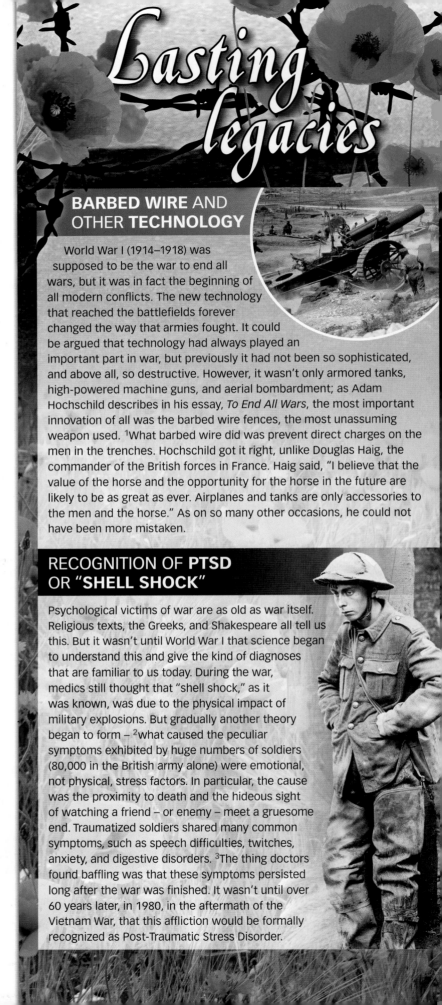

Lasting legacies

BARBED WIRE AND OTHER TECHNOLOGY

World War I (1914–1918) was supposed to be the war to end all wars, but it was in fact the beginning of all modern conflicts. The new technology that reached the battlefields forever changed the way that armies fought. It could be argued that technology had always played an important part in war, but previously it had not been so sophisticated, and above all, so destructive. However, it wasn't only armored tanks, high-powered machine guns, and aerial bombardment; as Adam Hochschild describes in his essay, *To End All Wars*, the most important innovation of all was the barbed wire fences, the most unassuming weapon used. [1]What barbed wire did was prevent direct charges on the men in the trenches. Hochschild got it right, unlike Douglas Haig, the commander of the British forces in France. Haig said, "I believe that the value of the horse and the opportunity for the horse in the future are likely to be as great as ever. Airplanes and tanks are only accessories to the men and the horse." As on so many other occasions, he could not have been more mistaken.

RECOGNITION OF PTSD OR "SHELL SHOCK"

Psychological victims of war are as old as war itself. Religious texts, the Greeks, and Shakespeare all tell us this. But it wasn't until World War I that science began to understand this and give the kind of diagnoses that are familiar to us today. During the war, medics still thought that "shell shock," as it was known, was due to the physical impact of military explosions. But gradually another theory began to form – [2]what caused the peculiar symptoms exhibited by huge numbers of soldiers (80,000 in the British army alone) were emotional, not physical, stress factors. In particular, the cause was the proximity to death and the hideous sight of watching a friend – or enemy – meet a gruesome end. Traumatized soldiers shared many common symptoms, such as speech difficulties, twitches, anxiety, and digestive disorders. [3]The thing doctors found baffling was that these symptoms persisted long after the war was finished. It wasn't until over 60 years later, in 1980, in the aftermath of the Vietnam War, that this affliction would be formally recognized as Post-Traumatic Stress Disorder.

BLOOD BANKS

The first blood banks, called "blood depots," were set up by Oswald Hope Robertson, a medical scientist and US Army Officer, while serving in France in 1917. Just before the war, in 1914, it had been discovered that transfused blood could be prevented from clotting if mixed with sodium citrate. In the same year it was established that blood could be stored in refrigerators. These two huge breakthroughs paved the way for Robertson's "blood depots." Prior to this, blood transfusions had had to be made vein to vein, directly from donor to patient. Medics used the "preserved" blood at casualty stations for wounded soldiers. However, survival rates were not good because [4]one vital thing they had overlooked was the importance of blood groupings (three blood groups, A, B, and O, had been identified in Vienna in 1901 by an Austrian, Karl Landsteiner). Nevertheless, the wartime advances led to a blood-donor service being established in London in 1922. Here all volunteers were tested for blood group and screened for diseases.

THE DECLINE OF ARISTOCRACY

World War I had a devastating impact on the British upper classes. The sons of the aristocracy fortunate enough to survive the war returned to find their place in society no longer automatically assured. Their numbers were severely reduced – even the prime minister's son was killed. This meant that in the immediate post-war period, those who had been expected to become leaders – particularly in politics and business – were no longer there.

There was also a fall in the number of those willing to work as their servants. History professor Joanna Bourke says, "In the past, the servant class in upper-middle-class homes were those people whose family tradition was to work there. When someone left, the cook would recommend her niece – and that no longer happened." The introduction of a draft had turned a professional army into a civilian one. New officers could now come from humble backgrounds and, like the many thousands of emancipated women, they were not prepared to abandon the possibility of social advancement that the war had brought them and go back to being shopkeepers and servants.

WOMEN'S EMANCIPATION

[5]Something that historians still wrangle over is how much World War I liberated women. In reality, women's work was already on the rise before 1914, and once the war was over many women went back to their old jobs. However, without a doubt, women successfully carried out a huge number of traditionally masculine roles during the war. And without a doubt, some of the post-war fashions, such as the flapper *garçonne* (*little boy*) look, flew in the face of pre-war feminine dress codes. Also, crucially, it was after the war that women in certain countries achieved the most important political right: the right to vote. In Great Britain, they could vote from the age of 30 in 1918. In Germany, they could vote in 1919. In the US, women could vote in all states from 1920. However, in France, women could not vote until 1944, towards the end of World War II.

"BROKEN FACES" – THE FIRST PLASTIC SURGERY

Modern surgery was born in World War I. Civil and military hospitals acted as theaters of experimental medical intervention, and the outbreak of war changed the course of plastic surgery forever. Trench warfare meant that the head and the face were especially exposed to enemy fire and received extensive trauma wounds. Countless veterans survived the war, but paid the price by ending up maimed, mutilated, and disfigured. These were the so-called "broken faces," named after an expression coined in France by Colonel Yves Picot, president of the *Union des Blessés de la Face et de la Tête*, which was founded in 1921.

By the end of hostilities, there were about 6.5 million war invalids in France. Surgeons from the warring countries faced a considerable flood of these "broken faces," and were charged with giving them human features again, to ease the plight of their reintegration into civil life. Missing flesh and bone were covered up with grafts, an innovation that came about by using skin from other parts of the body.

LANGUAGE FOCUS
Ways of adding emphasis

1 These sentences are similar to ones found in *Lasting legacies* on pages 46–47. Check them with the sentences in the texts. How exactly do they differ? What is the effect of the differences?

- ¹ Barbed wire prevented direct charges on the men in the trenches.
- ² Emotional, not physical, stress factors caused the peculiar symptoms exhibited by huge numbers of soldiers.
- ³ Doctors found it baffling that these symptoms persisted long after the war was finished.
- ⁴ They overlooked the importance of blood groupings.
- ⁵ Historians still wrangle over how much World War I liberated women.

GRAMMAR SPOT

Structures that add emphasis (1)

a I hate the waste of human life in war. (base sentence)

| What | | |
| The thing | I hate **about** war is the waste of human life. |

It's the waste of human life **that I hate**.

b War changes / The war changed people's lives forever. (base sentences)

What		
The thing	war **does is**	change people's lives
Something	the war **did was**	forever.

What happened was...

CD2 23 Listen and repeat the sentences so they *sound* emphatic.

▶▶ **Grammar Reference p. 146**

---

2 **CD2 24** Listen and identify the ways in which the speakers add emphasis to these sentences. Work with a partner. Can you think of any other ways of emphasizing each sentence?

1 I can't stand Bruce. He's so full of himself.
2 His lack of self-awareness amazes me.
3 You don't appreciate how exhausting traveling is.
4 The number of security checks drive me crazy.
5 The customs officer behaved so rudely. This upset me.
6 All the nurses were very sympathetic. I appreciated this.
7 You are always late. This really annoys me.
8 You should talk to Peter.

3 Read the question and answer below. Rephrase the *answer* to make it sound more **emphatic** using the expressions below.

Q What kind of vacation do you like?
A I like touring historic sites.

1 *One* thing …
2 What I …
3 Touring historic sites …
4 It's …
5 … something I …
6 There's nothing … more than …

CD2 25 Listen and check. What are the questions and comments that stimulate the different responses? Practice them with your partner, paying particular attention to the stress and intonation.

The Berlin Wall

Structures that add emphasis (2)

1 Negative inversion

Certain negative expressions can be put at the beginning of a sentence for emphasis. This happens more often in written or formal English.

I've never seen **Never have I seen**	such courage.
One rarely finds **Rarely does one find**	such clear explanations.
If it hadn't been for the war, **Had it not been for the war,**	women would not have gotten the vote.

2 Emphatic *do, does, did*

Finally, the war ended.   Finally, the war **did** end.

CD2 26 Listen and repeat the sentences so they *sound* emphatic.

▶▶ Grammar Reference pp. 146–147

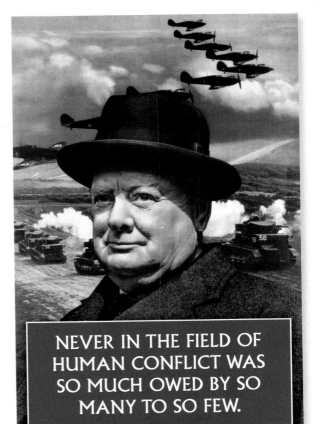

NEVER IN THE FIELD OF HUMAN CONFLICT WAS SO MUCH OWED BY SO MANY TO SO FEW.

4 Complete the sentences to make them more emphatic.

1 You don't often read any good news in the newspaper.
   Rarely _____

2 Churchill was a strong wartime leader and a brilliant orator.
   Not only _____

3 I didn't know what he'd been up to.
   Little _____

4 You won't get that job with an attitude like that.
   In no way _____

5 Fighting broke out as soon as the demonstration started.
   No sooner _____ than _____

6 Now I understand why you were so worried.
   Only now _____

7 If I hadn't seen it with my own eyes, I wouldn't have believed it.
   Had _____

8 You won't find a better heart specialist anywhere.
   Nowhere _____

Talking about you

5 Complete the remarks about you using an emphatic structure. Share ideas with the class.   *I've never gotten around to telling*

1 Something I've never told you is … [that I'm actually a secret agent.]
2 What I can't stand about …
3 What always surprises me is …
4 The thing that annoys me the most …   *gets to me*
5 It's not me who …
6 What the government should …   *gotten a chance*
7 Never in my life have I …
8 What I did after class yesterday …

CD2 27 Listen and compare your ideas.

Pronunciation: using stress to emphasize

Work with a partner. What do you think is the main stressed word in each of **B**'s replies?

1 **A** Peter hasn't told anybody.
  B He told me.

2 **A** I hope you didn't tell Clara.
  B I didn't tell anyone.

3 **A** I invited Anna, but she isn't coming.
  B I told you she wouldn't.

4 **A** Who told Tim about it?
  B I have no idea. I didn't tell anyone.

5 **A** John won't like it when you tell him.
  B If I tell him.

6 **A** It's the worst movie I've ever seen.
  B Tell me about it!

7 **A** He dumped me.
  B I told you he would!

8 **A** Have you heard the joke about the old man and his dog?
  B I told you it!

CD2 28 Listen and check. Practice with a partner.

💬 LISTENING AND SPEAKING
Peace and goodwill

1 What do you know about the First World War? How do people generally view it today?

2 **CD2 29** Listen to **Part 1**. It's an extract from a musical play called *Oh, What a Lovely War!*

 1 Who is fighting who? What nicknames do the two sides have for each other?
 2 Where are they standing? What two things do they hear?
 3 What is surprising about the interaction between these enemy soldiers?
 4 The scene depicts the beginning of the so-called "Christmas truce," which took place on Christmas Eve in the first year of the war. What do you think happened next?

3 **CD2 30** **Graham Williams** and **Harold Startin** fought in WWI and were on sentry duty on that Christmas Eve. Many years later they recorded their experiences that night.

Listen to **Part 2**. How is their account similar to the scene in the play? What is *no-man's land*?

In your own words

4 Use the prompts to tell the story to a partner.

 1 At the stroke of eleven o'clock lights … , and people started …
 2 Graham thought this was … , so he woke …
 3 Eventually both sides started communicating by …
 4 The next morning everyone …
 5 Harold says that he made friends with … despite …
 6 They helped each other in many ways. For example, they …

5 **CD2 31** How long do you think the truce lasted? Listen to **Part 3** and find out. Answer the questions.

 1 Who was John French?
 2 What was the significance of the rifle shots?
 3 Who was Otto?

What do you think?

• Do you find the story depressing or uplifting? Or both? Why?
• Do you think that commanding officers could become friends in the same way?
• Could such an incident happen in modern conflicts? If not, why not?

Tense review

Complete the summary of the story with a verb from below in the correct tense and form, active or passive.

be (x3)	believe	borrow	bury	conduct	make
~~go on~~	happen	help	join in	last	meet
sing (x2)	strengthen	take place	visit	wake	

The Christmas Truce

The war [1] _had been going on_ for only a few months when on Christmas Eve 1914, an extraordinary event [2] _____.
At midnight, the sleeping British soldiers [3] _____ by the sound of carols [4] _____ in the German trenches. They immediately [5] _____ with English carols and soon both sides [6] _____ together. The next morning they all [7] _____ in no-man's land, and in a very short time, many friendships [8] _____. Not only [9] _____ they _____ to bury each other's dead, but often German and British soldiers [10] _____ together in the same grave. Tools [11] _____ also _____ from each other, and defenses [12] _____. There was no fear or suspicion on either side. If there [13] _____ fear, such a truce [14] _____ never _____.

Incredibly, some friendships [15] _____ a lifetime. Harold Startin, who [16] _____ dead for many years now, [17] _____ regularly during his life by his friend Otto, from Stuttgart.

Nowadays, it [18] _____ generally _____ that such a truce [19] _____ impossible. Most modern warfare [20] _____ from the air.

▶▶ **WRITING** Writing for talking – Researching a period in history *pp. 110–*

VOCABULARY
Nouns formed from phrasal verbs

1 Complete the sentences with a compound noun formed from *up* at the end of the words in the box below.

> back   slip   shake   hold

1 *something used for support if the main one fails*
   At the end of the day, I make a copy of my work as a
   _____ .

2 *a careless mistake that spoils a plan*
   There was an administrative _____ , and the
   emails weren't sent in time.

3 *a situation in which a lot of changes are made*
   There's been a big _____ at work. They've fired
   six managers and restructured the whole company.

4 *a delay*
   Sorry for the _____ – we're having a few
   technical glitches with our software today.

Why do I always have to be the lookout?

2 Complete the sentences with a compound noun using the word in **bold** as the **first** word. Use the definitions to help.

out

1 *the final result of an election, or negotiations*
   We are all waiting for the _____ of the meeting.

2 *a set of clothes worn together*
   She bought a new _____ for the wedding.

3 *what is expected to happen in the future*
   The _____ for tomorrow's weather is bleak.

4 *a store or company through which products are sold*
   Starbucks has retail _____ in all the major cities
   throughout the world.

take

5 *a meal you buy in a restaurant to eat at home*
   Do you want to eat out or get _____ ?

6 *getting control of a company by buying most of its shares*
   Business sections of newspapers are full of company
   mergers and _____ .

down

7 *information obtained from the Internet*
   For free _____ , click here.

8 *failure or ruin following success*
   I usually eat a healthy diet, but chocolate is my
   _____ .

9 *a lot of rain that falls fast and heavily*
   I got soaked in yesterday's _____ .

break

10 *new and dramatic development*
   There have been great _____ in organ transplants
   in the last 20 years.

11 *a serious mental illness*
   After his mother died, Paul suffered from a complete
   nervous _____ .

12 *end of a relationship*
   Sarah was very depressed after the _____ of her
   marriage to Tony.

3 Choose some of the words in the box. Use a dictionary
if necessary and write a definition as well as an example
sentence with a blank. Test other students.

setback	upkeep	lookout	comeback	outburst
showdown	upturn	knockoff	drawback	knockout

Keeping the peace

1 We all have arguments. Look quickly through the four conversations. What are the people arguing about?

①
A What color do you call that?
B It says "pale sunlight" on the can.
A "Pale sunlight!" It's more like "dazzling daffodil!" I can't wake up to that every morning – it'd give me a headache.
B ¹_____ it is a little bit yellow. Oh, dear! I just wanted a kind of sunny glow in our bedroom.
A Don't worry. ²_____ Let's get some of those little sample cans from the paint store.

②
A We should have turned left there.
B Look! Who's driving this car? The GPS said "right."
A I know these streets better than any GPS.
B ³_____ The GPS is never wrong.
A Huh! You don't believe that any more than I do.
B Well, I am *not* turning around.
A OK, OK. ⁴_____ But don't blame me if we're late.

③
A I don't have a clue who to vote for in the next election. They are all a bunch of...
B But you have to vote. We can't let the opponents win.
A ⁵_____ They're all horrible.
B ⁶_____ Let the opponents win and taxes will skyrocket and prices will ...
A Come on! That happens with all of them.
⁷_____ . We can't ruin our friendship over this.

④
A Put that thing down!
B What?
A You spend your life in front of a screen.
B Hey! Hang on a minute – ⁸_____ You never go anywhere without your tablet and cell phone.
A Yeah, but I'm not always checking them. You've lost the art of conversation.
B I have not! ⁹_____
A Well, I've been telling you about my day, and you haven't heard a word.
B Uh? Sorry – what did you say?

2 We use many expressions in arguments to agree, disagree, and sometimes to compromise and make peace. Which of these expressions disagree? Which seek to make peace?

I couldn't disagree more.	Have it your way.
That's not how I see it.	You do not!
Let's just agree to disagree.	I guess ...
I really take offense at that.	Look who's talking!
I'm sure we can find a happy medium.	

3 Work with a partner. Complete the conversations with the expressions from exercise 2. Read them aloud to each other.

CD2 32 Listen and check. Act out some of the conversations for the class.

4 With your partner, create an argument about one of these topics. Try to reach a compromise or make peace at the end.

choosing a vacation	what to cook for friends
the other's boy/girlfriend	which is best – book or e-reader?
which movie to see	an item in the news

7 Lighten up!

Real and unreal tense usage • Phrasal verbs with *on* and *off* • Look on the bright side

 VIDEO **Graffiti life**

STARTER

1 Graffiti can sometimes lighten up everyday life. Work in pairs. Where in public might you read the signs in 1–12? Match them with the graffiti written on them in a–l. Which did you find the funniest?

1 Bill posters will be prosecuted.
2 **Parking area 2B**
3 These bathrooms will be closed on Monday.
4 Fly British Airways. Breakfast in London. Lunch in New York.
5 **Beauty blossoms with age.**
6 *Have you seen the Empire State Building?*
7 **This door is alarmed.**
8 **No smoking**
9 **Beware of the dog!**
10 Passengers are requested not to cross the lines.
11 *Headache? Nothing acts faster than Anadin.*
12 **SAY NO TO GRAFFITI!**

2 Look at the examples of works by the graffiti artist Shepard Fairey. What point do you think he's trying to make with them? Which do you find the most compelling? Why?

a unless you're on fire.
b Please don't startle it any further.
c The cat's not very trustworthy either.
d It takes hours to untangle them afterwards.
e Sign a partition!
f Not Photoshop.
g So take nothing instead.
h Bill Posters is an innocent man!
i Or not 2B
j Luggage in Nairobi.
k Please return to "Lost and Found."
l Please do as much as you can today.

How to be happier

1 What changes would you most like to make in your life in order to be happier? What do you think are the most common causes of unhappiness?

2 Read the captions in the pictures. What do you think sections 1–7 are about? Read the text quickly and check.

3 Read the text again. Which section talks about …?

1 having a negative view of your own performance
2 concentrating on the good things in your life right now
3 benefitting from difficult experiences
4 hearing voices in your mind
5 making your body feel better
6 imagining the future

In your own words

4 Use the prompts to summarize each section of the text.

1 self-criticism / useful / constant / human / qualities
2 compare / others / better / deceptive / inside / same
3 capitalism / expectations / unrealistic / dissatisfied / real
4 meaning to / nagging / to-do list / life changes / regret / learn
5 past / look forward / present / mindfulness / chatter
6 moan / problems / accept / difficult / natural / opportunities

5 Find words or phrases in the text that mean …

1 keep talking about your weaknesses or faults (*section 1*)
2 admit that you recognize something is true (*1*)
3 view behavior in a hard and unforgiving way (*1*)
4 not what they seem to be (*2*)
5 give a high opinion of you enthusiastically (*2*)
6 constantly demanding that you do something (*4*)
7 a responsibility that weighs heavily on you (*4*)
8 worrying about a decision for a long time (*4*)
9 feel better after a bad experience (*4*)
10 complain about things in an annoying way (*6*)

CD2 34 Listen to eight people talking. Which of the words or phrases describe what they say?

What do you think?

• Which advice in the text do you agree or disagree with? Why?
• What other advice would you give to people to make their lives happier?
• Is there someone you know or have met who's made you feel more positive about life? How?
• When were the times you felt happiest in life (so far!)? Why?

▶▶ **WRITING Informal writing – A letter to my younger self** *p. 112*

SEVEN WAYS TO MAKE YOURSELF HAPPIER

1 Be kind to yourself.

Self-criticism has its uses; on the whole, it's better to be too self-critical rather than not self-critical enough! But when that voice in your head goes on and on about your failings, you need to challenge it. Let's face it, if someone else were as constantly and savagely critical of our behavior as we ourselves can be, we'd tell them to back off! Remind yourself that you're doing your best and you're only human. And tell that voice that you'd be able to take its criticisms more seriously if it had ever acknowledged some of your good qualities!

Be kinder to others, too. It's easier to forgive if you remember that generally people "know not what they do." We often judge people harshly to make ourselves feel better, but it actually sucks all the joy out of our relationships.

2 Don't compare your insides with other people's outsides.

This is often one of the main reasons we're so hard on ourselves; we think other people are managing their lives so much better than we are. But you never know what's really going on behind the personas that other people project, and you've probably seen the shock others often show if you reveal to them how you really feel inside. Appearances can be so deceptive!

You might think all those confident people in that meeting at work wouldn't be singing your praises now if they'd known how anxious you were feeling at the time, after a sleepless night worrying about it all. Well, what if those other people were feeling exactly the same way? Would you have known?

We asked positive psychology experts to share their favorite insights into what makes us unhappy, and how we can bring more joy into our lives.

3 Happy people don't have more. They just appreciate what they have.

Consumer capitalism encourages us to focus on what we don't have. It can be good to have our expectations raised, but there is a formula that states that *happiness = reality minus expectations*. If constant advertising makes us wish we had things that we have no realistic chance of getting, the end result is unhappiness.

They say you don't miss what you don't know. If only you hadn't seen that sold-out pasta dish on the restaurant's menu of lunch specials. It wouldn't have occurred to you then to feel dissatisfied with the dish you ordered! Ads like to tell us what we're missing and the satisfaction it would bring us if only we had it. It might, but then again, it might not. Remember, it's all imaginary; don't let it distract you from the pleasures of the real things you *do* have.

4 Stop procrastinating.

How many things are there in the back of your mind that you need to do, but haven't done? How long have you been meaning to fix that broken door, or reply to that email? Notice what a nagging burden these "must-do's" are at some level. No time to do them? But how long would some of them *really* take? Been too tired? Well, feel how tiring it is to have them hanging over you, and remember the energy lift you get when you finally cross something off your to-do list. Just get it done!

Are there big changes in life you've been putting off? Maybe you're afraid you'd regret them, but we regret failing to do things more than we regret having done them. At least we then learn from things going wrong, which is better than agonizing over what might have happened if we *had* done something. And anyway, our worries about negative outcomes are usually exaggerated. Let yourself be pessimistic, and imagine the worst that could happen. Wouldn't you get over it?

5 Where is your mind?

How much of the time is our mind focused on the past or future, rather than the here and now? Even looking forward to something a lot, which seems positive, can take us away from the potential happiness of the present moment. As the musician Hélène Grimaud puts it, "Waiting for anything to happen, worrying that something may, or wishing that something had not happened, or will not happen, steals from every precious moment we are living in now … and now … and now … forever."

Try a simple mindfulness exercise for becoming present. Sit upright and relax your body, from your feet to your head. Then, *listen* to the sounds around you. You'll find yourself either listening to the constant chatter in your head instead, busy with the past and future, or really listening to the sounds and becoming still and present.

6 Life isn't supposed to be easy.

People often complain about their problems as if they shouldn't exist, as if having a problem is a reason to be unhappy. *The Road Less Traveled*, by M. Scott Peck, begins with the line, "Life is difficult." It sounds gloomy, but Peck explains that once we *truly* accept the fact that life *is* difficult, it stops being so, because we see problems as natural occurences and actually as opportunities for growth. It's the people who won't accept this that make their lives miserable. As Peck says, "Most do not fully see this truth that life is difficult. Instead, they moan more or less incessantly, noisily or subtly, about the enormity of their problems, their burdens, and their difficulties, as if life were generally easy, as if life should be easy."

P.S. If you get plenty of exercise, it'll make you feel great!

LANGUAGE FOCUS
Real and unreal tense usage

GRAMMAR SPOT

1 Which sentences describe possible situations in the real world? Which describe unreal ones?

a If I **go** to the gym straight from the office, I **forget** all about work problems.

b If you **decide** you want to join a gym, I'**ll take** you to visit mine.

c If there **was** a gym near my house, I'**d join** it.

d I **would have gone** to the gym today if I **hadn't been** so tired.

What *is* the real situation in the unreal examples? How do the tenses in those examples reflect the unreality?

2 Look at other examples of unreal situations. What is the reality? What tenses are used?

I **wish** I *didn't live* here. **If only** I *hadn't moved*. I **wish** *you'd speak* more slowly. **Suppose** you *got* sick? **It's time you** *got* some health insurance. He talks **as if** he *knew* everything. I'**d rather** Harry *didn't come* to my party.

Which two of these uses of *wish* are correct? Correct the wrong ones.

I wish you would be taller. I wish I had blond hair. I wish I would find a better job! I wish you would stop talking so much!

▶▶ **Grammar Reference pp. 147–148**

---

1 Which of these sentences refer to real past time?

1 Suppose I decided to live in Brazil?

2 If we ever had money as children, we spent it on toys.

3 I'd rather you'd not told everyone my news.

4 Isn't it time we took a break?

5 Everyone agreed that she'd just gotten lost and would arrive before long.

6 I wish you didn't have to go.

7 He behaves as if he owned the place.

8 Had he known the truth, he would never have signed the contract.

9 My mother would always bake a cake for our birthdays.

10 She looked at me as if I'd gone crazy.

2 Discuss whether the sentences are correct. Correct the wrong ones.

1 I wish you would have asked me before buying that picture.

2 He looks as if he's French.

3 If we were warned about the flood, we would have moved everything upstairs.

4 I'd rather you wouldn't have put that picture on Facebook.

5 If only she could have gotten tickets for the championship game!

6 I wish you didn't interrupt when I'm talking!

7 If we didn't have to work on the weekend, we would often go sailing.

8 It's time you get a haircut.

GRAMMAR SPOT

Mixed conditionals

In Zero, First, Second, and Third Conditional sentences, both clauses are often in a set pattern of present, past, or future. However, mixed conditionals can contain various combinations of time periods.

If you'**d read** the instructions, you **wouldn't be finding** it so hard to use.
   (past)   (present)

I'**d take** you to the airport tomorrow if my car **hadn't broken down**.
(future)   (past)

▶▶ **Grammar Reference p. 148**

---

3 What are the time periods in the clauses in these examples?

1 You'd have a better appetite if you hadn't eaten that chocolate.

2 If my exams weren't happening soon, I'd have come out with you all.

3 I'd have applied for that job in Lima if I spoke Spanish.

4 I wouldn't be going to Bali if I hadn't won that money.

5 If we hadn't called off the wedding, we'd be celebrating our anniversary next Monday.

4 Complete the mixed conditionals with the correct verb forms.

1 I _____ (give) Dave a ride again tomorrow if he _____ (not make) fun of my car this morning.

2 If you _____ (not sit) in that café when I walked in, we _____ (not live) together now.

3 If Mason _____ (be) born a week earlier, he _____ (start) school next week!

4 We _____ (buy) that house right now if the previous owner _____ (not paint) it pink!

5 If I _____ (not have) bad eyesight, I _____ (train) as a pilot after I graduated from college.

6 I _____ (mail) Maria's birthday present yesterday if I _____ (not visit) her next week.

CD2 35 Listen and check.

5 **Will** and **Zoe** are having an argument in a hotel. Put the verbs in parentheses in the correct verb form. Where there is no verb given, use an auxiliary.

"I wish we hadn't come here."

Zoe Ugh! This hotel is horrible! I wish we ¹_____ (not come) here. I've never seen such a dirty place in my life! It ²_____ (not be) so bad if the bathroom ³_____ (be) clean, but it ⁴_____ (be) filthy. I ⁵_____ (not even wash) my socks in it.

Will I know, but we'd been driving for hours, and I ⁶_____ (want) to stop. If we ⁷_____ , there might not have been another hotel for miles, and we ⁸_____ (still drive).

Zoe I wish we ⁹_____ (leave) earlier, so we ¹⁰_____ (get) to Carmel today. We ¹¹_____ (not get) there until tomorrow at lunchtime now. I told you we'd need to leave in the morning, but you ¹²_____ (listen)!

Will I had to finish some important work this morning. If I ¹³_____ , we ¹⁴_____ (can leave) earlier. Then we ¹⁵_____ (sit) in a nice hotel on the coast instead of this dump in the middle of nowhere.

Zoe Anyway, it's time we ¹⁶_____ (have) some food. If it ¹⁷_____ (not be) so late, I ¹⁸_____ (suggest) looking for a cute café, but I guess we ¹⁹_____ (have to) eat here. I wish we ²⁰_____ . It ²¹_____ (be) awful, I'm sure.

Will Oh, I wish you ²²_____ (stop) complaining!

Zoe OK, I'm sorry. I guess we're both tired. Come on, let's start enjoying the weekend!

CD2 36 Listen and check. Practice the conversation with a partner. Pay attention to short forms and contractions.

---

would

6 Which of these sentences describe real situations? Which use of *would* is expressed in them?

1 My car wouldn't start, so I took the bus.

2 I wouldn't use that milk if I were you – it smells funny.

3 When I was a student, I'd often get up at noon.

4 In Paris, Charles met Penny, who he would marry five years later.

5 I'm glad he didn't ask me to lend him the money. I would have refused.

6 We'd go windsurfing every weekend at the lake. Those were the days!

7 So he took the job? I knew he would!

8 Ideally I would go to the gym more often, but I just don't have time.

The history of the smile

1 Which smiles in the pictures do you like most? Why?

2 Read the text. Which pictures do the highlighted words describe? Why is it easy for a smile to go wrong?

Why we smile
A broad, beaming smile is a wonderful thing, but not something we can produce to order. When we force a smile for a photo, it can look like an anxious grimace, and with good reason. It's thought the smile evolved from the "fear face" seen in primates today, with the corners of the mouth pulled back. This shows submission to a hostile fellow primate, signaling, "I'm afraid of you. I'm not a threat." In humans this evolved into the smile, making others feel at ease. Achieving a good fake smile isn't easy; we can control the muscles around the mouth, but not those around the eyes, which give a smile its warmth. This fake, tight-lipped smile can easily become a grin or smirk, sending the wrong message entirely.

3 **CD2 38** Listen to **Part 1** of a radio program on the history of the smile. Answer the questions.
   1 What did W.C. Fields say about starting the day?
   2 How important is the smile to communication today? Was this always the case?
   3 What do you learn about pictures **c** and **e**? Why might the "Laughing Cavalier" in **e** *not* be laughing?
   4 What role did sugar play in posing for portraits?
   5 What did Madame Vigeé-Lebrun in **g** have that the "Laughing Cavalier" didn't? What was the reaction to her portrait?

4 How easy do you find it to smile for photos? What's the best way to get a natural smile when posing?

   CD2 39 Listen to **Part 2**. Answer the questions.
   1 What revolutionized the way we smile?
   2 Why were smiles so important when Hollywood shots became fashionable?
   3 What do you think *crow's feet* are?
   4 How does Olivia Mann get natural smiles?

5 **CD2 40** Listen to **Part 3**. What effect is dentistry having on smiles? What might this lead to in future?

In your own words

6 In pairs, use the prompts to summarize different sections of the program.

Student A	Student B
Smiles in early paintings closed / control / teeth / sugar / serious	**Smiles in photographs** instant photography / Hollywood / informal shots / natural smile
Smiles in later portraits 1786 / Madame Vigeé-Lebrun / open / dentist / toothpastes	**Modern smiles** dentistry / new attitudes / acceptable / perfect / irregularities / bigger

What do you think?

- In which jobs is smiling important? Why?
- Can smiles be annoying? What emotions can they express?
- Take real or pretend photos of each other as Olivia Mann suggests. Say what you were thinking of.

VOCABULARY
Phrasal verbs with *on* and *off*

1 Starting/stopping

What might people be talking about in these examples?

Try ***turning*** it ***off*** and ***on*** again.   Tom ***took*** some ***time off*** last week.
It suddenly ***came on*** in the night!   It ***went off*** after I burned the toast!

"In preparation for landing, please turn off your books."

Complete the sentences with the verbs and *on* or *off*: | put bring catch pay finish log |

1 Do you think smart watches will _____ ?
2 We _____ the entire pizza by ourselves!
3 The Clippers in the finals? _____ it ____ !
4 _____ before leaving your desk.
5 I'll _____ the kettle _____ for tea.
6 We've finally _____ all our debts.

2 Continuing/not continuing

Why would someone ... ?

1 ***carry on*** like a crazy person.
2 find a lecture ***dragging on***
3 ***go on and on*** about their new phone
4 ***cheer*** somebody ***on*** during a race
5 tell you to "***dream on***"
6 say it's time to ***get a move on*** with work

CD3 2 Listen and compare.

What or who ... ?

1 can be ***blown off***
2 ***wears off*** after a few hours
3 can be ***laid off*** in a company reorganization
4 might be ***broken off*** after a change of heart
5 can be ***called off*** after intense negotiations
6 might you ***go off*** after visiting a processing plant

CD3 3 Listen and compare.

"Couple of kooks, I guess. They carry on like that every time we pass here."

3 Closer to/further away

Ben is *gaining on* Leo.

He *drove off* without me!

Complete the sentences with *on* or *off*.

1 We went to the airport to see Dan ___ .
2 A man just grabbed my bag and ran ___ !
3 He snuck up ___ me and startled me.
4 Her hair's dark brown, verging ___ black.
5 You're too close, just back ___ a little!
6 The police advanced ___ the protesters.
7 Ssh! Quiet! Don't scare the birds ___ !
8 Can we put this ___ until tomorrow?

4 Connected/separated

Choose the correct particle.

1 My house has a ***fenced on / off*** yard and a ***built on / off*** garage.
2 Oak Street, which ***borders on / off*** the park, is ***closed on / off*** this week due to road work.
3 The police have ***cordoned on / off*** the criminal's house and ***sealed on / off*** the entire area.
4 The gym has ***added on / off*** a women's weight room, which is ***partitioned on / off*** from the men's.

5 **CD3 4** Listen to the questions and reply with a verb from the box + *on* or *off*. Then listen and compare/repeat.

So there isn't going to be a taxi cab strike now?

No, they've called it off.   No, it's been called off.

| drag | come | see | lay | ~~call~~ | blow |
| wear | put (x2) | catch | nod | seal | |

THE LAST WORD
Look on the bright side

Never mind!

1 **CD3 5** When we tell people our bad news, they often try to cheer us up and reassure us. Listen and complete **B**'s reply.

A I got soaked when that huge wave came in!
B *Never mind, it _____. At least* you can dry off in the sun.

2 Use the highlighted words to complete the replies.

1 end   cheer   work

   A The bank won't lend me any more money. I wish I'd never started my own business!
   B _____ up! *I'm sure it'll all _____ out for the best in the _____.*

2 gained   ventured   tried

   A If only I'd never asked Lucy out. She said no, and it's really awkward working with her now.
   B You'll get over it soon. *At least you _____. You know, nothing _____, nothing _____.*

3 stay   hang

   A I don't think I'm ever going to make it as an actor. I messed up another audition this morning.
   B It's not the end of the world. *_____ in there* and *_____ positive.*

4 done   forgotten

   A I can't believe what I've done! I sent an email complaining about my boss to her by mistake!
   B Don't worry about it. *What's done is _____. And it'll all be _____ in a few days.*

5 look   keep

   A I'd just had the cast taken off my leg, and now I've broken one of my fingers!
   B *_____ your chin up! Some day you'll _____ back on all this and laugh!*

6 good   easy

   A We'll have to be more careful. We've spent most of my year-end bonus money already.
   B Oh, well. *Easy come, _____ go. It was _____ while it lasted.*

7 could   win   beat

   A I'm so disappointed I didn't get the contract for the stadium. They gave it to another firm.
   B *You can't _____ 'em all. And you _____ always get a job with the other firm.*
   If you can't _____ 'em, join 'em!

8 best   disguise   gloom

   A It was depressing to lose the championship game on a goal scored in the last few seconds!
   B *It's not all doom and _____, though.* There's always next year. *And maybe it's for the _____.*
   If they focus on signing some new players, it might turn out to *be a blessing in _____.*

CD3 6 Listen and check. Which expressions are most similar to ones in your language?

3 Prepare some notes to talk about three bad things that have happened to you recently. Tell a partner what happened. Reply using expressions from exercise 1.

4 Work in pairs and write a dialogue that ends with one of these expressions. Read your dialogue to the class.

Still, better late than never!	Never mind. Better luck next time.
Oh, well. Live and learn.	Still, think of the money you've saved.

Oxford Online Skills Program
Log in for additional online learning

8 Gender matters?

Relatives and participles
Homonyms, homophones, and homographs • Clichés

VIDEO ◀ Ruth Shackleton: A life less ordinary

▶ **STARTER**

1 Look at the pictures. What is the message about gender roles in each one?

2 Read the statements in the quiz. Do you agree or disagree? Compare answers with a partner. Can you identify which gender-typical traits are being referred to in each one?

3 **CD3 8** Listen to a boyfriend and girlfriend checking their answers and check yours. How typical are they? How typical are you? Do you agree with the answers?

Are you a typical Male or Female?

1 ◯ I have lots of friends of my own sex.

2 ◯ I surround myself with things rather than people.

3 ◯ I usually remember people's birthdays.

4 ◯ I often forget people's names.

5 ◯ I'd rather communicate with friends via texts than call direct.

6 ◯ I'm good at figuring out how much to tip in a restaurant.

7 ◯ I'm good at multitasking.

8 ◯ I spend a lot of time talking about sports.

9 ◯ I find it easier to read maps by turning them in the direction I am going.

10 ◯ I find it easy to put myself in other people's shoes.

11 ◯ I'm good at working on a team, and I'm happy not to be the leader.

12 ◯ When I have a problem, I tend to keep it to myself.

13 ◯ I'm good at learning foreign languages.

14 ◯ I prefer to read non-fiction such as biographies and travel books rather than fiction.

4 What other statements could you add to the quiz to test gender traits? Make a list and share your ideas with the class.

DESPERATE HUSBANDS

"It's a dirty job," warns Hugo Carey. "When people talk about having an *anno horribilis*, they are not normally referring to the year in which they had their first children and got married. But for me that year was also the year in which I lost my job and became just one of the growing league of stay-at-home husbands."

READING AND SPEAKING
Jobs for the boys ... or girls?

1 In pairs, list jobs that are typically done by men or women. Which are typically done by both? Share ideas as a class.

2 Look at the titles of the two texts. What do you think they mean? Read the introductions. Which text(s) do you think these phrases come from?

flight deck	turbulent weather	air traffic controller
domestic issues	steep learning curve	career path
had to pull my weight	lost in admiration	tank-like stroller
slightly taken aback	swap the boardroom	exhibited prejudice
household chores	the breadwinner	hostile to the idea

3 Work in two groups.

> **Group A** Read about house husband **Hugo Carey**.
>
> **Group B** Read about **Cliodhna** /kliəna/ and **Aoife** /ifə/ **Duggan**, the female pilots.

Which words from exercise 2 are in your article? Were your ideas correct? What is their context?

4 Read your article again. Answer the questions about Hugo or the pilots, Cliodhna and Aoife.

1 In what ways is what they do not typical of their sex? What are the statistics concerning this?
2 What is the background for their current jobs or situation? Was it their choice?
3 Did they approach their roles confidently?
4 What problems did they face when they started?
5 What has been the attitude of people of the opposite sex?
6 What evidence is there of changing attitudes?
7 Which of these people are mentioned in your article? What do you learn about them?

a six-year-old girl	Susie	Yvonne Sintes	a technician
Dave Thomas	job center officials		their mother or father

In your own words

5 Work with someone from the other group. Ask each other the questions in exercise 4 to find out about the people in the other article. Explain any new vocabulary.

What do you think?
- How would you feel if the pilot on your flight was a woman?
- Whose lifestyle, the sisters' or Hugo's, do you think is most enviable? Why?
- Are there any jobs that you feel are best done by one of the sexes? Which? Why?
- In what ways is your lifestyle typical for your sex? In what ways is it not?
- How much have attitudes changed about gender roles over the years?

A **slow take-off** for female pilots

When two children, a six-year-old girl and an older boy, visited her flight deck last week, British Airways pilot **Aoife Duggan** asked if they would like to fly planes, too. The boy said yes, but the girl demurred, saying, "I think I'd like to be a flight attendant. Boys are pilots." A surprised Duggan says, "I was like, 'No! Come and sit in my seat, wear my hat.'"

Cliodhna and Aoife Duggan

According to figures from the Office of National Statistics, Hugo is one of over 220,000 house husbands – a figure that has leapt from fewer than 120,000 16 years ago. Although one of many, it still came as a shock for him to swap the boardroom for the baby-changing table. But he was used to bombshells. He'd faced one just two years earlier when he and his wife Susie went for their first baby ultrasound.

"Is this your first ultrasound?" asked the ultrasound technician. Hugo and Susie answered eagerly, "Yes, it is." "Well, it's two, twins." Stony silence was followed by convulsive laughter. They all started to giggle. Poppy and Thomas – now 18 months old – probably did, too. It was the start of a journey of discovery for Hugo. He was downsized when the twins were ten months old, and with Susie, a fashion consultant, now the breadwinner, there wasn't much choice. "I was just going to have to pull my weight and become a hands-on, full-time dad." He was unfazed, convinced he had a way with children. He now says, "Maybe I wouldn't have been so confident if I had known just how steep the learning curve was going to be."

For a start, their two-bedroom apartment, which doesn't have a yard, felt very small. His daily routine was exhausting at first. The twins woke each other up, so he had to be up and out of bed at 6 a.m. to let Susie sleep. And of course, the housework fell to Hugo. He had always been the chef in the family, so cooking wasn't a problem, but other household chores – cleaning, ironing, and shopping – and taking care of two small children, proved something of a challenge. He's now convinced that men don't have the same patience as women, but he's managed to raise his own level of patience. At first,

when out with the twins in their large, tank-like stroller, he would march them everywhere at an angry pace, but now he has learned to stop and let other sidewalk users pass by.

The humiliation of going down to the job center has also been somewhat diminished by the hilarity of entering accompanied by a couple of loud, hysterical children. Officials now hurry him through what is normally a long and tedious procedure.

After the twins' first birthday, he decided it was time to locate the nearest playgroup. "I think the moms were pretty excited to see a man, and I was asked if I wanted to attend their dinner get-togethers on the first Thursday of the month. They were probably just as bored as I was. I politely declined."

As the twins now approach their second birthday, Hugo can look back and admit that his role as a house husband took quite a bit of adjustment. At first, he yearned for office life, but now the rewards for his efforts have become much clearer. He says, "In fact, I am just grateful to have spent these crucial months with my children. I've seen them grow up, take their first steps, discover, and learn. I see lots of dads who obviously don't get to spend much time with their kids, and they don't seem to have a strong bond. I feel sorry for them."

One problem that's emerged is that because Hugo is now used to doing things for the kids, his methods don't always coincide with Susie's. However, his relationship with his mother has improved immeasurably. She had five children, and Hugo has nothing but admiration for her.

Yvonne Pope Sintes

Four decades after the first female pilot started work for a commercial airline, there are still relatively few women sitting in Duggan's seat. Of the 3,500 pilots employed by British Airways, just 200 are women, yet the airline still employs the highest proportion of female pilots of any UK airline. Globally, around 4,000 of the 130,000 airline pilots are women.

How much has changed since Yvonne Pope Sintes became Britain's first commercial airline captain in 1972?

She says, "Women are just as good as men, but they seem to have more domestic issues. I actually met someone, just a few months ago, who said he didn't know that there were any women pilots. I couldn't believe it."

When Sintes, now 83, started her career, airlines actively barred women. Inspired by watching the planes while growing up near an airport, she tried to join the military after school, but they wouldn't take women. So she became a flight attendant and earned her private pilot license with the Airways Aero Club. Then she became an air traffic controller and eventually, in 1965, a pilot. She says her male colleagues "didn't like me at all." Around half of them were hostile to the idea of a female pilot. "Someone actually said they'd resign if a woman joined. Unfortunately, he didn't." Later, it was the passengers who exhibited prejudice. "The men always looked slightly taken aback."

According to Aoife Duggan and her older sister Cliodhna, who is also a pilot, reactions to their gender are more likely to come from

passengers than colleagues. Only a couple of years ago, at her previous job for an airline in Asia, says Aoife, one man took one look at her and her female co-pilot and got off the plane. Cliodhna says she still sees some passengers' surprise.

"We've had pretty awful weather recently. My last landing was in Gatwick, and it was particularly turbulent … one of the passengers said, 'Oh my goodness, you look so small. I can't believe you just landed this giant plane.'"

For both women, flying was a part of their childhood. Their mother was a flight attendant, and their father an airline pilot. They grew up around a flying club. "There were some women at the club," says Cliodhna. "I was aware that there were women flying, and I didn't see my gender as a barrier." Aoife, seven years younger, grew up seeing her older sister's career path and decided to follow.

Why do they think so few women go into flying? "A lot of the time it's a matter of younger girls not being made aware that it's a career option open to them," says Aoife. "It's not the kind of thing people talk about in schools. You get young boys who say they want to be a pilot or an astronaut, whereas girls are not encouraged that way."

For the past couple of years, British Airways has been trying to increase its recruitment of women. "What we're after is the best person for the job," says Captain Dave Thomas, BA's chief pilot and head of training. They are having some success. The number of female candidates for jobs has gone from 5% to 15%. Thomas thinks the lack of women is mainly a cultural problem which needs to be tackled at an early age. "We did a little bit of research, surveying children between the ages of six and 12, and I think it came out as number two on the boys' list of top jobs, but I don't think girls think of it as an option."

LANGUAGE FOCUS
Relatives and participles

GRAMMAR SPOT

Defining and non-defining relative clauses

1 <u>Underline</u> the relative clauses in these sentences from the texts.
   a It was the passengers who exhibited prejudice.
   b According to Aoife and her sister, who is also a pilot, reactions are more likely to come from passengers.
   c It's a cultural problem which needs to be tackled at an early age.
   d Their two-bedroom apartment, which doesn't have a yard, felt small.
   e The mom who he was talking to invited him to the get-together.
   f Officials hurried him through what is normally a long procedure.

2 Answer the questions about sentences a–f.
   1 Which sentences still make complete sense if the relative clauses are removed? Which are defining relative clauses? Which are non-defining?
   2 In which sentences can *who* and *which* be replaced by *that*? Why?
   3 In which sentence can the relative pronoun be omitted? Why?
   4 In which sentence can *whom* replace *who*? Transform this sentence. What effect does this have?

3 **CD3** **9** Read the sentences in exercise 1 aloud. What is the role of the commas? Listen and check. What are the short responses? Practice the sentences with the response.
▶▶ **Grammar Reference pp. 149–150**

Discussing grammar

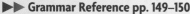

1 Discuss with a partner any differences in meaning and/or form between these sentences.

1 My sister, who's a flight attendant, is actually scared of flying.
   My sister who's a flight attendant is actually scared of flying.

2 The sailors whose cabins were below deck all drowned.
   The sailors, whose cabins were below deck, all drowned.

3 The girl who I shared a room with at college came from China.
   The girl with whom I shared a room at college came from China.

4 A few of the mothers who I met greeted me suspiciously.
   A few of the mothers that I met greeted me suspiciously.
   A few of the mothers I met greeted me suspiciously.

5 That's my cousin with the son who works in the White House.
   That's my cousin whose son works in the White House.
   That's my cousin who has a son who works in the White House.

6 People who are downsized often become depressed.
   People downsized often become depressed.

7 **A** There are still a lot of countries where women don't have the right to vote.
   B That's where you are wrong. There are only two.

2 Read these incomplete sentences. Discuss whether to complete them with a defining or non-defining relative clause, or either.

1 I don't like children …
2 The commute from work to home … took over three hours yesterday.
3 Politicians … aren't worth listening to.
4 The Taj Mahal … is built from exquisitely carved white marble.
5 These are the photographs …
6 We docked at the small port on the coast of East Africa …
7 My cousin … went paragliding last weekend.
8 We went on a white-water rafting trip on the Colorado River …

CD3 **10** Complete them with your ideas. Then listen and compare.

Participles (-ed and -ing forms)

Present and past participles can be used in many different ways.

1 As reduced relative clauses after nouns. Compare these examples from the texts:

*There are still relatively few women **sitting** in Duggan's seat.* (women who sit)

*Of the 3,500 pilots **employed** by British Airways, just 200 are women.*
(pilots who are employed)

2 As adjectives: *a **surprised** Duggan*   *an **interesting** statistic*

3 To express these ideas: **at the same time**   **because**   **if**   **after**

***Inspired** by watching the planes **while growing up** near an airport, she tried to join the military.*

▶▶ **Grammar Reference p. 150**

3 What ideas do the participles in these sentences express?

1 Having read the minutes of the meeting, I wrote a report.
2 Having read the minutes, I understood what the problem was.
3 I cut myself opening a can.
4 That portrait, believed to be by Rembrandt, sold for $26 million.
5 Cooked in a brown sauce, ostrich meat can be delicious.
6 Knowing my love of chocolate, she hid it away in her drawer.
7 Taken from his mother as a child, he's always had difficulty establishing relationships.
8 Browsing in our local bookshop, I was delighted to find a book called *Statistics for Dummies*.

4 Complete each pair with the present and past participle of the same verb.

1 a Flights _**booked**_ one month in advance have a 10% discount.
   b _**Booking**_ your flight in advance gives you a better deal.

2 a The new uniforms _____ by the pilots looked very professional.
   b Visitors _____ sleeveless tops will be denied entry.

3 a We took a shortcut, _____ an hour on our commute time.
   b With the money _____ from not eating out, I'm buying a bike.

4 a _____ all things into account, I've decided to resign.
   b _____ three times a day, these tablets will help your allergy.

5 a I fell on the ice, _____ my wrist.
   b The boy _____ in the car accident is in the hospital.

6 a _____ promises leads to lack of trust.
   b _____ promises lead to lack of trust.

7 a _____ away secrets won't win you any friends.
   b _____ the chance, I'd love to work in New York City.

8 a _____ up in the suburbs is healthy for young kids.
   b Strawberries _____ under polythene ripen more quickly.

CD3 11 Listen and check.

▶▶ **WRITING Adding style and cohesion – A folk tale** *p. 113*

5 There is something odd about the meaning of these sentences. Rewrite them to make them less ambiguous.

1 At the age of five, his mother remarried.

2 Coming out of the supermarket, the bananas fell on the sidewalk.

3 Riding along on my bike, a dog ran into me.

4 Skiing down the mountain, my hat flew off in the wind.

5 Having eaten our main courses, the waitress showed us the dessert menu.

Gender-neutral parenting

1 Discuss in groups. What did you like/not like about your upbringing? Did your parents have set ideas?

2 Look at the beginning of an article about "gender-neutral parenting." What do you think this is?

3 **CD3 12** Listen to **Ali** and **Luke** discussing the article. Who is the most scathing about it? Who are **Sam** and **Emma**? Who is **Storm**?

Bringing up Max

Parents raise son according to a technique known as *gender-neutral parenting*.

4 **CD3 12** Listen again. Are these statements true or false? Correct the false ones.

1 Both Max and Sam have sisters.
2 Luke used to worry about Sam wearing Emma's clothes.
3 Ali accuses Luke of criticizing Sam.
4 Sam is a difficult teenager.
5 Max's parents won't let him play with boys' toys.
6 Luke and Ali guessed that Max would be home-schooled.
7 Max's and Storm's parents are following exactly the same technique.
8 Ali believes the worst thing about Storm is the name.

Storm Witterick

What do you think?

• Do you agree with Ali's disapproving view of gender-neutral parenting or Luke's more accepting one?
• How many pros and cons can you think of in relation to bringing up a child this way?
• Is gender identity more about nurture or nature?

5 Turn to page 169. Read how Storm's mother reacted to criticism of her and her husband's ideas.

6 **CD3 13** Listen to and complete what **Dr. Eugene Beresin**, a child psychiatrist, says about baby Storm. Which of his views do you agree with? Why?

> 66 To raise a child not as a boy or a girl is creating, in some sense, a [1] _____. The Canadian couple's approach is a terrible idea because identity formation is really [2] _____ for every human being, and part of that is gender. There are many [3] _____ and social forces at play. Since the sexual [4] _____ of the 1970s, child development experts have embraced a more flexible view of gender. Before that, the stereotypes of boys were that they were self-sufficient, non-empathetic, [5] _____, and good at war. Girls were trained to be empathetic and [6] _____, and more nurturing. But since then, women have become more [7] _____, aggressive, and independent, and by the same token, men are allowed to cry. We often see hulking soccer players who are [8] _____. 99

SPOKEN ENGLISH *just*

1 What does *just* mean in these examples?
He's **just** a toddler.   It's **just** as I thought.

2 *Just* can have many different meanings. What does it mean in sentences 1–8?

| exactly recently right now simply only equally almost absolutely |

1 Don't worry. He's *just* as rude to me as he is to you.
2 A pair of red socks! That's *just* what I wanted!
3 We're *just* about out of coffee.
4 I'm *just* leaving now. See you soon.
5 *Just* listen to me for once!
6 I was *just* terrified!
7 I *just* heard the news.
8 Tom couldn't come, so it's *just* me.

Think of a context for each line. **CD3 14** Listen and compare.

VOCABULARY AND PRONUNCIATION
Homonyms, homophones, and homographs

Homonyms

1 Work with a partner. These sentences contain words that have homonyms in the text about pilots on pages 62–63. Find them. What are the two meanings?
1 This deck of cards has all the jokers missing.
2 This salad bar has every kind of vegetable you can think of!

2 Identify all the homonyms in these sentences. Make sentences for the other meanings.
1 Our company has branches all over the world.
2 We spotted a really rare bird in the forest.
3 Don't go making any rash promises that you can't keep!
4 I think we should scrap that idea. It's garbage.
5 Stop rambling and get to the point!

Homophones

3 Read these words aloud. Think of another word with the same pronunciation but a different spelling and meaning.

wail whirled bare heir site hire week sighed

4 Choose the correct homophone.
1 Public speaking makes my voice go *horse* / *hoarse*.
2 His *coarse* / *course* remarks upset all those present.
3 They tied their boat to the *buoy* / *boy* in the harbor.
4 I heard the long cry of a *loan* / *lone* wolf at sunset.
5 The thieves got away with a large *hall* / *haul* of gold antique coins.
6 Squirrels *berry* / *bury* nuts in woods and yards.
7 She lifted her *vale* / *veil* and smiled at her new husband.
8 This is only a *draft* / *draught* contract. You don't have to sign it.

Homographs

5 **CD3 15** Listen and write down the homograph you hear in each pair of sentences. What are the different pronunciations?

We're sitting way in the back, in **row** 102. /roʊ/
We had another **row** about our finances. /raʊ/

6 Divide into two groups. Use your dictionaries to find the two pronunciations and meanings of the words in your box. Make sentences to illustrate the meanings for the other group.

GROUP A			**GROUP B**		
wind	refuse	defect	wound	live	minute

THE LAST WORD
Talking in clichés

1 **CD3 16** A cliché is a phrase that has been used so often that it has lost much of its force. Read and listen to the conversations. Identify the clichés. What do they mean?

A Mom! Tommy's fighting with Ryan again!
B Oh, dear! I guess boys will be boys.

A Bye, Grandma! Jamie and I are going out for the evening!
B Have a great time! Don't do anything I wouldn't do.

A I'm thinking of getting another tattoo. A scorpion maybe, just above where it says "I ❤ Mom." What do you think?
B It's not for me to say. At the end of the day, it's your decision. You'll have to live with it.

2 Read the sentences in **A**. Match them with a response in **B**. Underline the clichés in **B**. What do they mean?

A	B
1 I just came across my very first girlfriend on Facebook.	a Hmm. You can't win for losing!
2 Larry failed his exam. Amy has the chicken pox. What's next?	b I bet that was a blast from the past.
3 Dad, I made the school soccer team! Varsity first string!	c Well, you know what they say: "No pain, no gain."
4 If I offer to pay, she'll say I'm old-fashioned. If I don't, she'll say I'm cheap.	d Good idea. Better safe than sorry.
5 I got a card from Jerry one week after my birthday.	e Better watch out! They say these things come in threes.
6 We're taking a complete break. Two weeks in the Caribbean!	f That's my boy! Like father, like son.
7 It took me ten years to build up my business. It nearly killed me.	g It takes all kinds.
8 I just need to go back in the house and make sure I turned off the oven.	h It boggles the mind! I can't even bear thinking about it.
9 They have ten kids! Goodness knows what their house is like.	i Oh, well. Better late than never.
10 Bob's a weird guy. He's going to live alone on a remote Alaskan mountain for a year.	j Sounds like just what the doctor ordered.

CD3 17 Listen and check. What is the next line in the conversation?

3 What do you think the following clichés mean? Try to use them in short conversations.

accidents will happen	a man (or woman) after my own heart	actions speak louder than words	it's all in a day's work
a fate worse than death	you can't have your cake and eat it too	behind every great man is a great woman	it's as clear as mud

4 Do you have any similar clichés in your language? Give examples.

Oxford Online Skills Program
Log in for additional online learning

9 The sound of music

Discourse markers • Rhyming words • The music of English

 VIDEO Silent movie music

PRODUCTION
DIRECTOR
SCENE | TAKE | ROLL
DATE

► STARTER

1 Look at the details of six scenes from upcoming movies. Your job is to choose soundtrack music for them. What genre and mood of music would you suggest for each one?

A Stylish spy thriller set in Prague. Opening scene with spy in dark subway, walking to meet with his contact.

B Science-fiction horror. Scene where girl put in trance by images beamed on TV walks into lake and is devoured by aliens.

C Action movie. Helicopter chase scene where government agent is hunted by secret service after uncovering conspiracy.

D Romantic drama set in New York City. Scene at end of day in Central Park on couple's first outing after falling in love.

E Quirky indie comedy about two sisters on road trip around US in rich uncle's car. Music for closing credits.

F Romantic drama. Final scene where relationship has to end because man is unable to get visa to stay in country.

2 **CD3 19** Listen to nine short clips of music. In pairs, decide which six you want to use for the movie scenes A–F.

3 **CD3 19** Listen again and share ideas as a class. Which choices were the easiest ones to agree on? Why?

4 **CD3 20** Listen to one more piece of music. Close your eyes and see what kind of movie scene comes to mind. Describe your scene to the class. Vote for the best suggestion.

You are the music

1 On a radio program called *Recommended Reads*, guests choose a book and say why they enjoyed it. Look at the book chosen by the guest, Rosie Garnett. What do the pictures tell you about the topics it contains?

You Are the Music

How Music Reveals What It Means To Be Human

Victoria Williamson

2 **CD3 21** Listen to **Part 1** of the program and answer the questions.

1 Why was Rosie's book not an obvious choice for her?
2 What is an *amusic*? What percentage of the population think they are amusical? What is the actual percentage?
3 When was music played for the babies in the experiment?
4 How did the researchers *know* that the babies recognized the music?
5 What is the everyday term for Infant Directed Speech (IDS)? What is it? Can you give examples of it?
6 Why do tone-deaf people struggle with language learning?

3 **CD3 22** Listen to **Part 2** and make notes. What does Rosie say about …?

Life memories	
Music and identity in adolescence	
Montreal	
YouTube	
The amygdala	
Movie music	
Musical instruments	

In your own words

4 In pairs, use your notes to talk about the different topics in exercise 3.

Vocabulary

5 **CD3 22** Listen again to **Part 2** and match the verbs in **A** with the phrases in **B**. What do they refer to in the program?

A	B
take somebody back	your attitude to music in subway stations
play	less self-conscious
go	from dementia
hang around	to a period of their life
hit	a role
suffer	haywire
come	on a solution
change	to life
feel	

What do you think?

• How good do you think you are at singing? Is it necessary to be musical to enjoy singing?
• Choose three songs or pieces of music that would be the top three on the soundtrack to your life so far. Talk in groups about the memories you associate with them.

LANGUAGE FOCUS
Discourse markers

1 Read this version of an extract from the program on page 70.

> **Rosie** [1] This book is an unexpected choice for me. [2] I don't consider myself a very musical person.
>
> **Clive** [3] It's not for music specialists, then?
>
> **Rosie** No, it's [4] geared for the general public, and [5] she makes the point that we're all far more musical than we might realize. I'm [6] one of those people she talks about who claim to be tone-deaf. [7] Nearly a fifth of the population believes that.

CD3 23 Listen to the actual extract and note the words that are used at points 1–7. What do they mean? How do they help to structure the discourse between the speakers?

GRAMMAR SPOT

Attitude adverbs

There are many adverbs and expressions that show the speaker's attitude to what they are saying.

Quite honestly, I think you should leave your job and try to make it as a professional singer.

Of course, it's a risk, and you'll probably earn less. But **surely** job satisfaction is more important than money?

Connectors

Connectors make the connection between independent clauses clear.

Growing your own vegetables saves money, and helps you stay in shape. **Above all**, it's fun!

You must pay that parking fine within 21 days. **Otherwise**, you'll have to pay double.

Explain the meaning of the connectors in **bold**.

▶▶ **Grammar Reference p. 151**

---

2 Choose the correct attitude adverbs to complete the conversation about a TV talent show.

A Have you been watching *Star Voices*?

B Well, [1]*funnily enough / as you'd expect*, I'̇ ~~~~ I caught last week's show and, [2]*seriou~~ ~~~*.

A So did you see the semi-final last ~~~~

B No, [3]*inevitably / unfortunat~~~~* Was it good?

A Well, [4]*actually / naturally ~~~~* [5]*Bizarrely / Frankly*, Anna, the ~~~~ make it to the final, even though s~~~~ was [6]*apparently / obviously* the best ~~~~ far. [7]*Surprisingly / Conveniently*, she seemed fine about it, though.

B Oh, she was my favorite, too! Well, [8]*no doubt / admittedly* she'll get a recording contract anyway. [9]*Alarmingly / Amazingly*, her performance from last week has had over a million YouTube hits.

CD3 24 Listen and check.

3 Which phrase follows the discourse markers in **bold**?

1 I'd thoroughly recommend that new pizzeria. The pizzas are amazing! **Mind you,** *it's cheap / it's expensive.*

2 I can't go skiing so soon after my accident. It's too much of a risk. **Besides,** *I can't really afford it. / I could come and enjoy the hotel spa!*

3 Why are you worried about asking Tom to lend you the money? **Surely**, he wouldn't say no to you. *It would be very unlike him. / He always does.*

4 **A** Tina must be upset about not getting promoted. **B** **Actually**, *she was disappointed. /she doesn't seem to care that much.*

5 The builders have done the job pretty quickly, **given that** *the work is poor quality. / the weather's been so bad.*

6 I think you expect too much of Amy. You need to be realistic about her behavior. **After all**, *she's still a teenager. / she could behave better.*

7 Guess what? Rob finally has a new girlfriend! **Apparently,** *he told me they met on vacation / he met her at a conference.*

8 So, I guess that's why Kyra's looking so happy these days. **Anyway,** *I guess I'd better be going. / I think she's enjoying her new job.*

9 It would be great if you got into drama school. **By the way,** *when will they let you know? / have you heard about Robin's plan to move into a new apartment?*

10 We didn't see a single whale or dolphin on our whale-watching cruise! **Still, at least** *the trip was very disappointing. / the weather was good.*

CD3 25 Listen and check.

4 Complete the conversation with either a discourse marker or a suitable phrase.

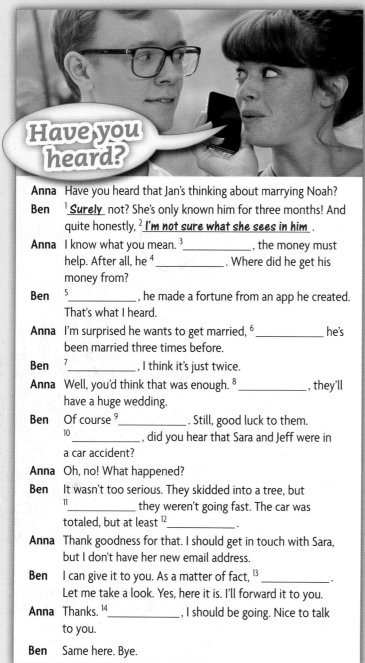

Have you heard?

Anna Have you heard that Jan's thinking about marrying Noah?

Ben [1] <u>Surely</u> not? She's only known him for three months! And quite honestly, [2] <u>I'm not sure what she sees in him</u> .

Anna I know what you mean. [3]_____ , the money must help. After all, he [4]_____ . Where did he get his money from?

Ben [5]_____ , he made a fortune from an app he created. That's what I heard.

Anna I'm surprised he wants to get married, [6]_____ he's been married three times before.

Ben [7]_____ , I think it's just twice.

Anna Well, you'd think that was enough. [8]_____ , they'll have a huge wedding.

Ben Of course [9]_____ . Still, good luck to them. [10]_____ , did you hear that Sara and Jeff were in a car accident?

Anna Oh, no! What happened?

Ben It wasn't too serious. They skidded into a tree, but [11]_____ they weren't going fast. The car was totaled, but at least [12]_____ .

Anna Thank goodness for that. I should get in touch with Sara, but I don't have her new email address.

Ben I can give it to you. As a matter of fact, [13]_____ . Let me take a look. Yes, here it is. I'll forward it to you.

Anna Thanks. [14]_____ , I should be going. Nice to talk to you.

Ben Same here. Bye.

CD3 26 Listen and compare your answers. Then practice the conversation in pairs.

5 **CD3 27** Work in groups. Listen to items 1–10. Agree on ways to complete them. Then listen and compare.

> Hello. Your face looks familiar. Have we met before?
>
> Actually, I don't think we have.

▶▶ **WRITING** Giving an informal opinion – A post on a comment thread *p. 114*

VOCABULARY AND PRONUNCIATION
Song, rhyme, and rhythm

1 Look at the photo on page 73. It depicts a scene that inspired the song *The Night I Heard Caruso Sing* by Everything but the Girl. What is incongruous about it? Where do you think it is?

2 Read the FACT FILES and answer the questions.

FACT FILE

Everything but the Girl

Lead singer/guitar:
Tracey Thorn

Guitar/keyboards/singer:
Ben Watt

Formed:
1982 in Hull, UK

Active: **1982–2000**

FACT FILE

Enrico Caruso (1873–1921)

Nationality: **Italian (born in Naples)**

First work: **apprentice mechanic and street singer**

First music lesson: **age 18**

Professional debut: **age 22**

Most appearances: **New York Metropolitan Opera (863)**

1 How long was Everything but the Girl together?
2 Who sang most of their songs?
3 What was Enrico Caruso's profession?
4 What was his background?

3 **CD3 28** Close your books and listen to *The Night I Heard Caruso Sing*. What is its message?

4 Read the lyrics and discuss in pairs which words you think are best to complete them. Think about rhyme and rhythm. Compare with others in the class.

5 **CD3 28** Listen to the song again and check.

What do you think?
- What stage of life was Ben at when he wrote the song?
- What does it mean that "the chains are loose"?
- How does the song reflect its period, the 1980s?
- Do you think its message is still true today? If so, how?

6 Read the background about the song on page 169.

THE NIGHT I HEARD CARUSO SING

The highlands and the lowlands are the routes my father _____,
The holidays at Oban and the towns around Montrose
But even as he sleeps, they're loading bombs into the _____,
And the waters in the lochs can run deep, but never still.

I've thought of having children, but I've gone and changed my _____,
It's hard enough to watch the news, let alone explain it to a child.
To cast your eye 'cross nature, over fields of rape and _____,
And tell him without flinching not to fear where he's been born.

Then someone sat me down last night and I heard Caruso sing.
He's almost as good as Presley and if I only do one _____,
I'll sing songs to my father, I'll sing songs to my child.
It's time to hold your loved ones while the chains are loose,
And the world runs _____.

But even as we speak, they're loading bombs onto a white _____.
How can we afford to ever sleep so sound again?

- takes / knows / goes
- hills / mountains / valleys
- ideas / mind / view
- wheat / barley / corn
- thing / act / deed
- wild / riot / amok
- submarine / train / plane

Rhyming words

7 Which word in each group of three doesn't rhyme with the other two?

1 knows / rose / lose
2 tough / cough / rough
3 foul / soul / poll
4 suit / route / foot
5 gloss / cross / gross
6 goose / choose / truce
7 flood / stood / blood
8 pour / roar / sour
9 word / sword / board
10 tow / dough / vow
11 card / ward / guard
12 rush / bush / push

Check using a dictionary (check any meanings you don't know at the same time).

8 **CD3 29** Listen to items 1–12, and complete them using one of the words from that number in exercise 7. Pay attention to your pronunciation! Then listen and compare.

> My favorite team is playing tonight. The players are in a slump right now, so ...

> I'm sure they're going to lose.

SPOKEN ENGLISH Rhyming expressions

Match words and phrases from **A** and **B** to make rhyming expressions. Think of ways to use them.

We spent five hours at the mall. We really shopped until we dropped!

A		B	
~~shop~~	nearest	the talk	and square
eyes	use it	and greet	on the prize
meet	blast	to zero	and shame
fair	walk	~~until you drop~~	and dearest
hero	name	or lose it	from the past

CD3 30 Listen and check/compare.

READING AND VOCABULARY
Hélène Grimaud

1 Look at the pictures of Hélène Grimaud and the headings in the text.
- What do you think she does for a living?
- What can you deduce about her life?

2 Read the text and check your ideas.

3 Statements 1–10 about Hélène Grimaud are *all* true. Find evidence in the text to support them.

1 Hélène felt she should have been born a boy.
2 Her parents worried about her behavior.
3 She didn't look forward to going to school.
4 She is sensitive to the suffering of animals.
5 She had disagreements with some of her professors at the Paris Conservatory.
6 Musical success didn't always bring fulfilment.
7 Hélène believes in fate.
8 She doesn't let fear dominate her approach to life and feels we have to take risks sometimes.
9 Hélène found it easy to identify with wolves.
10 She feels the quality of the instrument music is played on isn't so important.

Vocabulary

4 Read the highlighted words in the text and try to guess *roughly* what they might mean.

5 Match the words with their meanings.

A	B
1 compulsive	a too shocked to speak
2 scrawled	b stomach
3 smashed	c difficult to stop or control
4 tactile	d from prehistoric times
5 stunned	e drawn or written hurriedly
6 primeval	f using the sense of touch
7 belly	g broken into many pieces

What do you think?

- Why do you think wolves are "misunderstood"? How are they usually portrayed? What do you know about their real nature?
- Why do you think Hélène has a kinship with wolves? Which animal do you feel most kinship with? Why?
- Do you think someone needs to have suffered in life in order to be a great artist? Why/Why not?
- Have you discovered an activity that makes you feel more complete?

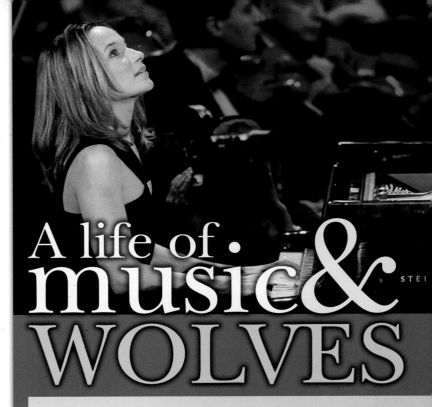

A life of music & WOLVES

As a child, Hélène Grimaud often heard a family of words she called the "uns." She was declared to be "uncontrollable." People also described her as "unmanageable," "unsatisfied," "undisciplined," and "unpredictable."

She was often an enigma even to her parents. It was decided she had too much energy, and judo, tennis, and ballet were the prescription. While the first two were tolerable to the tomboy Hélène, ballet – no way; the costume reminded her of the dolls she'd been given, and had smashed against her bedroom wall.

At school in Aix-en-Provence she had no playmates, and spent break times hiding behind the coats in the corridor. Her teacher expressed concern when an instruction to draw chickens on a farm resulted in Hélène's scrawled picture of wire mesh. Something did indeed seem caged inside her, yearning to be free. But what?

Hélène began to self-harm, discovering that acute physical pain gave her the intense sense of existence that she longed for. She also spent hours folding and refolding her clothes, and rearranged everything in her room endlessly. Psychologists would call this obsessive-compulsive disorder; Hélène now sees it simply as her desperate search for equilibrium.

Salvation in music

Finally, when she was seven, the energy trapped inside her found its outlet. Wondering if his daughter suffered from an excess of mental rather than physical energy, Hélène's father suggested music lessons. As Hélène listened to her teacher playing the piano, she felt something stir deep inside her: "I had the physical sensation of an opening; the impression that a path opened in front of me, as if a door had opened in the wall ..."

When she started the piano, her intensity found its home. "The tactile pleasure of playing, of seeking inside myself the emotion that I never, ever, in any way had been able to express or bring to a peak, this delicious pleasure completely satisfied me." Hélène recognizes just how important music was for her: "It saved me."

A rising star

She completed an eight-year piano curriculum in four years, and was accepted by the Paris Conservatory at 13, the youngest student by far. However, she eventually became bored with the piano studies she was given to play, and with the impetuosity of youth, returned to Aix to perform her first piano concerto in public. "I had the feeling that I was finally living, living in broad daylight, publicly – the thing I had been silently waiting for all my life." Her talent was recognized, and she recorded Rachmaninoff's Piano Concerto No. 2 when she was 15. She returned to the Conservatory, but left early, wanting to find her own style of playing, despite warnings that she wouldn't make it in the classical world without her professors' support.

Life in America

She had great success and there were more recordings, and yet she began to feel again that nagging sense of something missing in her life, and retreated into herself once more. When she received an invitation to play in the US, she jumped at it. She loved the experience and wanted to play more concerts there. Not speaking English was a problem, though, so she spent days watching rented videos in English, from war movies and historical epics to love stories and westerns, living on sandwiches. Six months later, she was able to hold all the conversations necessary to organize and perform a US tour.

She felt at home with Americans – no-one found her strange – and accepted an invitation to go and live in Tallahassee, Florida. Even though it wasn't her ideal city, she felt destiny had drawn her there, and that something important awaited her. At night, she walked her friend's dog in the rural outskirts of the city. Neighbors warned her that it was risky, especially in the area where a Vietnam veteran lived alone, a man they considered to be crazy and dangerous.

A fateful encounter

This only made Hélène curious. Out walking the dog at 2 a.m., she saw something that sent a shiver down her spine. It was the silhouette of a dog, yet it was unlike any dog she'd ever seen.

When its owner appeared, he explained that it was in fact a she-wolf. This was Dennis, the Vietnam veteran, who turned out to be a classical music lover. They talked about music, but Dennis fell silent when the she-wolf approached Hélène, who remained still as the wolf slipped its head under her palm. Hélène felt a spark radiate through her, the call of an unknown, primeval force, and then the wolf lay down, and offered Hélène its belly. Dennis explained his stunned silence. "It's incredible for a wolf to do that; it's a sign of recognition and trust, even a sign of submission. Wolves have a real phobia of humans. They never lay themselves open like that if they don't feel safe. Even with me, she's never acted like that."

Twin passions

Hélène had found her other passion and vocation. She began to learn everything she could about wolves and decided to create a center for the study and rehabilitation of this much misunderstood animal, with which she felt a strong kinship. For three years, she lived in the cheapest rooms she could find in the poorest areas of New York, content to rent whatever piano she could find for a couple of hours' practice, so she could save the money from her concerts to pay for her dream of protecting wolves. And so the Wolf Conservation Center was founded in 1999, in New York State, with Hélène playing a key role in its operation.

It continues with its educational mission today, though Hélène herself has since returned to her full-time profession as one of the world's top concert pianists. She describes the howling of wolves as a form of music, a social glue for the wolf pack, which "sends a lot of positive interactive feeling flying around." Her own performances clearly have a similar effect in the concert halls of the world.

The elements of music that lend themselves to language are **stress** (rhythm) and **intonation**.

Stress

1 **CD3 31** Listen to these sentences. Does the last sentence take much longer to say than the first sentence?

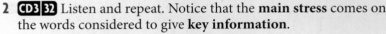
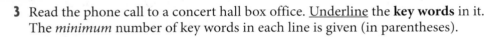

•	•		•
Mom	makes		cakes.
Our mom	makes		cakes.
Our mom	makes	the	cakes.
Our mom'll	make	the	cakes.
Our mom'll be	making	the	cakes.
Our mom'll be	making	all the	cakes.

English is a *stress-timed language*. This means the stressed syllables in a phrase have a regular rhythm. Any unstressed syllables between them are said quickly enough to fit into that rhythm.

2 **CD3 32** Listen and repeat. Notice that the **main stress** comes on the words considered to give **key information**.

3 Read the phone call to a concert hall box office. <u>Underline</u> the **key words** in it. The *minimum* number of key words in each line is given (in parentheses).

> **A** <u>Palace</u> <u>Theater</u>. How can I <u>help</u> you? (3)
> **B** Could I buy some tickets for the flamenco concert on Saturday? (4)
> **A** I'm afraid the Saturday concert is sold out. (3)
> **B** Oh, really? How disappointing! So are there tickets for the other dates? (5)
> **A** Yes. We have four tickets left for Sunday. Would you be interested in those? (4)
> **B** Yes, that would be great. I only need two tickets. (4)
> **A** Would you like seats on the floor or in the balcony? (2)
> **B** How much are the seats in the balcony? (3)
> **A** They're $40. The ones on the floor are $80, but they're great seats, very close to the stage. (8)
> **B** I'll take the seats on the floor. Can I pay with a debit card? (4)
> **A** Of course. May I have your card information? What's the number on the front? (6)
> **B** It's 5610 5910 8101 8250.
> **A** And the security number on the back? (3)
> **B** 713.
> **A** Thank you. Could you make sure you bring that card when you pick up the tickets? (7)
> **B** Sure. Thanks for your help. (3)
> **A** You're welcome. (1)

Friday, June 6 - Sunday, June

Palace Theate
Brookly

Ticke
$40, $8
on sale at th
box offic

Flamenco concert

4 Practice the dialogue in pairs, using **only** your <u>underlined</u> key words. Use **LOTS** of intonation.
CD3 33 Listen and repeat.

5 Now practice the full conversation, making sure you keep the main stress on the key words, and using plenty of intonation.
CD3 34 Listen and compare.

6 In pairs, write a short conversation in a store. Reduce it to the minimum number of key-word prompts and give it to another pair. Have the full conversation, using the prompts that you've been given. Pay special attention to stress and intonation.

10 Body and mind

Distancing the facts • Words to do with the body • Tag questions and replies

VIDEO **The science of sports**

> **STARTER**

1 Work in groups. Choose the correct facts in **bold** about the bod...

(handwritten note) pronunciation poem (rhyming / are) AHS

How well do you kno...

1

Every day the average person loses
25–50 / 50–100 / 175–200 hairs.
Blonds / Brunettes / Redheads
have the most hair.

...lower
...ster than /
...enails.
...ng nail
...iddle /

2
The average adult heart is
about the size of **one / two /
three** fists. The main artery
from the heart, the aorta,
is about the diameter of
a **drinking straw / ballpoint
pen / garden hose**.

6
Most people blink around
10 / 15 / 25 times a minute,
but that reduces by a half
when staring at a computer
screen. Babies blink only
**twice / four times /
six times** a minute.

3
Nerve impulses to and from the brain
travel as fast as **100 / 150 / 250** miles
per hour. Humans use **10% / 50% / 100%**
of their brains during a normal day.

7
Children have **twice / three
times / four times** as many
taste buds as adults. By the
age of 60, most people will
have lost about **a quarter /
a half / three quarters** of
their taste buds.

4
Babies are born with **20% /
30% / 50%** more bones than
adults. As adults, we are
about **1 / 2 / 3** centimeter(s)
taller in the morning than in
the evening.

8
The *three* most common reasons
for visits to the doctor are for
**headaches / skin problems /
a sore throat / joint problems /
back problems / the flu /
stomach problems**.

2 **CD4 2** Listen and check. What extra information do you learn about each topic?

READING AND VOCABULARY
The power of placebo

1 Discuss the questions in groups.

- What do you think are the best remedies for these ailments?

a cold the flu insomnia

- How do we *know* these remedies actually help? What other factors might be involved? What do you know about the *placebo effect*?

2 Read the first part of the text. Why was the cyclists' training session unusual? How many cyclists received a genuine supplement?

3 Read the rest of the text quickly. Find three things you *didn't* know about the placebo effect.

4 Look at the text again and say who …

1. received a placebo after being told it was likely to have a positive effect on them.
2. didn't perform any better after taking a placebo.
3. gave people placebos expecting them to have no effect whatsoever.
4. felt better as a result of medical malpractice.
5. developed the earliest theories on how major physical problems could have psychological causes.
6. has the opposite reaction to most people when given some placebo pills.
7. was eager to be given a supply of sugar pills.
8. can produce a similar effect to a placebo, using only words.

Vocabulary

5 Match the words from the text in **A** and **B** to make compound nouns associated with health.   *drug trial*

A		B	
~~drug~~	brain	benefits	anesthetic
pain	local	scan	suggestion
self	health	relief	back
broken		substance	~~trial~~
performance-enhancing			

6 Find words in the text that mean …

1. fascinated (*para. 1*)
2. limited (*4*)
3. notices (v) (*5*)
4. example (*5*)
5. gain access to (*7*)
6. ask strongly for (*8*)
7. making use of (*9*)
8. disadvantage (*9*)

What do you think?

- Do you think some forms of alternative medicine rely purely on the placebo effect? Which ones? Why?
- Would you ever take part in drug trials? Why/Why not?
- Have you ever felt unwell and suspected it was for psychological, rather than physical reasons? What was the situation?

THE PLACEBO EFFECT

Jessica Glanville reports on the strange world of imaginary medicine.

Some of the world's top cyclists are in training and are intrigued to hear that today they will be taking part in tests of a new and legal energy-boosting supplement. Unusually, the cyclists will have to complete two time trials around the velodrome. In time trials, cyclists have to give everything they have to achieve the fastest time possible, and no cyclist would normally attempt another time trial until the following day.

As the cyclists prepare for the second time trial, half receive what they are told are caffeine capsules. The other half are given the new supplement – apparently a special formula that the researchers say is reported to have improved performances significantly with other athletes. Even if the supplements worked, the tired cyclists would still be expected to go slower than on the first time trial, but amazingly, half of those who took the new supplement put in a faster time, with one cyclist achieving a personal best. Some seem to have found the second ride easier. "I felt really tired before I took it," says one, but then "I got a burst of energy and felt ready to go again." Everyone is excited about the new performance-enhancing substance … until the researchers tell them that none of the capsules contained any active ingredients. All the pills, even the "caffeine ones," were full of cornflour; they were placebos.

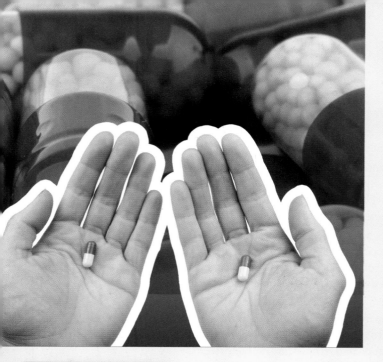

Unexpected outcomes

The term *placebo* comes from the Latin, *I shall please*. It was used in the 19th century to describe medical treatments whose goal was to please the patient, rather than provide any significant health benefit. While patients might feel better emotionally for having received some form of treatment, it was believed that placebos obviously had no real effect on their illness. However, doctors soon realized that placebos often led to significant improvements in patients' symptoms, and they were introduced into modern drug trials in order to show whether the drug being trialed brought greater benefits than those expected to occur from the placebo effect.

The effect isn't just restricted to drugs. For many years, patients with broken backs had surgical cement injected into their joints, and these operations appeared to have had amazing results. Eventually, one surgeon became suspicious when patients who'd had the wrong part of the spine treated by mistake still experienced significant benefits from the operation. He then experimented by giving some of his patients a fake operation; they were given local anesthetic and the surgeon talked them through the operation while doing absolutely nothing to the problem joint. None of the patients knew who'd had the real operation, but they all experienced equal amounts of pain relief and improved movement afterwards. It would seem that the million plus operations that had been carried out worldwide may have been a very expensive piece of theater.

Not just in the mind

It's often assumed that the placebo effect is purely imaginary, i.e., nothing has really changed in the body, but the mind perceives an improvement. And yet, as Freud showed over a century ago, there seem to be few limits to the physical symptoms the unconscious mind can produce. Psychosomatic illnesses are said to be "all in the head," but they can often manifest in very real physical conditions. Could placebo cures simply be a more positive demonstration of the mind/body connection?

Tests at high altitudes have shown that hikers who believe they are breathing in extra oxygen, but have in fact been given cylinders containing ordinary air, produce real chemical changes in their bodies, exactly like the ones that result from breathing in oxygen. Brain scans also show that when people are given placebo painkillers, the brain actually produces natural painkillers, just as it would if morphine was used.

It seems that placebos can tap into the brain's internal pharmacy in response to our expectations, helping with a variety of conditions such as depression, nausea, and even Parkinson's disease. The subtle details of placebo psychology are incredible. Capsule placebos have been shown to be more effective than simple tablets; tablets from more expensive packages produce a greater placebo effect than cheaper-looking ones. It appears that even color plays a role; red placebo pills are considered to be the best for treating pain, while blue ones are ideal for anxiety – unless you're an Italian soccer fan, in which case blue, being the color of the national soccer team, will act as a stimulant rather than a sedative!

The power of suggestion

It seems unfortunate that placebo drugs can't be used more widely by doctors, but of course, medical ethics forbid deception, and surely a placebo can't have its effect if the patient is told the truth about it! Well, never assume anything concerning the bizarre power of mind over body! Participants in a Harvard University experiment found it absurd to take pills prescribed by a doctor, knowing that they were placebos. "He wants me to take sugar pills," said one. "This isn't gonna work." Nevertheless, they experienced twice as much improvement with their digestive problems as those who took nothing during the same period. Some participants found that all their symptoms disappeared and begged for more placebos when the symptoms returned at the end of the experiment. Unfortunately the doctors weren't allowed to prescribe them.

Perhaps the solution lies in other ways of harnessing the power of self-suggestion, which is the foundation of the hypnotist's art, also sometimes used to alleviate health problems. The snag there is that not everyone is responsive to hypnotic suggestion. One thing we should certainly pay more attention to is the significance of the doctor-patient relationship. It seems that a caring and supportive doctor, talking encouragingly about the likelihood of improvement, is often likely to have as much effect on a patient's condition as the drugs or treatment being prescribed. We should also remember that many of the expensive drugs we buy have only slightly better results than those of placebos in trials. Then again, perhaps the more expensive they are, the more effective we will imagine them to be!

LANGUAGE FOCUS
Distancing the facts

Passive constructions

1 Rewrite these sentences from a news report about **Dr. Martin Crispin**, beginning with the words in *italics*.

1 It is reported that *a leading plastic surgeon* is under investigation for fraud.
2 People believe that *Dr. Martin Crispin* owns three private clinics in San Diego.
3 Patients say that *Dr. Crispin and his colleagues* charged up to $1,000 for a consultation.
4 It was supposed that *Dr. Crispin* had done his surgical residency in the Caribbean.
5 People now know that *he* never trained as a surgeon.
6 Everyone now assumes that *his board certification* is fake.
7 People considered that *he* was a specialist in cosmetic surgery.
8 We understand that *Dr. Crispin* has been sued recently by five different patients.
9 It is alleged that *two of his colleagues* performed unnecessary surgery on hundreds of patients.
10 People presume that *the doctor and his wife* went into hiding this morning.

CD4 3 Listen and check.

2 Change these sentences, beginning with the words in *italics*.

1 It seems *this road* is taking us nowhere.
2 It appears that *we* have taken a wrong turn.
3 Jake appeared to have taken the wrong medicine. (*It*)
4 He seemed to have felt better nevertheless. (*It*)
5 It would seem that *the government* has changed its policy.
6 It appears *they* are seriously worried about losing the next election.

Top surgeon in fraud scandal

Reporting the news

3 What's in the news today?

4 Work in pairs. Read the headlines and openings of the six articles below.
- What are they about?
- <u>Underline</u> examples of distancing the facts.
- Complete the last line of each of the openings. Share your ideas with the class.

5 Choose one of the articles and complete it with your own ideas, including some constructions for distancing the facts (80–100 words).

6 Work as a class.
- Decide on a running order for your stories on tonight's TV or radio news.
- Choose a news anchor and correspondents to read each item. The anchor will present the news and introduce each item.

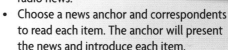
And now over to our sports/medical correspondent, Martina Diaz ...

Antibiotics losing effectiveness in every country, says WHO

Antibiotics are reported to be losing their power to fight infections in every country in the world, according to a new report from the World Health Organization (WHO). The situation could have devastating consequences for public health, and ...

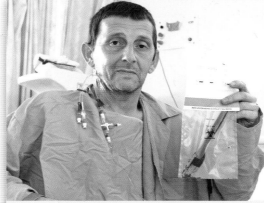

Fork found in man's stomach

A 40-year-old man who was thought to be suffering from stomach cramps was found to have a nine-inch plastic fork inside his stomach when doctors operated on him.

Lee Gardner appears to have swallowed the fork ten years ago, when ...

State Senate to vote on renewable energy bill

The State Senate will vote on a renewable energy bill in the next few days. The bill, which has the support of the governor, faces opposition from representatives in the southern part of the state.

Although the bill had been expected to pass comfortably, the news of ...

HURRICANE WINDS SET TO WREAK HAVOC OVER WEEKEND

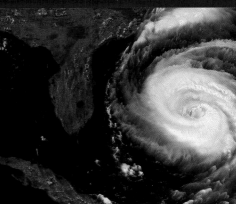

Athlete fails drug test and loses medal

Heptathlete Calvin Ackerman has failed a drug test after winning a gold medal at the National Track and Field Championships on Saturday. Ackerman (23) achieved a personal record in the event, but is alleged ...

PRICELESS PAINTINGS LOST IN FIRE TRAGEDY

Some of the world's greatest modern artworks are believed to have been destroyed in the fire that swept through the National Gallery in the early hours of the morning. The fire ...

Hurricane force winds are expected to reach southern areas of the country on Saturday morning and spread northwards over the following 24 hours. It's thought ...

LISTENING AND SPEAKING
Down to earth with a bump

1 **Guy Anderson** is a paraglider. Read a post from his Facebook page, written after a paragliding race in a remote area of the Rocky Mountains in the United States. What do you think happened to Guy during the race?

Guy Anderson
3 hrs ago

Guy Anderson is world champion hide-and-seek winner!
Huge thanks to all those who came to my rescue … Words don't express how humbled I feel by putting you all through the wringer for 48 hours. I certainly was pretty frightened out there, but knowing you were coming for me gave me the strength to wobble along. Big op on shoulder tomorrow; will let you know how it's going Friday.

2 **CD4 4** Listen to **Part 1** of an interview with Guy and answer the questions.
1 Why was Guy alone when the accident happened?
2 What role did the wind play in his crash?
3 Complete the table with details of his injuries.

Physical condition	
Ribs	
Pelvis	
Arms	
Nose	
Eyesight	
Lungs	

3 **CD4 5** Listen to **Part 2** and number the events in the order that they happened.

☐	he took photos	☐ 1	he crashed
☐	he sang out loud	☐	he got comfortable
☐	he started to nod off	☐	he saw a bear
☐	the bear kept away	☐	his radio malfunctioned
☐	he slept fitfully	☐	he heard growling

How would you describe Guy's character?

4 **CD4 6** Listen to **Part 3** and answer the questions.
1 How did he get to the bottom of the valley? How quickly? Why did he go there?
2 Why was it surprising that his friend Russell spotted him?
3 What did the search operation involve?
4 Can you explain his Facebook post about being "hide-and-seek champion" now?
5 Why does he keep flying?

In your own words

5 In pairs, act out an interview between a journalist and Guy's friend, Russell Ogden.

SPOKEN ENGLISH *quite*

1 What part of speech does *quite* modify in sentence **a**? What part of speech does *quite a few* modify in sentence **b**?
   a Your new sofa is quite comfortable.
   b There were quite a few people at the town meeting.

2 **CD4 7** Listen and repeat the sentences.
   1 In which sentence is there a reference to a large number?
   2 In which sentence does someone have an extreme feeling?
   3 Which word or words receive the stress in sentence **a**?
   4 Which word or words receive the stress in sentence **b**?

3 **CD4 8** Listen to the beginning of each conversation. Reply using *quite* and an adjective or *quite a* and a noun from the boxes. Then repeat the responses you hear.

Adjectives	big interesting successful sure

Nouns	bit musician surprise while

> That class wasn't as boring as I thought it would be.

> I agree! It was quite interesting!

VOCABULARY AND SPEAKING
Words to do with the body

1 Match the body parts to the figures.

elbow	sole	thumb	eyelash
shin	calf	cheek	
ankle	nostril	jaw	
waist	palm	thigh	
chin	chest	neck	
throat	hip	lung	
eyebrow	armpit	intestines	
spine	pelvis	knuckle	
forehead	wrist	veins	

What other body parts can you na...

2 Practice some of the parts of the body in exercise 1 in pairs.

Touch your ...

Poin...

3 Complete the sentences with the w... the box.

stomach	ribs	lip	chin	chest
thumb	elbow	palm	heels	toe

1 Come on, don't let it get you down. Keep your _____ up!

2 I tried to persuade Pete, but he dug his _____ in and refused to change his mind.

3 I find it hard to _____ when politicians half my age start preaching to me.

4 It varies, but as a rule of _____, I'd allow 20 minutes a mile on this walk.

5 The teachers in my school were pretty strict. They made us _____ the line.

6 Stacy has her parents eating out of the _____ of her hand. They'll buy her anything she wants.

7 I'm so ashamed, but I'm glad I told you. I needed to get it off my _____.

8 You must be starving after skiing all day, so I made some food that will stick to your_____.

9 The government talks as if they're concerned about the environment, but they're just paying _____ service.

10 These pots and pans aren't easy to clean. You'll need to use some _____ grease.

CD4 9 Listen and check.

▶▶ **WRITING** Debating an issue – An opinion piece *p. 115*

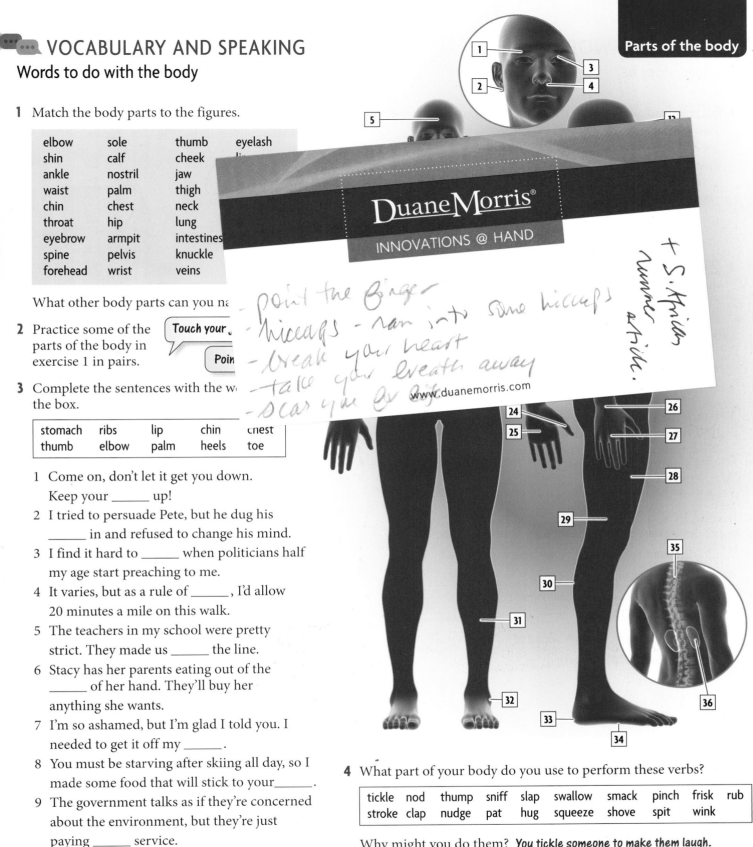

DuaneMorris®
INNOVATIONS @ HAND
www.duanemorris.com

(handwritten notes)
– point the finger
– hiccups – ran into some hiccups
– break your heart
– take your breath away
– scar you for life
+ S. African
runner a while.

4 What part of your body do you use to perform these verbs?

tickle	nod	thump	sniff	slap	swallow	smack	pinch	frisk	rub
stroke	clap	nudge	pat	hug	squeeze	shove	spit	wink	

Why might you do them? **You tickle someone to make them laugh.**

5 **CD4 10** Listen to the items. Which of the verbs in exercise 4 are they examples of?

6 Mime some of the verbs in exercise 4 for your partner to guess. Try not to look in the book when you're guessing.

1 **CD4 11** Read and listen to the questions from page 82. Does the intonation on the tag questions rise or fall?

> But you didn't get rescued before dark, did you?
> You must have been in terrible pain, weren't you?
> You decided to get moving, didn't you?

Which is a genuine question? Why are tag questions used in the others?

2 **CD4 12** Read and listen to these examples of tag questions. Which expresses the following?
• scepticism • aggression

a You've made a mess of this, Senator, haven't you?
b So you left your homework on the bus, did you?

How are the tag questions formed in each one? What are the intonation patterns in each tag question?

3 Match the sentences in **A** with the tag questions in **B**. Is the form similar to **a** or **b** in exercise 2? What feeling might be expressed in each? Say them with appropriate intonation.

A	B
1 You'll be careful,	will it?
2 So you were out with Lisa last night,	won't you?
3 You meant to kill the victim, Mr. Jones,	shall we?
4 I've been kind of stupid,	won't it?
5 So these are the spacious bedrooms,	didn't I?
6 That can't be right,	are they?
7 Oh yeah, camping will really appeal to Jo,	didn't you?
8 So that's all the help I'm getting,	can it?!
9 It won't hurt,	haven't I?
10 I beat him good,	is it?
11 Let's eat,	were you?

CD4 13 Listen and check/compare. What short answers do the replies begin with?

What's the situation in each? Practice the sentences in pairs, using the short answers in your replies.

4 Work with a partner. Decide where tags and replies can go naturally in these conversations. Do they rise or fall?

1 A You haven't seen my car keys?
  B No. You had them this morning.
  A That doesn't mean I know where they are now.
  B Well, let's look in the places you usually leave them.
  A I've already done that.
  B And ... here they are. Now, that wasn't hard.
  A Oh, thanks. You're the best!

2 B You forgot the shopping list.
  A Yes.
  B But I gave it to you as we were leaving.
  A Yeah. But I left it on the kitchen table.
  B You're so forgetful!
  A Oh, and you're perfect?

CD4 14 Listen and compare. Practice the conversations in pairs.

5 Respond to these statements in different ways.
1 Alex earns an absolute fortune!

> He does, doesn't he?   Does he? I had no idea.
>
> So he's really rich, is he?   Yes. He's a rich man.

2 Apparently Jane and John have moved to Australia.
3 Peter's new girlfriend works for a television company.
4 There's always something wrong with Alan. He's such a hypochondriac!
5 I'd definitely stay in this hotel again.

11 Our high-tech world

Future tenses and future in the past • Synonyms and antonyms • Ten really bad predictions

VIDEO◄ Survival skills

STARTER

1 What are *geeks*? Are they people or things? What is a *techno geek*? Do you know any?

2 Work in small groups. Go through the questions together and discuss your answers. How much variation is there in your answers?

3 **CD4 15** Listen to Pete talking about "his tech." How does he answer the questionnaire? How old do you think he is? What clues do you get about his age? Would you call him a *techno geek*?

You and your TECH!

1	Do you keep your phone with you most of the time? Are you lost without it? How often do you text?
2	Do you own a tablet? What do you use it for?
3	Which tech brands do you have? Which are your favorites?
4	How many apps do you have? Which do you use most often?
5	What's your all-time favorite computer game? Why?
6	How do you listen to music?
7	What other gadgets do you own? What are your favorites? Why?
8	Do you have a gadget that you bought but rarely use? Which?
9	Do you use a GPS device often? Would you ever use a print map?
10	Do you use social-networking sites? Which ones? How often?
11	How many emails do you receive or send in a week? Do you get much junk mail?
12	Do you think that technology isolates or connects people? How?
13	What would you make with a 3D printer?
14	If you could time travel, when and where would you go?
15	What technological advancements do you predict for the future?

Banksy, Bristol, 2014

THE INTERNET OF THINGS

1 *You and Yours* is a consumer radio program. Today it's about the early days of *The Internet of Things*. What is it?

2 **CD4 16** Listen to the program. Which things in the picture are mentioned? What are white goods? What do the speakers say about navigation apps?

3 **CD4 16** These sentences are from the program. Listen again and say what the words in *italics* refer to.

1 *They*'ll be connected to the Internet when *they*'re switched on …

2 I personally use an app that does *this*, an app which has been in the news a lot recently …

3 I can also see other drivers using *the same app* …

4 *It* enables you to document your day in images …

5 *All* wearing the same kind of technology I have around my neck …

6 I really like *this peer pressure* …

7 … *that's* been quoted for so long it's almost become a joke, hasn't it?

8 *This* may be a *naive question* …

4 Prepare questions. Then ask and answer them with a partner.

STUDENT A	STUDENT B
Read the audioscript of the program on pages 136–137. Write questions about it using these question words: *What? Where? Why? How? How many? Which?*	Read the audioscript of the program on pages 136–137. Write questions about it using these question words: *What? When? Who? Why? What … for? What kind of?*

CD4 17 Listen and compare questions. Answer any that you have not already asked and answered.

What do you think?
- Do you think *The Internet of Things* is a good thing? Why/Why not?
- What developments have you noticed already in your daily lives?
- What do you think the most useful developments will be in the future?
- What problems have you experienced with technology? Give examples.

SPOKEN ENGLISH *stuff*

The word *stuff* is widely used in spoken English. It means *random things where the name is not important.*

People now have lots of stuff that's linked to the Internet.

1 What kind of *stuff* do you carry in your bag?

2 Match the sentences in **A** and **B**. Try to extend the conversation.

3 **CD4 18** Listen, check, and compare.

A	B
1 Thanks for the great feedback on my report.	a You know me. I'm made of strong **stuff**.
2 What kind of stuff do you get with your new car?	b Come on. Cheer up! **Stuff** happens.
3 How do you cope with all that pressure at work and four kids?	c That's the **stuff** of nightmares. I would have been terrified.
4 Are you ready to go? We're late.	d I was impressed. You really know your **stuff**.
5 We were hiking in the mountains, and suddenly there was this huge bear heading towards us.	e I'm not sure. It looks like a lot of sticky, brown **stuff**.
6 What a day! I'm in a wreck. I lost my car keys and had to walk home in the pouring rain and …	f Oh, you know, all the usual **stuff**: GPS, bluetooth, leather seats.
7 Ugh! What's that on the rug?	g I'll just get my **stuff** and we can get out of here.
8 I did it! I can't believe it! Three *A*s!	h Good **stuff**!

LANGUAGE FOCUS
The future

Discussing grammar

1 What's the difference in meaning between the verbs?

1 Sue**'s leaving** tomorrow.
Her train **leaves** at 1:05 p.m.

2 **I'll give** you a ride to the station, if you like.
It's OK. John**'s going to give** me a ride.

3 We**'re going to have** dinner at 8:00.
We**'ll be having** dinner at 8:00.

4 The plane **will be landing** at 10:30 p.m.
The plane **will have landed** by 10:30 p.m.

5 The meeting **will finish** at five o'clock.
The meeting **will have finished** by five o'clock.

6 **I'm due to get** an upgrade on my phone.
I'm going to get a new phone soon.

7 I think Alison **will get promoted**.
I've heard that Alison **is going to get promoted**.

8 Run for cover! It**'s about to pour**.
It**'s going to be** a stormy night.

2 Complete the second sentence in each pair.

1 *I think their marriage will end in disaster.*
I predicted that their marriage _____ in disaster.

2 *Bob is going to move to Australia if he gets the job in Sydney.*
Bob _____ to Australia, but he didn't get the job.

3 *Ann's happy because she'll be seeing Tom tonight.*
Ann smiled to herself; she _____ Tom in an hour.

4 *The president is to make an announcement this evening.*
The president _____ an announcement that evening, but it was canceled.

3 Choose the correct ending to complete the sentences.

1 I was sure that the MRI …
would show that his heart was fine / will have been canceled.

2 I didn't call you with the news because …
we would meet later / we were meeting later.

3 The last time I saw Jim …
he was due to start a new job / he is leaving tomorrow.

4 There was to have been an investigation into the accident, …
but it never took place / and it was the driver's fault.

5 He believed that one day his newborn son …
would be running the business with him / was running the business with him.

What do you say?

4 `CD4 19` Listen. Complete the responses using *only* future forms.

1 *Hey, guys! I …*
2 *I really don't think I …*
3 *Hurry up! The play …*
4 *I know my hair's a mess, but I …*
5 *I'm really sorry. I know I …*
6 *Can you believe it? This time next week we …*
7 *I'm shooting for the moon. By the time I'm 40, I …*
8 *I'm so sorry. I was …*

`CD4 20` Listen and compare. Practice some conversations.

Too much science?

1 Work in small groups. Make a list of all the household appliances in your house. Compare your list with your group.

Who uses them? Which do you use most/least frequently? How old are they?

2 Look at the pictures and read the introduction and the descriptions of the appliances.
- What's your opinion of them?
- What does *"this $250 monument to excessive disposable income"* mean?
- What does it say about the journalist's style of writing?

3 Read the article quickly. Answer the questions.
1. What is *function inflation*? Give examples.
2. What is the problem it creates?
3. Is it driven mainly by consumers or manufacturers?
4. What is a *focus group*?
5. How have Apple products changed over the years?
6. How might one single button be used in years to come?

4 Read the article again. What do these phrases refer to? Why are some of them humorous?
1. ... parents too lazy to wash their babies in the bathtub.
2. ... all our appliances have learned new tricks.
3. ... an easy way to constantly relaunch essentially the same product.
4. ... the "job-endangering" snooze button, ...
5. ... rampant function hyperinflation has left many of us staring, ...
6. ... more cycles than we have outfits to wash.
7. ... on some customer feedback survey, at least two people piped up.
8. The marketplace rewards designers who edit a product down.

What do you think?
- Do you agree with the idea that household appliances are getting too complicated?
- Do you believe it's a generational thing and that younger people appreciate function inflation?
- Despite this inflation, are there any functions you would actually add to machines that you use?

▶▶ **WRITING Describing and evaluating –
An online product review** *p. 116*

ARE OUR HOUSEHOLD

**Toastière
Four-Slice
Toaster**

Six toast settings, independent slot operation, high-lift, cancel, defrost, and reheat functions, plus variable browning and illuminated controls.

**Who needs a vacuum cleaner with a flexi-crevice tool? A washing machine with baby and freshen-up functions? A toaster with six browning modes? What happened to the
5 good old days of the on/off switch?**

The modern washing machine has a dozen or more cycles that no one has ever used. The *baby cycle*, for example, aimed, presumably, at parents too lazy to wash their babies in the bathtub. Or, quoting from a variety of machines, the *duvet*, *sports*,
10 *bed and bath*, *reduced creases*, *allergy*, and *freshen-up cycles*.

The washing machine is hardly alone in this; all our appliances have learned new tricks. Posh kettles heat our water to a choice of temperatures, tumble dryers offer a variety of *dryness levels*, and even fairly basic toasters now proudly boast a *bagel*
15 *function*. At the top end of the market, you can buy a fridge with a built-in radio and voice recorder, proving we've reached the stage of combining functions entirely arbitrarily. It has all become a little overwhelming.

Function inflation is not, of course, confined to the kitchen.
20 We can see it in our computers and cars, our phones and televisions. "Fundamentally," says David Mattin, lead strategist at trendwatching.com, "I'd say function inflation is one consequence of the ever-increasing consumer thirst for the new – new products, services, brands, and yes, new features.
25 Throwing more functions and features onto an essentially standard product is an easy way to constantly relaunch essentially the same product and argue that their product is new."

APPLIANCES GETTING (TOO) COMPLICATED?

ZapVac AXV Family and Pet Bagless Cylinder Vacuum Cleaner

The ridiculous name aside, this $250 monument to excessive disposable income includes a crevice tool, dusting brush, turbo tool, stretch hose, and flexi crevice tool. You know, for cleaning your flexi-crevices.

Aqua Vivo Washing Machine

Although by current standards this model's total of 16 wash programs is relatively modest, the sheer range of them is baffling. It boasts both the aforementioned baby and freshen-up cycles, as well as duvet, allergy care, and bed and bath.

It is not without its benefits. Plenty of life-changing innovations, from the handy oven timer to the "job-endangering" snooze button, started out as added gimmicks on familiar household items. But, in the kitchen at least, things are moving a little too fast, and rampant function hyperinflation has left many of us staring, uncomprehending, at a washing machine control wheel with more cycles than we have outfits to wash.

In theory, all such functions are a response to consumer demand: if a washing machine has a *freshen-up* cycle, it is because in a focus group somewhere, or on some customer feedback survey, at least a couple of people piped up and said, "I want my clothes fresher, but not cleaned." Yet such demanding shoppers are in fact a small minority: Research shows that 70% of people use the same wash cycle almost every time, and nearly half of us are put off by complex multi-setting controls.

"The innovation is obviously being driven by manufacturers' desire to add value and to differentiate themselves," says analyst Neil Mason, head of retail research at market research company Mintel. "But from a consumer's point of view, what they want is convenience and simplicity. You run into trouble when you add all these extra functions and consumers just get perplexed as to how to actually use them."

New settings clearly continue to be seen as an easy road to higher sales. Yet, as Mattin points out, some of the most successful products on the market "succeeded specifically because they did not succumb to function inflation, indeed they made a virtue out of having very few functions."

Though Apple's app store is now a fast-moving bastion of user-controlled function inflation, the iPhone and iPad's predecessor began life as a reaction against it. "The iPod," says Mattin, "is a now-legendary example of a tech product that was beautiful in its simplicity. Compare earlier MP3 players, laden with various buttons and switches and features, with the iPod's click wheel."

"There's good evidence," he argues, "that the marketplace rewards designers who edit a product down until it does just what it should and no more. But that takes a few brilliant designers. Mediocre designers – that is 90% of them – just throw more and more functionality at consumers and see what sticks."

Perhaps, then, despite the current trend, the household of the future will be free of such baffling settings, switches, and dials. The ideal household gadget – be it a washer, dryer, or toaster – may one day sport a single, simple button marked *Sort this stuff out for me, will you?* The machines can figure out for themselves when, if ever, we merely want our clothes freshened up.

VOCABULARY
Synonyms and antonyms

1 We often use synonyms for reasons of style, to avoid repetition. Read the sentences below. Then find the synonyms in the texts on pages 88–89 that are used instead of the underlined words.

> Who needs a washing machine with a "freshen-up" *function*? A toaster with six browning <u>functions</u>?

> The washing *machine* is hardly alone in this; all our <u>machines</u> have learned new tricks.

> Posh kettles heat our water to a *choice* of temperatures, tumble dryers offer a <u>choice</u> of "dryness levels."

> In theory, all such functions are a response to consumer demand ... Yet such demanding <u>consumers</u> are in fact a small minority.

2 Find words in the article on pages 88–89 that mean approximately the same as those in the table below.

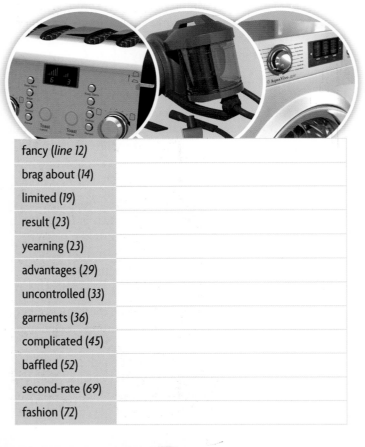

fancy (*line 12*)	
brag about (*14*)	
limited (*19*)	
result (*23*)	
yearning (*23*)	
advantages (*29*)	
uncontrolled (*33*)	
garments (*36*)	
complicated (*45*)	
baffled (*52*)	
second-rate (*69*)	
fashion (*72*)	

3 Complete the sentences with a word that has a similar meaning to the word in *italics*. Sometimes the word class changes.

1 By *present-day* standards the 10-wash program is modest; many _____ washing machines have 16.

2 "Did he *say* how his job's going?" "No. He didn't _____ it."

3 He *admitted* to deleting a number of classified emails. This _____ came after days of interrogation.

4 Progress will be *slow*, but if we persist, things will _____ improve.

5 You *can't count* on her. She's totally _____.

6 You want an *approximate* figure? If I had to give a _____ guess, I'd say there were about 50.

7 Massage *eased* the pain in my back and _____ the tension I've felt for so long.

8 He's made a *miraculous* recovery, but then he has _____ strength.

9 Soldiers *attacked* the enemy headquarters. The _____ took place before dawn.

10 Drugs can treat many *illnesses*, but there are some _____ that are incurable.

Yes, I did <u>say</u> you have the blood pressure of a teenager. Did I <u>mention</u> it's one who lives on junk food, TV, and the computer?

Antonyms

4 Complete the phrases with the synonyms and antonyms on the right that best collocate with the nouns.

	Synonyms	Antonyms			
OLD	an _____ civilization	an _____ travel guide	ancient	current	up-to-date
	_____ furniture	the _____ exchange rate	antique	original	antiquated
	an _____ farm tractor	an _____ idea			
FAIR	an _____ witness	a _____ ruler	biased	impartial	balanced
	an _____ opinion	a _____ referee	unjust	intolerant	objective
	a _____ view	an _____ law			
PERFECT	_____ taste	_____ judgement	flawed	second-rate	faulty
	an _____ kitchen	_____ wiring	immaculate	faultless	impeccable
	a _____ performance	a _____ author			
IMPORTANT	an _____ message	_____ pursuits	trivial	crucial	petty
	a _____ decision	a _____ comment	critical	urgent	frivolous
	a _____ playoff game	_____ cash			

5 Complete the sentences with a word that has the opposite meaning of the word in *italics*. Sometimes the word class changes.

1 One of my cats is *tame and domesticated*. The other is totally <u>wild</u> .

2 I've always been *successful* at work, but my private life is a total _____ .

3 His ability to make money is *admirable*. However, I have nothing but _____ for the appalling way he treats his employees.

4 At first they thought it was a *genuine* da Vinci sketch, but it turned out to be a _____ .

5 I find it difficult to *relax*. My life is so _____ . So much to do, so little time.

6 I was sure I'd seen her before. I *didn't recognize* her face, but her voice was _____ .

7 This road is *straight* for a while, but then it _____ uphill for two miles.

8 I know most people are *very excited* about traveling, but I really _____ it. I'd rather stay at home.

9 You thought she dropped the vase *accidentally*, but believe me, it was _____ .

CD4 21 Listen and compare.

THE LAST WORD
Ten really bad predictions

1 Work in groups. What predictions about the future of technology are being made today?

2 Read these really bad past predictions. Try to match them with a source and a date. What actually happened to each of the things predicted? Which do you think were the worst predictions?

PREDICTIONS	SOURCES and DATES
1 Computers of the future may weigh no more than 1.5 tons.	a Robert Metcalfe, inventor of Ethernet, *Infoworld* magazine, 1995
2 Rock 'n' roll will be gone by June.	b John Langdon-Davies, war correspondent, *A Short History of the Future*, 1936
3 Stock prices have reached what looks like a permanently high plateau.	c Margaret Thatcher, 1969
4 Democracy will be dead by 1950.	d *New York Times*, science section, 1920
5 It will be years – not in my time – before a woman will become prime minister.	e Irving Fisher, economist, October 1929
6 The cinema is little more than a fad. Audiences want flesh and blood on the stage.	f Charlie Chaplin, 1916
7 Rail travel at high speed is not possible because passengers – unable to breathe – would die of asphyxia.	g *Variety*, US entertainment magazine, Spring 1955
8 A rocket will never be able to leave the Earth's atmosphere.	h Plato, Greek philosopher and mathematician, 428 BC–348 BC
9 I predict the Internet will soon go spectacularly supernova and in 1996 catastrophically collapse.	i *Popular Mechanics*, technology magazine, 1949
10 The pen will produce forgetfulness in the minds of those who learn to use it because they will not practice their own memory.	j Dr. Dionysius Lardner, popular science writer, 1830

3 Are there any predictions about future technology that you doubt?

The past seen from the future

4 Read the extract from Margie's journal. What is the date? Who do you think Tommy is?

5 **CD4 22** Listen to the conversation between Margie and Tommy.
- What does Margie learn from Tommy that surprises her about the past?
- What other things about the world today do you think would surprise them?
- Do you believe that future schooling will be as described in their conversation?

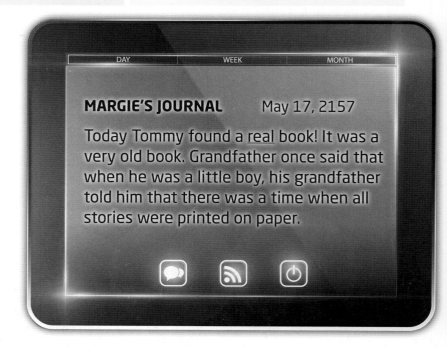

MARGIE'S JOURNAL   May 17, 2157

Today Tommy found a real book! It was a very old book. Grandfather once said that when he was a little boy, his grandfather told him that there was a time when all stories were printed on paper.

12 Turning points

Linking devices • Metaphors • Word linking and intrusive sounds

VIDEO **The Human Genome Project**

STARTER

1 Look at the photos of significant events. Can you put them in the order they happened? Why were they turning points in history? Check your answers on page 170.

2 Which three events do you think have had the greatest impact? What other events, including recent ones, would you say were key turning points in history?

3 **CD4 23** Listen to Justin Baines' eyewitness account of the fall of the twin towers. Where was he as events unfolded? What are some of his memories of that day? Do you have any memories of it?

1 First picture of Earth from lunar orbit

2 Founding of UN

3 Russian Revolution ДА ЗДРАВСТВУЕТ СОЦИАЛИСТИЧЕСКАЯ РЕВОЛЮЦИЯ!

4 Beatlemania

5 First women getting the vote

6 Fall of Berlin Wall

7 Atomic bomb

8 9/11

9 The invention of the cell phone

10 Discovery of penicillin

When man first saw the Earth

1 Read about the early *Apollo* missions. Why were *Apollo 8* and *9* special?

> *Apollo 11* and *13* are inevitably the NASA missions most people remember – the former for landing a man on the Moon, and the latter for its dramatic rescue of a stranded crew. However, it was *Apollo 8* that was arguably the most daring of the missions, taking humans out of Earth's orbit for the first time in 1968, into a new orbit 238,000 miles away (using an on-board computer with 32K of memory). Both *Apollo 8* and *9* resulted in photographs described as the most significant in human history.

2 You're going to hear part of a radio program about the legacy of the *Apollo* project. It includes seven clips of radio conversations between the astronauts (**A**) and Mission Control (**MC**). Complete the transcripts 1–7 below with the words in the box.

> pretty   running   visible   good
> view   color   lift-off   hand

3 CD4 24 Listen to the program and check. What effect did the photographs have on people?

4 Are the statements true or false? Answer as many as you can.
1 *Apollo 8* was the first *Apollo* mission with astronauts on board.
2 Humans had no idea what the far side of the Moon looked like before *Apollo 8*.
3 Astronauts had little training in the use of cameras.
4 The photo of Earthrise was taken spontaneously.
5 Rusty Schweickart's spacewalk happened because there were technical problems.
6 Rusty had spent some time preparing for his talk in New York.
7 His talk was primarily a technical one.
8 Rusty thinks there would be fewer wars if people respected each others' boundaries.

CD4 24 Listen again and check/complete your answers.

What do you think?
• Describe the effect looking at the photo *Marble Earth* has on you.
• Would a summit of world leaders in Earth's orbit give them a new perspective?
• Are manned space programs worthwhile? Why/Why not?
  Could the money for space exploration be better spent on Earth?

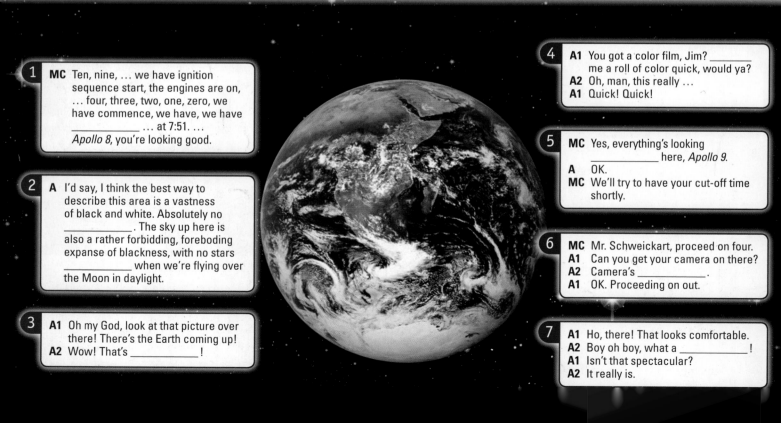

1 MC Ten, nine, ... we have ignition sequence start, the engines are on, ... four, three, two, one, zero, we have commence, we have, we have _____ ... at 7:51. ... *Apollo 8*, you're looking good.

2 A I'd say, I think the best way to describe this area is a vastness of black and white. Absolutely no _____. The sky up here is also a rather forbidding, foreboding expanse of blackness, with no stars _____ when we're flying over the Moon in daylight.

3 A1 Oh my God, look at that picture over there! There's the Earth coming up!
A2 Wow! That's _____!

4 A1 You got a color film, Jim? _____ me a roll of color quick, would ya?
A2 Oh, man, this really ...
A1 Quick! Quick!

5 MC Yes, everything's looking _____ here, *Apollo 9*.
A OK.
MC We'll try to have your cut-off time shortly.

6 MC Mr. Schweickart, proceed on four.
A1 Can you get your camera on there?
A2 Camera's _____.
A1 OK. Proceeding on out.

7 A1 Ho, there! That looks comfortable.
A2 Boy oh boy, what a _____!
A1 Isn't that spectacular?
A2 It really is.

VOCABULARY AND SPEAKING
Metaphorical language

1 Look at the sentences below from **CD4 24**.

> *The Moon landings **fueled** many people's imaginations.*
> *The images of Earth **fired** the imaginations of us all.*

What is the effect of the metaphorical use of *fuel* and *fire*? How can these words be used literally?

2 **CD4 25** Read **Conversation 1** and listen to a different version of it, **Conversation 2**. Which metaphors in **2** can you remember?

3 **CD4 25** Listen again and note the metaphors that replace the phrases 1–13 in **Conversation 1**. Practice the conversation in pairs, using the metaphors.

4 In pairs, discuss the literal meanings of the words in **A** below. Then use them as metaphors to complete the sentences in **B**. You may need to change the form.

Conversation 1

A Hi, Annie! What a nice surprise ¹*meeting you* here! I haven't seen you for a long time!

B I know. ²*Time goes by so fast,* doesn't it?

A It sure does. Is your business still ³*doing really well*?

B Yeah, ⁴*I'm working really hard* as usual. ⁵*We have lots of* orders right now, and I'm pretty much just ⁶*coping*. Still, I shouldn't complain. How's your company doing?

A OK. Things ⁷*didn't go so well* last year, and we had to ⁸*make some cutbacks,* but things are ⁹*improving* now. And how's life in your ¹⁰*quiet* little town?

B Very nice. It's such a good place to ¹¹*relax*. Look, ¹²*I have to go* now, but ¹³*I'll contact you* soon and have you over for dinner.

A That would be great. Hope to see you soon.

Light

Weather

Food

A	shining overshadow spark flash dawn shady bright	whirlwind flood hot cloud breeze foggy	bite off bland sour food grilling half-baked chew

B

1 It was the movie *Twelve Angry Men* that _____ *my interest* in law.	7 There's another article on Internet privacy here. It's a _____ *topic* right now.	13 My job interview lasted over an hour. They *gave me a* really good _____.
2 The team's victory was _____ *by* the serious injury to their star pitcher.	8 I was relieved to get the medical test results. It's been like a _____ *hanging over me.*	14 I'm struggling in this job. I think I've _____ *more than I can* _____.
3 I just had a _____ *idea*! It just *came to me in a* _____.	9 Don't ask me how to pronounce that word. I *don't have the* _____ *idea*!	15 Oh, another of your _____ *ideas*! You need to think things through more!
4 I don't trust that guy you met last night. He seems like a _____ *character*.	10 You don't need to worry about passing your driver's test. It'll *be a* _____ for you.	16 Fonseca's sports career *ended on a* _____ *note* when he broke his arm in the off season.
5 The space station is a _____ *example* of international cooperation.	11 It was a _____ *romance*, and Steve and Linda were married within six weeks.	17 It's a rather _____ autobiography. You don't learn anything very exciting.
6 I wondered why Bill's always so rude, and then it _____ *on me* that he was jealous.	12 I knew this would be my new home, and a feeling of happiness _____ *through me.*	18 Thanks for your suggestions. That's given me _____ *for thought.*

CD4 26 Listen and check.

LANGUAGE FOCUS
Linking devices

Linkers are used in various ways to make links between sentences, or parts of a sentence.

1 Read about **Rusty Schweickart**, the astronaut who took the famous photo of the Earth. Write the highlighted words and phrases in the table of linking devices below.

Shots of Earth

The astronaut Rusty Schweickart made a spacewalk in order to test an emergency procedure, in case the *Apollo* capsule and lunar module failed to connect. However, as the test began, there was a delay due to a technical problem, and as a consequence, Rusty had five minutes in space on his own while it was being fixed.

Although the astronauts hadn't been briefed to take photographs, when Rusty saw the Earth hanging in space, he was so awestruck that he immediately captured it on camera. Not only did these images affect the astronauts deeply, they also had a profound effect on the rest of mankind.

Time	Addition	Contrast	Reason	Result	Purpose	Condition
as soon as	as well as	(even) though	owing to	so	so that	if
after/before	in addition to	whereas	because of	therefore	so	unless
until	furthermore	while	as	as a result	so as to	so/as long as
once	what's more	nevertheless	since	thus	_____	otherwise
by the time	too	despite/in spite of	seeing as	_____		provided that
meanwhile	_____ (but) ... _____	yet	_____			supposing
in the end		all the same	_____ ... _____			_____
_____		_____				
_____		_____				
_____						

▶▶ **Grammar Reference p. 153**

Which linking devices in the table are usually found in more formal written English?

2 Answer the questions.

1 What does *while* mean in each sentence? Which can be replaced with *whereas*?
   a Jack likes to read the newspaper while Elaine practices the piano.
   b Jack likes to read newspapers, while Elaine prefers magazines.

2 Complete each of the sentences.
   a People who live in Boston often walk to work, even though _____ .
   b People who live in Boston often walk to work, whereas _____ .

3 In which three positions in the sentence can *however* be used? Where are commas necessary?
   The airline refused to refund my fare.
   (1) they (2) have (3) offered (4) me (5) $250 (6).

4 In which sentence can both *However* and *Nevertheless* be used? Which *one* can only be used in the other sentence? Why?
   a Jason promised to be more punctual. _____, he's arrived late twice this week.
   b I really wanted to be at work early today. _____, the bus was late, and I didn't get here until 9:30.

5 Which linker, *in case* or *if*, can complete the sentence?
   It's hot now, but I'll put my heavy coat on _____ it gets cold.

3 What happens when a social movement or trend reaches its *tipping point*? Quickly read the text about the book of that name. Why are social trends similar to medical epidemics?

4 Choose the correct linkers in the text. Sometimes one, two, or all three of the options are possible.

Malcolm Gladwell wrote *The Tipping Point* [1]*so as to/in order to/to* explain the way social trends suddenly take off, [2]*to use/uses/using* Hush Puppies shoes as his first example. [3]*Before/As soon as/Until* their comeback in the late 90s, Hush Puppies had been a dying brand, [4]*owing to/due to/since* the fact that they were seen as old-fashioned. [5]*While/As soon as/After* a few young "hipsters" began wearing them in the clubs of Manhattan in 1995 [6]*though/however/yet*, the fashion began to spread. [7]*Once/By the time/When* fashion designers started wearing them [8]*in addition/too/as well*, sales boomed and [9]*at the end/therefore/in the end* the shoes became one of the most popular fashion icons of the decade. This rapid turnaround in fortunes occurred [10]*even though/in spite of/while* the Hush Puppies company itself had played almost no part in it.

Gladwell compares such social trends to medical epidemics. [11]*Despite/Although/Whereas* they may begin with only a few people being "infected," [12]*provided that/if/so long as* these individuals are influential and well connected, the trend will slowly grow [13]*by the time/until/when* the "tipping point" is reached, at [14]*that/what/which* point the rate of spread accelerates enormously.

The Tipping Point made interesting reading for marketing executives, [15]*since/seeing as/as* it showed that [16]*however/whereas/while* widespread publicity may be achieved by expensive advertising campaigns, similar levels of exposure can be gained for far less [17]*because/due to/as a result of* word-of-mouth marketing. [18]*What's more,/As well,/Furthermore,* the advent of social media has greatly increased the role of viral marketing in starting social trends.

CD4 27 Listen and check/compare.

5 Link or rewrite the sentences in two or three different ways, using the words in *italics*.

1 *meanwhile   while*
   We'd been waiting for a long time for the bus. It had started to rain.
   We'd been waiting for a long time for the bus. Meanwhile, it had started to rain.
   While we were waiting for a long time for the bus, it started to rain.

2 *having   after*
   I saw the movie and enjoyed it, so I decided to read the book.

3 *whereas   however   though*
   Tony's very fussy about hotels. I don't mind as long as the bed's comfortable.

4 *so   so as not to*
   Celebrities often wear sunglasses in public. They don't want people to recognize them.

5 *since   seeing as*
   We should go to that museum. It's free.

6 *provided that   otherwise*
   Refunds will only be made on production of a receipt.

7 *even though   despite   yet*
   I've been on a strict diet for three weeks. I still haven't lost much weight.

8 *in case   as*
   Places should be booked early. The event may be very popular.

9 *nevertheless   although   all the same*
   He was penniless and starving, but he shouldn't have stolen the food.

10 *as a result   therefore*
   The freeway is closed. There has been an accident.

6 Complete the sentences in your own words.

1 As well as studying English, I …
2 Once this class is over, …
3 I know you're a good driver. All the same, …
4 I'm nervous about the exam, even though …
5 Seeing as there are lots of holiday sales, …
6 You can leave work early provided that …
7 I arrived on time in spite of …
8 By the time you wake up tomorrow, …

CD4 28 Listen and check/compare.

▶▶ **WRITING Connecting ideas – Writing a biography** *p. 117*

READING AND SPEAKING
Life-changing experiences

> *The Guardian* newspaper has a weekly article in its magazine called *Experience*, in which people recount an event that had a profound, life-changing effect on them.
>
> You will read about two people's experiences.

1 Work in groups.

Group A Look at the title in **A** below and check the vocabulary.

Group B Look at the title in **B** below and check the vocabulary.

A Running a marathon nearly killed me David Byrom	**B** Our plane was hijacked Nancy Traversy
peak fitness	shuddered
obsessed with	free fall
running through molasses	stalled
staggering	deranged
collapsed	passenger restraint kit
pull through	subdued
discharged	reeling
emotional wreck	ordeal
priorities	closure

Discuss what you think happened to the people in your story, using the vocabulary.

2 **Group A** Read the story on page 99 and compare your ideas.

Group B Read the story on page 100 and compare your ideas.

3 Make *brief* notes on your story in answer to the questions.

1 What was the background to the event?
2 When and where did it happen?
3 What happened?
4 How did the person react at first?
5 What did they do next?
6 What happened in the end?
7 What was the reason for the event?
8 How did the person feel in the period immediately after the event was over?
9 What long-term effect has it had on their life?

In your own words

4 Work in pairs, one student from **Group A** and one from **Group B**.

Use the vocabulary in exercise 1 and your notes in exercise 3 to tell each other your story. Ask and answer questions to get more information.

What do you think?

- Which story did you find most interesting? Why?
- Do you know anyone who's experienced a similarly traumatic event? How did it change their lives?
- Why do traumatic events often have a positive effect on people eventually?
- What have been the most life-changing events in your life so far, positive or negative?
- "In any case, while it is all very well to talk of 'turning points,' one can surely only recognize such moments in retrospect." Kazuo Ishiguro, *The Remains of the Day*. Do you agree? Why/Why not?

SPOKEN ENGLISH Emphatic expressions with *do/does/did*

1 Read the sentence from text **B** aloud. Why is *did* used? Which is stressed, *did* or the verb after it?

In the end, we *did* make the move to New York.

2 Match the sentences in **A** with the responses in **B**.

A	B
1 I didn't need *that* much detail about your operation!	a Maybe not. He did deserve it, though.
2 Didn't you think it strange that the car was so cheap?	b Well, I did warn you!
3 It's so embarrassing when Ken talks about his ten cats.	c Well, she does behave like one sometimes.
4 You didn't have to challenge Josh in front of everyone.	d Well, I did wonder.
5 You shouldn't treat Emma like a child.	e Yes, I do wish he wouldn't.
6 I can't believe how violent that DVD you lent me was!	f Well, you did ask!

CD4 29 Listen and check. Practice the exchanges in pairs.

Experience
Running a marathon nearly killed me

by **David Byrom**

I've been a runner all my adult life. At six feet, seven inches and 240 pounds, I don't fit the normal profile of a long-distance athlete, but I'm in good shape and experienced. Four years ago, at the age of 44, I was at my peak fitness.

It was my second London marathon and I was training hard – five days a week – aiming to run it in less than four hours. In the build-up, I did a couple of 20-mile runs, and my times suggested I could finish the marathon in around three hours and 40 minutes, which I was really happy about. I've always been pretty obsessed with my times: I'm a competitive person and, like many runners, believed that if you're not exhausted by the end of a race, you haven't tried hard enough.

On the day of the race, I felt fantastic. It was a sticky day, but a little bit of rain had cooled things off and everything was going to plan. But by mile 19, I knew something wasn't right. It was more psychological than physical: I started to feel that I wasn't completely with it. I felt confused. I remember being unaware of the crowds. I'd arranged to pass my wife and wave to her along the Embankment, at around the 24-mile mark, and forgot. By the time I saw Big Ben, just before the finish, I felt I was running through molasses. I wasn't aware of being in pain, but I was exhausted. I had to dig down to a level I hadn't done before.

When I turned the final corner on to the last 650 feet and saw the finish, I knew I was going to make it in less than four hours. And that's the last thing I remember. As soon as I'd seen the clock, I must have switched off. Witnesses said that when I crossed the line, I was staggering all over the place. I don't remember this, but I must have managed to collect my medal before taking myself to the medical tent, because it was around my neck when I checked in there. And that's when I collapsed. They inserted tubes to help me breathe, and then I went to St. Thomas's hospital by ambulance.

I had seriously overdone it, and my body had overheated, forcing my liver and kidneys to shut down. They put me in a medical coma for three days to allow my body to recover. I had also contracted pneumonia. The doctors said it was likely I'd had an infection on the day of the race and that was why my body had overheated. They later told me that people don't usually pull through this sort of condition and that the only reason I did was because I was in such good shape, and because of the work of the doctors at the finish line. They saved my life.

When I came around, I saw my wife, brother, and sister standing by my hospital bed. My first question was, "What time did I do?" (The answer was three hours, 55 minutes, and 46 seconds.) And my second one was, "Why am I here?" My wife had been by my side the whole time, and I put her through so much strain and worry. It was terrible for her. She still won't talk about it – and won't go back to London. I feel so guilty.

I was discharged a week later. I was an emotional wreck. The run-up to the race had defined me for so many months, and I felt I'd let down everyone who'd sponsored me. But most of all, I kept thinking, "How could this happen to me?" The race had nearly killed me. With hindsight, I should have listened to my body and walked, but then I would have been robbed of my finish time.

It was nearly four months before I started to feel better. During those weeks, I started to think about my priorities. I love running, but achieving certain times can become all-consuming, particularly if you're a club runner. Today, I have a clean bill of health. I stay just enough in shape. I swim, ride my bike, and go for runs locally with my dog, but I don't race. I'd never put my wife through anything like that again, and I've realized that times just aren't that important. The joy of running is taking in your surroundings and you can do that better from the back.

B Experience
Our plane was hijacked

by **Nancy Traversy**

It was my 40th birthday and, as a surprise present, my husband had arranged a vacation to Kenya. We were six hours into the flight and drowsing, my four children draped around me, when there was a loud grinding sound, and the plane shuddered violently. We all sprang awake, sat bolt upright, and looked around us. This wasn't turbulence; it was like nothing I'd experienced before. I fastened everyone's seatbelts. Then it happened twice more. We started to climb steeply, and then went into free fall.

My daughter, Kristen, had a window seat and could see the plane turning upside down. The ground was visible above us. The oxygen masks dropped down, and my heart went into my stomach. We were dropping out of the sky. All around us people were screaming, crying, and praying; everything in the cabin was flying around. So many thoughts were crowding in my mind. I said to my husband, "I think we're going to crash!"

I turned to my young son sitting across the aisle. My instinct was to hold him, but was he safer strapped in his seat? "Life doesn't always begin at 40" popped into my head. I was whispering goodbye to my husband, feeling weirdly calm, though I was sure we were going to die, when suddenly the plane leveled off. Seconds later, the breathless voice of the captain came over the speaker: "A madman has tried to kill us all, but we're going to be OK."

Relief flooded through me, and then the captain's voice came back on, much more composed this time: "A deranged man broke into the cockpit and tried to kill himself and all 400 people on board. He's now in a passenger restraint kit in the galley, and we'll be landing ten minutes behind schedule."

The atmosphere was buzzing. Everyone was talking and hugging. A flight attendant announced that breakfast was canceled because it was all over the cabin. My main concern was just getting off that plane.

It was 24 hours before my husband and I felt ready to talk about what had happened. It was hard to comprehend that we had nearly died.

We later learned that a six-foot, five-inch man had gone into the cockpit and attacked the pilot, trying to wrestle the controls from him. During the fight, the autopilot was disengaged, and the plane started to climb so steeply that the engines stalled. This caused the noises we heard. It then tipped upside down and plummeted 12,000 feet. If the plane had fallen for four seconds longer, the pilot would not have been able to save us. Luckily, a basketball player in business class managed to crawl to the cockpit and restrain the attacker, which allowed the pilot to restart the engines and level the plane, despite having had half his ear bitten off. No charges were brought against the attacker, who was found to have mental health problems.

Our vacation in Kenya was subdued. I looked into every conceivable way of getting home without flying, but it wasn't possible. Fortunately, the journey back was uneventful.

The whole experience left me reeling. I learned that our pilot never flew again, which didn't surprise me. I found myself questioning my decisions in life. I was about to move to the US to expand my publishing business, but was this a sign that I shouldn't?

In the end, we did make the move to New York City – just weeks before 9/11. I watched the footage of the planes involved in the attacks time and again, feeling so lucky to be alive, unlike those poor souls. In a way, it brought closure. I was able to draw a line under our ordeal and get on with life.

I still fly regularly for work, but wouldn't describe myself as relaxed. That one flight will remain etched in my memory forever.

THE LAST WORD
Word linking – the potato clock!

1 **CD4 30** Listen to a story about a question a Japanese student asked her English teacher. What do you think the student's roommate actually said?

CD4 31 Listen and check. Why is it easy to mishear words in phrases like this?

Linking sounds

2 Words beginning with a vowel sound link with the sounds before them.

CD4 32 Listen to and repeat the example.

Invention of the Year

This‿is‿an‿evening‿of‿anticipation‿and‿excitement.

3 Mark the links in these sentences from the acceptance speech.

1 It's an honor to present this award for best invention.
2 The name is in an envelope as usual.
3 I'll open it and read it right away.

CD4 33 Listen and check, and repeat the sentences.

Intrusive sounds

4 **CD4 34** Two vowel sounds are linked with /w/ or /y/.

a blue‿eyes	b two‿oranges	c go‿away
/w/	/w/	/w/
d my‿office	e the‿economy	f three‿apples
/y/	/y/	/y/

These sounds occur naturally, but when do we add /w/ or /y/?

5 Mark the links in these sentences and write the sound when two vowels are linked.

1 My officemate and I are leaving to eat lunch now.
2 Although it's the obvious answer, it isn't the easiest option.
3 This recipe calls for two onions and three avocados.

CD4 35 Listen and check, and repeat the sentences.

6 When we spell words out loud, for example our name, we use a lot of linking and intrusive sounds. Why?

CD4 36 Listen to the example.

J O H N   S P E A R S
/dʒeɪ‿oʊ‿eɪtʃ‿ɛn   ɛs piː‿i‿eɪ‿ɑr‿ɛs/
     /y/ /w/   /y/ /y/ /y/

Practice spelling your names to each other with speed and rhythm. Then, give yourself a new name and spell it to a partner.

The name's BOND. JAMES BOND. That's J‿A‿M‿E‿S ...
                                      /y/ /y/   /y/

7 **CD4 37** Listen and mark which sentence in each pair you hear. Compare with a partner.

1 a **It isn't easy to recognize speech!**
   b *It isn't easy to wreck a nice beach!*

2 a **This guy is the limit.**
   b **The sky is the limit.**

3 a **Some others will leave and say goodbye.**
   b *Some mothers will even say goodbye.*

4 a **Six students had a grade A.**
   b *Sick students had a gray day.*

5 a **Ice cream in a nice cold shower!**
   b *I scream in an ice-cold shower!*

Say a sentence from each pair to your partner. Can they identify which it is?

8 **CD4 38** Listen and write the sentences you hear. Compare with a partner. Can you figure out the other options? Check on page 170.

Writing Contents

1 Many people need to write a personal profile as part of an application for college or a job. Quickly read the profile. Who is it from? What is it for?

2 **CD1 9** There are many websites where you can get tips for writing these profiles. Read the tips that Jack found, and then listen to him reading his. Work with a partner and note the ways in which he has tried to follow the advice. Do you think he succeeds in all respects?

> **KEY TIPS** **to make your profile more interesting and dynamic**
>
> **1** Introduce yourself.
> **2** Get right to the point.
> **3** Keep it as short as possible: 200–400 words.
> **4** Keep it formal, but not too formal.
> **5** Don't be too modest – it's your chance to be noticed ...
> **6** ... but at the same time, don't go "over the top" and sound big-headed.
> **7** State your career goals.
> **8** If you can, use 1.5 line spacing to make your statements easier to read.
> **9** Read your profile aloud to ensure it reads naturally.

3 Work with a partner. These sentences have similar meanings to some of the sentences in the profile, but they are very informal. Find their more formal language equivalents.

1 I work hard and get good grades.
2 I do lots of other stuff to help my school.
3 I like reading all kinds of books.
4 I like doing plays and stuff, as well as reading books.
5 I really want to act in plays in college.
6 I've seen a ton of nice plays.
7 I've learned a lot about movies from Ben Brantley's blog.
8 I'm an athletic person and have played a lot for my school.
9 After college, I want to work in the media. Maybe I'll be a movie critic.
10 Getting an English degree will lead to a great job.

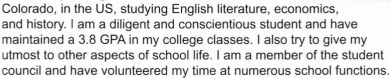

PERSONAL PROFILE **Jack Devoy (18)**

I am currently a student at Western Colorado Community College in Grand Junction, Colorado, in the US, studying English literature, economics, and history. I am a diligent and conscientious student and have maintained a 3.8 GPA in my college classes. I also try to give my utmost to other aspects of school life. I am a member of the student council and have volunteered my time at numerous school functions.

Literature has always played an important role in my life. I feel lucky to have been brought up in a family with a passion for books. I enjoy reading books from a wide range of genres, from Shakespearean comedies such as *The Taming of the Shrew* to historical investigations such as Douglas A. Blackmon's *Slavery by Another Name*. I particularly enjoy combining my interest in history with my love of literature and have read many historical books – a particular favorite being E.H. Gombrich's *A Little History of the World*. I often have strong views on any text I read, and this helps me when I analyze them for my studies.

In addition to my love of reading, I really enjoy drama and acting. This year, I ran a local drama competition, where I directed middle-school students in a short comedy play, *The Frog Prince*. I look forward to getting involved in any drama groups at a four-year college.

Outside of school, I have a strong interest in film and theater. I have seen numerous interesting plays, including *The 39 Steps* and *War Horse*, and I follow the blog of respected film critic Ben Brantley, which has given me an insight into the film industry. I would really like to combine my interest in film and theater with my study of English.

Alongside my studies, I feel I could contribute a great deal to life in general at a four-year college. I am an avid sportsman, and I have represented my school in soccer, golf, and track and field. Playing on numerous sports teams has taught me the importance of good teamwork and strong leadership. I would love to continue playing a variety of sports at a four-year college.

Looking ahead, I would really like to go into a career in the media, either in television and film, or journalism. As I have mentioned, I tend to have a strong view on most texts I read, so I could envisage myself becoming a literary or film critic. I know that a degree in English literature would be the springboard to success in these fields.

4 Write your own personal profile. Use the plan below to help you.

Paragraph 1: Introduce yourself and say what you do. Talk about your current responsibilities and skills.
Paragraph 2: Talk about your past experiences and achievements. Point out the main contributions you have made to your school/college/work.
Paragraph 3: Talk about your leisure activities. Think about how they contribute to the skills and experience you already have.
Paragraph 4: Say what you hope for your future career.

5 Read your profile aloud to the class.

1 Quickly read these opening paragraphs from three different stories.
Which most grabs your interest? Why?

2 Read them again and answer the questions with a partner.

1 How do the opening sentences attract the reader's attention?
What atmosphere do they create? How do the characters feel?

2 Which tenses are used in each story? Is direct speech used?
What effect does it have?

3 Who are the main characters in each story? What is their relationship?

4 How old are the main characters? How do you know this?

A New Year's Eve again. Joyce looked out of the frosted window at the bare, winter garden. A pair of sparrows were hopping through the frozen grass, searching for food. It'd been three long years and she still hadn't gotten over it. She sighed and pushed a wisp of white hair back behind her ear. The pictures on the mantlepiece were her only companions now, and she treasured them like nothing else. A few holiday cards kept them company, but as the years went by they were fewer and fewer. No, she'd never get used to it … but she didn't want to go into a retirement home, not yet. This house was her home, she thought fiercely as she walked unsteadily towards an old threadbare armchair and sat down next to the fire.

B Hannah glanced anxiously at her watch. It was 11:54 p.m. and the night train for Bangalore was leaving in six minutes. She peered along the dimly lit platform, searching for a familiar figure in faded jeans carrying a well-worn backpack. But the train station was deserted, apart from a tired-looking porter shuffling around aimlessly. She thought back to their conversation earlier that day. Perhaps he'd been serious after all? They'd argued many times during their three-month trip, and he'd often gone off on his own to "cool off." But then he'd always turn up later, and they'd work out their differences. Hannah fingered her ticket nervously. She didn't want to leave without Peter …

C "What was that?" whispered Jes, his eyes wide with fear. "Shhh," said Luis, slowly edging his way up the creaking stairs. "Probably just a rat." It had been Luis's great idea to explore "Fletcher's place" as it was known, named after the eccentric old man who last lived there. It was the archetypal haunted house and had been deserted for years – nobody brave enough to buy it or even break into it, Luis had said. They'd been laughing about it just that afternoon and had speculated wildly about the supposed murder that happened years before. School was out, and they were both in high spirits, so when Luis suggested a midnight raid, he'd readily agreed. Now, faced with the grim reality of a creepy, damp house, Jes was having second thoughts. "Was there really a murder here?" he wondered desperately.

Brainstorming ideas

3 Discuss with your partner and then as a class what you think happens next in the stories. Consider these questions:

- In each story, someone is facing a choice. What is that choice, and what decision do you think each person will make?
- What could be the consequences of that decision? How will it affect other people?
- What do you think will happen in the end?

4 Now read how story **A** continues. Make it more interesting by adding the adverbs below. There may be more than one possible answer.

> carefully   encouragingly   gently   instinctively
> softly   slowly   strangely

5 In what ways were your ideas for story **A** similar or different? What happens in the end? Which ending do you prefer and why?

6 Choose extract **B** or **C** on page 104 and complete the story in 200–300 words. Use the ideas you brainstormed in exercise 3 and follow the advice below.

- Plan your story carefully. Decide what happens next, the order of events, and how the story ends.
- Decide how the main characters will react to the events in your story and which verbs, adjectives, and adverbs will best describe their feelings and actions.
- Use linking words to order the events in your story.
- Use direct speech to vary the pace and focus.
- When you have finished, check your grammar carefully – make sure you have used past tenses and time adverbials correctly.

Ⓐ continued

It was his favorite chair, and as she sat there (1) _____ warming her hands, she smiled to herself. She could almost see him at the table, browsing through the Sunday papers. After a while, she fell into a deep sleep.

   "Joyce, Joyce," a voice whispered (2) _____ in her ear. Joyce opened her eyes. At first, she didn't know him – he looked younger and slightly different than she remembered – but she recognized his voice.

   "What's the matter, dear?" she asked almost (3) _____ .

   "Come on, sweetheart," he said. "Let's go for a walk." He helped her up and (4) _____ took her arm. She felt calm and (5) _____ light as they walked (6) _____ out of the room. "Almost there," he said (7) _____ , as he pulled at the latch on the front door. The door creaked open and warm sunlight streamed into the hall. Joyce smiled and stepped outside – it was a beautiful spring day.

1 Look at the pie chart and answer the questions.
- What does it show?
- How and why do you think it was produced?
- Do any of the results surprise you?
- What would be your answer to the question?

What is the primary way you watch TV?

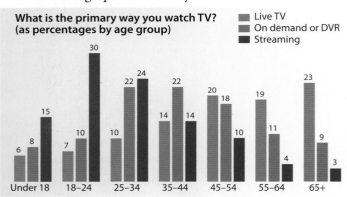

Other 9%

Online streaming (Netflix, Hulu Plus, etc.) 17%

DVR (record and watch later) 23%

On demand 4%

Live TV 47%

2 Which of the ways of watching TV in exercise 1 do you think is popular with older viewers? What about younger ones?

3 Look at the graph and check your ideas.

What is the primary way you watch TV?
(as percentages by age group)

- Live TV
- On demand or DVR
- Streaming

	Under 18	18–24	25–34	35–44	45–54	55–64	65+
Live TV	6	7	10	14	20	19	23
On demand or DVR	8	10	22	22	18	11	9
Streaming	15	30	24	14	10	4	3

4 How do you think a report based on the graph in exercise 3 would be organized – by age group, or by ways of watching TV? Read the report and check.

5 Read the report again and complete it with the discourse markers from the box.

Turning to   While   Conversely,   overall   respectively
Looking first at   with regard to   particularly

6 Discuss the questions in pairs.
1 Which two trends were considered to be unsurprising? Why do you think this is?
2 Why are the statistics in the pie chart likely to change? How soon is this expected?
3 Why does the report focus on the graph?
4 What kind of products would you recommend advertising on each of the modes of watching TV?

Analysis of primary TV watching habits

Aim

This report will analyze the results of a survey among different age groups on preferred ways of accessing TV programs and make recommendations to advertisers based on the findings.

Methodology

TV viewers of different ages were asked about their primary way of watching TV. The results can be seen in the pie chart, which shows that while live TV is still popular, it is now preferred by just under half of those surveyed. Watching recorded programs (DVR) is the second most popular option (23%), with online streaming in third place (17%).

Of the people who chose each of the three main viewing categories, the graph shows what percentage were in each of the seven age groups. To help advertisers seeking to target appropriate age ranges, the report will focus on the data shown in this graph.

Live TV

[1]_____ live TV, predictably, this traditional way of watching is significantly more popular with older viewers. Those under 18 account for only 6% of this category, with a slight rise for 18–24-year-olds. There is a small but steady increase through the 25–34 and 35–44 groups, until we reach 20% of those preferring this mode of viewing among 45–54-year-olds. There is then a slight fall for the 55–64 group, but this picks up again for respondents who are 65 or older, at 23%.

7 Complete the phrases with the correct prepositions from the box.

on   for   among   at   in   of   to   with

1 aimed _____ older people
2 a large proportion _____ TV viewers
3 this accounts _____ 20% of the total
4 DVDs are popular _____ older people
5 the report focuses _____ this area
6 make recommendations _____ advertisers
7 those who are younger _____ age
8 this is common _____ students

Streaming

² _____ the newest form of viewing, streaming via the Internet, is predictably much more popular with younger viewers. ³ _____ 15% of those preferring this option are those under 18, there is a sharp increase to 30% with 18–24-year-olds. The figures then drop gradually across the age ranges and plummet to only 4% and 3% for the 55–64 and 65 or older groups ⁴ _____ .

On demand or DVR

⁵ _____ on demand and ⁶ _____ DVR, the figures indicate that this category has the widest reach across age groups. Moderate proportions of those choosing this option are those under 18 and 18–24-year olds, with a substantial increase to 22% with the 25–34 group. This then remains stable through the next two age groups, before dropping gradually to 11% and 9% in the two oldest groups.

Conclusions

The survey shows that live TV viewers are still the largest group. They tend to be older in age, so advertising through this medium will be less effective for products aimed at younger people.

On demand/DVR viewers are more likely to be aged 25–44, but ⁷ _____ , this is the best category for advertisers aiming at a wide age range. However, ⁸ _____ DVR viewers, it should be remembered that they are likely to skip advertisement breaks when watching recorded programs.

Online streaming viewers are typically younger in age (under 25). While they currently account for less than a fifth of viewers overall, this figure is likely to rise in the immediate future, presenting great potential for targeted advertising. The rate of that rise will depend on the increased provision of superfast broadband, which is necessary for streaming high-definition TV.

Generally, it is likely that the figures for the three categories will become more equal in the not-too-distant future.

---

8 Look at the graph below. What does it show? How and why do you think it was produced?

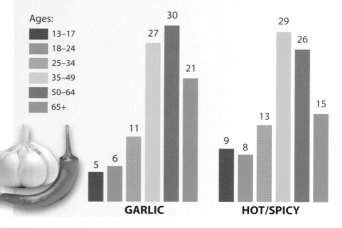

Percentage of respondents by age who want more of certain flavors on menus

Ages:
- 13–17
- 18–24
- 25–34
- 35–49
- 50–64
- 65+

GARLIC: 5, 6, 11, 27, 30, 21
HOT/SPICY: 9, 8, 13, 29, 26, 15

9 Write a report based on the graph, using the plan below to help you. Include discourse markers. Look at the ones below and match them with the ones used in exercise 5.

1 Starting with	4 generally	7 In contrast,
2 especially	5 Whereas	8 concerning
3 correspondingly	6 Moving on to	

Paragraph 1: Introduction. State the aims of the report and who you are writing it for.
Paragraph 2: Methodology. Explain the nature of the survey and the graphs resulting from it.
Paragraph 3: Analyze the findings for one of the categories in the survey.
Paragraph 4: Analyze the findings for the other category, noting similarities to and differences from the first category.
Paragraph 5: Conclusion. Summarize the key findings and make recommendations.

Formal emails

1 Apart from the absence of postal addresses and a date, the format of a formal email is largely the same as for a formal letter. Complete the details and tips with the options in the box.

> Tony   Mrs.   Take   informal
> Madam   formal   Sincerely

Greeting	Signing off
Dear Mr./ ¹_____ / Ms. Mitchell, →	⁴_____ care,
Dear Sir / ²_____, →	⁵_____ yours,
Dear ³_____ Hickson,	Best regards, Best,
To Whom It May Concern:	Regards, Kind regards,
	Your full name (and job title if relevant)

Tips

- Avoid ⁶_____ language and exclamation marks.
- Unless you want to sound very ⁷_____ you can use contractions occasionally, but they should generally be avoided.
- Use separate paragraphs for different points, and don't let any paragraph get too long.

2 **CD2 8** Listen to a phone conversation between two friends, Peter and Martin. What is the problem? What possible solution is suggested?

3 Read Martin's email to one of the conference organizers. How does he attempt to compensate for the problem he is causing?

> **From** Mart.Simmons@fastmail.org
> **To** Pat.Smithson@MedexConfOrg.com
> **Subject** Martin Simmons Conference Presentation October 18th
>
> Dear Mrs. Smithson,
>
> Thank you for your email outlining the technical resources available for my presentation at the Medex Conference in London on October 18th. Regretfully, I am writing to inform you that it is no longer possible for me to attend the conference on the 18th. I am very sorry about this and am aware of the inconvenience it will cause, but due to unforeseen circumstances, I will not be able to attend that day.
>
> I was wondering whether it might be at all possible for you to move my presentation to Sunday. I am able to attend the conference on the 19th, and if there is any possibility that you could rearrange the conference schedule, I would be delighted to give my talk on that day. Could you possibly let me know if this might be an option?
>
> Alternatively, I was thinking that I could perhaps brief one of my colleagues to deliver my presentation on the 18th. I have two colleagues who are well acquainted with the work I was planning to present, and I'm confident that both of them would act as more than adequate replacements in my absence.
>
> Once more, please accept my sincerest apologies for my non-attendance on the 18th and any inconvenience I've caused. I hope that my suggestions for possible solutions to the problem might be feasible, and I look forward to hearing from you in that regard.
>
> Best regards,
>
> **Martin Simmons**
> **Clinical Research Coordinator,**
> **Valley Medical Practice**
>
> **✚ VALLEY** medical practice

4 Find words or phrases in the letter that mean:

1	explaining briefly	6	give instructions to
2	be present at	7	give / present
3	trouble	8	familiar
4	an unexpected situation	9	possible choice
5	better than satisfactory	10	useable

5 Put the words in the correct order to make apologies and polite requests.

1 regret / my / like / to / express / behavior / deepest / for / I / my / would / .

2 for / I / having / your / apologize / time / only / can / wasted / wholeheartedly / .

3 inconvenience / my / caused / for / accept / I've / apologies / any / sincere / please / .

4 me / could / I / give / if / presentation / you / possibly / wonder / for / my / ?

5 record / that / chance / could / presentation / me / is / any / the / for / you / there / ?

6 we / your / convenient / tomorrow / it / be / session / until / would / postponed / if / ?

6 Write an email to the human resources department of a company concerning a job you applied for.

- Thank them for sending information about the interview you had agreed to attend.
- Apologize for being unable to attend the interview.
- Ask if it would be possible to have the interview on another date and give some options. Ask if you could do the interview online if that is not possible.
- Apologize again.

1 Divide into two groups. In two minutes, write down as many things as you can about:

Group A the United States

Group B Canada

Share your ideas. Which group had the most information? Why do you think this is?

2 Read the text about Canada and the US. Work with a partner from the other group. Which facts did you know already? Which are new to you?

3 Study the text again with your partner. Try to figure out the meaning of the highlighted words. Underline any words or phrases used to compare the two countries, e.g., *in neither country*.

4 Complete these sentences about the text to indicate similarity or comparison.

1 *Not only are* Canada and the US two of the world's largest countries, they …

2 The populations of Toronto and New York City *are far …*

3 Canada has a parliamentary system of government, *whereas …*

4 *Besides* speaking English, 21.3% of Canadians and 12% of Americans … *respectively.*

5 *Despite* … , they don't always share the same interests.

6 *While* Canadians are passionate about ice hockey, Americans …

7 *Generally speaking*, Canadians and Americans get along well as good neighbors … . *Nevertheless, …*

8 *Other than* the Canadians' love of ice hockey and their weird vowel sounds, Americans … at all.

5 Write a composition comparing your country with another country of your choice. You could include: location, size, people, language, government, culture, traditions, educational systems – the list is endless, but limit it to 300–400 words.

Canada *vs.* the United States

Two of the largest countries in the world, Canada and the United States, share the longest international border, 5,525 miles (8,891 km) and the world's largest waterfall, the Niagara Falls. In neither country is the capital city the largest city. In the case of Canada, its capital, Ottawa, has a population of over 800,000, nearly 2 million fewer than Toronto, its largest city. In the US, the capital – Washington, DC – has a population of a paltry 658,000 compared with New York City's 8.4 million.

While both countries are democracies, their style of government is different. Canada has a parliamentary system similar to the British model. The US, on the other hand, has a presidential system. Both countries have English as their main language. However, both English and French are official languages in Canada, used by 56.9% and 21.3% respectively, and in the US, Spanish is used increasingly; it is now the primary language for 38.3 million Americans, about 12% of the population. This is a result of a surge in the Hispanic population.

Although they are such close neighbors, Canadians and Americans don't always share the same interests, especially in sports. For Americans, football (American football, not "soccer"), baseball, and basketball are foremost in the popularity stakes, whereas for Canadians, ice hockey is the predominant winter sport, and lacrosse its oldest, and indeed official, summer sport.

Like many close neighbors, Canadians and Americans often poke fun at each other, usually in stereotypical fashion. Canadian television frequently portrays Americans as loud, self-opinionated people with limited knowledge of the world outside the US. Americans joke that they don't know much about Canadians at all, aside from their passion for ice hockey, their eternal winters, and the weird way they pronounce their vowel sounds, saying, "aboot the hoose" instead of "about the house."

It would be difficult to quantify whether Canada and the US, two of the largest and closest countries in the world, have more similarities or differences. However, recently *The Economist* magazine ranked Canada as the third most democratic nation worldwide, ahead of all the other countries in North and South America.

1 Write down three things you know about your country's history. Work in small groups and share your ideas. Which events interest you most? Which would you like to know more about?

2 **CD2 33** Close your books and listen to a student giving a talk about life on the Texas frontier. In what year did Texas join the United States? Which of these topics does she cover in her talk?

| crime and punishment | education | food | border conflicts |
| health | travel | pastimes | religion | wealthy people | wars |

3 **CD2 33** Listen again and read her talk. Answer the questions in your groups.

1 Which paragraphs cover which topics from exercise 2?
2 What prompted her interest in this period?
3 What might her "romantic notions" about the period have been?
4 Which facts that she researched do you think caused her to shed these notions?
5 Describe some of the hardships families and farmers experienced living on the Texas frontier. What problem did both poor and middle-class families share?
6 What are the different ways she introduces each new topic?

4 You are going to give a talk about a period in history that interests you.

- First, do your research. You can choose topics from exercise 2.
- Write your talk, limiting it to 250–400 words.
- Introduce it with reasons for your choice.
- Illustrate your chosen topics with examples (see below).
- End with some overall comments and a conclusion.
- Practice your talk by reading it aloud to yourself.

5 Give your talk to the class. Ask for questions at the end.

Ways of introducing topics	Ways of giving examples
A particular time in history that ...	for example, ...
My interest is a result of ...	for instance, ...
I've never been very interested in ... , but ...	... such as ...
	like ...
As you might know, ...	namely ...
You might not know that ...	the most famous
One other thing that ...	a classic / a typical example is ...
As for the way they ...	
A key moment / A turning point / A crucial battle in the war was ...	, including ...
	, in particular ...
	, especially ...
Something I discovered from my research is ...	... is a good example / illustration of ...
The thing that surprised me most was ...	... is a case in point.

★ LIFE ON

Something that has dismayed me when studying history is the tendency to concentrate on wars and conflicts. So, what I'd like to talk to you about today is the lives of ordinary people in the US about 115 years ago, specifically the Texas frontier. My interest in this period stems from childhood, when I used to spend my summer vacations at my aunt's ranch house in southern Texas. It was built around 1875, just 30 years after Texas joined the United States. I would lie in bed at night and imagine what life must have been like then. However, when I started researching the period, I soon shed any romantic notions I had of it.

In case you're not sure of your history, Texas became the 28th state in 1845. Texas was originally part of Mexico until its citizens decided to claim independence in 1836. Mexico never officially recognized Texas's independence and continued to treat it as part of its territory. Once Texas joined the United States, border disputes with Mexico ignited the Mexican-American War. In the end, Mexico gave up its claim on Texas as well as other parts of what is now the US southwest.

As you might imagine, life in Texas during the middle-to-late 1800's was difficult. Life mostly revolved around hunting for food, growing food like wheat on farms, or gathering food from the wilderness. Food wasn't just an all-encompassing problem for poor families. Even middle-class families constantly worried about it and planned out their supplies to last up to six months. Luckily, the Texas frontier was home to animals like antelope, bison, turkeys, and even squirrels for families to hunt. When rain was plentiful, people gathered fruits, berries, and nuts that they dried. This way the food would

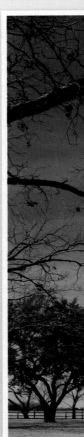

THE TEXAS FRONTIER

last a long time without going bad. Farmers found it easy to grow wheat because of the moderate climate, but turning wheat into flour was almost impossible. They often had to transport it to mills up to 100 miles away to have it ground into flour. That trip could take days and be very dangerous.

As for education, most children attended school if they had time after doing all their farm chores. The schools were often just one room, with one teacher overseeing children of all ages. Boys and girls sat on opposite sides of the room, and all children wrote with chalk on slates or blackboards. The school day typically lasted from 9 a.m. to 4 p.m. Children had a 15-minute break in the morning and afternoon in addition to an hour-long lunch break.

For entertainment, most Texans who lived far from towns enjoyed Saturday night hoedowns. Families would get together to eat, play guitar, dance, and play games. Other forms of daily entertainment included hunting and fishing as well as horse racing. Those who lived in towns had more opportunities for entertainment. They watched plays put on in theaters, attended political events and debates, and read newspapers.

There is so much more I could say about the Texas frontier people. I find their day-to-day lives fascinating—much more interesting than wars and conflicts. I hope that you've found this interesting, too. If anyone has any questions, I'd be happy to try and answer them. ✦

Writing a letter to your younger self has become a popular format. In these letters, people look back and offer themselves the guidance and support that hindsight provides.

1 **CD3 7** Read and listen to the letter by the 55-year-old Tom Sutcliffe to his 19-year-old self. Answer the questions.

1 Is the 19-year-old Tom's life easy?
2 What has his life been like so far?
3 Why shouldn't he wish things had been different?
4 Is Tom's life going to get much easier soon?
5 What do we learn about his love life?
6 What does he need to stop worrying about?
7 What advice does Tom give to his younger self concerning his …?
  • appearance • work life • finances

2 Tom's style is often very informal. Write the equivalents he uses for these phrases.

1 life isn't easy _____
2 an easy, comfortable state of affairs _____
3 a challenge _____
4 to end a relationship with someone _____
5 very beautiful _____
6 to subside _____
7 mustache _____
8 to resign from _____

3 In pairs, ask each other about:
  • what you were most worried about as a child
  • your biggest regret about your early life
  • the best thing to happen so far in your adult life
  • the worst character fault you've struggled with
  • what has surprised you most in life

4 Write a letter to your younger self – it could be any age from ten or upwards. Use a very informal style, whether the letter be serious or humorous (or a mixture of both).

When countering the misconceptions and delusions of your younger self, you can use:

| In reality, …   As a matter of fact, … |
| In actual fact, …   In truth, … |

Which three other ways does Tom do this in his letter?

Dear Tom,

I won't ask how you are – I remember all too well! I know life's no picnic right now, and all in all, you haven't exactly had an easy start in life.

My main advice is to stop wishing it had all been different. If it had, then you'd be different too, and hard as it is to believe, you're actually just fine as you are. In fact, it's the difficult experiences you've had that will give you the strength and insight to make the most of the wonderful opportunities that are coming your way.

Not that it's all a bed of roses from here on. There'll be no end of disappointments, but oh, if only you could realize that they're not as devastating as they seem! You get so upset when things don't go the way you think they need to! But hey, what gave you the idea that you know the best script for your life story? I've never figured out who or what writes the script, or indeed if there really is one, but looking back, it does all seem to work out pretty neatly.

For example, I know it's a stretch to believe this right now, but you will get over Sara dumping you. I know you think she's your one and only, and yes, she is sweet, and drop-dead gorgeous, and the heartache won't let up for quite some time. But boy, wait till you see who comes along later! I won't spoil it for you. But I promise, you'll find it was well worth the angst-filled wait. One tip – shave off that ridiculous 'stache now. She'll admit later that it almost made her think twice about you.

You'll make a few false starts with career choices, but I'm not going to help you avoid them. If you did, you might not appreciate just how lucky you are to have the job you'll wind up doing. Well, OK, maybe you could quit the job packing frozen chickens a little bit sooner …

It'll all get better once you stop agonizing over what everyone thinks of you. Look, your real friends will always think generously of you. As for the others, truth be told, most of them are too busy worrying about themselves to give you much thought.

It's how you feel about yourself that counts, and well, I am you, and I certainly feel a lot of affection for you as I write this.

Lots and lots of love,

Tom

P.S. Find out what 10^{100} is called, and when a company with a name that sounds like that appears, buy a few shares in it.

1 Which stories do you best remember hearing or reading as a child? Have you ever read stories to children yourself? Which are your favorites? Give the outline of a story to a partner.

2 Read this outline of the opening paragraph of a folk tale by the Brothers Grimm. Do you know the story? Can you guess what happens next?

> One day a princess went for a walk in a forest near the palace. She took her favorite toy, a golden ball, with her. She came to a pond and sat down beside it. She threw the ball into the air and it landed in the pond and sank. The princess was very sad. She said that she would give everything she had to get her ball back. Then a frog appeared.

3 Now read the full opening paragraph and compare it with the outline. What kind of language is used to make it more interesting? Find examples of writing style and word choice that you think are particularly suited to a traditional tale. How are participles used?

4 Find the highlighted words in the text that mean the same as the words in the box.

extremely sad	blinded by light	throw	shine	moaned
jumped	came across	lazily	emerged	sob

5 Read the outline for the rest of the story. What is the moral of the story?

> The princess didn't like the frog at all, but she told him what had happened. He said that he would get the ball for her if she let him live with her in the palace. She agreed and the frog dove into the water and got the ball. The princess was very happy. She ran back to the palace and forgot about the frog. The next day, she was having dinner when the frog knocked on the door. The princess opened the door. She was frightened and shut it immediately. Her father asked what had happened, and when she told him, he insisted that she should keep her promise to the frog. So the frog lived with the princess for three days, and then he said that he was leaving and asked the princess to kiss him goodbye. She kissed him and he turned into a handsome prince. An evil witch had turned him into a frog. The prince and the princess married and lived happily ever after.

6 Work in pairs. Rewrite the outline to improve the style and make it more interesting. Read it aloud to the class. You could include some of the words in the box.

slimy	retrieve	overjoyed	ignored
croaky	hopped	wicked	spell

7 **CD3 18** Listen and compare your stories.

8 Write a favorite tale from your childhood.

THE Princess AND THE Frog

One warm summer's evening, a beautiful young princess, feeling bored and lonely in the grand rooms of the palace, decided to take a walk in the nearby forest. With her, she took her favorite plaything, a golden ball, which she loved to toss up in the air and catch. After a while, she happened upon a shady pool of spring water, so she sat herself down to enjoy the cool shade and started idly throwing her golden ball high in the air, watching it glint in the evening sunlight. She reached out to catch it, but dazzled by the brightness of the sun, she missed and it splashed down into the center of the pond. Distraught, the princess leapt to her feet and, looking down into the black depths of the water, she began to weep. "Alas," she lamented, "if I could only get my ball again, I'd give all my fine clothes and jewels, and everything that I have in the world."

No sooner had she finished speaking when a frog's head popped up out of the water.

1 Why is music played in public places (stores, malls, airports, etc.)? How do you feel about it?

2 Read the beginning of an online article about music in public spaces. Which famous song does the article's title refer to?

The malls are alive …

Al Jenson   106 comments

I was shopping for an outfit to wear to a party the other day, and began to feel like I was already at one …

3 Read the comments thread that followed the article.
- What views do you think the writer of the article expressed?
- Which comments on the thread do you agree with the most?

4 The style of such comments is usually informal. Read the comments again, and choose the most appropriate linker in 1–7. Both are correct in meaning, but one is more informal.

5 People tend to use emotive and colorful language when expressing their opinions on forums. How do the comments express the phrases in *italics*?

1 store owners don't *deliberately annoy* their customers
2 music in restaurants sometimes *goes very quickly*
3 *it's no good complaining* continually about music in public
4 "elevator music" can be *very unpleasant*
5 banning public music would be *stupid*
6 stores are sometimes *empty*
7 the songs that are played are often *tasteless*
8 hearing music you don't like *is annoying*

6 Write two more posts on this comment thread.
- In your first post, reply to one of the earlier comments.
- In your second post, talk about another example of music used annoyingly – for example, on the phone when someone puts you on hold.
- Use linkers for adding points as well as other discourse markers throughout. Include some emotive language.

Comments   106 comments   sorted oldest first

 **MartyFry** ⬤Recommend 6   ⬤Report   ⬤Reply
July 08   10:17 a.m.

Interesting article, but it's not very balanced. It doesn't attempt to acknowledge why music is played in public places. ¹*For a start, / First and foremost,* it's simplistic to think that store owners choose to play music just to entertain customers or wilfully exasperate them. They do it because it influences the way people shop. Apparently, when romantic music was played in a flower shop for an experiment, sales were much higher! ²*Furthermore, / What's more,* they showed that people buy more food at restaurants when classical music is playing rather than pop music! ³*In addition, there is / Then there's* the effect of how fast the music is. Music that rattles along moves people through fast-food restaurants more quickly at peak times, whereas slow music gets them to stay longer and buy more when business is slow. Retailers will always use it if it can increase their turnover, so it's pointless whining about it.

 Greg100 ⬤Recommend 3   ⬤Report   ⬤Reply
July 08   10:21 a.m.

It's true that the worst kind of music can be obnoxious, and I agree with the point about music being simply noise if it's not wanted. But it's ridiculous to talk about banning it. Quite honestly, ⁴*apart from / with the exception of* rare occasions when I'm in a store for more than a few minutes, I can't say I notice the music. If I do, it's usually because I recognize a track I haven't heard for some time and that I look for as soon as I get home! ⁵*And let's not forget that / It should also not be overlooked that* if anyone, it's the salespeople who should be complaining. After all, they have to listen to it all day. Still, I suspect it actually helps to pass the time for them. Imagine the silence of a deserted store during long quiet periods.

 SheilaFeels ⬤Recommend 9   ⬤Report   ⬤Reply
July 08   10:43 a.m.

Music in any public place can be very annoying, but they could avoid people complaining about it by giving more consideration to the choice of music. ⁶*And it's not just that / Not only is it the case that* it should be decent quality (i.e., not cover versions of cheesy songs!). They should also mix tracks of various styles and artists so that you never have to listen to too much of someone you really don't like. ⁷*Moreover, / On top of that,* they should ask the people who have to listen to it all day what kind of music they want to hear. Having someone else's taste in music imposed on you is a pain, as the article rightly emphasizes, and it shouldn't be too difficult to ask salespeople and even customers what kind of stuff they'd like to hear.

Websites and magazines often tackle controversial issues by asking two people to write pieces about them: one *for* the argument and the other *against*.

1 Read the piece arguing **for** cosmetic surgery. What examples of hypocrisy does the writer give?

2 What do these figures in the text refer to?

90%	11	0.5	52	15

3 Put the words and phrases from the text in the correct column to make pairs with opposite meanings.

~~hideous~~	denounce	over the hill
tolerant	judgemental	~~attractive~~
calm down	profound	respectable
sanction	get riled up	sprightly
shallow	despicable	

	+	**−**
1	attractive	hideous
2		
3		
4		
5		
6		
7		

4 Look at the highlighted linkers in the text. They all have the same function. What is it? What ideas do they connect? Which are more formal?

5 Write your own piece to provide the argument **against** cosmetic surgery.
- In pairs, list all the points you can think of, and then share them with the class.
- Write the piece. Use some of the highlighted linkers for making similar points. You can also use contrastive linkers to refer back to points made in the **for** piece.

6 Read some of the pieces aloud in class. Then read the **for** piece again, and decide as a class which argument is most convincing.

For & against cosmetic surgery

FOR **Jenny Duffield**

Yes, I admit it. I've had cosmetic surgery! And I'm tired of being made to feel ashamed about it. I had a facelift when I was 52. I gather that it makes me a very shallow person, but it was bothering me that I no longer felt attractive when I looked at myself in the mirror. The results were life-changing. Just as it made me look younger, it made me feel younger, and I felt I could enjoy my looks for a while longer, instead of feeling middle-aged and "over the hill."

Likewise, over 15 million people a year spend billions of dollars on cosmetic procedures, and the rest of you really do need to get over it. Why does it make people so rabidly judgemental? Men spend billions every year on hair restoration, too, but no one seems to get riled up about that. Ninety percent of cosmetic surgery is done by women of course, and the fact that this is seen as a scandal suggests there is sexism at the root of this hypocrisy. Equally, there are double standards when women denounce their sisters for clinging to ideals of youthful beauty and refusing to grow old gracefully. These will often be the same women who sanction the use of hair dye and spend $11 billion a year on it. So what's happened to the demands that we all accept the ways of nature and focus on who we are inside rather than worrying about looks?

I accept that cosmetic surgery can reflect a preoccupation with the shallower aspects of life, but in the same way, spending a fortune on new cars and boats and ever-bigger TVs is hardly evidence of embracing the more profound aspects of our existence, is it? Again, that probably concerns mostly men, though, so it's not as despicable.

Then I hear people going on about how incredibly risky cosmetic surgery is. Well yes, there are risks involved, but similarly, skiing, horseback riding, and riding motorcycles are pretty hazardous ways of making yourself feel good. And in fact, the risk of serious complications with a cosmetic procedure is less than 0.5%. That's about the same risk as having an accident faced by every motorcycle rider.

We're becoming an increasingly tolerant society where we accept that people have the right to do whatever they choose with their bodies. If we accept this with regard to tattoos and body piercings − hideous in my opinion, but perfectly respectable nowadays − then by the same token we ought to calm down when people opt for surgery that makes their bodies more attractive. It's my body, and I'll do whatever I want with it.

1 People often read online reviews of the products they are about to buy. Have you read any? Were they helpful? Have you ever written one? Why?

2 Look quickly through the three reviews for the Galaxy Gear watch. Which are positive? Which are negative? Pick out one key phrase from each that illustrates the writer's opinion.

3 Read **Reviews 1** and **2**. What is the one thing they agree on? How do they express this?

4 These phrases are all taken from **Review 3**. Are they **positive** or **negative**? Write + or − beside each one.

> I wish Samsung had opted for −
> I'm pleasantly surprised +
> isn't to my liking
> better than expected
> feels like a gimmick
> sleek and elegant
> with a good deal of potential
> gorgeous premium feel
> basic yet intuitive at the same time
> stands out like a sore thumb
> these gestures are welcome
> to be honest, the camera is OK
> adds bulk to the device
> I would have preferred
> I really wanted to love the Gear

5 Read **Review 3** again. The writer calls it "OK but not quite there yet." In what ways is the product "not quite there"? In what ways does it excel?

6 Choose a gadget or a product that you know and write an online review about it. Use phrases from exercise 4. Compare your reviews.

SAMSUNG GALAXY GEAR wearable computer watch

REVIEW 1 ★★★★☆ 4 out of 5 stars   By **Markster**   Dec 15
An awesome piece of tech

The whole concept of making a phone call from your watch has been around for many years. For me personally, this watch is perfect. The screen is clear and the ringtones are good and loud. The camera is very good for 1.9 megapixels. Simple to use, and clear icons. Looks premium with brushed aluminium, and the strap is OK. Nice color collection.
I guess if I have to find negatives, they would be:
1 Not waterproof.
2 Not that many apps available, but what are, seem fine.
3 Not being able to make calls without being linked to smartphone.

REVIEW 2 ★☆☆☆☆ 1 out of 5 stars   By **Nirbhik**   Dec 22
Overrated, overpriced … few features

Unless you are one of those obsessed gadget geeks who doesn't know the difference between appearance and reality, it wouldn't take much effort to realize what an overrated, overpriced smart watch this really is. The annoying thing about this – lack of apps. So I had no other choice but to sell mine.

REVIEW 3 ★★★☆☆ 3 out of 5 stars   By **Shaun Dowdall**   Jan 11
OK but not quite there yet

Introduction   The Samsung Galaxy Gear is an intriguing piece of technology and perhaps one of the smartest wearables out there. With competition heating up and wearables fighting to become relevant in the marketplace, how does the Gear hold up?

Look and Feel   To start with, it's a beautiful device. It's sleek and elegant with a gorgeous premium feel to it. However, the strap isn't to my liking. The clasp on the bottom is too large. I constantly found myself getting caught on desk edges or on keyboards.

User Interface   It's pretty basic yet intuitive at the same time. Swipe to the left to show notifications or continue scrolling for other apps. You can also set quick gestures, for example, swipe up and your phone dialer will pop up. These gestures are welcome when it comes to such a tiny screen.

Sound quality needs a mention. It's good, very good in fact. During a call, I could hear everything clearly even when I was in a relatively noisy area. I didn't expect this and must admit I'm pleasantly surprised.

Camera   I would have preferred a front-facing camera, but Samsung opted to give us a spy camera shooter. To be honest, the camera is OK. It's not good, and it's not bad. The major issue I have with the camera is that it's relatively large and adds bulk to the device. It also stands out like a sore thumb, with many people asking why I have a camera on my watch.

Battery   I've heard some horror stories about the Gear's battery, but I got a solid two days on my Gear between charges. It's not fantastic, but it's better than expected.

Conclusion   I really wanted to love the Gear, but I just can't bring myself to fall for it completely. It's gorgeous and well-built, but it feels like a gimmick right now, with a good deal of potential. In my opinion, it just isn't yet ready for prime time, and my recommendation would be to wait for the second generation of the Gear.

> " When I woke up just after dawn on September 28, 1928, I certainly didn't plan to revolutionize all medicine by discovering the world's first antibiotic.
>
> One sometimes finds what one is not looking for. "

1 Work in pairs. Are the statements about the discovery of penicillin true or false?

1 Penicillin was discovered by an English scientist, Alexander Fleming.
2 Fleming worked as a shipping clerk.
3 Penicillin was discovered by accident.
4 Penicillin became widely available due to Fleming.
5 Penicillin was used in World War I.

2 Read the biography to check your answers to exercise 1. Answer the questions.

1 What does a *clerk* do?
2 How do you *enroll* for a course?
3 What can cause a *wound*?
4 How do you *apply yourself* to something?
5 What do you find *mold* on?
6 Where does *mass production* take place?

3 What's wrong with the style of Fleming's biography? In pairs, rewrite it using the linkers on the right of each group of sentences to make them into one sentence. Then organize the sentences into paragraphs.

Alexander Fleming was born in 1881 in Ayrshire, Scotland, where his father, who died when Alexander was seven, worked as a farmer.

CD4 39 Listen and compare.

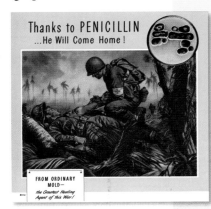

Thanks to PENICILLIN
...He Will Come Home!

FROM ORDINARY MOLD –
the Greatest Healing Agent of this War!

Alexander Fleming was born in 1881. He was born in Ayrshire, Scotland. His father worked as a farmer there. His father died when Alexander was seven.

Fleming left school. He worked as a shipping clerk for four years.

He received an inheritance. He was 20. He enrolled at St. Mary's Hospital Medical School. He wanted to pursue his interest in medicine.

He completed his medical degree in 1908. He won Gold Medal as the top medical student. He joined the research team at St. Mary's.

It was World War I. Fleming served in the Medical Corps in France. He worked in a hospital. It had been set up in a casino in Boulogne.

He saw many soldiers die from infected wounds. He decided to specialize in this area of medicine.

The war was over. Fleming returned to St. Mary's. He applied himself to research bacteria.

On September 28, 1928, Fleming was cleaning petri dishes in his laboratory. He wanted to be able to reuse them. He'd just returned from a vacation.

He was generally messy. The dishes had been left out in the warm laboratory. They were covered in bacteria. They were also covered in mold.

Fleming picked up one dish. He saw that no bacteria were growing around the mold. He decided to study it. It might prove to be an antibacterial agent.

Fleming had discovered the world's first antibiotic, penicillin. Two other researchers, Florey and Chain, brought it to mass production, in 1942. They changed the face of modern medicine.

The D-Day landings took place in 1944. Enough penicillin had then been produced. It treated all of the wounded Allied forces in World War II.

where
who

After

However
when
and
in order to

On
winning

During
working
set up

There
consequently

Once
and thereafter

having
so that

Owing to
and
therefore
as well as

As
so
in case

Although
it was
who
thus

By the time of
to

Audio Scripts

UNIT 1

CD1 2 The reunion
B = Bridget, M = Mark

M Hi, Bridget. Hey, how was your high school reunion? Wasn't that last weekend?

B Yeah, yeah. It was good. Well, it was OK – it's just that I didn't recognize a lot of the people and …

M Well, it's been close to 15 years.

B Yeah, I know, and boy do some people change! You know, I'd find myself talking to someone who obviously knew who I was, and I didn't have a clue who they were.

M And I don't suppose you could have asked.

B No, how rude would that have been? Oh, but I did recognize Judith. The dreaded, jolly Judith. She hasn't changed at all unfortunately! I tried to avoid her, but she cornered me during dinner.

M So?

B So, I'm like, "Hello, Judith. How are you?" Big mistake because then, of course, she starts talking – every detail of the last 15 years – you know, her ups and downs, her two failed marriages – no surprise there – her fabulous third husband, the operation on her sinuses, the time she was let go from her job, and on and on. Yeah, ask me anything me about Judith! I could write her biography.

M I bet you promised to keep in touch though.

B Well, you have to, right?

M You hypocrite!

B I know, but I managed to get away before giving my email address or cell phone number.

M Oh, good job!

B Hey, did you get the group picture I texted?

M Yeah, yeah, I did, but I could only identify you and Brendan – he looked good – tall, handsome as ever, but a little bit annoyed. You all looked pretty fed up to be honest.

B Well that's because we got the poor waiter to take our picture, and everyone kept giving him their phone or camera. And by the time he got to mine, well, we were all looking a little annoyed.

M It doesn't sound like a great success, this reunion.

B Oh, it was OK. I mean most people were really nice, but … do you want to know the worst thing?

M What?

B Well, when I got to the station to catch the train home, who came gushing up to me on the platform – "Oh, how nice, we can travel back together"?

M Oh, no. Not Judith!

B You got it! And, after I'd spent forever saying a polite goodbye to her.

CD1 3

1 He really thinks highly of himself. He thinks his own work on the project is the best.
2 Honestly, just listen to yourself. You never stop whining.
3 Don't put yourself down. Believe in yourself.
4 Take care of yourself. You've been looking a little tired lately.
5 I could kick myself. I didn't get her phone number.

6 Think for yourself. You don't have to agree with everything he says.
7 Suit yourself! You never listen to my advice anyway.
8 Just be yourself. Don't try to be something that you're not.
9 Think of yourself sometimes. You're always putting others first.
10 Don't flatter yourself! You didn't win because you're the best. Your opponent was terrible!

CD1 4

1 **A** You look fabulous in it. It's perfect for you.
  B I know, but look at the price!
  A Go on, treat yourself!
  B Oh, but …
  A Don't "but" me. Tell yourself that you deserve it.
  B OK then. I'll get it!
2 **A** You have to get over it. Move on with your life!
  B I can't. I think she's starting to realize that she made a big mistake.
  A Stop deluding yourself. It's over.
  B I don't know. Maybe I'll just give her a call.
  A Believe me. You're only making a fool of yourself.
3 **A** How's it going?
  B It's a challenge, a real challenge. I'm up planning lessons until midnight most nights.
  A You must be exhausted. You're going to have to learn to pace yourself or you'll get sick.
  B I can't. I gave up a good job in banking to do this, and I don't want to let myself or the kids down.
  A Yes, but it's not worth killing yourself. You won't be any use to anyone.
4 **A** Why did you do it?
  B Oh, believe me, I keep asking myself the same question.
  A You knew you'd never be able to pay it back. Now you've gotten yourself into a big mess.
  B I know, I know. And I've only got myself to blame.
  A What now?
  B I suppose I'll have to go to the bank of mom and dad!

CD1 5 See p. 9

CD1 6

1 When I'm asked what I do for a living, I often hesitate for a minute before answering because I'm never sure how people will react these days. Some people just think we're fat cats who make fast, easy money. But it's not like that. I work really hard, and there's a lot of risk involved, so it's really stressful. I get the 7:05 every morning – and I often don't get back until after ten at night, and that's not because I'm hanging out with the guys – oh no – I never get to put the kids to bed. I've faced being laid off several times, but I've been lucky so far. We have a huge mortgage, so we both have to work, but at least my wife has a steady job – she's a lawyer.

2 I don't like sleepovers. Everyone else does, but I just start to feel really sad at bedtime without my mom and dad there, and all my friends make fun of me. I don't mind play dates after school or something. Jason was at my house today, and we played Wii Sports until my mom told us to go outside and play. "Stop squabbling," she said, "and go get some fresh air and play soccer for real." But, I did beat Jason at the Wii, whatever he said. He's just a bad loser. Oh, it was freezing outside.

3 The one I was in closed down. They were so nice there. And I had a door in my room that opened onto the courtyard. I'd go out on a nice day and walk, with my walker of course, to a bench under a maple tree. I don't have a nice view from my room here, and the door's so narrow I can't get my walker through it easily. I asked for new batteries for my hearing aid, and I'm still waiting. They don't have the staff, you see. I stay in my room a lot. I don't like sitting in the lounge with the TV on all the time and people sitting around, falling asleep and snoring. My mind is still sharp. Some of them out there in the lounge aren't really with it anymore.

4 I get called a nerd. To be honest, it bothers me sometimes, but not often. Most of my classmates seem to take pride in being underachievers. The thing is, I like to have a good time – you know, clubbing and stuff – parties when I'm invited. But there's something I really want to shoot for. So, I've had an after-school job for the last couple of years. I've been working at Specsavers – just helping out and stuff – but it's fascinating. It's really the highlight of my week. And so now I've decided I'd like to be an optometrist. Does that sound boring? My friends think so, but I'm dead serious, and I was accepted to UC Berkeley to study optometry. I'm determined to do it. Everyone else doesn't have a clue what they want to do, so maybe I'm the lucky one.

CD1 7 See p. 10

CD1 8 See p. 10

CD1 9 See p. 103

UNIT 2

CD1 10 George Bernard Shaw

George Bernard Shaw (1856–1950) was an Irish playwright. He won the Nobel Prize in Literature in 1925. Shaw's instincts were to refuse this honor, but his wife persuaded him to accept it as a tribute to Ireland. He also won an Academy Award in 1939 for the movie version of his play *Pygmalion*. He is the only writer to win both awards. He wrote over 60 plays, but *Pygmalion* is probably his most famous work because, in 1956, after his death, it was adapted into the highly successful musical for stage and screen, *My Fair Lady*. He died at the age of 94 after falling off a ladder.

CD1 11 See p. 12

CD1 12 *Pygmalion*
Act II Scene 2 Professor Higgins's laboratory
H = Professor Higgins, L = Liza,
P = Pickering

H Say your alphabet.
L I know my alphabet. Do you think I know nothing? I don't need to be taught like a child.
H Say your alphabet!
P Say it, Miss Doolittle. You will understand presently. Do what he tells you; and let him teach you in his own way.
L Oh well, if you put it like that – Ahyee, beyee, ceyee, deyee –
H Stop! Listen to this, Pickering. This is what we pay for as elementary education. This unfortunate animal has been locked up for nine years in school at our expense to teach her to speak and read the language of Shakespeare and Milton. And the result is Ahyee, beyee, ceyee, deyee. Say "A, B, C, D."
L But I'm saying it. Ahyee, beyee, ceyee –
H Stop! Say "a cup of tea."
L A cappee-ee.
H Put your tongue forward until it squeezes against the top of your lower teeth. Now say "cup."
L C-c-c – I can't. … C-Cup.
P Good. Splendid, Miss Doolittle.
H By Jupiter, she's done it at the first shot. Pickering: we shall make a duchess of her. Now do you think you could possibly say "tea"? Not te-yee, mind: if you ever say beyee, ceyee, deyee again you shall be dragged around the room three times by the hair of your head. T, T, T, T.
L I can't hear no difference 'cept that it sounds more genteel-like when you say it.
H Well, if you can hear that difference, what the devil are you crying for? Pickering, give her a chocolate.
P No, no. Never mind crying a little, Miss Doolittle, you are doing very well; and the lessons won't hurt. I promise you I won't let him drag you round the room by your hair.
H Be off with you to Mrs. Pearce and tell her about it. Think about it. Try to do it by yourself: and keep your tongue well forward in your mouth instead of trying to roll it up and swallow it. Another lesson at half past four this afternoon. Away with you.

CD1 13 **Act III Scene 1 Mrs. Higgins's drawing room**

L = Liza, MRS. H = Mrs. Higgins,
P = Pickering, MRS. E-H = Mrs. Eynsford-Hill,
C = Clara, F = Freddy, H = Professor Higgins

L How do you do, Mrs. Higgins? Mr. Higgins told me I might come.
MRS. H Quite right: I'm very glad indeed to see you.
P How do you do, Miss Doolittle?
L Colonel Pickering, is it not?
MRS. E-H I feel sure we have met before, Miss Doolittle. I remember your eyes.
L How do you do?
MRS. E-H My daughter Clara.
L How do you do?
C How do you do?
F I've certainly had the pleasure.
MRS. E-H My son Freddy.
L How do you do?
MRS. H Will it rain, do you think?
L The shallow depression in the west of these islands is likely to move slowly in an easterly direction. There are no indications of any great change in the barometrical situation.
F Ha! Ha! How awfully funny!
L What is wrong with that, young man? I bet I got it right.
F Killing!
MRS. E-H I'm sure I hope it won't turn cold. There's so much influenza about. It runs right through our whole family regularly every spring.
L My aunt died of influenza: so they said. But it's my belief they done the old woman in.
MRS. E-H Done her in?
L Y-e-e-e-es, Lord love you! Why should she die of influenza? She come through diphtheria right enough the year before. I saw her with my own eyes. Fairly blue with it, she was. They all thought she was dead; but my father he kept ladling gin down her throat til she came to so sudden that she bit the bowl off the spoon.
MRS. E-H Dear me!
L What call would a woman with that strength in her have to die of influenza? What become of her new straw hat that should have come to me? Somebody pinched it; and what I say is, them as pinched it done her in.
MRS. E-H What does "doing her in" mean?
H Oh, that's the new small talk. To *do a person in* means to kill them.
MRS. E-H You surely don't believe that your aunt was killed?
L Do I not! Them she lived with would have killed her for a hatpin, let alone a hat.
MRS. E-H But it can't have been right for your father to pour spirits down her throat like that. It might have killed her.
L Not her. Gin was mother's milk to her. Besides, he'd poured so much down his own throat that he knew the good of it.
MRS. E-H Do you mean that he drank?
L Drank! My word! Something chronic.
MRS. E-H How dreadful for you!
L Not a bit. It never did him no harm what I could see. And always more agreeable when he had a drop in. When he was out of work, my mother used to give him four pence and tell him to go out and not come back until he'd drunk himself cheerful and loving-like. There's lots of women has to make their husbands drunk to make them fit to live with. Here! What are you sniggering at?
F The new small talk. You do it so awfully well.
L Have I said anything I oughtn't?
MRS. H Not at all, Miss Doolittle.
L Well, that's a mercy, anyhow. What I always say …
H Ahem!
L Well, I must go. So pleased to have met you. Good-bye.
MRS. H Good-bye.
L Good-bye, Colonel Pickering.
P Good-bye, Miss Doolittle.
L Good-bye, all.
F Are you walking across the park, Miss Doolittle? If so …
L Walk! Not bloody likely. I'm going in a taxi.

CD1 14

1 Poor Eliza was shabbily dressed in a tattered old coat and hat.
2 The return of the actor Bradley Cooper to the New York stage is eagerly awaited.
3 She was bitterly disappointed when she didn't get the part.
4 I work with a highly motivated sales team. We all work hard.
5 It's virtually impossible to get seats for a Yankees game.
6 I desperately need a vacation. I haven't had a break for three years.
7 Bad weather has severely affected the roads this weekend. Driving conditions are treacherous.
8 Don't you get it? It's blindingly obvious that he's in love with you.
9 I hate this cold climate. I'm sorely tempted to move south.
10 I distinctly remember telling you not to call me after ten o'clock.
11 Two people survived the crash with serious injuries, but unfortunately one man was fatally injured.
12 I've made my views on the subject of politicians perfectly clear. I don't trust any of them.

CD1 15

1 A You should have some breakfast. You'll be starving by lunchtime.
  B I did have breakfast! I had some delicious, brown, whole-grain bread with honey.
2 A There's been a break-in at the National Gallery.
  B Did they get much?
  A I don't think so. It just says, "Thieves stole a priceless, 19th-century, Impressionist painting" – but it doesn't say which one.
3 A Whoa! Did you see what happened to Camilla?
  B No, I didn't. What happened to her?
  A Well, she was wearing some fabulous, white, cropped, designer jeans and a waiter spilled spaghetti sauce all over them. She was absolutely livid!
  B I bet.
4 A Don't you think it's time we bought a new car? This one's a clunker.
  B Listen! I like my little, old, second-hand Honda, and it's not a clunker – at least not yet!
5 A You look wet and cold.
  B Well, we went on an exhausting, six-mile, coastal walk in the rain. Worth it, though – the views were stunning.
  A Hmm! Not my idea of a good time.
6 A How come you turned him down?
  B Where do I begin? First off – he wears cheap, revolting, smelly French cologne. I mean, really.
7 A I've never heard of Philippa Gregory.
  B Really? She's written a great, new, historical novel and lots of her stuff is adapted for TV.
  A I guess historical novels just aren't my kind of thing.
8 A Did you go over to meet the new neighbors?
  B I did. They're settling in well. They bought an amazing, massive, HD TV. It almost fills one wall, and it turns itself on when you speak to it.
  A What? How on earth does it do that?

CD1 16 *Jemima J.* by Jane Green
Chapter 1
I wish I were thin. I wish I were thin, gorgeous, and could get any man I want. You probably think I'm crazy, I mean here I am, sitting at work on my own with a massive double-decker club sandwich in front of me, but I'm allowed to dream, aren't I?

Half an hour to go of my lunch break. I finish my sandwich and look furtively around the office to see whether anyone is looking. It's OK, the coast is clear, so I can pull open my top drawer and sneak out the slab of chocolate.

Another day in my humdrum life, but it shouldn't be humdrum. I'm a journalist, for goodness sake. Surely that's a glamorous existence. I love the English language, playing with words, but sadly my talents are wasted here at the *Kilburn Herald*. I hate this job. When I meet new people and they ask what I do for a living, I hold my head up high and say, "I'm a journalist." I then try to change the subject, for the inevitable question after that is, "Who do you work for?" I hang my head low, mumble the *Kilburn Herald*, and confess that I do the *Top Tips* column. Every week I'm flooded with mail from sad and lonely people in Kilburn with nothing better to do than write in with questions like, "What's the best way to bleach a white marbled linoleum floor?" and "I have a pair of silver candlesticks. The silver is now tarnished, any suggestions?" And every week I sit for hours on the phone calling linoleum manufacturers, silver-makers, and ask them for the answers. This is my form of journalism.

Ben Williams is the deputy news editor. Tall and handsome, he is also the office Lothario. Ben Williams is secretly sought after by every woman at the *Kilburn Herald*, not to mention the woman in the sandwich bar who follows his stride longingly as he walks past every lunchtime. Ben Williams is gorgeous. His light brown hair is casually hanging over his left eye, his eyebrows perfectly arched, his dimples, when he smiles, in exactly the right place. He is the perfect combination of handsome hunk and vulnerable little boy.

CD1 17

1 A We couldn't help laughing. It was too funny for words.
  B I know – but it was her worst nightmare – wearing the same dress as someone else at a swanky party like that.
2 A I think he's boring. He has nothing to say for himself.
  B He may be a man of few words, but I think he's worth listening to.
3 A Pam just rambles on and on about herself. You can't get a word in edgewise.
  B I know. I thought she'd never shut up.
4 A Come on! You know you can trust me.
  B What? Trust you again? You're kidding. You don't know the meaning of the word.
5 A I got the latest Apple iPad Air. It's the last word in tablets. I love it.
  B Huh, lucky you! You always have the latest and greatest!
6 A No, I don't want anything for it. I don't need two computers. You can have it.
  B That's so kind of you. I'm at a loss for words. I can't thank you enough.
7 A Well! Not to mince words, but I don't think you stand a chance of getting that job.
  B Huh! Thanks for your vote of confidence!
8 A You said I had no chance. Well, you'll have to eat your words! I got the job.
  B You did? Well, go figure! You must be smarter than I thought!
9 A I think "selfie" is the latest buzzword. It's even in the *Oxford English Dictionary* now.
  B Yeah, I can believe it. Everybody's taking selfies. I just bought a selfie stick.

10 A This is just between you and me. Don't breathe a word to anyone else.
  B I won't tell a soul, I promise.

UNIT 3

CD1 18 World watch quiz

1 UN experts estimate that the total number of children in the world will remain at around two billion throughout this century. After a long period of constant increase, this peak level was reached at the end of the 20th century, as the average global fertility rate dropped from five babies per woman in 1950 to 2.5 in 2000.
2 Tragically, seven million of the 135 million children born each year die before the age of five, but the good news is that this is a huge drop to one in 25. This will not cause faster population growth, as women are more likely to limit the size of their families when child mortality drops.
3 The average life expectancy globally is 70 years. As recently as 50 years ago it was 60, and most of the longer lives were being lived in developed countries. Today, the average of 70 years applies to the majority of the world's population.
4 Today, 80% of adults in the world are literate. The biggest recent improvements in education have taken place for girls. In poorer countries such as Bangladesh, there are now as many girls attending primary and secondary schools as boys.
5 A family in extreme poverty cannot be sure of having enough food to eat on a daily basis. Figures from the World Bank show that the number of people living in extreme poverty has fallen from two billion in 1980 to just over one billion today.
6 In surveys over recent decades, self-assessment of where people feel they are on the happiness scale has resulted in slightly lower scores than half a century ago, despite significant increases in living standards.
7 During the first 12 years of this century, the average level of debt per adult increased by 45%. In some countries, the US for example, it increased to more than $225,000 per person.
8 The richest 10% in the world own 86% of global wealth. At the top of the pyramid, the concentration of wealth increases further, with the top 1% owning just over 50% of global assets.

CD1 19 Limits to growth
Part 1

H = Host, T = Tony Adams,
HA = Helen Armitage

H Hello. Welcome again to *Money Matters*. Now, we've had a few emails from listeners asking us to discuss the topic of economic growth. Margaret Bentley from Chicago writes, "It's disappointing to hear the economy has grown less than expected. But why do economies need to continue growing?" And David Adams from Nashville says, "Politicians are always promising to get the economy back to 'normal growth rates,' but surely our economy can't continue growing forever?" Well, I'm happy to say we have two people here today who are ideally suited to discuss this issue. Tony Adams is the head of the Center for Economic Policy.

T Hello.
H And Helen Armitage works for a think tank called Alternative Economies.
HA Hello.
H Tony, can you make the case for economic growth?
T Well, basically, just to maintain current living standards, the economy has to grow as fast as the population. If it doesn't keep up, there isn't enough work for everyone, and that means rising unemployment. But we want to keep improving living standards, not just maintain them, especially for the poorest in society. And the only way we can lift people out of poverty is through economic growth.
HA That's not strictly true, though, is it? Politicians want economic growth because it allows them to say they'll make the poor richer, without having to make the rich any poorer. Without economic growth, we have to start looking at the issue of income redistribution – letting the poor have a bigger piece of the pie. Of course, the people at the top are eager to avoid that, so they just keep trying to make the pie bigger and bigger.
H OK. Would you agree that growth is a way to avoid doing anything about inequality, Tony?
T Well of course, we need to avoid wealth redistribution if it means higher taxes on the rich. That reduces their motivation to invest, and so the economy then grows even less. We need to give everyone in society the opportunity to be better off, and that's what economic growth makes possible.
H Isn't that true, Helen, that growth keeps everyone happy?
HA You mean, "a rising tide lifts all boats"? That's such a familiar idea, along with the famous "trickle-down effect." But growth in recent decades hasn't reduced inequality; it's made it worse. Statistics show that the poorest in society haven't benefitted – the tide seems to have lifted only the big yachts, not all the boats.
T Well it's certainly made a huge difference in developing countries. The gap between rich and poor countries is much smaller than it used to be – most of the world's population now lives in middle-income countries.
HA Yes, but the inequality within countries has continued to increase. And anyway, it's wrong to assume that economic growth automatically leads to greater happiness. That may be true for the very poor – when you really don't have enough, more is definitely good. But overall, we've seen our economies grow 24 times bigger in the last century, and we're beginning to realize it hasn't made us that much happier. Studies show that at a certain level of income, the connection between more income and greater happiness disappears.
H Yes, I've heard that. And it starts to happen at a surprisingly modest level of income, too.
T But you're arguing against basic human psychology here. People always want more – they always have, and they always will. You see lots of relatively well-off people looking for new ways to make more money – why is that?
HA Because they can't help thinking that buying more stuff will make them feel happier. It's what our society encourages us to believe – just look at all the ads on TV. But if we stop to think about what gives us greatest fulfilment – does it always involve consumption? If you want to see what really makes you feel happier, go for a long walk with a friend. Try watching a

sunset one day this week. Organize a ball game with some friends in the park.

T Yeah, yeah, it all sounds very nice, but people won't stop wanting to buy more gadgets that will make their lives easier and more fun.

HA Do gadgets really do that, though?

CD1 20

Part 2

H So, Helen, are you saying that we need to have less growth, or no growth at all?

HA Well, the idea of endless economic growth is obviously a delusion. Economic growth of 2.5% a year sounds modest, but it means that GDP has to double every 30 years or so. You can't keep doing that forever – it's common sense.

T Common sense told us we couldn't continue growing as much as we have in the last 50 years. That's because we couldn't have predicted the technological advances that have made it possible, and who knows what technology we might develop in the future?

H And you think, Tony, that that will solve the problem of limited resources?

T Well, yes I do. We keep finding ways to use energy and resources more efficiently. Refrigerators now use half the energy they did 35 years ago. Family cars use half the fuel they did in the 1970s.

HA Fine, but we can't expect to keep making such huge improvements in efficiency. Our resources will remain limited, and that makes the idea of eternal growth a form of insanity. Look at those images of Earth from space, and it becomes blindingly obvious. The last year that the global economy was at a level the planet could support was 1983. We're now exceeding that capacity by more than 30%.

T Yeah, well, you know I remain an optimist. What's the alternative? No growth means more unemployment and less social spending because of lower tax revenues. And, if the environment needs protecting, no growth means having less money to spend on doing that.

H Yes, well maybe you should say something about the alternative, Helen.

HA The alternative is the "steady state economy," and even the great-grandfather of capitalism, Adam Smith, talked about it. He thought that once everyone had reached a reasonable standard of living, our economies would stop growing and reach a steady state. He assumed people would then prefer to spend more of their time on non-economic activities, things like art and leisure, and child rearing.

T Yeah, well, good luck with that. It's the happily unemployed fantasy – fine until you need some money to do something nice with your family.

HA No, it doesn't mean being unemployed. There would be less work available, but it can be shared, so we all do fewer hours a week. And as I said, the extra time can bring us much greater happiness.

H But people would have much less income.

HA Yes, but that's not such a problem if people accept they'll have to consume a lot less anyway. We could still buy new stuff, but we'd have to get used to buying a lot less of it, and keeping it for longer. It means getting things repaired more, instead of throwing them away and getting a new one – that's the way we used to live not so very long ago.

T Well, I just can't see it, personally.

HA Well, I can, so maybe I'm the optimist. And I think it's interesting to ask ourselves what we really want from life. Why are we hooked on producing and buying so much needless stuff? Why do we fill our lives with so much work that we don't have time to enjoy them? It's not as if we ever meant to create such a stressful way of life, so now's the time to look at doing things differently.

H You see managing without economic growth as a positive challenge, then?

HA Yes. We can't go back to the growth rates of recent decades, but it doesn't have to be a depressing prospect – exploring the alternatives can be exciting! We just need to give up the idea that consumerism is the central purpose of life.

H Well, thank you both. That is definitely an issue that isn't going to go away.

CD1 21

Spending on new cars rises sharply when people are in their 20s and presumably starting work. There's then a slight fall until mid-life, when there is a steady increase in people in their 40s and 50s buying new cars – perhaps men having their mid-life crises! Spending then drops back again to level off for 70-year-olds, before plunging sharply after people turn 80, when they are probably not so concerned about what they drive, if they're still driving at all.

CD1 22

The name Maria was reasonably popular in the 1880s, with just under 1,000 babies per million being given it. In the 1890s its popularity rose steadily to just below 1,500, and between the 1900s and 1920s it soared to over 2,500 before dropping again to around 2,000 in 1940.

The popularity of the name fluctuated over the next five decades, going up to 2,800 in 1960 and dropping again to 2,000 in 1980. Then there was a sharp increase up to over 3,000 between 1980 and 1990. There was a slight decrease to 3,000 during the 1990s, and the number of babies given the name Maria then plunged back to 2,000 by the end of the first decade of the 21st century. It is currently ranked as the 92nd most popular name for girls.

CD1 23

1 A This music's great, isn't it?
  B Turn it up – I can't hear it!
2 A Kids, quiet down!
  B Oh, Jeff. Leave them alone. They're just letting off steam.
3 A Why aren't you going out much these days?
  B I need to save up for a car.
4 A What's happened since your company was taken over?
  B They've cut down my hours.
5 A Speed up – it's a 70-mph zone!
  B It isn't. You can only do 60 on this road.
6 A Slow down – my legs are tired!
  B We'll never get to the youth hostel before dark if we don't walk faster!

CD1 24

1 A What will you do if you get downsized?
  B I'll set up my own business.
2 A What happened after the scandal broke?
  B The president stepped down.
3 A It's such a beautiful day. What should we do this afternoon?
  B Let's fire up the barbecue!
4 A What effect did it have on you, having to spend so much time abroad?

  B My marriage broke down.
5 A My laptop's so slow to boot up.
  B Try uninstalling programs that you never use.
6 A The drugstore's shut down.
  B I'm not surprised. It always seemed empty.

CD1 25

1 A I'm not talking to you until you say sorry.
  B Oh, grow up and stop acting like a child!
2 A I don't know why Diana hasn't replied to any of my texts this week.
  B You need to wake up and smell the coffee! It's obvious she isn't interested in you anymore.
3 A I've been sick, but I couldn't take much time off work.
  B Ah. You do look a little bit run down.
4 A Thank you all for coming during your lunch break. I want to talk to you about the …
  B Speak up! We can't hear in the back!
5 A I'm going to lose again. It's so depressing.
  B Oh lighten up, will you! It's just a game!
6 A How did you manage to drop my tablet? Oh, no! The screen is all cracked!
  B Calm down! I'll pay for the repair!
7 A Have you figured out what four across is? It's one of the best crossword clues ever!
  B It's too difficult. I give up! What's the answer?
8 A You promised you would get this report done by today.
  B I know. I'm sorry. I've let you down.
9 A I just don't want to confront her about it. I'm scared of her!
  B Man up, Tim, and stop being a wimp!
10 A Did you hear that the company's been taken over? No one seems to think it will change anything much.
  B The management's playing it down, but it's bad news.

CD1 26

1 Going forward, we're hoping to grow the business by at least 10% over the next year.
2 Jenny, can I task you with actioning all the points we've agreed on during this meeting?
3 This research phase is going to be mission-critical on this project, so I want to make sure that everyone is following best practice.
4 Supporting these charities will impact our tax situation positively, and also get us some great publicity – it's a win-win situation!

CD1 27 **Buzzword Bingo!**

OK, I thought I'd touch base and bring you up to speed on our bid to win the Delco advertising campaign. I know this is on all your radars, and as you know, this is mission-critical in terms of our attempt to grow the business this year. If we're proactive on this one and our bid is successful, it will impact our public profile in a big way and bring us serious bonuses – a win-win situation. I'm happy to see that Jeff's team has hit the ground running on this. I don't want to drill down into the ideas they've come up with so far, but let's just say they're certainly thinking outside the box, and I know Jeff will go the extra mile to get this contract. If any of you decide you have something to bring to the table on this, give me a heads-up, and I'll task you to action any good ideas you come up with. Going forward, we need to apply best practice throughout this bid, and if there are any new developments, you can be sure I'll keep you all in the loop. Danny, you don't look well. Are you feeling OK?

Sara

It's the macho action hero ones that get on my nerves the most. "Don't worry, it's on my radar." Actually, no, you don't have a radar because you're not a fighter pilot, and the upcoming presentation at the sales conference isn't really a potentially mortal threat. And before you tell me this is "mission-critical," we sell photocopy paper, and don't tend to go on many missions. There seems to be a desire to be associated with the heavy engineering boys, too – my boss has started asking me to "drill down" when he wants me to give him more information on something. And "growing the business" has become incredibly common, but it still sounds odd to me – I can only think of vegetables when someone talks about growing things. "Hit the ground running" is alright, though. I like that image because it does feel like that when you start a new project. And "go the extra mile" is something I often do for my customers, and I'm fine with it being described like that. Things like that, and "bring you up to speed," sound like perfectly normal language to me. The danger with all of them is that if you hear someone say exactly the same thing many, many times, you zone out.

Danny

I can't stand all this verbing of nouns. "Could you action this for me," as if "Could you do this for me" doesn't sound impressive enough. At least it's short, though. The ones that use an excessive number of words annoy me the most. "I'll keep you in the loop." Why not just "keep you informed"? "Going forward" is redundant most of the time, or you could just say "in the future." The only reason for using all this gobbledygook is the pathetic idea that it makes you sound like some high-flying managerial hot shot, but it can actually make you sound like a moron if you use too much of it. Some of the shorter ones can be useful – "best practice" means what it says and is neat, and "pro-active" is a good thing to be in business. I think "a win-win situation" has a really good feel to it. And I'm actually OK with "think outside the box," because in itself, it means something that I really like to do. It's just been overused so much and the kind of person who uses it is usually stuck inside a box labeled, "I copy what everyone else says."

UNIT 4

K = Karen, B = Beth

K Hey, Beth! You won't believe what happened in my jewelry store this morning!

B What?

K There was a woman buying a diamond necklace, and Jenny, the other assistant was helping her, and when she was paying for it, this guy, who I'd thought was just another customer, but I have to say, I had noticed he was behaving kind of strangely, well, he turned out to be a police officer, and arrested her for using counterfeit money, and …

B Whoa! Slow down! You've lost me! The woman was a customer?

K Yeah, and there were two men in the store who were actually plain-clothes police officers.

They'd been following her because she was part of a gang they'd been investigating for weeks – they were all buying stuff with counterfeit money – so they arrested her when she was paying with it.

B Wow! That's crazy! So was it a really expensive necklace?

K It was about four grand.

B And didn't anyone think that was a lot to pay in cash?

K Well, it's not that unusual at a jeweler's. And the police said the fake money was really convincing, so we probably wouldn't have spotted it.

B So what's happened to the woman?

K They've taken her down to the police station. They said they'd be back in a couple of hours to get full statements and bring the necklace back – they had to take that as evidence.

B Gosh! I know I shouldn't say it, but it's kind of exciting, isn't it?

K Yeah, I know what you mean. It wouldn't have been exciting if she'd gotten away with it, though. I'm not sure my manager would've been very understanding if he'd found out we'd been deceived.

K Oh, Beth, I'm so upset …

B What's wrong?

K You know how I said those police officers were coming back to the store with the necklace?

B Yeah.

K Well, … they never did – it turns out the whole thing was a scam!

B What? I don't understand.

K They weren't really police officers – they were all part of a gang, the two men and the woman.

B So, what, they … no, I don't understand, … they took their own counterfeit money …

K The money wasn't the point. They wanted the necklace, and I told you, they said they had to take it as evidence.

B Oh, … I get it. Oh, that's awful! … And tricky … I guess you were so grateful when they told you they were police officers, and what they were doing. I mean, you were hardly going to question them. You asked for their IDs though, right?

K We didn't need to, they held their badges up when they arrested the woman, but they must've been fake ones – they can't have been difficult for them to make if they were forgers, … though apparently they hadn't forged the money, it was real.

B Oh, no! And you weren't suspicious when they said they had to take the necklace with them?

K Well, no, I guess Jenny and I were in shock. I'm kicking myself about that now, though. I mean, why would they have needed to take it away as evidence?

B Oh, don't beat yourself up about it. I know I'd have fallen for it, too. So … what now? The real police are looking for all three of them, right?

K Yeah. And they're trying to get statements from any eyewitnesses. We have some security camera footage, but apparently one of the cameras wasn't working properly. Oh, what a horrible, horrible day!

Up until the 1970s, courts would often convict people of serious crimes purely on the basis of eyewitness evidence. Defense lawyers would try to argue that a witness might be mistaken on some of the details in their statement, but if the witness wouldn't accept this, the jury would usually believe them and assume the suspect was guilty.

Then, psychology professor Elizabeth Loftus began her work on the unreliability of memory and witness accounts. It showed that we shouldn't think of memory as an accurate and permanent record that we play back repeatedly. We will often change our memories by filling in new details about what must have happened, even though we didn't actually notice those details at the time.

Professor Loftus was also able to show how much the memories of eyewitnesses can be influenced by the questions they are asked, for example, "What color hat was the man wearing?" encourages a witness to "remember" that the man was wearing a hat, when in fact he wasn't. These are known as "leading" questions because they lead people to remember events in a certain way. Even the choice of words used in questions can be critical. Witnesses who were asked what speed two cars were going when they smashed into each other all gave higher speeds than those who were asked the speed when the cars hit each other.

Professor Loftus's work has led to restrictions on the use of eyewitness evidence. Suspects have the right to ask if they can speak to a lawyer before being interviewed. Police interviewers now have to follow strict guidelines and must not ask leading questions. Judges will often remind juries of the unreliability of eyewitness testimonies. However, they are still the leading cause of convictions that are later proven to be wrong.

1 **A** It's just a small gift to show how much I appreciate your help.
　B Oh, thanks, that's very thoughtful of you, but you really shouldn't have!

2 **A** I could have sworn I left the car here!
　B Well, I hope you're wrong because otherwise someone must have stolen it.

3 **A** Was Jake's party good?
　B It was OK. I got all dressed up, but I really didn't have to. No one else made an effort.

4 **A** Jenny will keep going on about my age!
　B I think she's just worried that you're trying to do too much.

5 **A** You might want to check that your shirt's buttoned up correctly.
　B Oh, no! Thanks! How embarrassing! I got dressed in a rush this morning.

6 **A** Oh, you can be so insensitive sometimes!
　B Me, insensitive? You should talk! You were the one who asked them why they'd paid so much for the house!

7 **A** Do you have to whistle all the time?
　B Oh, sorry! I didn't realize I was doing it!

8 **A** And who might you be?
　B I'm the new cleaner. Is it OK to do your office now?

9 **A** I want to apologize for the way I behaved.
　B I should think so! It was appalling what you did!

10 **A** Derek said the economic crash wasn't at all predictable.
　B Well, he would say that, wouldn't he? He works for one of the banks that needed bailing out.

RA = Radio Announcer, N = Narrator, Chris Blackwell, H = Houdini, CD = Conan Doyle, HW = Houdini's wife

RA And now the second part of our serialization of *Unexpected Friendships*. Chris Blackwell reads an extract telling of the unlikely friendship of Sir Arthur Conan Doyle and Harry Houdini.

N They seemed an unlikely couple, the six-foot-one British doctor and author, and the five-foot-six poorly educated American immigrant, but when Conan Doyle met Harry Houdini in 1920, they were immediately attracted to each other. Houdini had ambitions to be a writer himself, and was eager to mix with the literary elite. He was also intrigued to meet a highly intelligent man who believed in the supernatural. Doyle was convinced that Houdini's amazing talents could offer proof of supernatural powers, and was anxious to make use of Houdini's fame and popularity to publicize spiritualism.

Conan Doyle talked to Houdini about his own experiences of the supernatural, claiming to have spoken to his dead son on six occasions. Houdini showed great interest, and was enthusiastic about the possibility of Doyle finding him a true medium, telling him:

H I am very, very anxious to have a seance with any medium with whom you could gain me an audience. I promise to go there with my mind absolutely clear and willing to believe.

N But Houdini soon saw that the mediums Doyle introduced him to were simply using tricks to give the impression of communicating with spirits – the same tricks that he used in his own acts. Tactfully, he chose not to offend Doyle by exposing these mediums as fakes, saying on one occasion:

H I am afraid that I cannot say that all their work was accomplished by the spirits.

N Doyle was always confused as to why Houdini needed convincing of the supernatural, and asked him:

CD My dear chap, why go around the world seeking a demonstration of the occult when you are giving one all the time?

N In 1922, Doyle visited the US to give a lecture tour on life after death. He attracted huge audiences, and there was a sensation when newspaper reports of his New York lectures resulted in a number of suicides. It seemed that readers had found his accounts of the next world all too convincing and were eager to experience it as soon as possible.

Houdini decided to try and show Doyle that "supernatural phenomena," were not all they seemed, and arranged a private demonstration. Houdini performed an amazing trick in which a message that Doyle had written down in secret was written on a slate by a ball soaked in ink. No one was touching the ball. It seemed to be moved by an invisible hand as it wrote the words. Doyle was speechless. Houdini then told him that it had all been done by trickery, and said:

H I beg of you, Sir Arthur, do not jump to the conclusion that certain things you see are necessarily "supernatural," or the work of "spirits," just because you cannot explain them.

N But it was a lost cause. Doyle was convinced that Houdini could only perform such amazing tricks by using psychic abilities, saying:

CD It is an outrage against common sense to think otherwise.

N He assumed that Houdini had to deny his psychic abilities, because he would have been unable to continue as a magician if it was known that he had them. And of course, Houdini couldn't have revealed how he performed his tricks, as it is taboo for any magician to do so. He simply noted with regard to Doyle that:

H I have found that the greater a brain a man has, and the better he is educated, the easier it has been to mystify him.

N Doyle was determined to persuade Houdini that not all mediums were fakes, and arranged a seance in which his wife Jean would attempt to contact Houdini's dead mother. Houdini was excited about the possibility, and said:

H With a beating heart I waited, hoping that I might feel once more the presence of my beloved mother.

N Jean went into a trance and began to write messages to Houdini, saying that it was his mother speaking directly to him, and that she was simply moving Jean's hand to write the words. When the seance was over, Houdini wrote at the bottom of the page, which was filled with messages written in perfect English:

H My sainted mother could not write English and spoke broken English.

N She had always communicated with her son in German. Houdini never thought the Doyles were trying to deceive him, but were simply deluding themselves. However, when Doyle went on to write newspaper articles about the "messages" that Houdini had "received" from his mother, it was the final straw. He went public himself about how the whole thing had been a sham, saying:

H It is a pity that a man should, in his old age, do such really stupid things.

N And so their unusual friendship came to an end. Houdini dedicated himself to exposing mediums as fakes, while Doyle insisted that Houdini was using his special powers to prevent the mediums from performing properly. Doyle was clearly upset, and wrote to Houdini:

CD As long as you attack what I know to be true, I have no alternative but to attack you in return.

N The two men never met again. After Houdini's death, his wife wrote to Doyle, insisting that Houdini had not actually held any bad feelings towards him. She said:

HW He was deeply hurt whenever any journalistic arguments arose between you and would have been the happiest man in the world had he been able to agree with your views on spiritualism. He admired and respected you.

N Doyle referred to Houdini as:

CD The most curious and intriguing character whom I have ever encountered.

1 **A** I don't think she left him just because he forgot their anniversary.
  B No, but I think it might have been the final straw.

2 **A** Dan got back from traveling around Asia two months ago, and I think he's already thinking about another trip.
  B Yeah, he seems to have itchy feet again.

3 **A** I avoid using my credit card when I'm shopping for clothes – it's difficult to stop once I've started.
  B Yes, it's a slippery slope.

4 **A** Was Mia sad about moving across the country for her new job?
  B No, she didn't give it a second thought.

5 **A** I can't believe Dana went to Jack for help. She can't stand him!
  B I know, but he was her last resort. No one else who knows the program was in the office, and she had a deadline.

6 **A** I noticed you changed the subject when David started talking to Jane about house prices.
  B Yes, it's a sore spot for her right now.

7 **A** So you don't think it's worth me spending any more money trying to get this car back on the road?
  B No, I think it's a lost cause.

8 **A** It's not fair! My sister got to go to New York for her birthday, and all I got was a dinner and a movie.
  B Yes, it sounds like you got a raw deal there.

9 **A** Do you think Suzanne really has a chance of getting into the Boston Conservatory? She only started the piano three years ago.
  B No, it's just wishful thinking.

10 **A** I can never understand the rules about which future tense to use.
  B To be honest, not many people can. It really is a gray area.

DM = David Mitchell (host), GG = Graeme Garden, HW = Henning Wehn, JH = Jeremy Hardy, VCM = Victoria Coren Mitchell

DM Your subject, Graeme, is doctors: persons trained and qualified to diagnose and treat medical problems. Off you go, Graeme.

GG In 2009, a group of doctors opened a restaurant in Latvia, called Hospitalis. The dining room looked like an operating theater, the food came on hospital trolleys, with drinks in specimen beakers. On request you could be fed your meal by waitresses dressed as nurses, while you wore a straitjacket.

DM Henning.

HW Yeah, I believe that story.

DM You're right to believe it, because it's true! It closed because it was failing hygiene tests … but then, as we know, the hygiene requirements of a restaurant are much much higher than they are for a hospital.

GG In the 14th century, Henri de Mondeville believed that causing the patient to weep or scream would remove the cause of their illness, which is where clown therapy began.

DM Jeremy.

JH I think the first bit of that is true.

DM He believed that causing patients to weep or scream was a good idea?

JH Yeah.

DM No, he didn't.

JH OK.

DM No, but, no, this chap, Henri de Mondeville, he was one of the first surgeons to stress the need for a good bedside manner, so very much the opposite of making people weep and scream. He recommended that surgeons should keep each male patient cheery with false letters about the deaths of his enemies, or, if he is a spiritual man, by telling him he has been made a bishop. That's it, just, that's a way of cheering someone up – some bad medical news, … in other news, you have been made a bishop. Graeme.

GG When doctors in Brazil went on strike in 1973, the number of daily deaths dropped by a third.

DM Henning.

HW That sounds unfortunately entirely plausible.

DM It is true! Yes. Uh, it's believed a factor in the

reduced death rate could be the reduction in elective non-emergency surgery caused by the strike. Or, you know, they're doing more harm than good.

GG Back in the 1860s, one American doctor devised an ingenious way of getting rid of awkward patients. He invented the hand grenade. Doctors …

DM Victoria.

VCM I'm gonna guess that the person that invented the hand grenade was a doctor.

DM No, he wasn't.

VCM Oh, I'm so bad at this!

DM No, well you're … you're not …

VCM You told me that Henning always lost and this would be an easy one!

DM No, no, the hand grenade wasn't devised by a doctor, but the machine gun was invented by a doctor, Dr. Richard J. Gatling.

GG Doctors have always been applauded for the elegance and clarity of their handwriting. In a rare exception to the rule, the doctor who recorded the birth of Hollywood hunk Clark Gable was not a master of penmanship. As a result, Clark Gable's birth certificate listed him as female, and his name was deciphered as Joan Crawford.

CD2 4

T = Ted, M = Margaret, A = Attendant

T That one's incredible, isn't it, Margaret? She looks so real!

M Yes. I was wondering if it might be possible to take a photo of it. Do you think it would be alright?

T You might want to ask that attendant first.

M Oh, I thought he was one of the exhibits! Excuse me, could I possibly take a photo of that statue?

A Oh, we don't allow flash photography.

M I thought I might take it without flash. Would that be OK?

A Yes, that's fine.

M Thank you. Ted, you couldn't take one of me next to it, could you?

T Yes, of course. Just move a little bit to the left, would you?

CD2 5

A Excuse me, is there any chance I could take a look at your iPad? I was thinking I might buy one of those.

B Yes, of course. I'm really happy with it.

A Thank you. Do you think I could try typing on it? I was wondering if the keyboard would be big enough for my fingers.

B Sure, go ahead. My fingers are pretty big, and I don't have a problem typing on it.

A Mmm. It's nice. Would you mind telling me how much you paid for it?

B $499. You might want to take a look in PC World. They're on sale there right now.

A Oh, thanks very much. I think I might do that.

CD2 6

Would you mind not putting your feet on the table?

Do you think you could stop interrupting me?

Do me a favor and go, now!

Do you mind? That's my seat!

CD2 7

1 Excuse me, would you mind speaking more quietly?

2 Perhaps you'd like to explain this?

3 I'm afraid this isn't good enough.

4 Close the door, will you?

5 Could you possibly move your car?

6 Would you mind not making that noise?

CD2 8

M = Martin, P = Peter

M Hi, Peter!

P Hey, Martin. Good news! I finally did it! I popped the question!

M You asked Karen to marry you! You said you were going to do it this year! And the answer was obviously a big yes!

P Yup, so your stint as best man is coming very soon!

M When's the wedding?

P October, October 18th.

M Gosh, that's soon … oh, hang on, that could be a problem … let me check … oh, yeah, sorry, Peter, I can't do that Saturday.

P No!

M Yes, really, I have an annual international conference in London that weekend, and I'm scheduled to give a presentation. You can't have arranged anything yet – couldn't you move the wedding to another weekend in October?

P No – we spent hours finding a weekend that worked for both our families to come, and that really was the only one before the end of the year. Couldn't you ask them to move your presentation to Sunday?

M Not really. It's already scheduled, and it's in all the programs they sent out.

P They could change that, though – it wouldn't be such a big deal for them.

M I can hardly ask them to do that because I want to go to a wedding though, can I?

P Well, think of something else to tell them, and ask very, very nicely. Come on, I can hardly get married without you as my best man!

M Ooooh, I don't know …

UNIT 5

CD2 9

1 **A** Oh my goodness! Did you see that sign? What on earth does it mean?

B No idea. Do you think there's a river at the bottom of this hill?

A Yeah, a river full of crocodiles.

B Yes, but it seems like they only eat people in wheelchairs.

A Weird. Well, we'll see.

2 **A** You're holding everyone up!

B Look, I'm new at this. I can't figure out how to …

A Read the sign!

B It doesn't make sense! How can I hold my poles and do that at the same time? It's not possible.

A Well, everyone else can do it.

B Ouch! Ow! I give up. I'm going up on the gondola.

A Good idea. You do that.

3 **A** Ow! Careful! It's a speed bump! You're going too fast!

B No, I'm not!

A Ouch! You are! We just went over another one. I practically hit my head on the roof. Drive over them more slowly.

B I am.

A You're not. Ooh! … Phew! Thank goodness for that – we're on the open road again.

4 **A** Hey, slow down! I want to look out for ostriches.

B Uh, ostriches? You won't see any here.

A Well, that sign said we might.

B No, it didn't. I don't know what it was, but it wasn't an ostrich.

A Well, it looked like one to me.

5 **A** Ugh! Look at these traffic queues!

B "Lines" – remember we're in the US!

A OK, OK. I told you it wasn't a good idea to drive during rush hour.

B Don't "I-told-you-so" me! Just tell me which "line" to pull into.

A Not that one! We're paying cash.

B Why not?

A I think it's a drive-through lane. Try that one over there!

B OK, OK. This is …

6 **A** Why would that be banned?

B Well, obviously it's bad for you.

A But it's just a nut.

B Not just any nut. I'm pretty sure it's addictive and carcinogenic, and it makes your teeth red.

A Ew!

B Didn't you see that guy in that café we stopped at? His mouth was red.

A Yeah, I saw that, but I thought he had bleeding gums and just needed a trip to the dentist.

CD2 10 Papua New Guinea

Papua New Guinea is located in the southwest Pacific Ocean just north of Australia. Its population currently stands at approximately 7,500,000. This is made up of over 700 different tribes. Many of these are in the isolated mountainous interior or the rainforest and therefore have little contact with one another, let alone with the outside world. This is one of the reasons why Papua New Guinea is linguistically the world's most diverse country, with over 800 languages spoken – 12% of the world's total.

Eighty-two percent of its people live in rural areas with few or no facilities or influences of modern life. Cannibalism and headhunting were widely practiced until as recently as the 1950s, and polygamy is still part of the culture. It is still possible to buy a wife with seashells or pigs.

Papua New Guinea has strong ties with its southern neighbor, Australia, which administered the territory until independence in 1975. The government is led by an elected prime minister in the National Parliament, but, as the country is a member of the Commonwealth of Nations, Queen Elizabeth II is its head of state.

CD2 11

1 I tried to fix my car, but I couldn't. It needs a mechanic.

2 **A** You look awful. Why don't you see a doctor?

B I did. He just gave me some pills and told me to take it easy.

3 **A** Did you read this report?

B No, I didn't, but I will.

4 My car's being serviced right now. If it wasn't, I'd give you a ride. Sorry.

5 I'm so glad you told Sue exactly what you thought of her, because if you hadn't, I certainly would have!

6 **A** I think I'll call Rob.

B You should. You haven't been in touch with him for a long time.

7 I went to a party last night, but I wish I hadn't. It was awful.

8 My boyfriend insists on doing all the cooking, but I wish he wouldn't – it's inedible!
9 A Aren't you going to the beach for your vacation?
   B Well, we might, but we're still not sure.
10 A Andy got lost on his way to Anne's party and didn't show up until midnight.
   B He didn't! That's so typical of him.

CD2 12
1 A You met my sister last night.
   B Yes, I did. She thought we'd met before, but we hadn't.
2 A It's a long journey. Be careful on the freeway.
   B Don't worry. We will.
3 A Come on, John! It's time to get up!
   B Stop yelling at me! I am!
4 A The weather forecast said that it might rain this afternoon.
   B Well, we'll have to cancel the tennis match if it does.
5 A Did you get that job you applied for?
   B Yes, I did, and I really didn't think I would.

CD2 13
1 A Can you come over for dinner tonight?
   B Thanks. I'd love to!
2 A Did you mail my letter?
   B Oh, I'm really sorry. I forgot to!
3 A I can't take you to the airport after all. Sorry.
   B But you promised to!
4 A Was John surprised when he won?
   B He sure was. He didn't expect to!
5 A Why did you slam the door in my face?
   B It was an accident. I really didn't mean to!
6 A You'll be able to enjoy yourself when exams are over.
   B Don't worry. I intend to!

CD2 14 See p. 41

CD2 15 *Don't Log Off* with Alan Dein
Part 1
A = Alan, B = Bryan
A Hello.
B Hello!
A Hello! Is this Bryan?
B Yes, this is Bryan.
A Hi, How are you? I first spoke with Bryan 18 months ago.
B I dedicate my lunch hour normally to chat with my girlfriend, Anna, that I met online. I was just browsing profiles in Russia and I stumbled across the most beautiful woman in the world.
A But this was more than just a typical online romance. Do you speak Russian?
B No, I'm learning to speak Russian.
A And does Anna speak English?
B No, not yet. She's trying to learn English, too. I began to chat with her using Google translator.
A That's how the relationship continued. Bryan and Anna relying on online translation to communicate. Saying that you were both "lost in translation" but in fact you found each other though translation. This was the first of numerous conversations with Bryan. The next time he'd been to visit Anna in Russia.
B Let me tell you. It took me over 24 hours just to get there.
A Did you feel that it all was exactly how you thought it would be in your mind?
B Oh, yes. The physical, spiritual, mental connection – everything was there.
A Six months later. Hello!

B Hello, Alan!
A Bryan had some big news for me.
B We've just decided we were going to get married and …
A Anna and her two children would be leaving Russia and moving to America. And the amazing thing is, this whole relationship is still relying on online translation. Neither Bryan nor Anna speak each other's languages.
B She's left the only home she's ever known all her life basically …
A Anna and her children were on their way.
B She's coming to a country where she's never been. She's never even been on an airplane before.
A I spoke with Bryan at the airport on the night of their arrival.
B She should be here any minute. It had to have landed.
A They were all gonna come over on a three-month visa.
B There's some people coming up the escalator.
A Anna has to get married to Bryan within those three months. Otherwise Anna and the children have to return to Russia.
B Then I still don't see … You guys coming from New York? Ha! Here she is! There she is. I missed her! Oh! I missed you, too! Oh! She's here.
A Bryan, this is a very special moment.
B OK well, she just told me to get off the phone.
A Well, Bryan, may I wish you good luck, and I look forward to catching up with you shortly.
B OK, you can call me in the next few days.
A And it was then that I had an idea. I was thinking it would be a wonderful experience to visit you and Anna in Boise, Idaho.
B Oh, wow!
A To see you in person and to kind of capture your life with Anna now.
B That would be … that would be … that would be, uh, interesting, yes.
A But you never know – that might fit into your wedding plans.
B Yes, I think it would definitely take it up to the next level.
A Bryan set the wedding date for the 21st September, and I booked the plane ticket so I could be there. But then I received a rather worrying message. So this is really big news …

CD2 16
Part 2
A = Alan, B = Bryan
A This is really big news … The wedding that was planned for Saturday the 21st September is now off.
B Hello!
A Bryan, I got your message. Um, it's big news.
B It's a little bit difficult, but – uh …
A Yeah.
B Fortunately, we haven't made a lot of arrangements.
A Tell me how you both made the decision to postpone the wedding.
B I think the 21st was just a little bit too soon for her. She's been through a lot. She came half way around the world. She's only been here, just about a month and a half now, just a little shy of a month and a half. And I think maybe, perhaps – uh, things may not be as nice as she'd imagined, you know – uh …
A What is the cut-off point, Bryan?
B October 20th, I think would probably be the 90-day cut off.

A The clock is ticking, isn't it, Bryan?
B Yes, and I hope that she doesn't have second thoughts.
A But, wedding or no wedding, the plane tickets had been bought. Boarding the plane I had no idea quite how this story would unfold. 15 hours later. There I am, breathing Idaho air.
A Hi, Anna. How are you? It soon becomes clear to me that it's not been easy for Anna in these first few months in the US.
B Right now she really hasn't been anywhere by herself. She's always had me with her.
A So, when you're at work?
B When I'm at work she pretty much stays at home.
A Can you understand that?
B I can understand. She has been through a big change, and I don't want to add any stress to her life.

CD2 17
Part 3
A What have you got in that bag, Bryan?
B This is our wedding rings.
A Bryan and Anna are getting married. They've decided to go ahead with the wedding, but it's not quite the big day that Bryan had originally planned. It's going to be a very low-key affair in the court house. It's all very casual. Both Anna and Bryan are wearing jeans. It's an empty courtroom. The only people present at the wedding are Bryan and Anna, Anna's eight-year-old son, Ivan, myself, the producer, and the interpreter. And then Bryan had a surprise for us. Both myself and my producer, Lawrence, were called upon to be official witnesses at the wedding.
   I can't quite believe that from a random Skype conversation almost two years ago that I am now in Boise, Idaho, signing Bryan and Anna's wedding certificate. A wedding that would never have taken place without the advent of online translation.

CD2 18
Peter
I'm from Miami, and a few years ago I went to work in Prague, and on my very first day there I set off to walk to work. And I came to this butcher's shop, and I casually glanced at the special offers board on the sidewalk outside. I couldn't believe my eyes – it read, "ZEBRA, 65 Kc/kg." For me this was a big cultural difference. I'm no vegetarian, and I'll eat almost any meat. I don't have a problem with veal or rabbit, but I do draw the line at endangered species, so I checked the board again, and it really did say "zebra." I felt sick. I worried about it all the way to work. I'd always thought the Czechs were a civilized nation, and I wasn't sure what perturbed me the most; the idea of eating zebra or the fact that it was so cheap.
   Anyway, after I got to work and had a cup of coffee, I introduced myself to the pretty, young, Czech receptionist. And I just had to find out if Czechs really did eat zebra. So I said, "What's Czech for *zebra*?" "*Zebra*," she said, "Why?" Oh, dear, I was horrified, so I asked,
   "And it's a Czech delicacy?" "No," she said, "of course not. Why?" "Well, outside the butcher's, it said 'ZEBRA 65Kc/kg.'"
   She started laughing and finally she asked, "Did the z have a hacek?" "A what?" I asked. "A little hook, like this above the z." And she drew it for me. "You see, *zebra* is Czech for *zebra* BUT *žebra* with a hacek above the z means *ribs*." And

she pointed at her midriff to show me. I felt really foolish but very relieved. The Czechs really are a civilized bunch after all. So much so that I'm still here eight years later and … I'm married to Lenka – she's the pretty, young receptionist.

Sarah

I'm half-Korean and half-British, so I have a kind of dual identity. I was born in Seoul in South Korea, but I've lived in England for years, and now I find whenever I go back to Korea I'm faced with some unique cultural differences. I suppose I look about, uh, 80% Korean and 20% British – and Korean people are often a bit puzzled as to why I look slightly different from them. And one day the funniest thing happened, in this respect. I was in a department store in Seoul, just browsing through some clothes, and this woman came up to me, and she grabbed me by the arm and said, "Oh, please tell me, where did you get your nose done?" And I just looked at her and said, "What? What do you mean?" And I tapped my nose and felt very self-conscious. Then it struck me, because actually in Korea plastic surgery is quite a routine procedure. It's very common. There are plastic surgeons on every street corner, so this lady just assumed because my nose is a bit larger than usual – um, that I must have had plastic surgery done. I just said to her, "Oh no, no, sorry. Actually my father gave me this nose. He's British."

Elena

I'm originally from Oaxaca, Mexico, but I currently live in Germany with my German husband and our two children. We met and fell in love many years ago when we were college students in the United States. At the time, I never dreamed that I would live anywhere other than Mexico, but love has a funny way of changing your plans! One of the most delightful differences is experiencing four seasons of weather. In the part of Mexico I'm from, there are two seasons: the dry season and the rainy season. In Germany, I get to experience four seasons of weather. I must admit that I still haven't gotten used to the cold winters here, though. I'd pick Mexican weather over German weather any day! Another thing that I'm still trying to deal with is showing affection. Germans can sometimes be a little bit reserved. In Mexico, we hug and kiss our friends all the time. In Germany, I have to rely on words to express emotions. Sometimes it's very frustrating for me. It's also kind of difficult to make friends here. I have a few German friends that I've met through work, but I'm much closer to my friends back in Mexico.

Ethan

I'm Australian and about six years ago I spent two years living and working in Burma. Every day I'd catch a taxi to my work. Anyway, one day, not long after I arrived there I got into this taxi, a beautiful clean, shiny taxi. I sat down and – uh, I put my feet … well, it was difficult to find anywhere to put my feet. But I didn't look down and the taxi started moving, luckily a bit slowly. Suddenly, I found my feet because they'd started … sort of running. It was the weirdest feeling. I looked down and my feet were actually on the road and they had to run to keep up with the taxi. I looked again and saw a huge rusted hole in the floor of the taxi – my feet had gone right through it. Quick as a flash I pulled them back inside and positioned them firmly on both sides of the hole. But after that I noticed that a lot of the taxis had problems – they were really ancient cars, but their owners were really proud of them and kept them in beautiful condition where they could, but some things like doors or floors

they couldn't replace. I couldn't imagine taxis like these being allowed in Sydney. There didn't seem to be any health and safety regulations in Burma, but the taxis did their job just fine. Maybe it's different now.

CD2 19 See p. 44

CD2 20 See p. 44

CD2 21

1 A Do you have the time?
   B Yeah, it's five after four.
   A Did you say five of?
   B No, five *after* four.
2 A What are you gonna do on the weekend?
   B The usual stuff. Play soccer with my kids and rake the yard.
3 A Did you have a good vacation?
   B Yeah, real good.
   A How long were you away?
   B Five days in all. Monday through Friday.
4 A Where do you live?
   B We have a small apartment on the first floor of an apartment building downtown.
   A Do you have a yard?
   B No, we don't – just a parking lot around the back.
5 A Did you see Meryl Streep's new movie yet?
   B Yup. She was awesome in it. She played this homely, old woman who drifted around in her bathrobe all day.
   A Yeah, she's a great actor.
6 A Did they bring the check yet?
   B Yeah. They just did. But I can't read a thing. It's so badly lit in here. You need a flashlight.
7 A Do we need to stop for gas?
   B Sure do! Anyways, I need to use the bathroom.
8 A Did you enjoy the game?
   B Yeah, it was great, but we had to stand in line for half an hour to get tickets.

UNIT 6

CD2 22

1 "I came, I saw, I conquered," was said by Julius Caesar (100 BC to 44 BC). He was a Roman general who sent the famous message, *veni, vidi, vici* to the Roman senate in 47 BC, after a great military victory in Asia Minor, now known as Turkey.
2 "Happiness lies in conquering one's enemies, in driving them in front of oneself, in taking their property, in savoring their despair, in outraging their wives and daughters." This was said by Genghis Khan (1162–1227). He was the emperor and founder of the Mongol Empire. After his death, this became the largest empire in history.
3 "The supreme art of war is to subdue the enemy without fighting," was said by Sun Tzu (544 BC to 496 BC). He was a Chinese general who is credited with writing *The Art of War*, a book about military strategy which is still used today.
4 "It is not enough to say we must not wage war. It is necessary to love peace and sacrifice for it," was said by Martin Luther King, Jr. (1929–1968). He was a US minister, humanitarian, and activist who used nonviolent civil disobedience as a form of protest.

5 "War does not determine who is right, only who is left." This was said by Bertrand Russell, (1872–1970). Russell was a British philosopher, mathematician, historian, and pacifist. He won the Nobel Prize for Literature in 1950.
6 "The tragedy of modern war is that the young men die fighting each other, instead of their real enemies back home in the capitals," was said by Edward Abbey (1927–1989). Abbey was an American author, essayist, and anarchist, noted for his advocacy of environmental issues.
7 "No one is born hating another person because of the color of his skin, or his background, or his religion. People must learn to hate, and if they can learn to hate, they can be taught to love." This was said by Nelson Mandela (1918–2013). Mandela was a South African anti-apartheid revolutionary, politician, and philanthropist. In 1962, he was arrested and sentenced to life imprisonment. He served over 27 years in prison. He was finally released in 1990 following an international campaign. He then served as president of South Africa from 1994 to 1999.
8 "I know not with what weapons World War III will be fought, but World War IV will be fought with sticks and stones," was said by Albert Einstein (1879–1955). He was a German-born physicist who developed the general theory of relativity. In 1921, he received the Nobel Prize in Physics.
9 "In war, truth is the first casualty," was first said by Aeschylus (525 BC–456 BC). He was a Greek tragic dramatist. He is often described as the father of tragedy, being the first of the three ancient Greek tragedians whose plays are still read or performed. The others are Sophocles and Euripides.
10 "Mankind must put an end to war before war puts an end to Mankind," was said by John F. Kennedy (1917–1963), the 35th president of the US. It was part of a speech to the United Nations General Assembly on September 25, 1961.

CD2 23 See p. 48

CD2 24

1 The thing I can't stand about Bruce is the way he's always so full of himself.
2 It's his lack of self-awareness that amazes me.
3 What you don't appreciate is how exhausting traveling is.
4 Something that drives me crazy is the number of security checks.
5 The thing that upset me was the way the customs officer behaved.
6 What I appreciated was the fact that all the nurses were so sympathetic.
7 Something that really annoys me is the way you're always late.
8 It's Peter who you should talk to.

CD2 25

1 A What kind of vacation do you like?
   B *One* thing I like is touring historic sites.
2 A *I* like relaxing on a beach in the sun.
   B What *I* like doing is touring historic sites.
3 A *You* like adventure vacations, don't you?
   B No, no, *touring historic sites* is what *I* like.
4 A You like going on cruises, don't you?
   B No, it's touring historic *sites* that I like.
5 A I know you *hate* touring vacations.
   B Well, actually, touring historic sites is something I *like*.

6 A You *like* cultural vacations, don't you?
  B Yes, there's *nothing* I like more than touring historic sites.

CD2 26
Never in the field of human conflict was so much owed by so many to so few.
Never have I seen such courage.
Rarely does one find such clear explanations.
Had it not been for the war, women would not have gotten the vote.
Finally, the war did end.

CD2 27
1 Something I've never told you is that I'm actually a secret agent.
2 What I can't stand about modern life is the number of choices you have to make.
3 What always surprises me is the way we always seem to end up doing what you want to do.
4 The thing that annoys me the most is people who talk loudly into their cell phones in public places. Do they think it makes them look important?
5 It's not me who wanted to come to this dump on vacation! It may be cheap, but there's nothing to do.
6 What the government should do is stop listening to focus groups and get on with governing!
7 Never in my life have I been so happy to see someone. Do you have a key to the front door?
8 What I did after class yesterday was just go home and chill. I was exhausted.

CD2 28
1 A Peter hasn't told anybody.
  B He told me.
2 A I hope you didn't tell Clara.
  B I didn't tell anyone.
3 A I invited Anna, but she isn't coming.
  B I told you she wouldn't.
4 A Who told Tim about it?
  B I have no idea. I didn't tell anyone.
5 A John won't like it when you tell him.
  B If I tell him.
6 A It's the worst movie I've ever seen.
  B Tell me about it!
7 A He dumped me.
  B I told you he would!
8 A Have you heard the joke about the old man and his dog?
  B I told you it!

CD2 29 Part 1
Oh, What a Lovely War!
A, B, C, D, F = British soldiers, E = German soldier
A Hey, listen!
B Yeah, they're coppin' it down Railway Wood tonight.
A Nah, not that. Listen. What is it?
C Singin' innit?
B It's those Welsh bastards in the next trench.
C That's Jerry, that is.
B Yeah, it is Jerry. It's comin' from over there.
D Sing up, Jerry! Let's 'ear yer!
C Oh, nice, weren't it?
E Tommy? Hello Tommy!
B Eh! 'E 'eard us!
C 'Ello?
E *Fröhliche Weihnacht!*
C Eh?
B What?

E Happy Christmas!
ALL Oh! 'Appy Christmas!
F Hey, yeah, it's Christmas!

CD2 30 Part 2
Graham Williams and Harold Startin's account of the Christmas truce
I = Interviewer, GW = Graham Williams, HS = Harold Startin
I That scene from the West End musical of the 1960s *Oh, What a Lovely War!* is a pretty accurate illustration of the kind of thing that happened in several places on the Western Front on that Christmas Eve of 1914. Listen to the account of someone who was actually there. Graham Williams, a rifleman with the London Rifle Brigade, was on sentry duty that night.
GW On the stroke of eleven o'clock, which by German time was midnight, 'cause they were an hour ahead of us, lights began to appear all along the German trenches, and uh … then people started singing. They started singing *Heilige Nacht, Silent Night.* So I thought, "Well, this is extraordinary!" And I woke up all the other chaps, and all the other sentries must have done the same thing, to come and see what was going on. They sang this carol right through, and we responded with English Christmas carols, and they replied with German again, and when we came to *Come All Ye Faithful,* they joined in singing, with us singing it in Latin, *Adeste Fideles.*
I So by the time you got to that carol, both sides were singing the same carol together?
GW Both singing the same carol together. Then after that, one of the Germans called out, "Come over and see us, Tommy. Come over and see us!" So I could speak German pretty fluently in those days, so I called back … I said, "No, you come over and see us," I said, "*Nein, kommen … zuerst kommen Sie hier, Fritz!*" And nobody did come that time, and eventually the lights all burned out, and quieted down and went on with the usual routine for the night. Next morning I was asleep, when I woke up I found everyone was walking out into no-man's land, meeting the Germans, talking to them, and … wonderful scene … couldn't believe it!
I Further along the line in the perfect weather, Private Harold Startin of the Old Contemptibles was enjoying that morning, too. He couldn't speak any German, but that didn't stop him making friends.
HS We were "Tommy" to them, and they were all "Fritz" to us. If you'd have met your brother, they couldn't have been more cordial towards you, all sharing their goodies with you. They were giving us cigars about as big as your arm, and tobacco.
I Were you frightened at first? Were you suspicious at all? Because these were people …
HS No!
I … that you'd been trained to hate, weren't they?
HS No! There was no hatred, we'd got no grudge against them, they'd got no grudge against us. See, we were the best of pals, although we were there to kill one another, there were no two ways about that at all. They helped us bury our dead, and we buried our dead with their dead. I've seen many a cross with a German name and number on and a British name and number on. "In death not divided."

I Did you do other work during the truce as well? Was it just burying the dead, or were there other things …
HS Oh, there was strengthening the trenches, borrowing their tools …
I You actually borrowed German tools to strengthen your trenches?
HS We borrowed German tools. They … then … they'd come and help you strengthen your defenses against them.

CD2 31 Part 3
How the truce ended
I = Interviewer, HS = Harold Startin
I Not only was the truce more extensive than anyone has realized before, it also lasted much longer than has been believed until now. In some areas, the war started up again on New Year's Day, but in the part of the line where Harold Startin was, the truce lasted a lot longer than that.
HS Ours went on for six weeks. You can read in the history books about Sir John French, when he heard of it, he were all against it. But our truce went on for six weeks. And the Württemberg Regiment, they got relieved before we did, and they told us they thought it were the Prussian Guards goin' to relieve them, and if it was, we should hear three rifle shots at intervals, and if we only heard three shots we should know that the Prussian Guards, that were opposite us then, and we'd got to keep down.
I Because they would be fiercer than …
HS Yes!
I … than the Württembergers?
HS Yes!
I Can you remember particular Germans that you spoke to? Over six weeks you must have made friends?
HS I spoke to one, Otto, comes from Stuttgart, 'as … 'as been over to England to see me.
I So you made friends during the truce and kept in touch after the war?
HS We made friends during the truce, and friends after.

Goodbyee! (Soldiers' song from the 1914–1918 war.)
Goodbyee! Goodbyee!
Wipe the tear, baby dear, from your eyee!
Though it's hard to part, I know,
I'll be tickled to death to go.
Don't cryee! Don't sighee!
There's a silver lining in the skyee.
Bonsoir, old thing! Cheerio! Chin-chin!
Au revoir! Toodle-oo! Goodbyee!

CD2 32 Keeping the peace
1 A What color do you call that?
  B It says "pale sunlight" on the can.
  A "Pale sunlight!" It's more like "dazzling daffodil!" I can't wake up to that every morning – it'd give me a headache.
  B I guess it is a little bit yellow. Oh, dear! I just wanted a kind of sunny glow in our bedroom.
  A Don't worry. I'm sure we can find a happy medium. Let's get some of those little sample cans from the paint store.
2 A We should have turned left there.
  B Look! Who's driving this car? The GPS said "right."
  A I know these streets better than any GPS.
  B You do not! The GPS is never wrong.

A Huh! You don't believe that any more than I do.

B Well, I am not turning around.

A OK, OK. Have it your way. But don't blame me if we're late.

3 **A** I don't have a clue who to vote for in the next election. They are all a bunch of …

B But you have to vote. We can't let the opponents win.

A That's not how I see it. They're all horrible.

B I couldn't disagree more. Let the opponents win and taxes will skyrocket and prices will …

A Come on! That happens with all of them. Let's just agree to disagree. We can't ruin our friendship over this.

4 **A** Put that thing down!

B What?

A You spend your life in front of a screen.

B Hey! Hang on a minute – look who's talking! You never go anywhere without your tablet and cell phone.

A Yeah, but I'm not always checking them. You've lost the art of conversation.

B I have not! I take offense at that.

A Well, I've been telling you about my day and you haven't heard a word.

B Uh? Sorry – what did you say?

CD2 33 See pp. 110–111

UNIT 7

CD2 34

1 I'm so fed up with living in this town. It's so boring, there's just nothing interesting to do here. And I wish we hadn't bought this house – it's so dark and depressing.

2 Look, it's really time you cleaned your room. When are you going to do it? If I've asked you once, I've asked you a thousand times!

3 I was really upset when I didn't do well on the SATs, but I feel OK about it now. I guess it's not the end of the world.

4 I think it was appalling the way Selena behaved. I'm not interested in her excuses. She should be ashamed of herself.

5 OK, OK, you made your point. Maybe I did behave badly tonight.

6 I'm not very good at explaining things to people. I'm impatient, and I get very frustrated if they don't understand right away.

7 Everyone's saying how wonderful your presentation was! Derek says you're one of the best presenters he's ever seen.

8 Oh, I still don't know whether to take that job or not! I hardly slept last night thinking about what to do. Do you really think I should take it?

CD2 35

1 I'd give Dave a ride again tomorrow if he hadn't made fun of my car this morning.

2 If you hadn't been sitting in that café when I walked in, we wouldn't be living together now.

3 If Mason had been born a week earlier, he'd be starting school next week!

4 We'd buy that house right now if the previous owner hadn't painted it pink!

5 If I didn't have bad eyesight, I would have trained as a pilot after I graduated from college.

6 I would've mailed Maria's birthday present yesterday if I wasn't going to visit her next week.

CD2 36

Z = Zoe, W = Will

Z Ugh! This hotel is horrible! I wish we hadn't come here. I've never seen such a dirty place in my life! It wouldn't be so bad if the bathroom was clean, but it's filthy. I wouldn't even wash my socks in it.

W I know, but we'd been driving for hours, and I wanted to stop. If we hadn't, there might not have been another hotel for miles, and we'd still be driving.

Z I wish we'd left earlier, so we could have gotten to Carmel today. We won't get there until tomorrow at lunchtime now. I told you we'd need to leave in the morning, but you wouldn't listen!

W I had to finish some important work this morning. If I hadn't, we could have left earlier. Then we'd be sitting in a nice hotel on the coast instead of this dump in the middle of nowhere.

Z Anyway, it's time we had some food. If it wasn't so late, I'd suggest looking for a cute café, but I guess we'll have to eat here. I wish we didn't. It'll be awful, I'm sure.

W Oh, I wish you'd stop complaining!

Z OK, I'm sorry. I guess we're both tired. Come on, let's start enjoying the weekend!

CD2 37

1 **A** There isn't very much, if any, chicken in this sandwich – it's all lettuce.

B I know. Mine's the same. I'd have ordered the vegetarian option if I didn't want meat!

2 **A** We rarely, if ever, watch reality TV shows.

B We don't either. I find I get enough reality in everyday life.

3 **A** He's a born loser if ever I saw one.

B Oh, that's a terrible thing to say. He's just going through a difficult period in life.

4 **A** You should find my house easily. If not, give me a call, and I'll give you directions.

B It's OK. I never find things easily myself, but my GPS usually does the job.

5 **A** Jo seemed interested in the idea, if not exactly enthusiastic.

B Oh, I think she's very eager. She just doesn't show her feelings very much.

6 **A** See if that dress fits you. If so, you should definitely buy it.

B You know, I think I might just do that. It's about time I bought some new clothes.

7 **A** Creepy Carlos asked me for a date! As if!

B Oh, come on! He's not that bad! I'd be interested in him if he dressed little better.

CD2 38 The history of the smile

Part 1

H = Host, KW = Kate Williams,
CJ = Colin Jones, LC = Laura Cumming

H The historian and author Kate Williams goes in search now of the modern winning smile.

KW W.C. Fields's advice might have been to start the day with a smile and get it over with, but the power of the smile should not be underestimated. The broad and confident smile is at the heart of our communication, and central to how we interact with people in today's society. However, this hasn't always been the case, as Colin Jones, professor of history at Queen Mary University of London, explains:

CJ Since the Renaissance, there's been a tremendous emphasis on forms of politeness and civility, which emphasize control. All that sort of conduct literature emphasizes closure of the mouth. Of course one smiles at all sorts of circumstances, the crucial thing is to control that smile, and to keep the lips firmly shut, so that the mouth is closed and the teeth are undisplayed.

KW Just because they were restrained doesn't mean they didn't have a good time. As a historian, I'm fascinated by how images of our ancestors as straight-faced and serious makes us think that they were dour. From Elizabeth I to Queen Victoria, it is almost as if we think those before us never smiled. Art critic Laura Cumming, author of *A Face to the World*, has examined smiles in portraiture from across the centuries.

LC Most smiles that I can think of in portraiture are closed-lipped. It seems to me that that's quite significant. Clearly teeth are an issue in the medieval era, and they become an issue very strongly with the arrival of sugar, and in Flemish art, in which there are lots of smiling portraits, there's a suggestion that the open mouth smile is indicating speech and sometimes indicating age. There are wonderful paintings, Lucas Cranach and so on, where the sitter is opening their mouth to show, either rather beautiful flashy white teeth, in which case they're showing their teeth off, or they're showing the crumbling teeth like a faltering/falling skyline. Most smiles, closed.

KW Professor Colin Jones feels there's one portrait in particular that has great significance in the history of the toothy smile we know today. *Self-portrait in a Turban with Her Child*, by the French court painter Élisabeth Louise Vigée-Lebrun, painted in 1786 and first shown a year later at the Louvre, where it still remains.

CJ It really crystallizes the change, which has probably been going on in the previous years, about the meaning of the smile – the smile with an open mouth showing teeth, that is. She's sitting in a very sort of casual way with her rather beautiful child on her lap, looking directly at the viewer, with a very charming smile, and she's showing white teeth. It provokes quite a storm. There are people who write in about this and say, this is quite radical, it's quite disgraceful that she's showing herself in this way. By focusing on the smile, I think we've definitely got something which is changing, it's something which is a very significant moment, I think, in the representation of the smile in Western art, but it also is flagging up a change in the way that people think about the relationship between their smile and their basic identity.

LC Vigée-Lebrun is not the first by any means. What she is, however, is the first to make a real style of it.

CJ What is also interesting about this smile, is that it's flagging up Madame Vigée-Lebrun is a woman who can afford a dentist. She could act as almost like an advertisement for some of these Parisian dentists who are seen as Europe's greatest practitioners in the 18th century, or for the tooth powders or pastes and toothbrushes which are emerging precisely at this time.

Part 2

AT = Angus Trumble, KW = Kate Williams,
CJ = Colin Jones, OM = Olivia Mann

AT   The greatest single factor governing the development of modern smiling habits, apart from dentistry, was the invention of photography, and in due course, the invention of motion picture photography.

CJ   The emergence of Hollywood studio shots, where the smile is seen as something which is absolutely vital to the person's charisma. It's really in the late 19th and definitely much more in the 20th century that the idea comes forward that the informal shot, which can be picked up by instant photography, becomes a way in which individuals can register their individuality.

KW   We have our photographs taken all the time, weddings, Christmas, holidays, but it's actually quite difficult to get that perfect natural smile. So to find out how to look good on camera, I'm here in a photography studio in North London, to meet the photographer Olivia Mann, and we're going on a mission for the perfect natural smile.

OM   Great, that's fantastic.

KW   So, Olivia, you specialize in wedding photography, and when you're out there photographing the wedding, how do couples feel about smiling on their wedding day?

OM   I have brides coming to me and saying, "Oh, I'm really worried about my crow's feet, and if I smile too much, then that's going to make me look awful." What is actually a nightmare for me is that if someone is worrying about their crow's feet, then what they tend to do is tighten up and clench all their facial muscles, so they actually look quite scary, which is the last thing you want in your wedding photographs.

KW   So Olivia, I can't put it off any longer. I'm going to have my photograph taken. What will you do to say, to get me to make that perfect natural smile?

OM   What I want you to do is, just sit there for a moment, and just start relaxing everything. Yeah, first of all, your forehead. Everyone holds a lot of tension in their forehead. Really relax the muscles around your eyes and your cheekbones, and just let your lips fall open. If you could just imagine a moment in your life where you felt particularly happy, confident and attractive.

KW   I'm in Italy, in a little village by the sea, and having a large plate of pasta, and it's beautiful weather, and I'm with friends and it's just, it's just a wonderful evening.

OM   So, now I want you to hold on to all of those feelings, but you're now in the studio and you're ready to be photographed, so open your eyes and let's go! … That's absolutely lovely … and just drop your chin a tiny touch, yeah, that's the shot, that's lovely.

KW   Oh, I'd love to see it. Can I have a look? Oh, that's great! That's fabulous! I love it! So there's me thinking of Italy. I think I'm going to try this from now onwards. Every time I have to have my photograph taken, I'm going to start thinking about eating pasta in Italy by the sea!

Part 3

AT = Angus Trumble, MF = Martin Fallowfield, KW = Kate Williams

AT   The profound transformation of whole societies by what can be achieved now in the dentist's chair is giving rise to completely new attitudes about what is beautiful and what is acceptable and what is desirable in our smile. So in a way, the medical and the cultural are traveling in parallel.

KW   One man who has our smiles literally in his hands is dentist Martin Fallowfield. So is there such a thing as the perfect smile?

MF   There are those who argue that the perfect smile is an imperfect smile. The very, very best technicians will be building in tiny irregularities when they're building a full mouth smile. This wall-to-wall symmetrical dentistry that we're seeing, actually doesn't look that good.

KW   So what's the future for our smiles? Bigger? Whiter? Wider? Angus Trumble.

AT   If you look at the difference between Rita Hayworth and Julia Roberts, it is impossible not to be startled by an amplification. The dial on the meter marked "smiling" is being turned up and there's no reason to suppose that it will stop being turned up. It will get bigger, possibly fiercer, certainly whiter, and possibly even broader.

KW   So one day we might be like the Cheshire Cat, big and smiley and the grin remains!

AT   Yes, and in that situation a solemn or somber person may strike us as not just bizarre but mad.

1 **A**   How did the meeting with your boss go?
   B   Not very well. I just carried on like a crazy person. I don't think I said anything that made sense!
2 **A**   Oh, no, I feel like I've heard this lecture before!
   B   I know, it's dragging on, isn't it? And his voice is so monotonous!
3 **A**   I finally managed to get away from Alan. He was going on and on about his new phone.
   B   I know. He's been wanting one of those for a long time, so he's pretty excited about it.
4 **A**   Are you going to the 5K charity run?
   B   Of course I am! Maddie might not win the race if I'm not there to cheer her on!
5 **A**   I think there's a chance I can get out of my speeding ticket if I tell them I was late for a really important medical appointment.
   B   Oh, yeah, dream on. You think they haven't heard that one before?
6 **A**   Well, I guess we'd better get a move on.
   B   Absolutely. It's almost three o'clock, and we're only half way through.

1 I'm going to blow off going to the gym. I'm too tired to exercise.
2 These pills really help my migraines, but they wear off after about four hours, and I don't want to keep taking more of them.
3 About a third of our workers were laid off in the company reorganization.
4 I can't believe Denise has broken off her engagement. She seemed so happy with Jason.
5 The postal service strike was called off at the last minute after intense negotiations.

6 I went off chicken for a while after visiting a chicken processing plant on our school trip. It was enough to put anyone off.

1 **A**   So there isn't going to be a taxi cab strike now?
   B   No, it's been called off.
2 **A**   A lot of people are eating quinoa now, aren't they?
   B   Yes, it really seems to have caught on.
3 **A**   These painkillers don't work for very long, do they?
   B   No, they wear off after about three hours.
4 **A**   Did you stay up late last night?
   B   I did. That's why I nodded off during Professor Taylor's lecture this morning.
5 **A**   Would you like a cup of tea?
   B   Yes, I'll put the kettle on.
6 **A**   When does the heater start working?
   B   It comes on at nine o'clock.
7 **A**   Did you meet Jack for lunch today?
   B   No, I didn't. He blew me off.
8 **A**   How come you lost your job?
   B   I got laid off.
9 **A**   Are you taking Suzie to the airport?
   B   Yes, I'm going to see her off.
10 **A**   You haven't written that essay yet?
   B   No, I keep putting it off.
11 **A**   Oh, I thought that lecture would never end! It was so boring.
   B   Yes, it did drag on.
12 **A**   Why can't you drive down Main Street? Is it because of that awful traffic accident?
   B   Yes, the police have sealed off the area.

1 **A**   I got soaked when that huge wave came in!
   B   Never mind, it could be worse. At least you can dry off in the sun.

1 **A**   The bank won't lend me any more money. I wish I'd never started my own business!
   B   Cheer up! I'm sure it'll all work out for the best in the end.
2 **A**   If only I'd never asked Lucy out. She said no, and it's really awkward working with her now.
   B   You'll get over it soon. At least you tried. You know, nothing ventured, nothing gained.
3 **A**   I don't think I'm ever going to make it as an actor. I messed up another audition this morning.
   B   It's not the end of the world. Hang in there and stay positive.
4 **A**   I can't believe what I've done! I sent an email complaining about my boss to her by mistake!
   B   Don't worry about it. What's done is done. And it'll all be forgotten in a few days.
5 **A**   I'd just had the cast taken off my leg, and now I've broken one of my fingers!
   B   Keep your chin up! Some day you'll look back on all this and laugh!
6 **A**   We'll have to be more careful. We've spent most of my year-end bonus money already.
   B   Oh, well. Easy come, easy go. It was good while it lasted.
7 **A**   I'm so disappointed I didn't get the contract for the stadium. They gave it to another firm.
   B   You can't win 'em all. And you could always get a job with the other firm. If you can't beat 'em, join 'em!

8
A It was depressing to lose the championship game on a goal scored in the last few seconds!

B It's not all doom and gloom, though. There's always next year. And maybe it's for the best. If they focus on signing some new players, it might turn out to be a blessing in disguise.

CD3 7 See p. 112

UNIT 8

CD3 8 **Are you a typical male or female?**

G = Girlfriend, B = Boyfriend

G Let's see. Number one. Oh, yes. Definitely female. That's so totally me. I have lots of amazing girlfriends – friends I've had since high school.

B But I do, too. All my high school and college buddies go back for years.

G Yeah, but you can't call you and your buddies typical, can you? All that male-bonding is kind of rare, don't you think?

B Whatever.

G What about number 2? Now that is absolutely a male thing. You're the original "gadget man."

B Hey! Not just gadgets! I like people just as much as things.

G I still think gadgets win for you. And the next two – names and birthdays – we're both absolutely typical for our sex with those. I'm always the one who remembers birthdays and you …

B OK, I know. I have a real problem with names and birthdays …

G Huh! What about 5?

B Everyone I know just texts these days.

G Yeah. I don't think that's a male/female thing. Everyone texts all the time, but I do talk on the phone more than you. There's nothing like a nice long talk!

B If you say so! What's next? Number 6, right? Ah, yes! I'm definitely good with numbers. I never have a problem figuring out percentages.

G Me neither. I'm the one who studied math, remember!

B You never let me forget.

G Mm, now for 7 and 8. Oh, exactly! Everyone knows that women are much better at multitasking, and …

B OK, I'll give you that. And I know, I know, very typically, I do talk about sports a lot.

G A lot? You and your buddies never stop. You go on and on and …

B OK, OK. So we like our sports. Let's look at number 9. Now come on. You have to admit you are a lousy navigator. That is surely typical for many females.

G I'm not that bad. Anyway, who needs maps? Everyone has a GPS these days. And … moving on, number 10 … yeah, definitely, I'm sympathetic to others and their feelings so 10 is correct.

B That's not fair. I'm a sympathetic kind of guy. I understand people's feelings.

G OK, OK, you're a nice guy. Oh, but look at 11 … you do prefer to work alone and not on a team. But then I do, too actually. I'm not happy on a team, and if I am on a team I like to lead. Now, on to 12. Oh, I definitely don't do this. I like to talk about stuff that's worrying me, especially with my sister. You know what they say: "A problem shared …"

B Yeah … "is a problem halved." I know that. I just don't go around spilling my guts about my problems. I'm a typical guy, I guess.

G Yeah. Your mom complains to me that you keep too much to yourself.

B Yeah, yeah. Now, what about 13? Now I'm definitely the linguist. You're not!

G I know. I'd love to speak French like you do. Oh, neither of us is typical for 13.

B But we definitely are for the last one.

G I'll say. I have no idea what you find interesting about *Great Train Journeys in Outer Mongolia* and …

B Come on, it wasn't "Outer Mongolia."

G It was somewhere like that.

B Well, I don't know what you see in all those crime novels and chick lit.

G I do not read chick lit. I read well-written modern romances … Anyway, let's add up our answers. How typical are we?

CD3 9

a **A** It was the passengers who exhibited prejudice.
   B I can believe that.

b **A** According to Aoife and her sister, who is also a pilot, reactions are more likely to come from passengers.
   B Two sisters who are pilots! That's got to be unusual.

c **A** It's a cultural problem which needs to be tackled at an early age.
   B What is?
   A The lack of female pilots.
   B That's true of many jobs.

d **A** Their two-bedroom apartment, which doesn't have a yard, felt small.
   B I bet it did, especially with twins.

e **A** The mom who he was talking to invited him to the get-together.
   B Did she? What would his wife say?

f **A** Officials hurried him through what is normally a long procedure.
   B Which procedure is that?
   A Oh, all the stuff you have to do and forms you have to fill in when you're looking for a job.

CD3 10

1 I don't like children who always interrupt their parents' conversations and whose parents never tell them to be more polite.

2 The commute from work to home, which is always a nightmare, took over three hours yesterday. I'm going to have to find a new job or move to a new house.

3 Politicians who make impossible promises just to get elected aren't worth listening to.

4 The Taj Mahal, which took 22 years to complete, is built from exquisitely carved white marble.

5 These are the photographs my grandma gave me from when she was a young girl with her grandma – so that's my great, great grandma. Apparently, her name was Rosemary.

6 We docked at the small port on the coast of East Africa, where my parents lived 25 years ago, and where both my brother and I were born.

7 My cousin, who's afraid of heights, went para-gliding last weekend. I thought he was crazy, but he said it was fine – not the same as being on a cliff or at the top of a tall building.

8 We went on a white-water rafting trip on the Colorado River, which I wasn't really excited about, but in fact I had a great time, despite the cold weather.

CD3 11

1 **A** Flights booked one month in advance have a 10% discount.
   B Booking your flight in advance gives you a better deal.

2 **A** The new uniforms worn by the pilots looked very professional.
   B Visitors wearing sleeveless tops will be denied entry.

3 **A** We took a shortcut, saving an hour on our commute time.
   B With the money saved from not eating out, I'm buying a bike.

4 **A** Taking all things into account, I've decided to resign.
   B Taken three times a day, these tablets will help your allergy.

5 **A** I fell on the ice, injuring my wrist.
   B The boy injured in the car accident is in the hospital.

6 **A** Breaking promises leads to lack of trust.
   B Broken promises lead to lack of trust.

7 **A** Giving away secrets won't win you any friends.
   B Given the chance, I'd love to work in New York City.

8 **A** Growing up in the suburbs is healthy for young kids.
   B Strawberries grown under polythene ripen more quickly.

CD3 12 **Bringing up Max**

A = Ali (wife), L = Luke (husband),
S = Sam (Ali and Luke's teenage son)

A Have you seen this? Poor little guy!

L What? Who's a "poor little guy"?

A This poor kid. He's just a toddler, one year old. How can they do this to him?

L What are you talking about? Who are "they" and what on earth have they done?

A Just look at these pictures!

L Yeah? So? What are you bothered about? He looks really cute, don't you think? I like his plaid lumber-jack shirt. And he has his big sister's pink tutu on. Good for him! I remember when Sam wanted a bow in his hair like Emma. He loved wearing all those costumes she had for dressing up, especially the Cinderella one. Remember, we thought it was funny, but Emma ripped him to shreds.

A Yeah, that's what big sisters do. But this is different. Max – his name is Max – and he doesn't have a sister. And it seems the pink tutu was bought specifically for him. It says here that wearing costumes is all part of his parents' plan to bring him up to be "gender neutral."

L "Gender neutral"? He's a little boy. I don't get it. What does it mean?

A It's supposed to be a radical new technique for child rearing, where boys and girls are treated exactly the same. His mother, her name is Lisa, says, and I quote, "We're doing it because gender stereotyping can be so damaging. It teaches little boys to be aggressive." Well, all I can say is that I'm glad we didn't know that when we were raising Sam.

L "Gender stereotyping," eh? Well, I guess there could be a point to that.

A So, you think our son is aggressive?

L No, of course not. I didn't say that. Sam's a great kid. He's full of life. He's your typical happy, energetic, goofy teenager. It's just that …

A It's just what? And it's a ludicrous idea. Max's parents are actively encouraging him to be more girl-like, and they're not only OK with him wearing girls' clothes, but they also want him to play with conventionally female toys … as well as boys' toys. I mean, they're totally OK with it if he wants to wear a pink tutu and fairy wings. And if he decides not to play soccer and wants to paint his fingernails with glittery polish, they will view it as a form of "cute self-expression." That's a direct quote from the article.

L Why are they doing all this?

A They think it will help boost his confidence.

L How is wearing a tutu a boost to a boy's confidence? But look, you know as well as I do, all toddlers will try anything that tickles their fancy. It doesn't matter if it's for boys or girls. They don't care. They're just too young to bow to peer pressure.

A Exactly. You don't have to actively encourage toddlers one way or the other. They just do their own toddler thing.

L Let me see this article. Oh, right. I remember … You know, that Canadian couple a while back? They made headlines when they refused to reveal the sex of their newborn baby. They called it "Storm" and dressed it "neutrally" so that no one would stereotype it.

A Ugh, that's awful. I don't mean calling the baby Storm, but calling him or her "it" all the time. That's not just awful, it's weird.

L They said that what they were doing was, and I quote, "a tribute to freedom and choice."

A Whose choice? Their choice and not the baby's. It's the same for this boy, Max. It's not his choice. And what about when he goes to school? I mean, what will …

L Here we are! Yes, it's just as I thought. Max's parents say that they are planning on educating Max at home so that he won't have to wear gender-specific clothes when he starts school.

A No surprise there. Don't you think he might be in danger of growing up to be a lonely, confused little boy?

L That remains to be seen. How long can his parents keep this up, though? And those Canadian parents! I can't believe they'll be able to continue calling their child "it" forever. I'd like to see into the future. What will these kids be like in ten years?

A Yeah, and what will their parents be doing? It's as if they're using their kids as guinea pigs. I don't think it's fair to the kids.

S Hi, Mom! Hi, Dad! We won again! And I'm starving.

L There's our flawless offspring! What can we get you to eat? Your wish is our command!

S Huh? What's up with you two?

CD3 13 Dr. Eugene Beresin

To raise a child not as a boy or a girl is creating, in some sense, a freak. The Canadian couple's approach is a terrible idea because identity formation is really critical for every human being, and part of that is gender. There are many cultural and social forces at play. Since the sexual revolution of the 1970s, child development experts have embraced a more flexible view of gender. Before that, the stereotypes of boys were that they were self-sufficient, non-empathetic, tough, and good at war. Girls were trained to be empathetic and caring, and more nurturing. But since then, women have become more competitive, aggressive, and independent, and by the same token, men are allowed to cry. We often see hulking soccer players who are bawling.

CD3 14

1 A Did you hear that? Andy called me "useless" and "inefficient."
  B Don't worry. He's just as rude to me as he is to you.

2 A A pair of red socks! That's just what I wanted!
  B I'm so glad you like them. You can't go wrong with socks as a present. They're always useful.
  A Yeah …

3 A Can I have mine black with two sugars?
  B Ah … We're just about out of coffee.
  A No problem. I'll have tea instead.
  B Actually …

4 A Where are you? You were supposed to be here hours ago.
  B I'm just leaving now. I got held up with a conference call. See you soon.

5 A I come home from work absolutely exhausted, and look at this mess! You haven't even washed the breakfast things and …
  B Just listen to me for once! It isn't my fault. The baby was sick just after you left, and I had to call the doctor, and …

6 A Did you see that movie *Fargo* on TV last night?
  B I couldn't watch it after the first few minutes. I was just terrified!

7 A I just heard the news. You got that job after all!
  B I know. I'm thrilled. I didn't hear back from them for months, so I thought they'd found someone else. Then suddenly I was called for a second interview.

8 A Hi! Great to see you! Oh, where's Tom?
  B Tom couldn't come, so it's just me.
  A Oh, no. You two have been arguing again, haven't you?

CD3 15

1 A We're sitting way in the back, in row 102.
  B We had another row about our finances.

2 A That was never him singing live. He was miming.
  B "Live and let live" is my philosophy.

3 A Close that window! That's one cold draught.
  B You're not even close to getting the answer.

4 A I soon got used to working the late night shift.
  B I don't trust used car-dealers. I'd never buy a car from one.

5 A It's impossible to tear open this package. Give me a knife.
  B A single tear ran silently down her cheek as she waved goodbye.

6 A He always looks so content and carefree.
  B The content of your essay was excellent, but there were a lot of spelling mistakes.

7 A The teacher complained to the parents about their son's conduct in class.
  B Keith Lockhart is going to conduct the Boston Pops Orchestra this evening.

8 A Could you record the next episode for me? I'm going to be out that night.
  B He broke the Olympic world record for the 100-meter dash.

CD3 16 See p. 68

CD3 17

1 A I just came across my very first girlfriend on Facebook.
  B I bet that was a blast from the past. Are you going to "friend" her?
  A Mmm. I'm not sure. Looks like she's changed quite a bit.

2 A Larry failed his exams. Amy has the chicken pox. What's next?
  B Better watch out! They say these things come in threes.
  A I don't want to hear that.

3 A Dad, I made the school soccer team! Varsity first string!
  B That's my boy! Like father, like son.
  A What do you mean? You only made junior varsity second string!

4 A If I offer to pay, she'll say I'm old-fashioned. If I don't, she'll say I'm cheap.
  B Hmm. You can't win for losing!
  A Yeah, it's a tricky situation.

5 A I got a card from Jerry one week after my birthday.
  B Oh, well. Better late than never.
  A Argh! You think so? I'm afraid it's the last straw.

6 A We're taking a complete break. Two weeks in the Caribbean.
  B Sounds like just what the doctor ordered.
  A In fact, the doctor did order it! He said Bill would have a nervous breakdown if we didn't take some time off.

7 A It took me ten years to build up my business. It nearly killed me.
  B Well, you know what they say: "No pain, no gain."
  A Yes, but nothing is worth ruining your health for.

8 A I just need to go back in the house and make sure I turned off the oven.
  B Good idea. Better safe than sorry.
  A Yeah, otherwise I'd be worrying all the way through the movie.

9 A They have ten kids. Goodness knows what their house is like.
  B It boggles the mind! I can't even bear thinking about it.
  A Yeah, I only have two, and it's chaos most of the time.

10 A Bob's a weird guy. He's going to live alone on a remote Alaskan mountain for a year.
  B It takes all kinds.
  A You can say that again.

CD3 18 The Princess and the Frog

One warm summer's evening a beautiful, young princess, feeling bored and lonely in the grand rooms of the palace, decided to take a walk in the nearby forest. With her she took her favorite plaything, a golden ball, which she loved to toss up in the air and catch. After a while she happened upon a shady pool of spring water, so she sat herself down to enjoy the cool shade and started idly throwing her golden ball high in the air, watching it glint in the evening sunlight. She reached out to catch it, but dazzled by the brightness of the sun, she missed and it splashed down into the center of the pond. Distraught, the

Audio Scripts   131

princess leapt to her feet and, looking down into the black depths of the water, she began to weep.

"Alas," she lamented, "if I could only get my ball again, I'd give all my fine clothes and jewels, and everything that I have in the world."

No sooner had she finished speaking when a frog's head popped up out of the water, and he inquired, "Princess, why are you weeping so bitterly?"

"Ugh!" she thought, "A disgusting, slimy frog!" But she sniffed and cried, "My golden ball is lost forever in the deep, dark water."

The frog said, "I don't want any of your finery; but if you will love me, and let me live with you and eat from your golden plate, and sleep on your bed, I will retrieve your ball."

"What ridiculous nonsense this silly frog is talking," thought the princess. "He'll never be able to leave the pond to visit me. However, he may be able to get my ball." So she said to the frog, "If you bring me my ball, I'll do all you ask."

The frog dove deep into the water; and after a little while he emerged carrying the ball in his mouth, and threw it onto the edge of the pond.

The princess was overjoyed. She ran to pick up the ball and without any sign of gratitude or a backward glance at the frog, ran home as fast as she could. The frog called vainly after her. "Stay, princess! What about your promise?" But she ignored his plea.

However, the next day, just as the princess was sitting down to dinner, there was a strange noise outside. Something was coming up the marble staircase. Then came a gentle knock at the door, and a croaky voice cried out:
"Open the door, my princess dear,
Open the door to thy true love here!
And mind the words that thou and I said
By the fountain cool, in the greenwood shade."

The princess ran to the door and opened it, and there stood the frog. She had forgotten all about him and now the sight of him frightened her. She slammed the door in his face and hurried back to her seat. The king, alarmed at his daughter's distress, asked her what was the matter.

"There is a disgusting, slimy frog at the door," she said. "He helped me get my ball back when it fell into the pond, and I promised he could live with me here, but …"

The frog knocked again and called out again:
"Open the door, my princess dear,
Open the door to thy true love here!
And mind the words that thou and I said
By the fountain cool, in the greenwood shade."

The king was an honorable man and he admonished his daughter. "If you have given your word, even to a frog, you must keep it; you must invite the frog in."

Very reluctantly she obeyed her father, and the frog hopped into the room, next to the table where the princess sat.

"Lift me onto the chair and let me sit next to you," he commanded the princess.

As soon as she had done this, the frog said, "Put your plate next to me so I may eat out of it."

This she did, and when he had eaten as much as he could, he said, "Now I'm weary, take me upstairs, and put me onto your bed." And most unwillingly the princess picked him up and carried him up to her room. She laid him on her pillow where he slept soundly all night long. Then, as dawn broke, he jumped up, hopped down the stairs and out of the house.

The princess sighed with relief. "Oh, at last he is gone. I'll be troubled no more."

But she was mistaken. For when night came again she heard the same tapping at the door; and she heard the familiar croaky voice.
"Open the door, my princess dear,
Open the door to thy true love here!
And mind the words that thou and I said
By the fountain cool, in the greenwood shade."

The princess opened the door and the frog came in, slept on her pillow as before, until the morning broke. This pattern continued for three nights and the lonely princess became used to his company and spoke more kindly to him. On the third morning, the frog thanked her for her friendship and announced that he would be leaving her for good. He asked if she would kiss him goodbye. Still a little reluctant, she closed her eyes tightly and bent to kiss his slimy lips. To her absolute amazement, when she opened her eyes again, she found herself gazing into the loving eyes of the most handsome prince. He told her his sad tale: a wicked witch had turned him into a frog and cast him into the pond. Only the kindness of a princess for three days and nights could save him.

"You," said the prince, "have broken the witch's cruel spell, and now I have nothing to wish for but that you should go with me to my father's kingdom, where we will marry, and love each other as long as we both live."

The young princess was overjoyed. Hand in hand they went together to see her father, who rejoiced at his daughter's happiness. She took her leave of him sadly but full of excitement, and set out for the prince's kingdom, where they married and lived happily ever after.

UNIT 9

CD3 19 and **CD3 20** See p. 69

CD3 21 *Recommended Reads*
Part 1

H = Host, Chris Morrison, R = Rosie Garnett, M = Matt Davis

H Welcome to *Recommended Reads*. I'm Chris Morrison, and my two guests this week are the philosopher Matt Davis …

M Hello.

H And TV cook Rosie Garnett.

R Hello.

H Rosie, you're going to start us off. Which book would you like to tell us about?

R I'm going to talk about *You Are the Music*. It's by Victoria Williamson, a music psychologist. To be honest, it's an unexpected choice for me, given that I don't consider myself a very musical person, but I heard Victoria talking on another radio program and found it fascinating, so I decided to read this book.

H Presumably it's not for music specialists, then?

R No, it's basically geared for the general public, and besides, she makes the point that we're all far more musical than we might realize. I'm one of those people she talks about who claim to be tone deaf. Apparently, nearly a fifth of the population believes that, but it's unlikely to be true. Actually, less than 4% of people are tone deaf, and they're called amusics. They suffer from a neurological condition called amusia. It

seems most people who say they can't sing to save their lives just lack confidence, probably from being told they couldn't sing when they were children.

H So, there's still hope for you, then?

R Well, I'm not banking on getting a recording contract yet, but the author thinks that a few singing lessons would help most people. Anyway, the thing I'd never thought about before is how musical life is from the outset, that right back when we were babies in the womb, we heard the world as a kind of music, with rising and falling sounds and rhythmic beats.

M That doesn't mean that babies in the womb can register musical patterns, though, does it?

R Well, yes. Apparently they can. In one study they played a relaxing melody twice a day to mothers in the last weeks of pregnancy. They then played that melody to the babies when they were six weeks old, while they were asleep. The babies' heart rates dropped noticeably, showing that they felt more relaxed.

H Surely that could have happened even if they hadn't heard it before, though?

R They did check for that, and while all babies showed some signs of relaxation when they played the music, the effect was twice as strong with the babies who'd heard it in the womb. So, they were recognizing it.

H Amazing!

R And the other thing I hadn't realized was how important musical awareness is to learning a language. And again, that's something that babies register very early. Apparently, babies cry in their own language!

M What do you mean?

R It's been shown, in another study, that French babies cry with more rising pitches, whereas German babies' cries have more of a falling pitch, and that reflects the most common intonation patterns that adult speakers of those languages use.

H How funny!

R And then you realize how important intonation is for early communication. I mean, just listen to people talking to babies and small children. We call it "baby talk," but in the book she calls it IDS, Infant Directed Speech. We all do it with babies to some extent, and it is very musical – big rises from low to high pitch, and a really strong rhythmic pattern. "Look who's here to see you!" And we do it because babies respond to it so well. They just love it, smiling and giggling away. I realize I still do it with my four-year-old when I want to communicate something with a lot of feeling. "Don't do that," and "It's OK. Mommy's here!"

M So what happens with those people who truly are tone deaf, then? Does that make language learning difficult?

R Well, yes. They can struggle to recognize what's being implied by different pitch and intonation patterns. Maybe they can't hear much difference between "good job" and "Good job!"

CD3 22
Part 2

R Another thing I could really relate to was what the book says about music and life memories, that different pieces of music become a soundtrack to our lives. As I said, I don't see myself as someone who's especially into music, but if I hear certain songs, they take me back to different periods of my life immediately, and very vividly.

H Do you think that's true for all periods of your life, even childhood?

R Yes, and for that matter, it seems that the earlier you go back, the more powerful the memory! The book emphasizes that music plays a very big role in the life of adolescents. Teenage girls in particular say that music is an important way of regulating their moods, at a time when emotions do tend to go haywire.

M It's an important way of defining what group you belong to, too.

R Yes, that's interesting because it's an important way of defining your individuality as a teenager to say, "I'm into heavy metal, or soul, or rap music," but at the same time it gives you an important sense of belonging to a group, which adolescents crave. It becomes almost tribal, and most teenagers can't stand the "wrong" type of music. I love the fact that in Montreal, the authorities were trying to stop large groups of young people from hanging around in subway stations, and they eventually hit on the solution of playing classical music!

H Oh, interesting!

R You can also really see the power of musical memory with people suffering from dementia. I checked out some videos about this on YouTube, and it really is incredible. There's this one guy in a nursing home who's completely lifeless. He barely speaks to anyone, and he can hardly remember anything about his past life. And yet, if the nurses play some music from his past, he suddenly comes to life. His eyes light up, he starts moving to the music, singing it, and even when it's finished, he keeps talking about all the memories associated with it.

M I've seen something similar. It seems to connect with something very deep in the brain.

R Yes, I learned that there's a part of the brain called the amygdala, which is linked to our deepest emotional responses, and music has a direct channel to that. That's why movie music is so powerful. It can make you cry or feel scared in a way that the movie scenes wouldn't do on their own. And after all, someone did once say that music is, essentially, recorded emotion.

H So has it changed your attitude to music, Rosie, reading this book?

R Yes, I guess it has. It's made me realize it's never too late to learn to play a musical instrument, so I have a nice fantasy of me playing the piano. And above all, it's made me feel less self-conscious about not knowing much about music. I realize I can enjoy a piece of classical music, even though I don't know anything about the composer, or the musical form and period it was written in.

H Well, you've certainly made me want to read this book. Thank you. Now Matt, tell us about your book …

CD3 23

R = Rosie Garnett, C = Chris Morrison

R To be honest, this book is an unexpected choice for me, given that I don't consider myself a very musical person.

C Presumably it's not for music specialists, then?

R No, it's basically geared for the general public, and besides, she makes the point that we're all far more musical than we might realize. I'm actually one of those people she talks about who claim to be tone deaf. Apparently, nearly a fifth of the population believes that.

CD3 24

A Have you been watching *Star Voices*?

B Well, funnily enough, I've just gotten into it. I caught last week's show and, predictably, I'm hooked.

A So did you see the semi-final last night?

B No, unfortunately I was out, but I recorded it. Was it good?

A Well, actually I was a little bit disappointed. Bizarrely, Anna, the blond girl, didn't make it to the final, even though she was obviously the best by far. Surprisingly, she seemed fine about it, though.

B Oh, she was my favorite, too! Well, no doubt she'll get a recording contract anyway. Amazingly, her performance from last week has had over a million YouTube hits.

CD3 25

1 I'd thoroughly recommend that new pizzeria. The pizzas are amazing! Mind you, it's expensive.

2 I can't go skiing so soon after my accident. It's too much of a risk. Besides, I can't really afford it.

3 Why are you worried about asking Tom to lend you the money? Surely he wouldn't say no to you. It would be very unlike him.

4 **A** Tina must be upset about not getting promoted.
   B Actually, she doesn't seem to care that much.

5 The builders have done the job pretty quickly, given that the weather's been so bad.

6 I think you expect too much of Amy. You need to be realistic about her behavior. After all, she's still a teenager.

7 Guess what? Rob finally has a new girlfriend! Apparently, he met her at a conference.

8 So I guess that's why Kyra's looking so happy these days. Anyway, I guess I'd better be going.

9 It would be great if you got into drama school. By the way, have you heard about Robin's plan to move into a new apartment?

10 We didn't see a single whale or dolphin on our whale-watching cruise! Still, at least the weather was good.

CD3 26

A = Anna, B = Ben

A Have you heard that Jan's thinking about marrying Noah?

B Surely not? She's only known him three months! And quite honestly, I'm not sure what she sees in him.

A I know what you mean. Mind you, the money must help. After all, he is a millionaire. Where did he get his money from?

B Apparently, he made a fortune from an app he created. That's what I heard.

A I'm surprised he wants to get married, given that he's been married three times before.

B Actually, I think it's just twice.

A Well, you'd think that was enough. Presumably, they'll have a huge wedding.

B Of course they will. Still, good luck to them. By the way, did you hear that Sara and Jeff were in a car accident?

A Oh, no! What happened?

B It wasn't too serious. They skidded into a tree, but luckily they weren't going fast. The car was totaled, but at least neither of them was injured.

A Thank goodness for that. I should get in touch with Sara, but I don't have her new email address.

B I can give it to you. As a matter of fact, I have it on my phone. Let me take a look. Yes, here it is. I'll forward it to you.

A Thanks. Anyway, I should be going. Nice to talk to you.

B Same here. Bye.

CD3 27

1 **A** Hello. Your face looks familiar. Have we met before?
   B Actually, I don't think we have.

2 I'd like to be famous. All those girls wanting to go out with you, all those parties. Mind you, it must be awful never having any privacy.

3 We forgot to bring the GPS with us, and we didn't have a road map in the car, and inevitably, we got completely lost.

4 Yes, it was one of the best games I've seen, and they deserved to win it. By the way, are you going to Jeff's farewell party on Friday?

5 **A** Why did Susan break up with Peter?
   B Well, basically, she was fed up with him working all the time.

6 **A** That was such a good movie, wasn't it?
   B To tell you the truth, I didn't really enjoy it. It was too long, and I thought the plot was pretty implausible.

7 I just had my blood pressure checked. Alarmingly, it's way higher than it should be.

8 You can't really make judgments about Maria's work performance at this point. After all, she's only been in the job for a month.

9 I can't believe that Aaron is thinking of buying your old wreck of a car! Surely he's not that stupid!

10 I'm not very excited to go on vacation next month. I'd like to do some work on the house, and I don't want to be too far away from my parents right now. Besides, I can't afford it.

CD3 28 *The Night I Heard Caruso Sing*

The highlands and the lowlands are the routes my father knows,
The holidays at Oban and the towns around Montrose
But even as he sleeps, they're loading bombs into the hills,
And the waters in the lochs can run deep, but never still.
I've thought of having children, but I've gone and changed my mind,
It's hard enough to watch the news, let alone explain it to a child.
To cast your eye 'cross nature, over fields of rape and corn,
And tell him without flinching not to fear where he's been born.
Then someone sat me down last night and I heard Caruso sing,
He's almost as good as Presley and if I only do one thing,
I'll sing songs to my father, I'll sing songs to my child.
It's time to hold your loved ones while the chains are loose,
And the world runs wild.
But even as we speak, they're loading bombs onto a white train.
How can we afford to ever sleep so sound again?

CD3 29

1 My favorite team is playing tonight. The players are in a slump right now, so I'm sure they're going to lose.

2 I didn't think the exam was easy! I thought it was really tough.

3 We should have gotten a free kick before they scored that goal. It was a definite foul.

4 We didn't drive back the same way. We took a different route.

5 Ugh! Keith dropped his burger on the floor, picked it up, and continued eating it. It was really gross!

6 I don't mind where we go on vacation this year. You can choose.

7 After six days of constant heavy rain, there were terrible floods.

8 The apples on that tree aren't ready to eat yet. They taste really sour.

9 I like fantasy video games because people don't usually fight with guns. They use swords.

10 My car broke down again. Could you help me tow it to the garage?

11 Let's visit Jenny and her new baby in the hospital. I'll call the maternity ward to find out her room number.

12 That door won't open if you pull it. You have to push.

CD3 30

1 We spent five hours at the mall. We really shopped until we dropped!

2 The reason Christy is so successful is that she constantly keeps her eyes on the prize.

3 We actually saw all the stars after the movie! They were doing a quick meet-and-greet in the movie-theater foyer!

4 No, I did not cheat at all when I beat Jim at tennis. I won fair and square!

5 Gosh, it's hard to remember how popular this governor was after the election. He's gone from hero to zero in less than six months.

6 We're not inviting many people to the wedding; just our nearest and dearest.

7 You should go to Cabo San Lucas for a weekend if your Spanish is getting rusty. Use it or lose it!

8 Wow! Running into Sam at the restaurant was a blast from the past! I hadn't talked to him in years!

9 Derek is full of plans and ideas, but he needs to walk the talk and show us what he can do.

10 I want to know exactly which companies are avoiding paying tax in this country. They should be named and shamed!

CD3 31 and **CD3 32** See p. 76

CD3 33

A Palace Theater … help?
B Buy tickets, flamenco Saturday?
A Saturday sold out.
B Really? Disappointing! Tickets other dates?
A Yes. Four, Sunday. Interested?
B Yes, great. Two tickets.
A Floor, balcony?
B How much balcony?
A $40. Floor $80. Great seats, very close stage.
B Take floor. Debit card?
A Of course. Card information? Number, front?
B 5610 5910 8101 8250.
A Security number, back?
B 713.
A Thank you. Bring card, pick up tickets?
B Sure. Thanks help.
A Welcome.

CD3 34 See p. 76

UNIT 10

CD4 2 **How well do you know your body?**

1 Every day the average person loses between 50 and 100 hairs, but you would have to lose over 50% of the hairs on your head before anyone would notice. Blonds have more hair – about 140,000 hairs on their head. Brunettes average about 110,000, people with black hair about 108,000, and redheads come in last with about 80,000 average hairs on their head.

2 The average adult heart is about the size of two fists. The main artery from the heart, the aorta, is about the diameter of a garden hose. The human heart creates enough pressure to squirt blood up to a distance of 30 feet.

3 Nerve impulses to and from the brain travel as fast as 250 miles per hour. The fastest messages are to the brain's pain receptors, telling you that metal is hot! It's a common myth that we use only a small part of our brain. It may be as little as 10% when resting, but during the course of a typical day, we use 100% of our brain.

4 Babies are born with 50% more bones than adults have. Many of these bones then fuse together, making larger bone structures that would have made it impossible for the baby to be born. As adults, we are about one centimeter taller in the morning than in the evening, when our joints have settled and become thinner.

5 Fingernails grow roughly twice as fast as toenails, and both now grow 25% more than they did 70 years ago, as a result of our protein-rich diet. The fastest growing nail is on the middle finger. The longer the finger, the faster the nail grows.

6 Most people blink around 15 times a minute, but that reduces by half when staring at a computer screen, which is why long-term computer users often suffer from dry-eye syndrome. Babies blink only twice a minute.

7 Children have three times as many taste buds as adults, which is why they often find bitter vegetables inedible, and why older people enjoy them more. The number of taste buds varies widely between people, with some people having four or five times as many as others. By the age of 60, most people will have lost about half of their taste buds.

8 According to a study by the Mayo Clinic in the US, the three most common reasons for visits to the doctor are for skin complaints and joint problems (for example, arthritis and back problems). Another common complaint is referred to by doctors as TATT (T, A, T, T) – "tired all the time."

CD4 3

1 A leading plastic surgeon is reported to be under investigation for fraud.

2 Dr. Martin Crispin is believed to own three private clinics in San Diego.

3 Dr. Crispin and his colleagues are said to charge up to $1,000 for a consultation.

4 Dr. Crispin was supposed to have done his medical residency in the Caribbean.

5 He is now known never to have trained as a surgeon.

6 His board certification is now assumed to be fake.

7 He was considered to be a specialist in cosmetic surgery.

8 Dr. Crispin is understood to have been sued recently by five different patients.

9 Two of his colleagues are alleged to have performed unnecessary surgery on hundreds of patients.

10 The doctor and his wife are presumed to have gone into hiding this morning.

CD4 4 **Down to earth with a bump**
Part 1
I = Interviewer, GA = Guy Anderson

I So you took off OK. What went wrong?
GA Yeah, I took off fine, and I was doing very well in the race. Um, I was going along with a bunch of others, and it was getting progressively windier, and we were jumping from mountain range to mountain range, and um, I split up with the people I was flying with, and I got stuck in a little windy valley, and I got lower and lower, and really, uh where the wind mixes with the mountainscape, you get a lot of turbulence, and I was just at the wrong height. We carry a reserve with us, and normally you can throw your reserve if you, if it, if it, the wind collapses …
I So that would be a parachute effectively?
GA A parachute, yeah, and you can come down under that, or normally the wing will reopen itself anyway, but I was at the height where the reserve wouldn't open, and it was still high enough to hurt when I hit the ground.
I So how far did you fall, do you think?
GA Probably about 60 feet, I should think.
I Oh my goodness. And what was the impact like? What do you remember of it?
GA I remember bouncing quite a lot. And I rolled over a few times and came to, came to rest underneath a few bushes, and uh, but generally I was pretty well bashed up. I'd broken all the ribs on my left, uh, my pelvis in about five places, and my left arm completely snapped off, my, the humerus, the ball joint on my, …
I Goodness, you must have been in terrible pain, weren't you?
GA So I was in a lot of pain, uh, and I was a bit shocked, really, uh …
I You were wearing sunglasses, weren't you, as well at the time?
GA Yeah, my sunglasses, my nice new sunglasses dug into my nose and so my face was bleeding quite a lot. And, so yeah, generally bashed up.
I So when you, kind of came to a standstill, what was going through your mind?
GA Um, well I just looked around and checked that I was still alive. I checked my, all my limbs, and uh, thought well, basically, I'm bashed, but I'm not, uh, you know, I'm still here. I had a strange thing where my eyesight started to degrade. Uh, I'd been looking around the clouds and the mountains just to see if anybody had seen me crash, and there was nobody, and then after a while, all I could see was maybe a hundred yards into the grass, and then that came right down to just twigs around me, and …
I Why was that happening?
GA It was shock, and I had this weird voice saying, "Oh, Guy. This is a classic sign of shock. You need oxygen now," and I said, out loud, "Ooh, that's lucky, I've got some oxygen with me," so I reached into my pack – we fly very very high in Idaho, so you do need oxygen from time to time – so I reached into my pack,

found my oxygen tube, turned it on full blast, and snorted some of that, and uh, ten minutes later I was, it's like a computer rebooting and all my vision came back, and …

I How did you know that?

GA I didn't know it. I just, it must have gone in at some point.

I Some instinct?

GA Yeah, and I'd remembered it.

I That's tremendous. That's quite amazing. And did you have any way of calling for help? Did you have a radio? Did you have a mobile telephone?

GA No, I'd punctured a lung as well, so I did yell "Help," but it didn't come out very loud.

CD4 5

Part 2

GA = Guy Anderson, I = Interviewer

GA Uh, I had a mobile phone, but there was no signal. I had a radio, but that obviously malfunctioned when I hit the ground, and um, I had no, what I did need was a satellite tracker, um, the organizers of the competition had given us trackers, but that, they worked off the mobile phone signal, and that didn't work either, so I was completely stuck in the middle …

I You're completely isolated, in the middle of nowhere, no means of communication. Did you panic?

GA Uh, no, I just lay there, I got … made myself as comfortable as I could in my harness, and thought, well if I get rescued, uh, before, before dark, I might get away with my wife and kids not, not finding out about what predicament I was in.

I But you didn't get rescued before dark, did you? You had to spend the night there. What was that night like?

GA Well, that was, as it, I was sort of quite comfortable …

I It was the first night in fact, wasn't it?

GA Yeah, the first night, and so I crashed at about three o'clock in the afternoon, and the first night, it was fine. I was reasonably comfortable, and I just thought, I was starting to nod off, to have a snooze, and um, then I heard this awful growling noise.

I Right! What did you think that was?

GA I didn't know what it was, I looked up behind me, sort of, I could just crane my neck round, and saw, up on the side of the hill, a huge great big bear …

I Ah …

GA Uh, that really concentrated the mind for a while, so I tried to make where I was look to the bear like it was a little hunting camp, so I took pictures with my mobile, the flash on my mobile phone …

I What, trying to frighten it with the light?

GA Yeah, and I sang, "She'll be coming round the mountain when she comes."

I Because you thought the noise would frighten the bear off?

GA Yeah, well I just hoped that they would think that there were maybe more than one person.

I And is that what happened? Did the bear go away and leave you?

GA Well, it didn't like … also my canopy was fluffing around in the wind, so it didn't like that either, so it didn't come any closer. I heard it later in the night, crashing about in the trees below me but uh, …

I I bet you didn't get much sleep.

GA No, I sort of, a bit fitful.

CD4 6

Part 3

I Then the next day, you decided to get moving, didn't you?

GA Yeah, I decided that you can, you can't last that long without water. I had a few liters of water, and it looked like there was a nice river at the bottom of the valley, so uh, I thought at least if I could get next to the water, I'd be fine, and uh …

I How did you move, though, you'd broken your pelvis?

GA Yeah, I pushed with my good arm and pulled with my legs, and I managed to make my way through the grass, and, it was quite painful but uh, …

I Quite painful? It's setting my teeth on edge just thinking about that!

GA But I got, I got all the way down to the bottom of the valley, and uh, it was completely dry, so I knew I had to start walking somehow, so I reached out a hand and there was this amazing stick, um, so it took me a couple of hours, very painful hours, to get to my feet, um …

I Two hours to get to your feet?

GA Yep. Um, but this, with this stick, armed with the stick I was able to make very slow progress. I'd move the stick, swing one leg, swing the other one, and on I go, so I made about a mile that, that day, and um, um, in the evening it, the, uh, the weather started to break down and it's a very desert area, and it hardly ever rains there, but that evening there was a huge, huge thunderstorm, so I just lay on the ground and got completely drenched, um, with this thunder and lightning going on all night.

I What was the first clue that you might be going to be rescued?

GA Um, the first clue was the next day, I heard a helicopter, uh coming into my valley, um, at about three in the afternoon, and um I, it came into my valley and then flew straight out the other side, so I just thought, well, they've missed me and that's the end of that. But in fact there was a friend of mine, Russell Ogden, a very old paraglider. He's a bit of a legend in the paragliding world, and he had seen me out of the corner of his eyes. He's got terrible eyesight but he'd still seen me, and he'd yelled at the helicopter pilot to go round. They went round and landed, and I didn't hear that because there was a bend in the valley and they'd landed, um, seen my canopy and landed, but, Russ jumped out of the helicopter, and nearly broke an ankle, and um, then raced down, saw my track and raced down the valley, find, trying to find me, and um …

I And what did you find out later about the nature of the search operation that had been launched, 'cos I mentioned earlier, it was quite an extensive operation.

GA There was a huge operation going on. I had no idea, but there were probably a hundred people up in the mountains all out on mo-, mountain bikes and, um, there were light planes up. There were just people on their days off who, who'd heard about it and were out looking and it was um, when eventually I got found, the helicopter eventually came down the valley and did find me, um, when it went out on the radio there were hoops of, uh, of joy amongst the people looking so it was a great, big moment …

I Goodness, and what about your family? You said you'd hoped that they might not find out, presumably they'd have been told and they'd be very worried.

GA They had a horrible 24 hours at home, uh, all waiting. They were, they were very stoic and quite brilliant, uh, and, we're a very close family and, uh, it was very difficult for them, I know.

I And I gather that after the rescue you updated your Facebook profile with the words "Guy Anderson is world champion hide-and-seek winner" …

GA Yeah.

I … which shows a sense of humor!

GA A few people thought I actually was.

I How long did it take you to recover from your injuries?

GA Uh, it, I'd, where I'd crashed I'd actually just got enough points to get me into the big race of the year, which is the World Cup Superfinal, so I had between August when I crashed and January when the Superfinal was, to get better enough to compete in the, the big race of the year, so I, uh yeah, just, just under six months.

I And you had no doubt at all about going back?

GA I had plenty of doubts, and uh, I, I, it's really, uh the worst thing is for my family, and uh, I know that I put them through hell, but it's uh, a horrible addiction that I have to flying, but it does put you in places that um you can only dream of and um, I can't stop it.

I Guy, it's an amazing story. Thank you very much indeed for joining us.

CD4 7

A Your new sofa is quite comfortable.

B There were quite a few people at the town meeting.

CD4 8

1 **A** That class wasn't as boring as I thought it would be.
  B I agree! It was quite interesting!

2 **A** How long did you have to wait in line for the tickets?
  B Quite a while … about three hours actually.

3 **A** How did your interview go? Did you get the job?
  B It was quite successful, actually. And yes, I got the job. I start next Monday.

4 **A** This spaghetti sauce is really spicy. How much pepper did you put in it?
  B Quite a bit … about three tablespoons, I think. I like spicy food!

5 **A** I really enjoy listening to the guitar player at the coffee shop.
  B I know, right? He's quite a good musician.

6 **A** Did you watch the game last night? I was devastated that our team lost.
  B Ugh. I thought for sure they'd win, so it was quite a surprise when they lost by 20 points.

7 **A** How did you do on the history test?
  B Not great. I wasn't quite sure what to study, so I played video games instead.

CD4 9

1 Come on, don't let it get you down. Keep your chin up!

2 I tried to persuade Pete, but he dug his heels in and refused to change his mind.

3 I find it hard to stomach when politicians half my age start preaching to me.

4 It varies, but as a rule of thumb, I'd allow 20 minutes a mile on this walk.

5 The teachers in my school were pretty strict. They made us toe the line.
6 Stacy has her parents eating out of the palm of her hand. They'll buy her anything she wants.
7 I'm so ashamed, but I'm glad I told you. I needed to get it off my chest.
8 You must be starving after skiing all day, so I made some food that will stick to your ribs.
9 The government talks as if they're concerned about the environment, but they're just paying lip service.
10 These pots and pans aren't easy to clean. You'll need to use some elbow grease.

CD4 10

1 Oh, what an adorable cat …
2 So wonderful to see you again!
3 Psst! Look over in the corner at what that man's wearing?
4 Phugh! Puh! Ugh! Sorry, I really couldn't eat that!
5 Gulp! Mmm, these tablets are huge!
6 Yes! Yes! Definitely!
7 How dare you!
8 Mmm? It's cinnamon, I think. Or maybe cloves.
9 Move over!
10 Terrific! What a great shot!
11 Stop it! I give up!
12 Could you step this way, sir? And hold out your arms …

CD4 11 and CD4 12 See p. 84

CD4 13

1 A You'll be careful, won't you?
   B Of course I will. It's not a very difficult climb. It's only 1,500 feet.
2 A So you were out with Lisa last night, were you?
   B What if I was? And I'm still not going to tell you what happened!
3 A You meant to kill the victim, Mr. Jones, didn't you?
   B Absolutely not! It was a horrible accident.
4 A I've been kind of stupid, haven't I?
   B You haven't! It's so easy to be taken in by Internet scams.
5 A So these are the spacious bedrooms, are they?
   B Yes, they are. Though the other real estate agent did describe them as "cozy."
6 A That can't be right, can it?
   B Uh, it is. We did have appetizers, and we had dessert.
7 A Oh yeah, camping will really appeal to Jo, won't it?
   B Well, it'll have to. We can't afford to stay in a hotel this year.
8 A So that's all the help I'm getting, is it?
   B Unfortunately, it is. I've painted three walls! I really have to pick up the kids from school now.
9 A It won't hurt, will it?
   B Not much. It's a very small needle.
10 A I beat him good, didn't I?
   B You did! Wow, good job! Those tennis lessons were obviously worth it!
11 A Let's eat, shall we?
   B Yes, I'm starving!

CD4 14

1 A You haven't seen my car keys, have you?
   B No. You had them this morning.

A That doesn't mean I know where they are now though, does it?
B Well, let's look in the places you usually leave them, shall we?
A I've already done that.
B And … here they are. Now, that wasn't hard, was it?
A Oh, thanks. You're the best!
2 B You forgot the shopping list, didn't you?
A Yes, I did.
B But I gave it to you as we were leaving, didn't I?
A Yeah. But I left it on the kitchen table.
B You're so forgetful!
A Oh, and you're perfect, are you?

UNIT 11

CD4 15 Me and my tech

I'm totally lost without my phones. I have two – uh, for personal stuff and work. And these days I use my tablet – an Apple iPad – for writing stuff more than I use my computer. I think it's easier. I'm kind of an Apple "fanboy." I have the iPad, the iPhone, and the iMac. And I have literally hundreds of apps – lots of weather apps and games. My favorite game is Defender. It's my favorite because it's the game I played as a child … when computer games first came out. My wife says I'm the original gadget man. You name it and I have it. I like PlayStations for games, fitness gadgets like Withings and Wireless Weighing scales. I've kind of started to take my health seriously, must be an age thing, oh, and music gadgets like Sonos. I have a Sonos system at home. Yeah, and I stream music everywhere, downstairs and in our bedroom. I use Spotify and Internet radio for this, but I still have a "normal" radio in my car and a GPS, of course. I have two – one in my car and one on my phone – it's much better because it gives traffic info as well. I haven't used a map for a long time.

I guess in some ways I'm a techno geek, but I'm not a great social networker, although I have used LinkedIn for work and jobs. One thing I could do without is so many emails. I get thousands a week, mainly work, but it really bugs me the way colleagues in the same office email you rather than pick up the phone or walk over and have a face-to-face conversation. It's weird. Technology both connects you and isolates you at the same time. You can connect with friends and family all over the world. You can Facebook or Skype them, and that's great, but then you see couples in restaurants, both on their phones and not communicating with each other. My wife and I make a point of conversing across the table when we're out together, more than we do at home.

There's so much tech around already. It's difficult to keep pace with it all, so I have no idea what the future holds. Time travel would be pretty awesome. I'd like to go backwards, not forwards – maybe to Hollywood in the 1950s. That would be interesting or better still, back to a really great World Series, like the year the Mets won. I'm not sure about 3D printers. My son, he's eight, says he'd use one to make all the Lego blocks he's lost – sounds like a good idea to me. I guess the future is this "Internet of Things" thing – you know where you can run your whole house via the Internet – sit at work and turn the oven on or mow the

lawn with a robot lawnmower. But heck, we'll all become so out of shape, so unhealthy. Mind you, I suppose I'll still have my fitness app. Actually, I've changed my mind. I'd like to time travel a hundred years into the future just to see what happens technology-wise. What on earth will the world be like?

CD4 16 The Internet of Things
H = Host, CP = Christian Payne,
WW = William Webb

H This is *You and Yours* Radio 4's consumer program …
If you've got a smart phone and a laptop, they'll be connected to the Internet when they're switched on, and it's predicted that by 2020 lots and lots of other things we use will also be connected. Things as varied as rubbish bins, car parks, roads, and fridges. It's being called "The Internet of Things" and Ofcom, the communications regulator, is predicting that up to 50 billion things will be linked to the Web by the end of this decade. Lots of people have stuff that's linked already. Here's Christian Payne. He's a technology blogger.
CP It's early days for the *Internet of Things* and yet there are so many "things" talking on the Internet right now – more things than people in fact. Stood at the side of a busy road in London, and it wouldn't surprise me at all to find out that many of these cars and vehicles are at this moment connected to the Internet, whether it be through their tracking devices or their navigation apps, which are logging and reporting and recording data not just for the user in the vehicle but also other people wanting to know about traffic conditions and journey times ahead. I personally use an app that does this, an app which has been in the news a lot recently called Waze. I find it vital for me to get to where I want to go faster and quicker. It also notifies me in real time should there be speed traps, but obviously I, I drive within the parameters of the law. I can also see other drivers using the same app, and it's kind of comforting to know that there are people as geeky as me logging data as they drive. Around my neck at the moment I have an "autographer," an automatic camera which for bloggers it's a normal device. It enables you to … to document your day in images which can connect to your mobile phone and be shared very easily to social spaces where you can keep a record of events, that you want to remember personally but you can also share that with anybody with an Internet connection. I'm standing in Regent's Park, and just in the last minute I've seen 15 or so runners passing me by, all wearing the same kind of technology I have around my neck – a fitness computer. Some of them are just using their mobile devices, some of them have wristbands, but what these little computers are doing are logging speed, location in some instances, how many calories they're burning, how active they are, and this will stream to the Internet perhaps through their mobile device and enable them to compete with their friends. If I'm sat too long at my desk in my office, I can get a notification from a friend telling me maybe I should get up and have a walk. I really like this, this peer pressure, forcing me to be more active. This is just the beginning of connecting our bodies to the Internet in this way. Health is gonna … gonna be revolutionized by where

we choose to place this data, whether it be with our local doctors or organizations who are researching anything to do with the body.

H Christian Payne. And we wondered if this technology is just for serious enthusiasts like him or for everyone, and we decided to ask William Webb. He's deputy president of the Institute of Engineering and Technology. William. This talk of 50 billion devices by the end of the decade suggests some kind of revolution's about to happen to us. Do you think it is?

WW I think it is, but it's more gonna happen to machines than to us. Now, of course, we interact with machines a lot so what we'll notice is lots of things just working better. Uh, our car will take us better to the place we want to get to; our washing machine will work better. But I don't think it will impact us as obviously and as immediately as something like the iPhone and the change to smartphones did, and indeed the whole idea of this really is to work in the background to make our world a better, easier place to live in, rather than to be in our face the whole time.

H We had some practical examples there from Christian Payne, but tell us what would be the benefit of a fridge communicating with the Net.

WW Oh, the fridge has been an example that's been quoted for so long it's almost become a joke, hasn't it? Um, there are a lot of reasons why we might want to start connecting many of our white goods in our home. Most of those actually revolve around either maintenance or energy usage, so for example the fridge could, could know that its compressor was starting to labor harder, and as a result, it was probably going to break at some time in the next few months. In fact, it's quite easy to spot imminent breakdown of these kinds of components, and it could send a message out to the manufacturer or to the retailer warning them that this was happening, and you could have someone effectively ring you up and say, "I need to come and maintain your fridge" before it actually failed, and you lost all the goods that were in the fridge.

H This may be a naive question, but won't these gadgets crowd out the space available, overload the system?

WW They could overload our existing cellular phone systems, which is why a number of people including myself are looking at alternative wireless technologies that are optimized very specifically for these machines.

H Some people worry that all this reliance on technology, even as we have it now, relying on a satnav rather than a map, um, that we're making ourselves vulnerable to attack. Are they right?

WW Well, we're certainly getting much more reliant on all sorts of technology now. Of course, this is nothing new. We've become reliant on electricity over the last century. Uh, we've become reliant on the Internet over the last decade, and if either of those two systems went down, I think people's lives would be dramatically altered. And I think what tends to happen is at first people don't rely too much on these new things, so when you first got your satnav you probably also kept the map in the car, just in case the satnav didn't work, and then progressively over time you become more reliant on it as you see that it is more reliable. Um, but we do need to make sure absolutely

that we are safe against all kinds of potential failure, either from terrorists or failure that might be caused by software errors, or, or lack of electricity or similar kinds of things.

H William Webb, we must leave it there. William Webb, deputy president of the Institute of Engineering.

CD4 17

1 When might billions of things be connected to the Internet? What kind of things?
2 Who are Christian Payne and William Webb?
3 What does Christian find comforting?
4 Where does he wear his "autographer"?
5 What does he wear it for?
6 How many runners did he see?
7 How does William Webb think white goods will mainly interact with the Internet?
8 Which thing is quoted so often that it's become a joke?
9 Why is he looking at alternative wireless technologies?

CD4 18

1 **A** Thanks for the great feedback on my report.
   B I was impressed. You really know your stuff.
   A Do you think so?
   B Oh, yes. You're destined for great things at this firm.
2 **A** What kind of stuff do you get with your new car?
   B Oh, you know, all the usual stuff: GPS, bluetooth, leather seats.
   A Doesn't sound like the usual stuff to me. You should see my old jalopy.
3 **A** How do you cope with all that pressure at work and four kids?
   B You know me. I'm made of strong stuff.
   A And you never complain.
   B Well, there's no point. I just have to put my head down and go.
4 **A** Are you ready to go? We're late.
   B I'll just get my stuff and we can get out of here.
   A OK, I'll be waiting in the car.
5 **A** We were hiking in the mountains, and suddenly there was this huge bear heading toward us.
   B That's the stuff of nightmares. I would have been terrified.
   A Believe me! We were!
6 **A** What a day! I'm a wreck. I lost my car keys and had to walk home in the pouring rain and …
   B Come on. Cheer up! Stuff happens. Let me make you a cup of tea.
   A Make sure it's nice and hot. I'm still shivering from the rain.
7 **A** Ugh! What's that on the rug?
   B I'm not sure. It looks like a lot of sticky, brown stuff.
   A Gross! It's melted chocolate. One of the kids must have dropped it.
8 **A** I did it! I can't believe it! Three As!
   B Good stuff! All that hard work paid off.
   A It did. I can really enjoy my school break now.

CD4 19

1 You offer to buy pizza for everyone in the office.
2 You think you have no chance of passing the exam.
3 Your theater ticket says *Hamlet* 7:30 p.m.
4 You made an appointment to get your hair cut tomorrow.

5 You arranged to help your friend move to a new apartment, but now you can't.
6 Next week you will be on vacation. You can see yourself sitting in the sun by the swimming pool.
7 You can see yourself at 40. You've started your own business, and it's already successful.
8 You didn't get in touch with a friend because you had the flu.

CD4 20

1 **A** Hey, guys! I'm going to treat the office to pizza for lunch.
   B Thanks, Kev. What's the occasion?
   A I just got a promotion!
2 **A** I really don't think I have a chance of passing the exam. I'm definitely going to fail.
   B No, you won't. You say that every time and you do really well.
3 **A** Hurry up! The play starts in half an hour.
   B I can't find my ticket anywhere.
   A We don't have them. We ordered them online. We're picking them up them at the box office.
4 **A** I know. I know. My hair's a mess, but I'm getting it cut on Saturday.
   B Not before then?
   A You should talk! Look at yours!
5 **A** I'm really sorry. I know I was going to help you out with your move, but …
   B Yeah, and boy do I need help.
   A I know you do, but I just found out I'm working in the New York office next week, and I can't get out of it.
   B Oh, never mind. It was nice of you to offer.
   A But I'll help you with the decorating when I get back.
   B Thanks. That'd be great.
6 **A** Can you believe it? This time next week we'll be sitting in the sun by a swimming pool.
   B Yeah, before going out for an amazing meal in an amazing restaurant overlooking the water.
   A I know, right! And paying amazing prices!
7 **A** I'm shooting for the moon. By the time I'm 40, I'll have set up my own business, and I'll be earning a fortune.
   B Wow! You've really got your future figured out!
   A Yeah, I simply won't consider failure.
   B I admire your confidence. I don't have a clue as to what I'll be doing when I'm 40.
8 **A** I'm so sorry. I was going to get in touch and say let's meet for coffee, but I've had the flu.
   B Not to worry. I'll meet you next week. Just say where and when!
   A Well, I was going to suggest the Café Nero near your office.
   B Fine! Is Tuesday OK for you?

CD4 21

1 **A** One of my cats is tame and domesticated. The other is totally wild.
   B Ouch! You can say that again.
2 **A** I've always been successful at work, but my private life is a total failure.
   B Oh, you're being too hard on yourself.
3 **A** His ability to make money is admirable. However, I have nothing but contempt for the appalling way he treats his employees.
   B I agree 100 percent.
4 **A** At first they thought it was a genuine da Vinci sketch, but it turned out to be a fake.
   B How embarrassing!

5 A I find it difficult to relax. My life is so hectic. So much to do, so little time.
   B You need to learn to slow down.
6 A I was sure I'd seen her before. I didn't recognize her face, but her voice was familiar.
   B Who was it then?
7 A This road is straight for a while, but then it winds uphill for two miles.
   B Ugh. Uphill? This is the last bike ride I'll ever go on with you!
8 A I know most people are very excited about traveling, but I really loathe it. I'd rather stay at home.
   B You would? I wouldn't.
9 A You thought she dropped the vase accidentally, but believe me, it was on purpose.
   B No way! She'd never do that.

CD4 22 Margie's journal

T = Tommy, **M** = Margie, **MM** = Margie's mother, **MT** = Mechanical teacher

T Oh, man. What a waste! When you're finished with the book, you just throw it away, I guess. Our television screen must have had a million books on it, and it has room for plenty more. I wouldn't throw it away.
M Where did you find the book?
T In my house. In the attic.
M What's it about?
T School.
M School? What's there to write about school? I hate school. Why would anyone write about school?
T Because it's not our kind of school, silly. This is the old kind of school that they had hundreds and hundreds of years ago. Centuries ago.
M Well, I don't know what kind of school they had back then. Did they have a teacher?
T Sure they had a teacher, but it wasn't a regular teacher. It was a man.
M A man? How could a man be a teacher?
T Well, he just told the boys and girls things and gave them homework and asked them questions.
M But a man isn't smart enough.
T Sure he is. My father knows as much as my teacher.
M He can't. A man can't know as much as a teacher.
T My dad knows almost as much, I betcha.
M Well, I wouldn't want a strange man in my house teaching me.
T You don't know much, Margie. The teachers didn't live in the house. They had a special building and all the kids went there.
M And all the kids learned the same thing?
T Sure, if they were the same age.
M But my mother says a teacher has to be adjusted to fit the mind of each boy and girl it teaches, and that each kid has to be taught differently.
T Just the same, they didn't do it that way then. If you don't like it, you don't have to read the book.
M I didn't say I didn't like it.
MM Margie! School!
M Not yet, Mom.
MM Now! And it's probably time for Tommy, too.
M Tommy, can I read the book some more with you after school?
T Maybe …

MT Today's math lesson is on the addition of fractions. Please insert yesterday's homework in the slot. When we add the fractions ½ and ¼ …
M Oh, how the kids must have loved it in the old days with a real teacher and other kids. I bet it was a lot of fun.

UNIT 12

CD4 23 The fall of the twin towers

… The day started much like any other day. I got on the subway. We went across the bridge, and I remember noticing what a beautiful day it was with the bright blue sky. I remember coming out of the subway as I usually did, and I saw a cloud, or what looked like a small cloud, white cloud, and I remember thinking "Gosh that's unusual because this sky is so totally clear," but I didn't think much more of it, and I started walking to my office. I didn't get far. I got to the first block, and on the corner there were a couple of people looking up, staring up at the tower, so I looked at what they were looking at and noticed that there was, what seemed to be, to me, at the time, anyway, a small hole, and you could actually see some flames around the edge, and I asked these two people what happened. One of them said that a plane had flown into it, and I remember thinking, "Ah, no, that can't be true." As I walked there was more and more smoke coming out, but I made it to my office and went up to the 16th floor. So I went into the office, and there were lots of my colleagues there. Obviously there was a lot of sort of confusion, so I went to one of these offices with the clearest view, and I looked out, and I remember thinking, "Gosh! I don't remember that. There's a hole in the other side." Quite a few people who were in the office earlier than me that morning, they'd seen both of them. They started telling me about this second one that went down the river and sort of exploded towards them because it came from the south. Soon you could start to see – they obviously started to evacuate – and there were just thousands of people walking straight up towards us, just pouring, pouring up towards us. I tried to call my family and friends, but none of the phones seemed to work. So I sent out an email; that seemed to be the one thing that was still working. I did speak to my wife once when I first got in and told her to wake up and turn on the television and see what was happening. I was unable to get through to her after that. These sort of surreal goings on, sending these emails back and forth about what was happening outside my very window. And it was while I was writing an email I heard some screams, and I ran around just to see sort of this huge, huge cloud of smoke and people just shouting and screaming, "It collapsed! It collapsed!" This huge cloud of dust came, you could see it pouring up the avenues, and it sort of burst out through Battery Park, right out into the Hudson River, because I remember seeing lots of the ferries were all doing evacuations, taking people from every point they could, and they just got enveloped in this huge cloud of dust. There was so much dust you didn't know, you know whether – how much it had fallen, whether it was just the top. I guess we were all expecting to see something still there. We could still see the other one standing because it had

the big antenna, the big aerial on top of it. So as we stood there watching it, no idea how long for, and then of course, the other one collapsed. You could clearly see, there's a very particular design, this long, long kind of metal work. I remember seeing that sort of explode out, and then you just saw the great big top with this giant antenna on it, just drop straight down and you'd see all this other stuff just peeling away from the sides. You could see just each corner of it peeling back and this giant top just smashing down through it and obviously there was all the dust and everything and more screaming. We all thought because we'd seen so many, so many thousands of people walking north that maybe everyone had gotten out because there was this, you know, non-stop procession of people. In fact, I think our brains didn't even think about the fact that there were people inside it, you just sort of looked at it as a building, and you just assumed that there was no one in it. You just don't actually want to think about that. It was, you know, unlike any feeling you've ever had. There wasn't really – there was no panic in the office, and also a very clear acknowledgement that something had changed. Something had changed in the world today, and we were sitting staring at it. It was the most incredible thing, and from what was just a normal beautiful New York fall day, it's just incredible how much changed in that morning.

CD4 24 When man first saw the Earth
MC = Mission Control, **CR** = Chris Riley, **A** = Astronaut, **H** = Host, **RP** = Robert Poole, **RS** = Rusty Schweickart

MC Ten, nine, … we have ignition sequence start, the engines are on … four, three, two, one, zero. We have commence, we have, we have lift-off … at 7:51 …
CR The inspirational effect of *Apollo*, which touched so many of us watching from Earth, was largely driven by the pictures which these missions returned. Views of human explorers on an alien world fueled our imaginations, and those images of our home planet, filmed by men who were so far away from home, had an even more profound effect.
MC *Apollo 8*, you're looking good.
CR In December 1968, *Apollo 8*, only the second manned *Apollo* mission, was sent straight to the Moon. It was the first time any astronauts had left low-Earth orbit, and if everything went to plan, Frank Borman, Jim Lovell, and Bill Anders would become the first humans to see the far side of the Moon with their own eyes.
A Actually, I think the best way to describe this area is a vastness of black and white. Absolutely no color. The sky up here is also a rather forbidding, foreboding expanse of blackness, with no stars visible when we're flying over the Moon in daylight.
H But it wasn't their unique views of the Moon which these missions became most famous for; it was their views of the Earth, rising over the barren lunar surface, which fired the imaginations of us all. Historian Robert Poole is the author of *Earthrise: How Man First Saw the Earth*.
RP The NASA head of photography, Dick Underwood, was keen on getting photographs of the Earth. He'd had a lot of experience, but he was pretty much a lone voice in NASA, so although he'd done his best to prepare them for taking photographs, they weren't prepared in any professional kind of way. So, when they

did actually see the Earth rise from, from lunar orbit, it did take them completely by surprise, and you can hear the surprise in their voices, "Wow, look at that!"

A1 Oh my God, look at that picture over there! There's the Earth coming up!

A2 Wow! That's pretty!

CR Yes, it's about the fourth orbit or something, isn't it? And there's a real scramble for the camera and some color film, I think.

A1 You got a color film, Jim? Hand me a roll of color quick, would ya?

A2 Oh, man, this really …

A1 Quick! Quick!

RP Yes, they didn't have a camera ready. They only had black-and-white film in the one that they were using, the spaceship had only just turned round to face the right way, they were busy doing something else, and suddenly one of them said, "Look, there's the Earth!" What in retrospect was the most significant moment possibly of the entire *Apollo* program, looking back and seeing the Earth in context.

CR The fact that no one planned those pictures seems extraordinary now, but the astronauts' encounter with the Earth would inspire future *Apollo* crews to look back with new eyes on their home planet.

MC Yes, everything's looking good here, *Apollo 9*.

A OK.

MC We'll try to have your cut-off time shortly.

CR *Apollo 9* was intended to test the entire *Apollo* flight system in Earth orbit and astronaut Rusty Schweickart would make a spacewalk to test an emergency procedure for transferring between the *Apollo* capsule and the lunar module in case the two failed to connect.

MC Mr. Schweickart, proceed on four.

A1 Can you get your camera on there?

A2 Camera's running.

A1 Good.

A2 Proceeding on out.

CR On board, his colleagues Jim McDivitt and Dave Scott would capture his progress on camera. But as his test began, their camera broke, and while they were fixing it, Rusty ended up with five minutes outside on his own.

A1 Ho, there! That looks comfortable.

A2 Boy oh boy, what a view!

A1 Isn't that spectacular?

A2 It really is.

RS During that five minutes that Dave took to try and repair the camera, which frankly never happened, I held onto the handrail only with one hand, my left hand, and I sort of swung around to get a full view of the Earth and the horizon, just spectacular beauty of the Earth, I mean the, the blackness is so black and the horizon is this brilliant thin band of blue, which is the atmosphere above the blue and white Earth. I mean, the contrast, the reality of what you're looking at, I mean it is incredibly impressive.

CR This would have been a wholly personal experience if Rusty hadn't been invited to speak at a major conference organized by the Lindisfarne Association in Long Island, New York, a couple of years later. Despite preparing for several hours, he had no idea what he was going to say until he found himself on stage.

RS And then I opened my mouth and I talked, and it was as, as if I was sitting in the audience going through the experience of flying in space, at many different levels actually, the physical level, sort of a technical diary almost, and then finally at, at a kind of spiritual level,

and I had absolutely no plan to do that, I mean, it just came out that way, and by the time I was done – uh, half of the people in the audience were crying, including me.

You look down there, and you can't imagine how many borders and boundaries you cross, again and again and again, and you don't even see them. There you are, hundreds of people in the Middle East killing each other over some imaginary line that you're not even aware of, that you can't see. And from where you see it, the thing is a whole, and it's so beautiful. You wish you could take one in each hand, one from each side in the various conflicts, and say, "Look! Look at it from this perspective. Look at that! What's important?"

CR That spontaneous lecture, later titled *No Frames, No, Boundaries*, and transcribed as an essay about the Earth and us, resonated with the burgeoning peace and environmental movements of the time. And the images of Earth that poured back from the eight subsequent *Apollo* flights to the Moon continued to raise our awareness of just how fragile our home planet seems to be.

CD4 25

Conversation 2

A Hi, Annie! What a nice surprise bumping into you here! I haven't seen you for a long time!

B I know. Time flies, doesn't it?

A It sure does. Is your business still booming?

B Yeah, I'm killing myself as usual. We're snowed under with orders right now, and I'm pretty much just keeping my head above water. Still, I shouldn't complain. How's your company doing?

A OK. Things went downhill a little last year, and we had to tighten our belts, but they're picking up now. And how's life in your sleepy little town?

B Very nice. It's such a good place to unwind. Look, I'm in a rush now, but I'll be in touch soon and have you over for dinner.

A That would be great. Hope to see you soon.

CD4 26

1 It was the movie *Twelve Angry Men* that sparked my interest in law.

2 The team's victory was overshadowed by the serious injury to their star pitcher.

3 I just had a bright idea! It just came to me in a flash!

4 I don't trust that guy you met last night. He just seems like a shady character.

5 The space station is a shining example of international cooperation.

6 I wondered why Bill's always so rude, and then it dawned on me that he was jealous.

7 There's another article on Internet privacy here. It's a hot topic at the right now.

8 I was relieved to get the medical test results. It's been like a cloud hanging over me.

9 Don't ask me how to pronounce that word. I don't have the foggiest idea!

10 You don't need to worry about passing your driver's test. It'll be a breeze for you.

11 It was a whirlwind romance, and Steve and Linda were married within six weeks.

12 I knew this would be my new home, and a feeling of happiness flooded through me.

13 My job interview lasted over an hour. They gave me a really good grilling.

14 I'm struggling in this job. I think I've bitten off more than I can chew.

15 Oh, another of your half-baked ideas! You need to think things through more!

16 Fonseca's sports career ended on a sour note when he broke his arm in the off-season.

17 It's a rather bland autobiography. You don't learn anything very exciting.

18 Thanks for your suggestions. That's given me food for thought.

CD4 27 *The Tipping Point*

Malcolm Gladwell wrote *The Tipping Point* in order to explain the way social trends suddenly take off, using Hush Puppies shoes as his first example. Until their comeback in the late 90s, Hush Puppies had been a dying brand, owing to the fact that they were seen as old-fashioned. After a few young "hipsters" began wearing them in the clubs of Manhattan in 1995, though, the fashion began to spread. When fashion designers started wearing them too, sales boomed, and in the end the shoes became one of the most popular fashion icons of the decade. This rapid turnaround in fortunes occurred even though the Hush Puppies company itself had played almost no part in it.

Gladwell compares such social trends to medical epidemics. Although they may begin with only a few people being "infected," provided that these individuals are influential and well connected, the trend will slowly grow until the "tipping point" is reached, at which point the rate of spread accelerates enormously.

The Tipping Point made interesting reading for marketing executives, as it showed that while widespread publicity may be achieved by expensive advertising campaigns, similar levels of exposure can be gained for far less as a result of word-of-mouth marketing. What's more, the advent of social media has greatly increased the role of viral marketing in starting social trends.

CD4 28

1 As well as studying English, I'm taking an evening class in photography.

2 Once this class is over, I'm going to take a vacation in Florida.

3 I know you're a good driver. All the same, I think you should drive more slowly on this road.

4 I'm nervous about the exam, even though I've done tons of studying for it.

5 Seeing as there are lots of holiday sales, I'm going to spend the afternoon shopping.

6 You can leave work early provided that you've finished all those jobs I gave you.

7 I arrived on time in spite of all the traffic.

8 By the time you wake up tomorrow, I'll be in New York!

CD4 29

1 **A** I didn't need *that* much detail about your operation!
  B Well, you did ask!

2 **A** Didn't you think it strange that the car was so cheap?
  B Well, I did wonder.

3 **A** It's so embarrassing when Ken talks about his ten cats.
  B Yes, I do wish he wouldn't.

4 **A** You didn't have to challenge Josh in front of everyone.
  B Maybe not. He did deserve it, though.

5 **A** You shouldn't treat Emma like a child.
  B Well, she does behave like one sometimes.

6 A I can't believe how violent that DVD you lent me was!

B Well, I did warn you!

CD4 30 **A potato clock**

I was teaching an intermediate class and there was a Japanese girl in it, Keiko, who was sharing an apartment with an English-speaking girl. One day Keiko came up to me after class and said, "Excuse me, what is a potato clock?"

I was a little bit baffled, and said, "I'm sorry. A what?"

She repeated, "A potato clock. My roommate told me she has to get one tomorrow. But I didn't understand."

I just had to admit to her that I had no idea what a potato clock was, and that she'd better ask her roommate to explain.

It was only later that it dawned on me what her roommate had said!

CD4 31

I have to get up at 8 o'clock tomorrow.

CD4 32 See p. 101

CD4 33 See p. 101

CD4 34 See p. 101

CD4 35 See p. 101

CD4 36 See p. 101

CD4 37

1 It isn't easy to wreck a nice beach!
2 This guy is the limit.
3 Some others will leave and say goodbye.
4 Sick students had a gray day.
5 I scream in an ice cold shower!

CD4 38

1 I have known oceans of danger.
2 It's important to give children an aim.
3 I told the mail carrier I only accept addressed mail.
4 We discussed the subject of youth in Asia.
5 Don't tell me that's tough!

CD4 39

Alexander Fleming was born in 1881 in Ayrshire, Scotland, where his father, who died when Alexander was seven, worked as a farmer.

After leaving school, Fleming worked as a shipping clerk for four years. However, he inherited some money when he was 20, and enrolled at St. Mary's Hospital School in order to pursue his interest in medicine.

Upon completing his medical degree in 1908, winning Gold Medal as the top medical student, he joined the research team at St. Mary's.

During the First World War, Fleming served in the Medical Corps in France, working in a hospital set up in a casino in Boulogne. There he saw many soldiers die from wound infections and, consequently, decided to specialize in this area of medicine.

Once the war was over, Fleming returned to St. Mary's and thereafter applied himself to research bacteria.

On September 28th, 1928, having just returned from a vacation, Fleming was cleaning petri dishes in his laboratory so that he could reuse them. Owing to his general messiness, the dishes had been left out in the warm laboratory for a month and were therefore covered in bacteria, as well as mold. As Fleming picked up one dish, he noticed that no bacteria were growing around the mold, so he decided to study it, in case it proved to be an antibacterial agent.

Although Fleming discovered the world's first antibiotic, penicillin, it was two other researchers, Florey and Chain, who found a way to bring it to mass production in 1942, thus changing the face of modern medicine. By the time of the D-Day landings in 1944, enough penicillin had been produced to treat all of the wounded Allied forces in World War II.

Grammar Reference

UNIT 1

Tense review

English tenses have two elements of meaning: time and aspect.

Time

Is the action present, past, or future? Does it refer to all time?

It is important to remember that time and tense are not always the same in English. Present tenses often refer to the present time, but not always; similarly past tenses do not always refer to past time.

*Your plane **leaves** at 10:00 tomorrow morning.*
(present tense form referring to the future)
*In the book, the heroine **goes** back to her youth.*
(present tense form referring to the past)
*I wish I **knew** the answer, but I don't.*
(past tense form referring to the present)
*I **could** come tomorrow, if you like.*
(past tense form referring to the future)

Aspect

The three aspects add another layer of meaning to the action of the verb.

Simple The action is seen as a complete whole.
Continuous The action is seen as having a particular duration.
Perfect The action is seen as completed before another time.

Choosing the correct tense

The choice of verb form depends on many factors, and not on a set of rigid grammatical rules.

1 The nature of the action or event
Because of the use of various aspects in English, events can be viewed with a multiplicity of implications. Look at this sentence:
I have been asking my husband to fix this door for two years.

In some languages, this verb form is in the present – *I ask my husband* ..., which indeed conveys the same basic message. But English has added on two aspects. The perfect aspect emphasizes both past and present, so that the enormity of this persistent lack of DIY can be appreciated. The continuous aspect expresses the repetitive nature of the wife's requests. She hasn't asked once, but countless times, over the course of two years. Neither of these ideas is expressed by the present tense alone.

2 How the speaker sees the event
Look at these sentences:
a He always buys her flowers.
b He's always buying her flowers.
c I'll talk to Peter about it this afternoon.
d I'll be talking to Peter about it this afternoon.

In each pair of sentences, the actions are the same, but the speaker looks at them differently.

In sentence *a*, the Simple Present expresses a simple fact. The Present Continuous in sentence *b* conveys the speaker's attitude, one of mild surprise or irritation.

In sentence *c*, *will* expresses a promise or a decision made at the moment of speaking. In sentence *d*, the Future Continuous is interesting for what it *doesn't* express. There is no element of intention, volition, or plan. The speaker is saying that in the natural course of events, as life unfolds, he and Peter will cross paths and talk, independently of the will or intention of anyone concerned. It is a casual way of looking at the future, which is why we can find it in questions such as *Will you be using the computer for long?*, which is much less confrontational than *Are you going to be using the computer for long?*

3 The meaning of the verb
In some cases, the choice of verb form might be suggested by the meaning of the verb. A verb such as *belong* expresses a state or condition that remains unchanged over a period of time. Other such verbs are *mean, understand, believe, adore, remember*, etc. It would therefore be more likely to find them in simple verb forms.
*This house **belonged** to my grandfather. Now it **belongs** to me.*
Similarly, verbs such as *wait* and *rain* express the idea of an activity over a period of time, and so are often found in continuous verb forms.
I've been waiting for you for hours!
It's raining again.

▶ 1.1 The simple aspect

The simple aspect describes an action that is seen to be complete. The action is viewed as a whole unit.
*The sun **rises** in the east.* (= all time)
*I've **read** the book and **seen** the movie.* (complete)
*My father always **wore** a suit to work.* (habit)
*He **died** in 1992.* (action completed in the past)
*This store **will close** at 5:30.* (simple fact)
Notice that in the first three examples, a specific time period isn't particularly relevant – the focus is on the fact that the action takes/took place.

Because the simple aspect expresses a completed action, we must use it if the sentence contains a number that refers to "things done."
*I **drink** five cups of tea a day.*
*She's **written** three emails today.*

▶ 1.2 The continuous aspect

Continuous verb forms express activities, or a series of activities, viewed at some point between their beginning and end. The continuous aspect focuses on the duration of an activity: we are aware of the passing of time. The activity is not permanent, and its duration is limited.
*I'm **staying** with friends until I find a place of my own.* (temporary)
*Why **are** you **wearing** that silly hat?* (in progress)
*I've **been learning** English for years.* (duration)
The activity may not be complete.
*I've **been painting** the kitchen.* (We don't know if it's finished.)
*He **was dying**, but the doctors saved him.* (He didn't "finish" dying.)
*Who's **been drinking** my tea?* (There's some left.)
Compare: *Who's **drunk** my tea?* (It's all gone.)
The continuous aspect is generally avoided with state verbs, which by their nature express permanence, and not specific duration.
*I **understand** your situation.   I **love** chocolate.*

The action of many verbs, by definition, lasts a long time, for example, *live* and *work*. The use of the continuous aspect gives these actions limited duration and makes them temporary.
*Miguel **is living** in Los Angeles while he's learning English.*
*I'm **working** as a waiter until I go to college.*
The action of some other verbs lasts a short time. These are often found in the simple aspect.
*She's **cut** her finger.*
*He **hit** me.*
In the continuous aspect, the action of these verbs becomes longer or repeated.
*I've **been cutting** wood.* (for a long time)
*He **was hitting** me.* (again and again)

Note
It has become common recently to use the continuous aspect even with state verbs, to add a sense of immediacy in a colloquial context.
*I'm **liking** your new hairstyle!*
*I'm really **wishing** she hadn't come!*

1.3 The perfect aspect

The perfect aspect expresses two ideas:

1 **An action completed before another time**
I've read his latest book. (some time before now)
When I arrived, Mary had prepared the meal. (some time before I arrived)
I will have learned my lines before the play starts. (some time before then)

2 **An action producing a result or a state of affairs relevant to a later situation**
I've read his latest book. (I know the story now.)
When I arrived, Mary had prepared the meal. (It was on the table then.)
I will have learned my lines before the play starts. (I'll know them in time for the play.)

An important characteristic of perfect verb forms, therefore, is that they explicitly link an earlier action or event with a later situation. If we want to direct attention specifically to the result or state produced by the earlier action, without drawing attention to the activity that has produced that state, we don't use a perfect form.
I know the book. It's good. (present)
The meal was ready. I ate it. (past)
I will know my lines. I'll give a good performance. (future)

Another characteristic of perfect verb forms is that the exact time of the action or event is either irrelevant or disregarded. The important elements are not *time when*, but the occurrence of the action itself and the results or state of affairs produced by it.

1.4 Active and passive

The passive is frequently used in English to express ideas that require a reflexive or impersonal construction in other languages, and in many cases is also used where other languages use the active.
English is spoken all over the world.
His books are sold in South America.

Passive sentences move the focus of attention from the subject of an active sentence to the object.
Shakespeare *wrote* Hamlet *in 1599.*
Hamlet, *one of the great tragedies of all time, was written in 1599.*

In most cases, *by* and the agent are omitted in passive sentences. This is because the agent isn't known, isn't important, or is understood.
This house was built in the seventeenth century.
The escaped prisoner has been recaptured.

Sometimes we prefer to end a sentence with what is new.
"What a beautiful painting!" "Yes, it was painted by Canaletto."

In informal language, we often use *you* or *they* to refer to people in general or to no person in particular. In this way, we can avoid using the passive.
You *can buy anything in Target.*
They'*re building a new airport soon.*

1.5 Future forms

English has several forms that express future events. The main forms and meanings are given in Grammar Reference Unit 11 on page 152.

1.6 Reflexive verbs

Reflexive verbs feature the pronouns *myself, yourself, himself, herself, itself, oneself, ourselves, yourselves,* and *themselves.*

These reflexive pronouns can be used:
1 where the subject and object are the same person.
We watched ourselves bungee jumping on video. (*We watched us ...)
I finished my work on time. I'm really happy with myself.
2 to give emphasis.
She spoke to the manager himself.
The food itself was good, but the restaurant was a little sketchy.
3 with *by* – meaning "without help" or "all alone."
He put up the shelf all by himself.
She lives by herself.

Notes
• The passive is used in English where reflexives are often used in other languages.
English is spoken here. (*English speaks itself here.)
Breakfast is served from 7:00 a.m. (*Breakfast serves itself from 7:00 a.m.)
• *"themselves"* or *"each other"*?
Peter and David blamed themselves for the mistake.
(= Peter blamed Peter / David blamed David)
Peter and David blamed each other for the mistake.
(= Peter blamed David / David blamed Peter)

UNIT 2

Position of adverbs

2.1 Adverb + adjective

When an adverb qualifies an adjective or past participle, it comes immediately before it.
The hotel is completely full.
We were deeply disappointed with his performance.

2.2 Adverb + verb

When an adverb qualifies a verb + object, we do not usually put the adverb between the verb and its object.
I like Mozart very much. (*I like very much Mozart.)
I usually have lunch at 1:00. (*I have usually lunch at 1:00.)

2.3 Front, mid, or end position?

There are three usual positions within a sentence for adverbs.

1 Front (at the beginning of the clause)
Today *we're studying adverbs.* **Obviously** *it's difficult.* **However,** *we're having fun.*
2 Mid (before the main verb, but after the verb *to be*)
I sincerely hope you can come to the party.
Pat and Peter are always late.
3 End (at the end of the clause)
They told me the news yesterday.
She speaks three languages fluently.

Different kinds of adverbs go in different positions, and many can go in all three. The rules about this are complicated, and you should consult a good grammar book for details. However, here are their common positions.

Manner (quickly, sincerely, gently)	end or mid	She **quickly** cleaned the room. She cleaned the room **quickly**.
Place (here, outside, upstairs)	end	They're playing **outside**.
Point in time (tomorrow, yesterday, tonight)	end or front	We're going to Paris **tomorrow**. **Tomorrow** we're going to Paris.
Indefinite time (already, still, just)	mid / Some can go in the end position.	I've **already** seen the movie. I **still** don't understand. I've seen the movie **already**. I haven't seen it **yet**.

Frequency (always, never, seldom)	mid	*I **always** drink tea in the morning.*
Attitude (clearly, obviously, naturally)	front or mid	***Obviously** I got it wrong.* *I **obviously** got it wrong.*
Linking (however, so, although)	front	***Although** it was raining, we went out.*
Degree/Intensifier (very, nearly, really)	before the word they qualify	*I **really** like you.* (before a verb) *I'm **really** hot.* (before an adjective) *You **very nearly** hit me!* (before another adverb)

Notes

- Some adverbs can be both attitude and manner. The position depends on which use it is.
  *I can see the boat **clearly**.* (manner)
  ***Clearly** you need to curb your spending.* (attitude)
  *Many herbs grow **naturally** in hot climates.* (manner)
  ***Naturally**, I'll pay you back the money I owe you.* (attitude)
- Some adverbs express how complete something is. They come in mid-position.
  *I have **completely** forgotten her name.*
  *We have **almost** finished our work.*
- If there is more than one adverbial in the end position, the normal order is manner, place, time.
  *He played **well yesterday**.*
  *I watched the sun rise **slowly above the horizon**.*
  *I was **at home yesterday**.*

2.4 Adverb collocations

Adverbs can go with certain verbs or adjectives because there is a link in meaning between the two. For example, emotions can be deep, so we often find the adverb *deeply* with words that express feelings.
***deeply** regret*   ***deeply** embarrassing*   ***deeply** hurt*
Here are some more examples.

freely admit	desperately anxious	highly recommended
feel strongly	severely damaged	walk briskly
easily confused	sadly missed	

2.5 Adverbs with two forms

Some adverbs have two forms, one with and one without *-ly*. Sometimes the two meanings are connected:
*We were flying **high** over the ocean.*
*I think very **highly** of Joe and his work.*
*Hold **tight**! The train's going to move.*
*We control our expenditure **tightly**.*
Sometimes the two meanings are not connected:
*We work **hard**.* (a lot) / *I **hardly** recognized her.* (= almost not)
*Turn **right** around.* (= completely) / *If I remember **rightly**, they live here.* (correctly)
*We arrived **late**.* (not punctually) / *I've noticed that **lately**.* (recently)
*We get along **fine**.* (OK) / *Chop the carrots **finely**.* (in small pieces)
***Sure**, I'll help.* (certainly) / ***Surely** it's illegal?* (isn't it obvious that?)
*I'm aiming **high**.* (not low) / *She's **highly** respected.* (extremely)
*You ate **most** of the pizza.* (more than anyone) / *It was **mostly** sunny.* (generally)
*His shot went **wide**.* (off target) / *We've traveled **widely**.* (extensively)
*It could go **wrong**.* (badly) / *You were **wrongly** informed.* (incorrectly)
*Go **easy** on him.* (gently) / *We won **easily**.* (without difficulty)
*She doesn't play **fair**.* (by the rules) / *I'm **fairly** sure.* (very)
*Don't come **near** me!* (close) / *You **nearly** ran me over!* (almost)
*It's **pretty** easy.* (very) / *She smiled **prettily**.* (attractively)
*Kids go in **free**.* (with no charge) / *He spoke **freely**.* (with no reserve)
*Don't stand so **close**!* (near) / *Watch **closely**.* (carefully)

2.6 Adjective order

Generally speaking, value adjectives (which indicate personal opinion) come first, followed by size, age, color, shape, nationality, and material.

Compound nouns (e.g., *washing machine*; *coffee pot*) are never separated.

There are several examples below of noun phrases with adjectives in this order.
two beautiful, black, leather riding boots
a priceless, 19th-century, Impressionist painting
their huge, circular swimming pool
my Swedish, wooden salad bowl
the dirty, old, metal garden seat
one tiny, L-shaped utility room
Jane's pretty, Victorian writing desk
his charming, sundrenched beach house

UNIT 3

Verb patterns

3.1 Verb patterns with the infinitive or base form

Verb + infinitive

The pattern of verb + infinitive is used:

1   After certain verbs

agree   ask   offer   promise   refuse   want

*He **asked to do** it.*

2   After certain verbs + object

ask   beg   encourage   order   persuade   tell   want

*They **asked** him **to do** it.*

Note
Some verbs can take both of the above patterns.

ask   beg   want   help

*She **wanted to do** it.*
*She **wanted** him **to do** it.*

Verb + base form

help   let   make

*They **made** me **do** it.*
*We **let** her **stay**.*

Notes
- *Help* can be used with *to*, but it's optional.
  *She **helped** me **pack**. / She **helped** me **to pack**.*
- The passive of *make* takes *to*.
  *I was **made to do** it.*
- The passive of *let* is *allowed to*.
  *I was **allowed to** do it.*

Adjective + infinitive

The infinitive form is used after adjectives.
*Are you **happy to see** me?*
*You'll be **disappointed to hear** my news.*

3.2 Verb patterns with the gerund

The gerund or -*ing* form is used:

1 After certain verbs

| admit | deny | regret | suggest |

He **admitted** *stealing* the money.

2 After prepositions, prepositional verbs, and phrasal verbs
After leaving school, he joined the army.
She **apologized for arriving** late.
I've **given up eating** processed foods.

Note
The preposition *to* (not *to* as part of the infinitive) can cause problems. This is because *to* + -*ing* is a strange combination.
I'm **looking forward to seeing** you.
I'm **not used to driving** on the right.
Do you **feel up to going** out this evening?

3.3 Verb + *that* + clause

In some (not all) of the above examples, a *that* clause can be used after the main verb in place of a gerund or infinitive. There is no change in meaning. *That* itself can be omitted.
She **admitted (that) she had made** a mistake.
He **promised (that) he would do** it.
They **suggested (that) we should have** a long break.

Notes
• *Suggest* has special problems. These constructions are also possible.
They **suggested (that) we have** a long break.
They **suggested (that) we had** a long break.
• *He wanted that I do it* is a common mistake.

3.4 Verb + infinitive or gerund with little or no change of meaning

The verbs *begin*, *continue*, and *start* can take either the infinitive or gerund and mean the same.

| It | began
continued
started | to rain.
raining. |

Notes
The choice may be governed by style or the nature of the following verb.
It's just *starting to rain*. (*starting raining*)
He slowly *began to understand* the situation. (*began understanding*)
Many verbs that express feelings and attitudes (*like, love, prefer, can't stand*, etc.) can be followed by either the infinitive or gerund, and the distinction in meaning is small.
I **like traveling** by train. (general truth)
I **like to travel** by train when I go to my grandmother's. (a little more particular)
Like + gerund can mean *enjoy*. *Like* + infinitive can express what you think is the right thing to do.
I **like cooking**.
I **like to pay** my bills on time.

Note
The infinitive is always used with *would like/prefer*, etc.
I'd **like to travel** by train when I next visit her. (one particular occasion)

3.5 Verbs + infinitive or gerund with a change of meaning

1 After the verbs *remember*, *forget*, and *regret*, the gerund refers to an action earlier in time than the main verb; the infinitive refers to an action at the same time or later.
I **remember giving** her the message when I saw her.
Please **remember to give** her the message when you see her.

I **regret saying** that because I upset her.
I **regret to say** we can't offer you the job.

2 After the verb *stop* and the phrasal verb *go on*, the gerund refers to an existing action; the infinitive refers to a following action.
We **stopped walking**.
We **stopped to take** a rest.
He just **went on repeating** the question.
After rejecting my proposal, he **went on to explain** why.

3 After verbs of the senses, *see*, *hear*, etc., + object, the gerund signifies an action in progress; the base form signifies a completed action.
We **saw him cutting** the hedge. (He was in the middle of doing it.)
We **saw him cut** the hedge. (We saw the whole event from start to finish.)

4 After *try*, the gerund refers to an action that isn't difficult and is done as an experiment; the infinitive refers to an action that is difficult and may not even be possible.
Try calling him at work – he might be there.
Try to lift this 20-pound weight with one hand!

5 After *need*, the gerund refers to a passive action.
The car **needs cleaning**. (It needs to be cleaned.)
The infinitive can be used with either a passive or active meaning.
Tom **needs to be supervised** more.
Tom **needs to supervise** his staff more.

6 *Suggest* + gerund can refer to an action that includes the person making the suggestion; *suggest* + object + infinitive (in fact, the subjunctive form) refers to an action that is suggested for others to perform.
Carol **suggested getting off** the bus and walking to her house.
The bus driver **suggested we get off** and walk.

3.6 Perfect and passive forms

The gerund and infinitive also have perfect and passive forms.
I **don't remember having said** that.
She **suffered from having had** a difficult childhood.
He **doesn't like being told** what to do.

UNIT 4

Modal auxiliary verbs

Modal verbs are a very rich and subtle area of the English language. They can all express degrees of probability/speculation about present or future time. *Will* is the most certain, and *might* and *could* are the least certain. Certain modals can also express other areas of meaning (see "Other use" below).

4.1 Modal verbs for speculation in the present and future

The main modal verbs that express present and future probability are given here in order of degrees of certainty with *will* being the most certain and *might/could* being the least certain.

1 **will**
Will and *won't* are used to predict a future event that is seen as certain, a future fact.
I'**ll** be on vacation next week. I **won't** do any work at all.
The semester **will** end on May 8th.

Will and *won't* are also used to express what we strongly believe to be true about the present. They indicate an assumption based on our knowledge of people and things: their routine, character, and qualities.
Is that the phone? It'**ll** be John. He said he'd call around now.
"I wonder what Meg's doing now?" "It's 7:00. I suppose she'**ll** be getting ready to go out."
Don't take the meat out of the oven. It **won't** be ready yet.

2 *must* and *can't*

Must is used to assert what we infer or conclude to be the most logical or rational interpretation of a situation or events. We have a lot of evidence, but it is less certain than *will*.
*Wow, look over there! That **must** be John's new car.*
*You **must** be joking! I just don't believe you.*
The negative of this use of *must* is *can't*.
*She **can't** be in the office today. She flew to Boston yesterday!*

3 *should*

Should expresses what may reasonably be expected to happen. It also carries the meaning that we want whatever is predicted to happen, and is therefore not used to express negative or unpleasant ideas. It can also suggest a conditional. If everything has gone/goes according to plan, then (x) should happen.
*Our guests **should** be here soon.* (if they haven't gotten lost)
*This homework **shouldn't** take you too long.* (if you've understood what you have to do)
*We **should** be moving into our new house soon.* (as long as all the arrangements go smoothly)

4 *may*

May expresses the possibility that something will happen or is already happening.
*We **may** go to Greece for our vacation. We haven't decided yet.*
*We **may not** have enough money to go away this year.*

5 *might*

Might, like *may*, expresses possibility, but in a more tentative way.
*It **might** rain. Take your umbrella.*
*I **might not** be back in time for dinner, so don't wait for me.*

6 *could*

Could is used in a similar way to *might*.
*It **could** rain, but I doubt it.*
*That indie movie **could** be worth seeing, but it didn't get very good reviews.*
The negative, *could not*, is NOT used to express future possibility. *Might not* is the negative of *could* in this use.
*It looks like it could rain, but it **might not**.*
*He **might not** come.*
The negative *couldn't* has a similar meaning to *can't* in 2 above, only slightly weaker.
*She **couldn't** be in the office today. She flew to Boston yesterday.*

7 *can*

We use *can* to express what is generally true, and logically possible.
*Riding a bike in town **can** be dangerous.*
Can cannot be used to predict future possibility. We must use *will be possible* or *will be able to*.
*In years to come, it'**ll be possible** to take vacations on the moon.*
*We'**ll be able to** travel by spaceship.*

4.2 Modal auxiliaries in the past

All the modal verbs given above are also used with *have* + past participle (the perfect base-form verb) to express varying degrees of certainty about the past. Again, *will/would* is the most certain and *might/could* the least certain. *Can* is a special case (see below).
*You met a man with a big, black mustache? That **would have been** my Uncle Tom.*
*It **won't have been** Peter you met at the party. He wasn't invited.*
*It **must have been** Kevin. He looks a lot like Peter.*
*It **can't have been** a very interesting party. No one seems to have enjoyed it.*
*Where's Henry? He **should have been** here hours ago! He **may have gotten** lost.*
*He **might have decided** not to come. He **could have had** an accident.*
*He **can hardly have forgotten** to come.*
Can have is only used in questions or with *hardly, only,* or *never*.
*Where **can he have been** all this time?*
*They **can only have known** each other for a few weeks.*

4.3 Other uses of modal auxiliary verbs, present and past

Obligation

Must/have to express strong obligation. The past is expressed by *had to*.
*You **must** try harder!   I **had to** work hard to pass my exams.*
Must can express an "internal obligation," based on the speaker's opinion.
*I **must** get this jacket cleaned soon.*
Have to expresses an external obligation, based on rules and regulations or another person's authority.
*You **have to** be 16 to learn to drive.*
*My boss says I **have to** work this weekend.*
Must not expresses negative obligation. *Don't have to* expresses the absence of obligation.
*You **must not** take photos inside the museum.*
*You **don't have to** have a degree to do this job.*
Need has two past forms.
Didn't need to (+ base form) expresses an action that was not necessary, but we do not know if it was in fact completed or not. The context usually makes this clear.
*I **didn't need to do** any food shopping because I was eating out that night.*
Needn't have (+ past participle) expresses an action that was completed but that wasn't necessary. This is chiefly used in British English.
*You **needn't have bought** any butter. We have plenty.*

Advice

Should is used to express advice, or milder obligation. The past is expressed by *should have* (+ past participle).
*You **should** rest.   You **should have taken** it more seriously.*

Permission

Can, could, and *may* are used to ask for permission. *May* sounds more formal than *could*. *Might* is extremely formal or tentative and is more likely to be used rather sarcastically in many contexts.
***Can** I come with you?*
***Could** I ask you a question?*
***May** I ask what the purpose of this visit is?*
***Might** I ask why you haven't answered any of my emails?*
The past of *may* and *can* is expressed by *was allowed to*. *Could* can only be used to report permission.
*I **was allowed to** do whatever I wanted when I was young.*
*My parents said I **could** stay out until after midnight.*

Ability

Can is used to express general ability; the form in the past is *could*.
*I **can** swim.   I **could** swim when I was six.*
To express a particular ability on one occasion in the past, *could* is not used. Instead, *was able to* or *managed to* is used.
*The prisoner **managed to** escape by climbing onto the roof.*
*I **was able to** give the police a full description.*

Refusal and willingness

Won't expresses a refusal. The past is *wouldn't*.
*He was angry because she **wouldn't** lend him any money.*
We also use *won't* for inanimate things when we see their incapacity to function properly as a form of "refusal."
*The car **won't** start.   I'm sorry, the printer **wouldn't** do these in color.*

Habit/Characteristic behavior

Will is used to express habitual or characteristic behavior. The past is expressed by *would*.
*He'**ll** sit for hours staring into the fire.*
*My grandma **would** always bring a present when she came to visit.*
If *will* is stressed, it suggests criticism and irritation.
*David **will** leave his homework until the last minute. It's infuriating.*

4.4 Softening the message

We can "soften our message" and sound more polite and indirect by using certain constructions.

A past tense
I **wondered** if you were free tonight? I **thought** we could go to the movies.

The continuous
I **was hoping** you could tell me the answer.
When **will** you **be arriving**?
We **were thinking** it might be nice to go out for dinner.

would
Would it be possible for you to come back tomorrow?
Wouldn't it be better if you did it my way?
I **would** say/think she's in her seventies.
I **would** have said/thought she was about …
I **wouldn't** be surprised if Jack didn't come soon.
I just thought I'**d** call to see if you were alright.
You'**d** have thought she could have remembered my birthday.

Polite requests
A variety of ways of making polite requests are dealt with on page 36. In actual fact, all degrees of politeness and formality can be covered with the use of *can* and *could* (*possibly*).
Can I borrow your dictionary for a second? (Informal, not tentative)
Could I borrow your umbrella? (Very formal/polite, tentative)
Could I **possibly** borrow your car on Saturday? (Formal/polite, very tentative)

UNIT 5

Avoiding repetition

To avoid repetition in many languages, it is common for words to be left out. This is called ellipsis. In English, it is common for the main verb to be left out, leaving just the auxiliary, and this can cause problems.

5.1 Using auxiliaries to avoid repetition

In short answers

When a *Yes/No* question is asked, we use the auxiliary on its own when answering rather than repeating the whole verb form.
"Will it rain this afternoon?" "Yes, I think it will (rain this afternoon)."
"Should I study for this test?" "Yes, I think you should (study for the test)."

Commenting on given information

When we make comments in conversation, we usually avoid repeating information that has just been given.
"Mary's coming." "I know she is."
"Angela can speak Arabic and Spanish." "She can't, can she?"

Note

Where there is no auxiliary verb in Simple Present and Simple Past positive statements, *do/does/did* is used to reply. This is to avoid repeating the full verb.
"I love Mexico." "I do, too, and so does Ryan."
"I thought the movie was wonderful." "I didn't. I hated it."

Responding with a different auxiliary

To know which auxiliary verb to use, it is necessary to reconstruct the part of the sentence that is missing, and to consider carefully the meaning and the time of the events in the sentence.
"I didn't see the movie." "Oh, you should have (seen the movie). *It was great.*"
"You should see the Renoir exhibition. It's excellent!" "I have (seen it)."
"I wish you'd lock the door when you leave." "But I did (lock it)."

Using more than one auxiliary

When there is more than one auxiliary, we usually use more than one when responding, too.
"He could have been lying." "Yes, he could have been."
"Would I have enjoyed it?" "No, I don't think you would have."
We always use more than one if there is a change in auxiliary.
"You should be given a raise." "Well, I haven't been."
"She can't have told him yet." "She must have."

5.2 Reduced infinitives

We can use *to* instead of the full infinitive in replies.
"Did you do the dishes yet?" "No, but I'm going to."
"Are you coming for a walk?" "No, I don't want to."
The verb *to be* is not usually reduced to *to*.
She's less moody than she used to be.
I wasn't as impressed as I'd expected to be.

UNIT 6

Adding emphasis

6.1 Structures that add emphasis

Sentences can be emphasized by adding certain structures. They are called cleft or divided sentences. Look at this base sentence:
Lucy moved to Los Angeles.
We can emphasize different parts of the sentence according to which element is the most important:
What Lucy did was move to Los Angeles. (*What* = the thing which/that)
All (that) Lucy did was (to) move to Los Angeles. (*All* = the only thing)
The (only/first) thing Lucy did was move to Los Angeles.
Where Lucy moved to was Los Angeles. (*Where* = the place which/that)
Why Lucy moved to Los Angeles was because … (*Why* = the reason why)
It was Lucy **who/that** moved to Los Angeles. (*who* = the person who/that)

Or we can emphasize the whole sentence:

What happened was that	
What surprised me was the fact that	Lucy moved to Los Angeles.
What interests me is why	

6.2 Negative inversion

Sentences can be given emphasis by negative inversion, which can take place:

1 after negative adverbials such as *never, nowhere, not for one minute, not since, not until, never again, rarely*. It is mainly used in written English but can also be used to emphasize points in more formal spoken English, such as when making speeches.
Not until 1920 did American women get the vote.
Never had he eaten such a huge meal.
Nowhere will you come across a more hospitable nation.
Nothing do they appreciate more than a trip to the beach.
Rarely do you meet a man of such integrity.

2 in certain established sentence patterns.
Hardly had he begun to speak **when** the majority of the guests departed.
No sooner had we sat down for dinner **than** the doorbell rang.
Little did anyone realize the seriousness of the situation.

3 after expressions with *only* and *no*.
Only *when I myself became a parent did I realize the value of my parents' advice.*
Not only *did she write short stories,* **but** *she was* **also** *a painter of talent.*
At no time *was I ever informed.*
In no way *can this government deny its guilt.*
On no account *will I compromise my ideals.*

▶ 6.3 Pronunciation

Of course, a major way of adding emphasis in spoken English is by stressing individual words. In English, a change of word stress changes the meaning of a sentence. Look at this base sentence:
John likes the brown shoes.
John *likes the brown shoes.* (Tom doesn't.)
John **likes** *the brown shoes.* (He doesn't hate them.)
John likes the **brown** *shoes.* (Not the black ones.)
John likes the brown **shoes**. (Not the brown sandals.)

Note
It is possible to stress the word *the* (pronounced /ði/) when it means that something is so superior to the alternatives, it can be considered the only real choice.
If John wants brown shoes, Jimmy Choo shoes are **the** *brown shoes to buy.*

▶ 6.4 Emphatic *do*, *does*, *did*

Do, *does*, and *did* can be used to give emphasis in positive statements in the Simple Present and Simple Past, and also in the imperative.
John **does** *like the brown shoes.* (You were wrong!)
Do *come with us on vacation. We'd love you to.*
I **do** *love you, really I do.*
He **does** *seem rather upset.*
They **did** *question him very thoroughly, didn't they?*

UNIT 7

Real and unreal tense usage

Introduction

1 English tense usage can be divided into two categories: tenses used to refer to fact, and those used to refer to non-fact. Fact is what is considered to be real or quite possible; non-fact is what is supposed or wished for, which is either unreal or improbable.

Fact	*I work in a restaurant, but I don't earn much.*
	If I find a better job, I'll take it.
Non-fact	*I wish I had a lot of money.*
	If I had a lot of money, I would open my own restaurant.

2 Tenses used to refer to fact are related to real time. For example, a past verb form refers to the past.
I **took** *a great vacation in Thailand last year.*

3 Tenses used to refer to non-fact are not related to real time. Generally speaking, this unreality is expressed by shifting the verb form "backwards," for example from present to past.
If I **had** *a car, I* **could** *visit my friends.*
Here the past verb form does not refer to the real past, but to the "wished for" present and future. It has the effect of distancing the meaning from reality.

▶ 7.1 Type 1 conditional sentences (real)

It is important to understand this difference between fact and non-fact when discussing conditional sentences.
- Type 1 conditional sentences are based on fact in real time. They express a possible condition and its probable result.
  If it rains, I'll get wet.
  If he doesn't come soon, we'll miss the bus.
- *Will* is not usually used in the condition clause. However, it can appear when *will* expresses willingness (or in the negative, refusal).
  If you **'ll wash** *the dishes, I'll put them away.* (if you are willing to)
  If Peter **won't give** *you a ride, I will.* (if Peter isn't willing to)
- *Should* and *happen to* can be used in the condition clause to suggest that something may happen by chance, but is unlikely.
  If you **should come across** *Pearl, tell her to text me.*
  If you **happen to find** *my keys, leave them on the table for me.*
- There are several other links with meanings similar to *if* that can introduce Type 1 conditional sentences.
  Provided/Providing *I have the time, I'll give you a hand to fix it.*
  Supposing *you miss the plane, what will you do?*
  I'll come tomorrow **unless** *I hear from you before.* (if I don't hear from you)

▶ 7.2 Type 2 conditional sentences (unreal)

1 Type 2 conditional sentences are not based on fact. They express a situation that is contrary to reality in the present and future; a hypothetical condition and its probable result. This unreality is shown by a tense shift "backwards":
Present → Past, *will* → *would*
If I were taller, I'd join the police force. (In reality I am not, and never will be, tall enough to join the police force.)
If you saw a ghost, what would you do? (I don't believe in ghosts, so I don't think you will ever see one.)

2 The difference between Type 1 and Type 2 conditional sentences is not related to time. Both can refer to the present or the future. By using a past verb form in Type 2, the speaker suggests that the situation is less probable, or impossible, or imaginary.
Compare the following.
If it rains this weekend, I'll … (Said in England, where rain is common.)
If it rained in the Sahara, the desert would … (This would be most unusual.)
If there is a nuclear war, we will … (I am a pessimist. Nuclear war is a real possibility.)
If there was a nuclear war, we would … (I am an optimist and I think nuclear war is very unlikely to happen.)
If you come to my country, you'll have a good time. (Possible.)
If you came from my country, you'd understand us better. (Impossible – you don't come from my country.)

Notes
- *Were* is often used instead of *was*, especially when the style is formal. It is also commonly used in the expression *If I were you …* when giving advice.
  If he **were** *more honest, he would be a better person.*
  If I **were** *you, I'd cook it for a little longer.*
- The Type 2 conditional can make a suggestion sound less direct and hence more polite.
  Would it be convenient if I called this evening around 8:00?
  Would you mind if I opened the window slightly?
- *Would* is not usually used in the condition clause. However, as with *will* in Type 1, it can appear when it expresses willingness. Again, it makes a suggestion sound more polite.
  I **would** *be grateful if you would give this matter your serious attention.*
- *Were to* can be used in the condition clause to suggest that something is unlikely to happen.
  If you **were to find** *that your neighbors were famous movie stars, what would you do?*

7.3 Type 3 conditional sentences (unreal)

Type 3 conditional sentences, like Type 2, are not based on fact. They express a situation that is contrary to reality in the past. This unreality is shown by a tense shift "backwards":

Past → Past Perfect, *would* → *would have*

If I had known his background, I would never have employed him.
(I didn't know his background and I did employ him.)
If I hadn't seen it with my own eyes, I wouldn't have thought it possible. (I did see it with my own eyes, so I knew it was possible.)

 ### 7.4 Type 2 and Type 3 mixed

1   It is possible for each of the two clauses in a conditional sentence to have a different time reference, and the result is a mixed conditional.
    If we had brought a map with us, we would know where we are.
    If we had brought … is contrary to past fact (we didn't bring a map).
    … we would know … is contrary to present fact (we don't know).
    If I didn't love her, I wouldn't have married her.
    If I didn't love her … is contrary to present fact (I do love her).
    I wouldn't have married her … is contrary to past fact (I did marry her).
2   Care needs to be taken when the Type 2 conditional refers to the future.
    I'd go to the party next Saturday if I hadn't made plans to go to the theater.
    This conditional is sometimes "unmixed" to regularize the tense sequence.
    I would have gone to the party next Saturday if I hadn't made plans to go to the theater.

Hypothesizing

There are certain other constructions that have a hypothetical meaning and, as in conditional sentences, the unreality that they express is again shown by shifting the verb form "backwards."
I wish I knew the answer. (But I don't know.)
If only I hadn't behaved so badly. (But I did behave badly.)

 ### 7.5 Hypothesizing about the present and future

The Simple Past tense form is used for present and future time reference. Notice that *were* is often used instead of *was*, especially in formal style.
*I wish I **were** taller!   If only he **were** here now!*
*Supposing/Suppose you **had** a million dollars? What would you do?*

Present state vs. present action or event

When we hypothesize about a present state, the Simple Past tense form is used.
*I wish you **lived** closer.   If only I **had** a car!*

When we hypothesize about a present action or event, *would* is used.
*I wish you**'d help** more in the house.*
*If only she **wouldn't wash** her socks in the sink!*

Would here expresses willingness in the first sentence, and annoying habit in the second.

I wish/If only

Notice that it is unusual to say *I wish/If only I wouldn't …* because we can control what we want to do. However, we can say *I wish/If only I could …*
*I **wish I could remember** where I put my glasses.*
If only I could give up checking my smartphone 100 times a day.
We can say *I wish/If only … would* to refer to a definite time in the future, but only if we think that the action will probably not happen.

I wish she'd come with me tomorrow.
If only you'd fix the car this weekend, we could go for a drive.
If it is possible that our wish will be realized, then a different structure such as *I hope* is needed.
*I **hope it doesn't rain** tomorrow.*

Fact vs. non-fact

Notice the difference between fact and non-fact in the following pair of sentences.
*He looks **as if he is** French.* (Fact – it is possible that he is.)
*He looks **as if he were** French.* (Non-fact – we know he isn't.)
The same distinction is found with other *as if/as though* structures.
*Why is that girl smiling at me **as though she knew** me?*
*He behaves **as if he owned** the place.*

It's time

It's time can be followed by an infinitive.
*It's **time to go** to bed.   It's **time for us to go**.*
It is also possible to use a past tense.
*It's **time we went** home.   It's **time I was** going.*
When we want to say that it is time for someone else to do something, the past tense is often used.
*It's **time you got** your hair cut.*

would rather

Would rather can be followed by a base form verb.
*I'**d rather have** ice water, please.*
When *would rather* is followed by another person, the construction *would rather* + person + past tense form is used.
*I'**d rather you kept** this a secret.*
*She **would rather you paid** with cash.*

 ### 7.6 Hypothesizing about the past

The Past Perfect tense form is used for past time reference.
*I wish she **hadn't been** so mean.*
*If only the police **had looked** in the attic, they would have found him!*
*Supposing/Suppose we **had missed** the plane? What would we have done?*

would rather

Would rather + the Past Perfect is possible, but it is more usual to express the same idea using *wish*.
*I'**d rather** you'd left.   I **wish** you'd left.*

Fact vs. non-fact

Notice the difference between fact and non-fact in the following sentences.
*He looked as if he **was** tired.* (Fact – this is probably how he felt.)
*He looked as if he **had seen** a ghost.* (Non-fact – very improbable.)

would like

Would like can be used with a perfect infinitive to talk about things we wish we had done.
*I **would like to have lived** in the eighteenth century.*
This can also be expressed by *would have liked* followed by either an ordinary infinitive or a perfect infinitive.
I would have liked to live
I would have liked to have lived │ *in the eighteenth century.*

The same forms can be used to refer to the present and the future if it is contrary to fact.
I would like to have stayed home
I would have liked to stay home │ *tonight, instead of going out.*
I would have liked to have stayed home

7.7 would

Would can express past habits.
When I was a kid, we'd go looking for mushrooms.
*My grandfather **would** sit in his armchair and nod off.*
*My sister **would** borrow my clothes without asking. It really annoyed me.*

Stressed *would* can be used to criticize a single past action. The meaning is "that's typical of you/him/her."
*Did she say I hit her? She **would** say that. I hate her.*

Would is used to express the future in the past (see p. 57). It reports speech and thoughts.
You promised you'd help me.
*I knew you **wouldn't** like it.*

Wouldn't can express a refusal on a particular past occasion.
*I asked him if he was going out with anyone, but he **wouldn't** tell me.*
*The printer **wouldn't** stop printing, so I unplugged it.*

UNIT 8

Relative clauses

Introduction

It is important to distinguish between defining and non-defining relative clauses. Defining relative clauses are an essential part of the meaning of a sentence and therefore they cannot be left out. They define exactly who or what we are talking about.
*There's the woman **you were telling me about.***

Non-defining relative clauses add extra information of secondary importance, and can be left out of a sentence.
*Mrs. Bottomley, **who was an extremely cheap person while she was alive,** has left all her money to a cats' home.*

Non-defining relative clauses are mainly found in written English, where sentences are carefully constructed. In spoken English, they sound rather formal, and can easily be expressed by simpler sentences.
*Did you know Mrs. Bottomley left all her money to a cats' home? It's incredible, really. She was such a **cheap** person.*

8.1 Defining relative clauses

These are the main forms used. The forms in parentheses are possible, but not as common.

	Person	Thing
Subject	who (that)	that (which)
Object	— (that)	— (that)

Notice that English likes to drop the relative pronoun when it defines the object of the clause.
*The doctor **who helped me most** was Dr. Clark. (subject)*
*The doctor **I found most helpful** was Dr. Clark. (object)*
*The treatment **that** helped me most was acupuncture. (subject)*
*The treatment **I liked best** was acupuncture. (object)*

Notice that there are no commas before and after defining relative clauses when written, and no pauses when spoken.

that

That is usually used as a subject after the following: superlatives, *all*, *every*(thing), *some*(thing), *any*(thing), *no*(thing), and *only*.
*He wrote some of the best poetry **that's ever been written.***
***All that's needed** is a little more time.*
*Don't take **anything that's valuable.***
*The **only thing that matters** is that you're safe.*

We often omit *that* when it is the object.
She's one of the nicest people I know.
Is there anything I can do to help?

Prepositions

Prepositions can come either before relative pronouns or at the end of the relative clause. In spoken English, it is much more common to put the preposition at the end (and to drop the pronoun).
This is the book I was talking to you about.
The people I work with are very helpful.

Second relative clause

A second relative clause, introduced by *and* or *but*, usually takes a *wh*-pronoun, not *that*.
Someone that I greatly admire, but who I've never met, is Professor Keats.

8.2 Non-defining relative clauses

These are the main forms used. The form in parentheses is possible, but not as common.

	Person	Thing
Subject	... , who ... ,	... , which ... ,
Object	... , who ... (, whom ...)	... , which ...

*Mr. Jenkins, **who has written several books,** spoke at the meeting last night. (subject)*
*Peter Clark, **who the governor fired from his staff,** has become the president of Redland Bank. (object)*
*My favorite food is chocolate, **which is one of Indonesia's most profitable exports**. (subject)*
*I gave him a sandwich, **which he ate greedily.** (object)*

Notice that there are commas around non-defining relative clauses when written, and pauses before and after them when spoken.

Prepositions

Prepositions can come at the end of non-defining relative clauses, but in a formal style they are usually put before the relative pronoun.
*The lecturer spoke for two hours on the subject of Weingarten's Theory of Market Forces, which none of us had ever heard **of**.*
*The privatization of all industry, **to** which this government is deeply committed, is not universally popular.*

which

Which can be used in non-defining clauses to refer to the whole of the preceding clause.
*He passed the exam, **which** surprised everyone.*
*The elevator isn't working, **which** means we'll have to take the stairs.*

whose

Whose can be used in both defining and non-defining relative clauses to refer to possession.
*There's the woman **whose** son was killed recently. (defining)*
*ABC Airways, **whose** fares across the Atlantic were lower than anybody else's, has just declared itself bankrupt. (non-defining)*

what

What is used as a relative pronoun instead of *the thing that* in some sentences.
*Has she told you **what's** worrying her?*
*I have to do **what** I believe is right.*

when and where

When and *where* can be used to introduce both defining and non-defining relative clauses. In defining relative clauses, *when* can be left out.
*Can you tell me the exact time (**when**) you hope to arrive?*

Where cannot be left out unless we add a preposition.
*That's the hotel **where** we're staying.*
*That's the hotel we're staying **at**.*

In non-defining relative clauses, *when* and *where* cannot be left out.
We go swimming after 5:00, **when** *everyone else has gone home.*
He shops in Atlanta, **where** *his sister lives.*

why

Why can be used to introduce defining relative clauses after the word *reason*. It can be left out.
Do you remember the reason **why** *we are arguing?*
We can also say *Do you remember why we are arguing?*, where the clause beginning with *why* is the object of the verb.

Participles

▶ 8.3 Participles as adjectives

Present participles describe an action that is still happening.
He dove into the water to save the **drowning** *child.*
They watched the **burning** *forest.*
Past participles describe the result of an action that has happened.
She looked at the **broken** *chair.*
The **completed** *statue looked very lifelike.*

▶ 8.4 Participles as reduced relative clauses

When participles come after a noun, they are like reduced relative clauses.
I met a woman **riding** *a donkey.* (who was riding)
The cash **stolen** *in the raid was never recovered.* (that was stolen)
The man **being interviewed** *by the police is suspected of arson.* (who is being interviewed)

▶ 8.5 Participles in adverb clauses

1   Participle clauses can describe actions that are going on simultaneously.
She sat by the fire **reading** *a book and* **sipping** *a mug of coffee.*
He went to the party **dressed** *as a monkey.*
2   Participle clauses can describe actions that happen consecutively.
Opening *his suitcase, he took out his jacket.*
Released *from its cage, the lion prowled around.*
3   If it is important to show that the first action has finished before the second begins, the perfect participle is used.
Having finished *lunch, we set off.*
4   Participle clauses can express the idea of *because*.
Being *a cheap person, he never spent more than he had to.*
(Because he was a cheap person …)
Not knowing *what to do, I waited patiently.* (Because I didn't know …)
Weakened *by years of bad health, she could hardly sit up in bed.*
(Because she had been weakened …)
5   Participle clauses can express the idea of result.
It rained every day for two weeks, completely **ruining** *our vacation.*
6   Participle clauses can express the idea of *if*.
Taken *regularly, aspirin can reduce the risk of a stroke.*
Participle clauses can be introduced by *while, when, after, by, on,* and *since*.
While studying *at Georgetown, he met the woman he was to marry.*
When leaving *the plane, remember to take your belongings with you.*
After saying *goodbye, he ran to catch the train.*
I paid my debts **by taking** *on another job.*
On entering *the room, I noticed that everyone was looking at me.*
Since arriving *in Seoul, I've made a lot of friends.*

Note
In all participle clauses, the subject of the clause and the subject of the main verb must be the same.

▶ 8.6 Participles after certain verbs

Many verbs can be followed by an *-ing* form.
I **spent** *the evening* **decorating***.*
He **spends** *his money* **shopping** *on the Internet.*
Don't **waste** *time* **thinking** *about what might have been.*
Let's **go swimming***.*

▶ 8.7 *just*

Just has several meanings.

exactly	*This house is* **just** *right for us.*
only	*He isn't a man. He's* **just** *a boy.*
a short time before	*I* **just** *tried texting you.*
right now	*I'm* **just** *getting dressed.*
simply, only	*I* **just** *want you to go.*
	I'd **just** *like an egg for breakfast.*
equally, no less	*You're* **just** *as bad as David.*

Just about means *almost*.
*"Are you ready to go?" "***Just about***."*
It can express something that is almost not possible.
I can **just about** *reach the top shelf.*
Sometimes it doesn't mean very much. It just emphasizes what you're saying!
Just *what do you think you're doing?*
It's **just** *incredible!*

UNIT 9

▶ 9.1 Discourse markers

Discourse markers are words and expressions that show how a piece of discourse is constructed. They can:

- show the connection between what is being said now to what was said before.
- show the connection between what is being said now to what is about to be said.
- show the speaker's attitude toward what has been said.
- show the speaker's attitude toward what they are saying.
- clarify, direct, correct, persuade, etc.

Here are explanations of the meaning of some common discourse markers.

> **Naturally**, you'll do what you think is best.
> (Of course, this is what I would expect.)
>
> **Basically**, you're spending too much money.
> (This is the most fundamental point.)
>
> **Apparently**, it's going to be very hot tomorrow.
> (I've heard this, but I don't know if it's true.)
>
> **Admittedly**, it would take a long time to do it this way.
> (I know this point goes against my main argument.)
>
> **Surely**, you understand why I'm saying this?
> (I'm almost certain of this point, but I need reassurance.)
>
> **Actually**, my name's Shauna, not Shona.
> (I'm correcting you as politely as possible.)
>
> **After all**, Manhattan is an island.
> (Don't forget this seemingly obvious point. It's a key one.)
>
> **As a matter of fact**, it's cheaper to send it by air.
> (This is a fact that might surprise you.)
>
> **Mind you/Still**, it won't be easy.
> (It occurs to me that this contrasts with what I just said.)
>
> **Given that** you studied so little, it's surprising you passed.
> (I'm taking this fact into consideration.)
>
> **By the way**, have you heard the news about Sara?
> (This isn't connected to what we've been talking about.)
>
> **All in all**, finding an interesting job isn't easy.
> (I'm considering every part of the situation.)
>
> **At least** the room was cheap, even if the view was awful.
> (This is one good point, amongst the bad ones.)
>
> **Besides**, Jess doesn't really like chocolate.
> (This strong point makes the previous ones unnecessary.)
>
> **Above all**, we need to make this decision quickly.
> (This is the most important point to consider.)
>
> You'll need the receipt, **otherwise** you won't get a refund.
> (Because if you don't, this will be the result.)
>
> **Anyway**, it's up to you. So, should we leave now?
> (I'm concluding, and not talking about that anymore.)

UNIT 10

Reporting with passive verbs

We can report words and actions using the passive voice in various ways.

▶ 10.1 *It* + passive verb + *that* clause

It **is said** that Bet Molam, the writer, earns $1 million a year.
It **is reported** that she is living in a rented house in Malibu.
It **has been alleged** that she married her third husband last week.
It **is known** that she has been working on a new book.
It **is said** that the book is based on her experiences in the Far East.
It **is understood** that she has been given an advance of $500,000.

Other verbs that follow this pattern are:

agree	calculate	discover	hope	show
allege	claim	estimate	know	suggest
announce	consider	expect	presume	suppose
assume	decide	fear	propose	suspect
believe	declare	feel	recommend	think

With some verbs we can use an infinitive instead of a *that* clause.
It was **agreed** to buy the company for $500 million.
It is **hoped** to find a solution to the problem soon.
It has been **decided** to relocate.
It is **planned** to move our manufacturing plant to Mexico.

▶ 10.2 Subject + passive verb + infinitive

Bet Molam is said **to earn** $1 million a year. (Simple Present infinitive)
She is reported **to be living** in Malibu. (Present Continuous infinitive)
She is alleged **to have married** her third husband. (perfect infinitive)
She is known **to have been working** on a new book. (perfect continuous infinitive)
The book is said **to be based** on her experiences. (present passive infinitive)
She is understood **to have been given** an advance. (perfect passive infinitive)

Other verbs that follow this pattern are:

allege	consider	know	say	suspect
assume	estimate	presume	suggest	think
believe	expect	report	suppose	understand

Notice this transformation with *there*:
It is thought that there has been a plane crash this afternoon.
There is thought to have been a plane crash this afternoon.
It is estimated that there are one million unemployed.
There are estimated to be one million unemployed.

▶ 10.3 *seem* and *appear*

We can use *seem* and *appear* to give information without stating categorically that we know it to be true.

They can be used in two patterns.

1 *It + seem/appear + that* clause
> It **seems that** she's upset.
> It **appears that** she's crying.
> It **seems that** I made a mistake.
> It **appeared that** his car had been stolen.

2 Subject + *seem/appear* + infinitive
> She **seems to be** upset.
> She **appears to be crying**.
> I **seem to have made** a mistake.
> His car appears **to have been stolen**.

We can make the statement more tentative with the use of *would*.
It **would seem** the problem has been nipped in the bud.
I **would appear** to have mislaid my keys.

10.4 Tag questions

Tag questions and replies

It has been said that a solid grasp of the systems of auxiliaries is essential to mastery of spoken English.

Falling intonation

With a falling intonation on the tag, this is not a real question. It means "Agree with me; talk to me."

It's a beautiful day, isn't it?

The movie was great, wasn't it?

Note

We can reply to a statement with a tag question.
"Beautiful day today!" "Yes, it is, isn't it?"
"You're filthy!" "Yes, I am, aren't I?"
"Their kids have good appetites." "Yes, they do, don't they?"

Rising intonation

With a rising intonation on the tag, we really want to know something because we aren't sure of the answer.

You didn't say that to him, did you?

They wouldn't take my car away, would they?

Notes

• Notice the auxiliaries in these tag questions.
  Let's go, shall we?
  Give me a hand, will you?
  Don't forget to buy some milk, will you?
  Nobody called, did they?

• These tag questions can be used in requests.
  You couldn't lend me a few bucks, could you?
  You haven't seen Peter anywhere, have you?

Same way tag questions

These occur after affirmative sentences. The tag question is positive and the intonation rises. The speaker repeats what they have just heard and uses the tag question to express interest, surprise, concern, or some other reaction.

So you're Kevin's sister, are you? I've heard a lot about you.

So you like rap music, do you? Well, just listen to this.

 10.5 Replies

Short answers

Short answers are used in reply to *Yes/No* questions.
"Did you have a good time?" "Yes, I did. It was great."
"Have you been to Thailand?" "No, I haven't, but I'd like to."

Reply questions

We use reply questions to show interest and to show we're listening.
"I had a terrible day today." "Did you, sweetheart?"
"My boss was in a horrible mood today." "Was he?"

Avoiding repetition

This was dealt with in Unit 5.
"Who wants some ice cream?" "I do." (I want some ice cream.)
"Who came to the party?" "Everybody did."

UNIT 11

Future forms

English has several forms that express future events, and which one the user selects depends on how they see the event as much as its certainty or nearness to the present.

 11.1 *will*

Will can function as an auxiliary of the future in simply predicting a future event.
*The first lady **will open** the new hospital next Thursday.*
*Tomorrow **will be** warm and sunny everywhere.*
Will can also function as a modal auxiliary to express ideas of willingness and spontaneous intention.
***Will** you **help** me for a minute?*
*"There's no more milk!" "**I'll go** and get some."*

 11.2 *going to*

Going to expresses a premeditated intention.
***I'm going to paint** the bathroom this weekend.*
*The government **is going to build** a new monument in memory of the fallen war heroes.*
Going to is also used to predict a future event for which there is some evidence now.
*Great news! **I'm going to have** a baby!*
*The crowd is very angry. I think there**'s going to be** a riot.*

 11.3 The Present Continuous

The Present Continuous is used to express an arrangement, usually for the near future.
*"What **are you doing** tonight?" "**I'm going out** to eat."*
It is wrong to use the Simple Present in this sense. We cannot say **What do you do tonight?* or **Do you go to the party on Saturday?*

The Present Continuous cannot be used to express an event that has not been arranged by human beings. We cannot say **It is raining tomorrow.* or **The sun is rising at 5:00 tomorrow morning.*

 11.4 The Simple Present

The Simple Present is used to express a future event that is seen as being certain because of a timetable or calendar.
*What time **does** the movie **start**?*
*My train **gets in** at 11:00.*
*The World Championship **takes place** on April 13.*

11.5 The Future Continuous

The Future Continuous expresses an activity that will be in progress around a specific time in the future.
Don't call at 8:00. I'll be eating dinner.
At this time tomorrow, I'll be flying to Hong Kong.
The Future Continuous also expresses an action that will occur in the natural course of events, independently of the will or intention of anyone directly concerned.
In a few minutes, we will be landing at LAX. (Of course the pilot has not just decided this!)
Hurry up! The bus will be leaving any minute!
The Future Continuous is often used to express a casual or polite question about someone's future plans. The speaker is trying not to impose their will in any way. This is related to the use of the Future Continuous described above, i.e., that it can express an action that will occur independently of the will or intention of the people concerned.

Compare:
Will you bring Kate to the party? (Perhaps a request.)
Will you be bringing Kate to the party? (I'm just asking.)

11.6 The Future Perfect

The Future Perfect expresses an action that will be completed before a definite time in the future.
I'll have finished my work by the time you get back.
Most of the leaves will have fallen by the end of November.

11.7 is/are to

In formal contexts, an arrangement is sometimes referred to as something that *is to happen.* This usage is frequently found in news reports.
The first lady is to give the commencement speech at the local college this weekend.
World leaders are to meet in Geneva on Saturday.

11.8 The future in the past

Sometimes when we are talking about the past, we want to refer to something that was in the future at that time. This is called the "future in the past," and it is expressed by *was/were going to*, the Past Continuous, or *would*, and *was/were to. Would* is very common in reported speech and thought.
The last time I saw you, you were going to start a new job. Did you?
I was in a hurry because I was catching a plane that afternoon.
He said he'd give me a ride.
It was announced that the coach was to resign after the World Cup.
The uses of these four forms are exactly parallel to *going to*, the Present Continuous, and *will*, and *is/are to*, as used to refer to the real future.
I'm going to start a new job. (intention)
I'm catching a plane this afternoon. (arrangement)
I'll give you a ride. (offer)
The coach is to resign. (formal arrangement)
The future in the past is often found in narratives.
Alice smiled as she thought of the evening to come. She was meeting Peter, and together they were going to see a play at the Adelphi Theater. She was sure the evening would be enjoyable.

 UNIT 12

Linking devices

12.1 Result

so and such

It was raining, so we went home.
The play was so boring that I fell asleep.
It was such a boring movie that I fell asleep.

as a result, therefore, and consequently/as a consequence

As a result, therefore, and *consequently/as a consequence* can also express the result of something.
He worked hard all his life. As a result, he amassed a fortune.
The dollar has gone down against the yen. Therefore/Consequently,/As a consequence, Japanese goods are more expensive for Americans. (more formal)

thus

Thus is even more formal than *therefore* and is used in formal writing, often to draw a conclusion resulting from certain facts and evidence.
In tests, fewer than 1% of the devices were found to have this minor fault. Thus, it has not been deemed necessary to recall the product.

Participles

As we saw in Unit 8, participles can also express result.
He fell off his motorcycle, breaking his leg and injuring his arm.

Note
It is important to use a comma before *so* in order to produce the meaning of result. Without the comma, this meaning of *so* can easily be confused with that of purpose (when *so* is a shorter form of *so that*).
I studied German, so I could read Hesse's work in the original.
(The ability to read Hesse's work is a (possibly unintended) result of studying German.)
I studied German so I could read Hesse's work in the original.
(The ability to read Hesse's work is the reason why I studied German.)

12.2 Reason

as and since

As and *since* are used when the reason is already known to the listener/reader, or when it is not the most important part of the sentence.
As it was getting late, we decided it was time to leave.
Since he had very little money, James decided he should look for work.
Both these clauses are very formal. In an informal style, we would be more likely to use *so*.
It was getting late, so we decided it was time to leave.

because

Because puts more emphasis on the reason and most often introduces new information.
Because she was getting frail in her old age, she went to live with her daughter.
When the reason is the most important part of the sentence, the *because* clause usually comes at the end.
I went to live in Mexico City because I wanted to learn Spanish.

for

For introduces new information, but suggests that the reason is given as an afterthought. A *for* clause could almost be in parentheses.
We should plan ahead carefully, for the future is almost upon us.

because of, as a result of, due to, and owing to

Because of, *as a result of*, *due to*, and *owing to* can also express the cause of something.
*We had to stop playing tennis **because of** the weather.*
*Services have been cut **as a result of** the government's austerity policy.*
***Due to** the economic situation, fewer people are taking vacations this year.*
***Owing to** a lack of funds, the project will be discontinued next year.*

seeing as

Seeing as is an informal way of giving a reason for doing something, often used in spoken English.
***Seeing as** you've been so nice to me today, I'll give you a ride home.*

Participles

As we saw in Unit 8, participles can also express reason.
***Being** an inquisitive person, I love to start conversations with strangers.*
***Deprived** of oxygen, the animal soon died.*

12.3 Purpose

The infinitive

The infinitive on its own is the most common pattern in informal English for expressing purpose. *In order to* is a longer form of the infinitive of purpose, and *so as to* is a more formal version.

I went to Mexico	to learn in order to learn so as to learn	Spanish.

We cannot use the infinitive alone in the negative.

I tiptoed upstairs	*~~not to~~* so as not to in order not to	wake anyone up.

so (that)

We can use *so (that)* + *can/could* or *will/would* to express purpose. The *that* is often dropped in more informal contexts, in which case there is no comma before the *so*:
*Daylight Saving Time (DST) was introduced **so that** people could take advantage of the long summer evenings.*
*I went to bed at 9:00 **so** I could get up really early and prepare my talk.*
*I left for work early **so** I could avoid the rush hour.*
We also use *so (that)* when there is a change in subject.
*Henry called a taxi **so (that)** his daughter would arrive on time.*

12.4 Addition

also and and

Also and *and* are the most simple and common ways of adding a further point.

Contrary to widespread belief, it is perfectly good style to begin a sentence with *And*.
*Schoolchildren are often told, wrongly, that they shouldn't begin sentences with conjunctions. **And** this isn't the only myth about style that many teachers perpetuate. There's also …*
And can also be used together with another linking device that expresses addition.
*This car is one of the most comfortable we've tested. **And what's more**, it's very fast!*

furthermore, what's more, in addition to, and as well as

Furthermore and *in addition to* are more formal equivalents of *what's more*, and *as well as*.
*The software has proven its reliability in testing. **Furthermore**, it can run on a variety of networks.*
*Swimming's a great way to exercise without putting too much strain on the body. **What's more**, it's one of the cheapest sports you can do.*
***In addition to** the booking fee, there is a 2% surcharge for payment by credit card.*
***As well as** being fun, dancing is a good way to stay in shape.*

too

Also can be used at the end of a sentence, but *too* is more common in this position.
*We're going to Worton Farm Café for lunch. Nadine is coming **too**.*
The use of a comma before *too* at the end of a sentence is optional. By introducing a pause, it tends to add emphasis.
*They sell delicious sandwiches – and it's near my office, **too**!*

12.5 Contrast

but, although, though, and even though

But is the most common way of expressing contrast. *Even though* is more emphatic than *although*. *Though* is more formal than *although*.

There was a transit strike, **but** **Although** there was a transit strike,	most people managed to get to work.

***Even though** there weren't any trains, I was only an hour late.*
*The trip back home was all right, **though** it wasn't easy.*
Though can be used as a comment adverb.
*"That meal was expensive." "It was good, **though**."*

however, nevertheless, yet, all the same, and even so

All the same and *even so* express contrast informally, while *however*, *nevertheless*, and *yet* are more formal.

I know he's a difficult person.	**All the same,** **Even so,**	I'm very fond of him.

The results were very discouraging initially.	**However,** **Nevertheless,**	they persevered.

*The results were very discouraging, **yet** they persevered.*

in spite of and despite

In spite of and *despite* can also express contrast.

We enjoyed our picnic	**despite** the rain. **in spite of** the rain.

***Despite being** over 80, my grandmother enjoyed the party.*
If a verb form other than the gerund is used, *despite* and *in spite of* are followed by *the fact that* + subject.
***Despite the fact that** we checked the document several times, there were still some typing errors in it.*

while and whereas

While is commonly used to make a contrast.
While *the idea of writing my book on a Greek island is appealing, I'm not sure I'd get much work done!*

However, *while* is avoided for contrasts if the meaning could easily be confused with *while* for time and sequence, e.g.,
While *Mary enjoys baking cakes, I like to bake bread.*
It is better expressed as a contrast using *whereas*.
Whereas *Mary enjoys baking cakes, I like to bake bread.*

While can be used to make contrasting statements about the same subject, or different ones, but *whereas* always involves a contrast between two different subjects.
Whereas cats *tend to be reserved,* **dogs** *have no reservations about showing their owners affection.*

Notes

- In most contexts, *however* can be replaced with other contrast linkers (with a change of form in some cases).
  We were told that the area was dangerous. **However,/Nevertheless,/Even so,/In spite of this,** *we had no choice but to pass through it.*

- In some contexts though, only *however* should be used. This is the case when a contrast exists between two statements, but there is actually no possible causative link between them.
I needed to be at work by 8:00 this morning. **However,** *the train was late, and I didn't get there until 8:15.*

It would be wrong to say …
I needed to be at work by 8:00 this morning. ***Nevertheless,*** *the train was late, and I didn't get there until 8:15.*

… because there is no reason why my wishing to be at work on time should affect the punctuality of the train. Similarly, the train can't be late *in spite of* my wishes.

As was stated earlier regarding *and*, it isn't necessarily bad style to begin a sentence with *but*.

But can also be used along with another contrast linker (with the exception of *however*). This can be a useful way to avoid the need to begin a new sentence.
The weather was disappointing, **but nevertheless,/even so,/all the same,** *we had a wonderful time.*

 ## 12.6 Time and sequence

Linkers

The following linkers are conjunctions of time.
When *I saw the time, I realized I was late.*
As soon as *I got up, I took a shower.*
After *I took a shower, I got dressed.*

As / **While** | *I was getting dressed, I thought about the day to come.*

Before *I went to work, I read the mail.*
Once *I'd fed the cat, I left the house.*
I worked **until** *I had finished my report.*
I've been working on this project **since** *I joined the company.*

as soon as and the moment

These emphasize the immediacy with which one event follows another (and are therefore not used with continuous tenses).
As soon as *the alarm went off, she jumped out of bed.*
The moment *I saw him, I knew he was a troublemaker.*

by the time

The meaning of *by the time* means that clauses containing it are often accompanied by examples of the past perfect or future perfect.
By the time *we'd arrived, night had fallen.*
You'll have finished your class **by the time** *I see you again.*

meanwhile

Meanwhile is similar in meaning to *while*, but introduces a new sentence.
Whisk the eggs **while** *the butter is melting in the pan.*
Melt the butter in the pan. **Meanwhile,** *whisk the eggs.*

in the end

In the end has a particular meaning; it does not simply refer to a final action or event. It describes a final outcome that was different from the one intended.
We'd made plans for a three-week trip, but **in the end** *we could only get two weeks off work.*

Participles

As we saw in Unit 8, participles can also express links of time.
Grabbing *my briefcase, I left to catch my train.*
Having bought *a ticket, I went onto the platform.*

12.7 Condition

The following linkers are used to express a condition.

If *you want a few days off, let me know.*

Providing / **Provided** / **As long as** / **So long as** | *you keep it clean, you can stay in my apartment.*

Even if *I'm there, I don't mind.*
I'll presume you're coming **unless** *I hear from you.*
Whether *you come* **or not,** *it would be nice to see you soon.*

However *late it is,* / **No matter how** *late it is,* | *just call me.*
(no matter who/what/when …)
Supposing *you ever ran out of cash, I could help.*

in case/in case of

In case has a very different meaning from *if*.
I'll do X **if** *Y happens.*
(Y must happen first in order for X to happen.)
I'll do X **in case** *Y happens.*
(X happens first, and isn't dependent on Y happening. It is a precaution.)
We'll eat in the house **if** *it rains.*
We put up a canopy in the yard **in case** *it rains.*

In case of + noun is a formal construction that does mean the same as *if*. It is usually found in notices and regulations.
In case of *a fire, leave the building by the nearest fire exit.*

Phrasal Verbs

1 Multiple meanings
Phrasal verbs can have multiple meanings.

a She **worked out** the plot of her book. (= devise, plan)
b **Work out** how much I owe you. (= calculate)
c Their marriage didn't **work out**. (= wasn't successful)
d I'm sure you'll **work out** your differences. (= resolve)
e She **works out** at the gym every day. (= do physical exercise)

2 Degrees of metaphorical use
There can be different degrees of metaphorical use.

a **Take off** your coat.   **Literal**
b The sick sailor was **taken off** the ship.
c They're **taking** 10 percent **off** the retail price.
d We're **taking off** two weeks to travel this summer.
e The plane **took off**.
f His business is **taking off**.   **Metaphorical**

Sentence *f* is an example of transference, in that it derives from the meaning of *take off* in sentence *e*. This is typical of the way in which the meaning and use of phrasal verbs grow and change.

3 Transferred or metaphorical meanings
The transferred (or metaphorical) meanings of phrasal verbs are often derived from the literal meaning.

The court **stood up** when the judge came in. (literal)
You should **stand up for** what you believe in. (transferred)

Come around to the side door, please. (literal)
She's **coming around** to my point of view. (transferred)

She **gave away** her money. (literal)
Don't **give away** my secret. (transferred)

4 The grammar of phrasal verbs
There are four types of phrasal verbs.

Type 1: verb + adverb (no object)
a He **went out**. (literal)
b I didn't put enough wood on the fire, so it **went out**. (metaphorical)

Type 2: verb + adverb + object (separable)
a I **put up** the picture on the wall. (literal)
b I **put up** my sister for the night. (metaphorical)

Type 2 phrasal verbs are separable. The object (noun or person) can come between the verb and the adverb.
I **put** the picture **up**.   I **put** my sister **up**.

But if the object is a pronoun, it always comes between the verb and the adverb.
I **put** it **up**. (*I put up it.*)   I **put** her **up**. (*I put up her.*)

If the object is a long noun phrase, a noun with a qualifying clause, or a noun clause, the adverb comes immediately after the verb. This avoids the adverb being too far separated from the verb.
They **turned down** the majority of the applicants for the job.
She **told off** the children who had stolen her apples.
You should **think over** what I've been talking to you about.

Type 3: verb + preposition + object (inseparable)
a She **came across** the street. (literal)
b She **came across** an old letter while she was cleaning her desk. (metaphorical)

Type 3 phrasal verbs are inseparable. The object (noun or pronoun) always comes after the preposition even when it is a pronoun.
She **came across** a letter.
She **came across** it.   *She came it across.*

Type 4: verb + adverb + preposition + object
Don't just sit there! **Get on with** your work. (Continue with it.)
I have to **cut down on** my spending. (reduce)

Type 4 phrasal verbs are almost all metaphorical. The object cannot change position. It cannot come before the adverb or the preposition.
I'm looking forward to it.   *I'm looking forward it to.*

5 The meaning of certain particles
Phrasal verbs are difficult to learn because the combination of verb + particle can seem random. When we *take after* a parent or a family member, why is it *after*? Why is it *up* when we *put up with* a difficult situation? There is no apparent reason in these cases.

However, as shown on pages 25 & 59, it is sometimes possible to see consistent categories of meanings with the use of some particles, even though the differences between them are not always easy to discern and define.

An awareness of these meanings can help you to understand and remember certain phrasal verbs. It also makes it possible sometimes to figure out the meaning of unfamiliar phrasal verbs, including ones that are newly created as the language evolves. For example, one meaning of the particle *out* is "completely" or "to the limit."
I'm afraid we don't have any candles. We're **sold out**.
You've **worn** these jeans **out**. You need a new pair.
I'm going to bed. That walk really **tired** me **out**.

This meaning is commonly applied to verbs in a creative way, to suggest that we can't engage in any more of the activity suggested by the verb, having reached our limit. The verbs themselves are often created from nouns.
"Coffee?" "No, thanks. I'm **coffeed out**. I've had six cups today!"
We ate so much breakfast in the hotel. We really **pigged out**!

Here are some examples of the meanings of particles.

across
to find unexpectedly
    I **came across** these old photos in the attic.
    We **stumbled across** this vase in a thrift shop.
to communicate
    He's not good at **getting** his message **across**.
    She **comes across** as being arrogant.

back
to return
    We **drove back** a different way.
    If it's broken, **send** it **back**.
to reciprocate
    You're being bullied, and you need to **fight back**.
    You're six. Do as you're told and don't **talk back**!
to restrain
    I could see that she was **holding back** the tears.
    The police were trying to **keep** the crowd **back**.

in

to enter a place
> *Our new neighbors **moved in** last week.*
> *Someone **broke in** to our house and stole my laptop.*

to mix together
> ***Stir in** the milk until the mixture is smooth.*
> *You're very chic, so you'll **blend in** in Paris.*

out

to leave a place
> *Come on, let's **eat out** tonight.*
> *We **slipped out** when no one was looking.*

to withdraw
> *He **pulled out** of the race due to an illness.*
> *I **dropped out** of college and got a job.*

to reach a solution
> *I finally **found out** why he was so hostile.*
> *Have you **worked out** the answer yet?*

to become public
> *The movie **comes out** on DVD in June.*
> *The news **got out** that they'd gotten engaged.*

to reach the limit
> *Dinosaurs **died out** after a meteor strike.*
> *You really **lucked out** with this job!*

over

to be finished
> *Jo's got a new boyfriend, Sam. It**'s over**.*
> *You can invite Jo. I**'m over** her now.*

to analyze
> ***Check over** your work very carefully.*
> *Don't decide now. You should **think** it **over**.*

to transfer
> *She's **taken over** responsibility for the account.*
> *The salesperson **handed over** the keys to the car.*

up/down
See p. 25

on/off
See p. 59

6 Register

Learners of English are sometimes given the impression that phrasal verbs are used mainly in informal spoken English. This is misleading. There are some phrasal verbs that are distinctly informal, e.g., *to hang out with a friend*, but in these cases the informality is as much to do with the choice of verbs as the fact that they come with a particle. There are a large number of phrasal verbs that are frequently found in formal contexts, e.g., news reports and academic writing.

It is true that many phrasal verbs have one-word synonyms that are more formal in register (usually because they are of Latinate origin), e.g.,
to put up with = to tolerate
to leave out = to omit
to give away = to donate

This is why some non-native speakers of English can sound excessively formal when speaking as a result of using the Latinate form that they are more familiar with instead of the equivalent phrasal verb.

In many cases, the Latinate form is indeed more likely to be found in formal writing. In others, the phrasal verb will be used because the Latinate equivalent can sound *overly* formal.
*The results of the investigation showed that the train had been **slowing down** prior to the derailment.* (not ***decelerating***)

Sometimes phrasal verbs are used in more formal contexts because there is no suitable equivalent. Any available equivalents may be long-winded, very low frequency, or simply unable to capture the same meaning.
*The president's deputy is to **stand in for** him at the forthcoming climate conference.* (not ***act as his replacement***)
*The opposition leader asked to see the cost of the project **broken down**.* (not ***separated into component parts***)
*But Lady Mount Severn had not **brought** him **up** to be dutiful.* (not ***raised***)

Word List

UNIT 1

act *n* /ækt/
adoration *n* /ˌædəˈreɪʃn/
affectionate *adj* /əˈfɛkʃənət/
all along *idiom* /ɔl əˈlɔŋ/
animal kingdom *n* /ˈænəml ˈkɪŋdəm/
anthropologist *n* /ˌænθrəˈpalədʒɪst/
anticipate *v* /ænˈtɪsəpeɪt/
anxiety *n* /æŋˈzaɪəti/
ape *n* /eɪp/
astonishment *n* /əˈstanɪʃmənt/
attempt *n* /əˈtɛmpt/
awkward *adj* /ˈɔkwərd/
ballad *n* /ˈbæləd/
bleed *v* /blid/
blow (somebody) away *idiom* /bloʊ (…) əˈweɪ/
blush *v* /blʌʃ/
boastfulness *n* /ˈboʊstflnəs/
book bag *n* /ˈbʊk bæg/
capacity *n* /kəˈpæsəti/
carriage *n* /ˈkærɪdʒ/
cart *n* /kart/
check *v* /tʃɛk/
chief *adj* /tʃif/
cold caller *n* /koʊld ˈkɔlər/
comb *v* /koʊm/
couch potato *n, coll* /ˌkaʊtʃ pəˈteɪtoʊ/
cram *v* /kræm/
crawl *v* /krɔl/
curiosity *n* /ˌkyʊriˈasəti/
dexterity *n* /dɛkˈstɛrəti/
diaper *n* /ˈdaɪpər/
digest *v* /daɪˈdʒɛst/
disappointment *n* /ˌdɪsəˈpɔɪntmənt/
dismayed *adj* /dɪsˈmeɪd/
empathy *n* /ˈɛmpəθi/
enable *v* /ɪˈneɪbl/
ensure *v* /ɪnˈʃʊr/
eventful *adj* /ɪˈvɛntfl/
feat of *n* /fit əv/
fencing *n* /ˈfɛnsɪŋ/
flatter *v* /ˈflætər/
flourish *v* /ˈflɔrɪʃ/
follicle *n* /ˈfalɪkl/
forebears *n* /ˈfɔrbɛrz/
free up *v* /fri ʌp/
function *n* /ˈfʌŋkʃn/
fury *n* /ˈfyʊri/
fuss *n* /fʌs/
gesture *n* /ˈdʒɛstʃər/
get through to *v* /gɛt θru tə/
gratitude *n* /ˈgrætəˌtud/
gut *n* /gʌt/
heartbroken *adj* /ˈhart,broʊkən/
hectic *adj* /ˈhɛktɪk/
high heels *n* /haɪ hilz/
imply *v* /ɪmˈplaɪ/

indignation *n* /ˌɪndɪgˈneɪʃn/
infant *n* /ˈɪnfənt/
insomnia *n* /ɪnˈsamniə/
irritation *n* /ˌɪrɪˈteɪʃn/
keep up *v* /kip ʌp/
kick yourself *idiom* /kɪk yərˈsɛlf/
locomotion *n* /ˌloʊkəˈmoʊʃn/
lose it *idiom* /luz ɪt/
make up *v* /ˈmeɪk ʌp/
manly *adj* /ˈmænli/
mean the world *idiom* /min ðə wərld/
merely *adv* /ˈmɪrli/
mistress *n* /ˈmɪstrəs/
mode of *n* /moʊd əv/
modesty *n* /ˈmadəsti/
morality *n* /məˈræləti/
naked *adj* /ˈneɪkəd/
nose *n* /noʊz/
oath *n* /oʊθ/
oblivion *n* /əˈblɪviən/
paradox *n* /ˈpærəˌdaks/
pelvis *n* /ˈpɛlvəs/
perplexing *adj* /pərˈplɛksɪŋ/
pick a fight *idiom* /pɪk ə faɪt/
pick on *v* /ˈpɪk an/
play date *n* /pleɪ deɪt/
portly *adj* /ˈpɔrtli/
posture *n* /ˈpastʃər/
pot belly *n* /ˌpat ˈbɛli/
precisely *adv* /prɪˈsaɪsli/
put our heads together *idiom* /pʊt ar hɛdz təˈgɛðər/
put (somebody) down *v* /ˈpʊt (…) daʊn/
puzzling *adj* /ˈpʌzlɪŋ/
rather *adv* /ˈræðər/
reassurance *n* /ˌriəˈʃʊrəns/
relative to *adj* /ˈrɛlətɪv tə/
rely on *v* /rɪˈlaɪ an/
reproduce *v* /ˌriprəˈdus/
sarcasm *n* /ˈsarkæzəm/
scene *n* /sin/
scrape *v* /skreɪp/
set (something) apart *v* /sɛt (…) əˈpart/
shift *v* /ʃɪft/
sigh *v* /saɪ/
slam *v* /slæm/
sleep in late *idiom* /ˈslip ɪn leɪt/
sleepover *n* /ˈslip,oʊvər/
so far *idiom* /soʊ far/
social bond *n* /ˈsoʊʃl band/
spirituality *n* /ˌspɪrətʃuˈæləti/
status *n* /ˈstætəs/
stir *v* /stər/
stop by *v* /stap baɪ/
suit yourself *idiom* /sut yərˈsɛlf/
symbolic *adj* /sɪmˈbalɪk/
teeter *v* /ˈtitər/
tell me another one *idiom* /tɛl mi əˈnʌðər wʌn/
territorial *adj* /ˌtɛrəˈtɔriəl/

think highly of yourself *idiom* /ˈθɪŋk haɪli əv yərˈsɛlf/
think on your feet *idiom* /θɪŋk an yər fit/
thrilled to pieces *idiom* /θrɪld tə ˌpisəz/
thrive *v* /θraɪv/
tool *n* /tul/
trace *n* /treɪs/
trait *n* /treɪt/
transmission *n* /trænsˈmɪʃn/
unite *v* /yʊˈnaɪt/
unwillingly *adv* /ʌnˈwɪlɪŋli/
vocal *adj* /ˈvoʊkl/
woeful *adj* /ˈwoʊfl/
works *n* /wərks/
yet *conj* /yɛt/

UNIT 2

a man of few words *idiom* /ə mæn əv fyu wərdz/
acknowledge *v* /əkˈnalɪdʒ/
affair *n* /əˈfɛr/
alas *adv* /əˈlæs/
appoint *v* /əˈpɔɪnt/
apprehensive *adj* /ˌæprɪˈhɛnsɪv/
arched *adj* /artʃt/
articulate *adj* /arˈtɪkyəˌleɪt/
at a loss for words *idiom* /æt ə ˈlɔs fər wərdz/
at the end of the day *idiom* /æt ðə ɛnd əv ðə deɪ/
avoid (something/somebody) like the plague *idiom* /əˈvɔɪd (…) laɪk ðə pleɪg/
awfully *adv* /ˈɔfli/
be flooded with *idiom* /bi ˈflʌdəd wɪð/
become of *v* /bɪˈkʌm əv/
belief *n* /bɪˈlif/
bitterly *adv* /ˈbɪtərli/
bleach *v* /blitʃ/
blindingly *adv* /ˈblaɪndɪŋli/
bodice *n* /ˈbadəs/
breathe a word *idiom* /brið ə wərd/
busybody *n* /ˈbɪzibadi/
buzzword *n* /ˈbʌzwərd/
by word of mouth *idiom* /baɪ wərd əv maʊð/
chic *adj* /ʃik/
choreograph *v* /ˈkɔriəgræf/
cliché *n* /ˈkliʃeɪ/
Cockney *n* /ˈkakni/
cocky *adj, coll* /ˈkaki/
come to *v* /kʌm tə/
come to be *idiom* /kʌm tə ˈbi/
compassionate *adj* /kəmˈpæʃənət/

condescending *adj* /kandəˈsɛndɪŋ/
confess *v* /kənˈfɛs/
constitute *v* /ˈkanstətut/
craftsman *n* /ˈkræftsmən/
crop *v* /krap/
deliberately *adv* /dɪˈlɪbrətli/
derelict *adj* /ˈdɛrəlɪkt/
desperately *adv* /ˈdɛsprətli/
dimple *n* /ˈdɪmpl/
diphtheria *n* /dɪfˈθɪriə/
dirt *n* /dərt/
divine *adj* /dəˈvaɪn/
do *n* /du/
do (somebody) in *v* /du (…) ɪn/
docile *adj* /ˈdasl/
dreary *adj* /ˈdrɪri/
eagerly *adv* /ˈigərli/
eat your words *idiom* /it yər wərdz/
editor *n* /ˈɛdətər/
fade *v* /feɪd/
fatally *adv* /ˈfeɪtəli/
flattery *n* /ˈflætəri/
flower girl *n* /ˈflaʊər gərl/
from the word go *idiom* /frʌm ðə wərd goʊ/
funny *adj* /ˈfʌni/
furtively *adv* /ˈfərtɪvli/
genteel *adj* /dʒɛnˈtil/
get a word in edgewise *idiom* /gɛt ə wərd ɪn ˈɛdʒwaɪz/
glamorous *adj* /ˈglæmərəs/
go over *v* /goʊ ˈoʊvər/
graveyard *n* /ˈgreɪvyard/
haughty *adj* /ˈhɔti/
have the face to *idiom* /həv ðə feɪs tə/
high-society *adj* /haɪ səˈsaɪəti/
hitchhiker *n* /ˈhɪtʃ haɪkər/
honor *n* /ˈanər/
humdrum *n* /ˈhʌmdrʌm/
hunk *n* /hʌŋk/
imposing *adj* /ɪmˈpoʊzɪŋ/
impressionable *adj* /ɪmˈprɛʃənəbl/
Impressionist *n* /ɪmˈprɛʃənɪst/
in want of *idiom* /ɪn want əv/
inevitable *adj* /ɪnˈɛvətəbl/
insist *v* /ɪnˈsɪst/
instinct *n* /ˈɪnstɪŋkt/
jot down *v* /dʒat daʊn/
lacing *n* /leɪsɪŋ/
literary *adj* /ˈlɪtəreri/
longingly *adv* /ˈlɔŋɪŋli/
Lothario *n* /ləˈθarioʊ/
not mince words *idiom* /nat mɪns yər wərdz/
muffled *adj* /ˈmʌfld/
mumble *v* /ˈmʌmbl/
mythology *n* /mɪˈθalədʒi/
naive *adj* /naɪˈiv/

not know the meaning of the
word *idiom* /nɑt noʊ ðə ˈminɪŋ
əv ðə wərd/
of no consequence *idiom* /ʌv noʊ
ˈkɑnsəkwɛns/
pass off as *v* /pæs ɔf əz/
pedant *n* /ˈpɛdnt/
phonetics *n* /fəˈnɛtɪks/
phonology *n* /fəˈnɑlədʒi/
pinch *v, coll* /pɪntʃ/
playwright *n* /ˈpleɪraɪt/
ramble on *v* /ˈræmbl ɑn/
revolting *adj* /rɪˈvoʊltɪŋ/
rhetorical question *n* /rɪˈtɔrɪkl
ˈkwɛstʃən/
roll *n* /roʊl/
row house *n* /ˈroʊ haʊs/
saucy *adj* /ˈsɔsi/
say the word *idiom* /seɪ ðə wərd/
scaffold *n* /ˈskæfəld/
screen *n* /skrin/
sculpt *v* /skʌlpt/
selfie *n* /ˈsɛlfi/
severely *adv* /sɪˈvɪrli/
show up *v* /ʃoʊ ʌp/
slab *n* /slæb/
slyly *adv* /ˈslaɪli/
sneak out *v* /snik aʊt/
snigger *v* /ˈsnɪgər/
sorely *adv* /ˈsɔrli/
soul *n* /soʊl/
split *v* /splɪt/
spy *n* /spaɪ/
stand a chance *idiom* /stænd ə
tʃæns/
steer clear of *v* /stɪr klɪr əv/
straightforward *adj*
/streɪtˈfɔrwərd/
strain *n* /streɪn/
straw *n* /strɔ/
stride *n* /straɪd/
strike *v* /straɪk/
subject *n* /ˈsʌbdʒɛkt/
take it or leave it *idiom* /teɪk ɪt
ɔr liv ɪt/
take over *v* /ˈteɪk oʊvər/
take (something) in *v* /teɪk (…)
ɪn/
tap *v* /tæp/
tarnish *v* /ˈtɑrnɪʃ/
tattered *adj* /ˈtætərd/
the coast is clear *idiom* /ðə koʊst
ɪz klɪr/
have the last word *idiom* /həv ðə
læst wərd/
the Middle Ages *n* /ðə ˈmɪdl
eɪdʒəz/
throat *n* /θroʊt/
transcribe *v* /trænˈskraɪb/
treacherous *adj* /ˈtrɛtʃərəs/
underprivileged *adj*
/ˌʌndərˈprɪvəlɪdʒd/
utterly *adv* /ˈʌtərli/
vehemently *adv* /ˈviəməntli/
virtually *adv* /ˈvərtʃuəli/
virus *n* /ˈvaɪrəs/
vulnerable *adj* /ˈvʌlnərəbl/
whole-grain *adj* /ˈhoʊl greɪn/

UNIT 3

a rising tide lifts all boats *idiom* /ə
ˈraɪzɪŋ taɪd lɪfts ɔl ˈboʊts/
a win-win situation *idiom* /ə wɪn
wɪn ˌsɪtʃuˈeɪʃn/
action *v* /ˈækʃn/
affluent *adj* /ˈæfluənt/
alternative *n* /ɔlˈtərnətɪv/
anonymous *adj* /əˈnɑnəməs/
assessment *n* /əˈsɛsmənt/
at a time *idiom* /æt ə taɪm/
attitude *n* /ˈætətud/
authorize *v* /ˈɔθəraɪz/
average *adj* /ˈævərɪdʒ/
avoid *v* /əˈvɔɪd/
be hooked on *v* /bi hʊkt ɑn/
be on somebody's radar *idiom* /bi
ɑn (…) ˈreɪdɑr/
beneficiary *n* /ˌbɛnəˈfɪʃiˌɛri/
benefit *v* /ˈbɛnəfɪt/
best practice *n* /bɛst ˈpræktəs/
boot up *v* /ˌbut ˈʌp/
bring somebody up to speed
idiom /brɪŋ (…) ʌp tə spid/
bring something to the table
idiom /brɪŋ (…) tə ðə ˈteɪbl/
broadly *adv* /ˈbrɔdli/
brush up *v* /brʌʃ ʌp/
charitable foundation *n*
/ˈtʃærətəbl faʊnˈdeɪʃn/
coin *n* /kɔɪn/
collapse *v* /kəˈlæps/
cut down *v* /kʌt daʊn/
debt *n* /dɛt/
delusion *n* /dɪˈluʒn/
donate *v* /ˈdoʊneɪt/
dress down *v* /drɛs daʊn/
dress up *v* /drɛs ʌp/
drill down *v* /drɪl daʊn/
dumb down *v* /dʌm daʊn/
duty-free *adj* /ˈduti fri/
eccentric *adj* /ɪkˈsɛntrɪk/
economic growth *n* /ˌɛkəˈnɑmɪk
ˈgroʊθ/
efficiently *adv* /ɪˈfɪʃntli/
element of *n, coll* /ˈɛləmənt əv/
embarrassing *adj* /ɪmˈbærəsɪŋ/
establishment *n* /ɪˈstæblɪʃmənt/
estimate *v* /ˈɛstəˌmeɪt/
extravagant *adj* /ɪkˈstrævəgənt/
extreme *adj* /ɪkˈstrim/
fall on hard times *idiom* /fɔl ɑn
hard taɪmz/
figure out *v* /ˈfɪgyər aʊt/
fix up *v* /ˈfɪks ʌp/
fluctuate *v* /ˈflʌktʃueɪt/
gap *n* /gæp/
give away *v* /ˈgɪv əweɪ/
give people a heads-up *idiom* /gɪv
ˈpipl ə hɛdz ʌp/
give up *v* /gɪv ʌp/
go the extra mile *idiom* /goʊ ðə
ˈɛkstrə maɪl/
going forward *v* /ˈgoʊɪŋ
ˈfɔrwərd/
good causes *n* /gʊd kɔzəz/
gradual *adj* /ˈgrædʒuəl/
grateful *adj* /ˈgreɪtfl/

grow the business *v* /groʊ ðə
ˈbɪznəs/
hardship *n* /ˈhardʃɪp/
have it tough *idiom* /həv ɪt tʌf/
hit the ground running *idiom* /hɪt
ðə graʊnd ˈrʌnɪŋ/
hooked *adj* /hʊkt/
household *n* /ˈhaʊshoʊld/
impact (something) *v* /ɪmˈpækt
(…)/
in full swing *idiom* /ɪn fʊl swɪŋ/
income *n* /ˈɪnkʌm/
inequality *n* /ˌɪniˈkwɑləti/
inflation *n* /ɪnˈfleɪʃn/
interest rate *n* /ˈɪntrest reɪt/
issue *n* /ˈɪʃu/
keep (somebody) in the loop
idiom /kip (…) ɪn ðə lup/
let (somebody) down *v* /ˈlɛt (…)
daʊn/
life expectancy *n* /ˈlaɪf
ɪkˌspɛktənsi/
literate *adj* /ˈlɪtərət/
live down *v* /lɪv daʊn/
living standards *n pl* /ˈlɪvɪŋ
ˈstændərdz/
median *adj* /ˈmidiən/
mess around with *v* /mɛs əˈraʊnd
wɪð/
midlife *n* /mɪdˈlaɪf/
mission-critical *adj* /ˈmɪʃn
ˈkrɪtɪkl/
modest *adj* /ˈmɑdəst/
payback *n* /ˈpeɪbæk/
peak *n* /pik/
philanthropy *n* /fəˈlænθrəpi/
pick up *v* /ˈpɪk ʌp/
piece of the pie *idiom* /ˈpis əv
ðə paɪ/
pin down *v* /pɪn daʊn/
plaque *n* /plæk/
plummet *v* /ˈplʌmət/
plunge *v* /plʌndʒ/
poverty *n* /ˈpɑvərti/
presumably *adv* /prɪˈzuməbli/
progress *n* /ˈprɑgrɛs/
proportion *n* /prəˈpɔrʃn/
prosperous *adj* /ˈprɑspərəs/
public functions *n* /ˈpʌblɪk
ˈfʌŋkʃnz/
radical *adj* /ˈrædɪkl/
rags to riches *idiom* /ˈrægz tə
ˈrɪtʃəz/
rate *n* /reɪt/
recall *v* /rɪˈkɔl/
redistribution *n* /ridɪstrɪˈbyuʃn/
relatively *adv* /ˈrɛlətɪvli/
remain *v* /rɪˈmeɪn/
remarkable *adj* /rɪˈmɑrkəbl/
rocket *v* /ˈrɑkət/
set out to *v* /sɛt aʊt tə/
set to *v* /sɛt tə/
share prices *n* /ʃɛr praɪsəz/
sharp *adj* /ʃɑrp/
shelter *n* /ˈʃɛltər/
shut down *v* /ʃʌt daʊn/
significantly *adv* /sɪgˈnɪfəkəntli/
slightly *adv* /ˈslaɪtli/
soar *v* /sɔr/

speed up *v* /ˈspid ʌp/
spoiled *adj* /spɔɪld/
stable *adj* /ˈsteɪbl/
stand down *v* /stænd daʊn/
steady *adj* /ˈstɛdi/
stressful *adj* /ˈstrɛsfl/
strict *adj* /strɪkt/
strive *v* /straɪv/
substantial *adj* /səbˈstænʃl/
task somebody *v* /tæsk ˈsʌmbɑdi/
tax revenue *n* /tæks ˈrɛvənu/
think outside the box *idiom* /θɪŋk
ˈaʊtsaɪd ðə bɑks/
throw away *v* /ˈθroʊ əweɪ/
touch base *idiom* /tʌtʃ beɪs/
track down *v* /træk daʊn/
trade-off *n* /ˈtreɪdɔf/
tragic *adj* /ˈtrædʒɪk/
transform *v* /trænsˈfɔrm/
trend *n* /trɛnd/
trickle-down effect *idiom* /ˈtrɪkl
daʊn ɪˈfɛkt/
turn up *v* /ˈtərn ʌp/
use up *v* /yuz ʌp/
wake up and smell the coffee *idiom* /weɪk ʌp ənd smɛl ðə ˈkɔfi/
wind up *idiom* /ˈwaɪnd ʌp/

UNIT 4

amusingly *adv* /əˈmyuzɪŋli/
alcoholic *n* /ˌælkəˈhɔlɪk/
alter *v* /ˈɔltər/
basis *n* /ˈbeɪsɪs/
bedridden *adj* /ˈbɛdrɪdn/
bishop *n* /ˈbɪʃəp/
blow *n* /bloʊ/
clown *n* /klaʊn/
cold feet *n* /koʊld fit/
comedian *n* /kəˈmidiən/
contestant *n* /kənˈtɛstənt/
contort *v* /kənˈtɔrt/
contract *n* /ˈkɑntrækt/
court *n* /kɔrt/
crate *n* /kreɪt/
criminal justice system *n*
/ˈkrɪmənl ˈdʒʌstəs ˈsɪstəm/
deduction *n* /dɪˈdʌkʃn/
delude *v* /dɪˈlud/
detailed *adj* /dɪˈteɪld/
disguise *v* /dɪsˈgaɪz/
document *n* /ˈdɑkyəmənt/
eager *adj* /ˈigər/
eliminate *v* /ɪˈlɪməneɪt/
expose *v* /ɪkˈspoʊz/
eyewitness *n* /ˈaɪwɪtnəs/
fairy *n* /ˈfɛri/
fill in *v* /fɪl ɪn/
final straw *n* /ˈfaɪnl strɔ/
fine line *n* /faɪn laɪn/
folder *n* /ˈfoʊldər/
foregone conclusion *n* /ˈfɔrgɔn
kənˈkluʒn/
formative *adj* /ˈfɔrmətɪv/
frustrated *adj* /frʌˈstreɪtəd/
go on *v* /goʊ ɑn/
gray area *n* /ˌgreɪ ˈɛriə/

guidelines *n pl* /ˈgaɪdlaɪnz/
hand grenade *n* /ˈhænd grəneɪd/
handcuffs *n pl* /ˈhændkʌfs/
harbor *n* /ˈhɑrbər/
hospital trolley *n* /ˈhɑspɪtl trɑli/
hypochondriac *n* /ˌhaɪpəˈkɑndriæk/
illusionist *n* /ɪˈluʒənɪst/
inauspicious *adj* /ˌɪnɔˈspɪʃəs/
insanity *n* /ɪnˈsænəti/
itchy feet *n* /ˈɪtʃi fit/
justified *adj* /ˈdʒʌstəfaɪd/
last resort *n* /læst rɪˈzɔrt/
level playing field *idiom* /ˈlɛvl ˈpleɪɪŋ fild/
likelihood *n* /ˈlaɪklihʊd/
long shot *n* /ˈlɔŋ ʃɑt/
lost cause *idiom* /ˌlɔst ˈkɔz/
make an impression *n* /meɪk ən ɪmˈprɛʃn/
medium *n* /ˈmidiəm/
mistaken *adj* /mɪˈsteɪkən/
mixed blessing *n* /ˌmɪkst ˈblɛsɪŋ/
offend *v* /əˈfɛnd/
outcome *n* /ˈaʊtkʌm/
outcry *n* /ˈaʊtkraɪ/
paradoxical *adj* /ˌpærəˈdɑksɪkl/
problematic *adj* /ˌprɑbləˈmætɪk/
purely *adv* /ˈpyʊrli/
raw deal *n* /rɔ dil/
saving grace *n* /ˌseɪvɪŋ ˈgreɪs/
seance *n* /ˈseɪɑns/
second thought *n* /ˈsɛkənd θɔt/
sham *n* /ˈʃæm/
shore *n* /ˈʃɔr/
slippery slope *n* /ˈslɪpəri sloʊp/
smuggle *v* /ˈsmʌgl/
so-called *adj* /soʊ ˈkɔld/
sore spot *n* /ˈsɔr spɑt/
specimen beaker *n* /ˈspɛsəmən ˈbikər/
spirit *n* /ˈspɪrət/
stage *n* /ˈsteɪdʒ/
statement *n* /ˈsteɪtmənt/
straitjacket *n* /ˈstreɪtˌdʒækət/
strike *n* /straɪk/
supernatural phenomena *n pl* /ˌsupərˈnætʃrəl fəˈnɑmənə/
take turns *idiom* /teɪk tɜrnz/
temporary *adj* /ˈtɛmpəˌrɛri/
thoughtful *adj* /ˈθɔtfl/
uncanny *adj* /ʌnˈkæni/
wake-up call *n* /weɪk ʌp kɔl/
wishful thinking *n* /ˌwɪʃfl ˈθɪŋkɪŋ/
withstand *v* /wɪðˈstænd/

UNIT 5

administer *v* /ədˈmɪnəstər/
advent *n* /ˈædvɛnt/
astounded *adj* /əˈstaʊndəd/
awesome *adj* /ˈɔsəm/
barren *adj* /ˈbærən/
bathrobe *n* /ˈbæθroʊb/
bill *n BRE* /bɪl/
biscuit *n BRE* /ˈbɪskət/

bombard *v* /bɑmˈbɑrd/
broad-mindedness *n* /ˌbrɔd ˈmaɪndədnəs/
browse *v* /braʊz/
cannibalism *n* /ˈkænəbəlɪzəm/
carcinogenic *adj* /ˌkɑrsənəˈdʒɛnɪk/
caution *n* /ˈkɔʃn/
check *n* /tʃɛk/
chemist's *n BRE* /ˈkɛmɪsts/
chew *v* /tʃu/
choke *v* /tʃoʊk/
circumstance *n* /ˈsɜrkəmˌstæns/
civilized *adj* /ˈsɪvəˌlaɪzd/
concession *n* /kənˈsɛʃn/
consensus *n* /kənˈsɛnsəs/
courtroom *n* /ˈkɔrtrʊm/
crisps *n pl BRE* /krɪsps/
cupboard *n BRE* /ˈkʌbərd/
decline *v* /dɪˈklaɪn/
dedicate *v* /ˈdɛdəˌkeɪt/
delicacy *n* /ˈdɛlɪkəsi/
diminutive stature *idiom* /dɪˈmɪnyətɪv ˈstætʃər/
diverse *adj* /dəˈvɜrs/
doll *n* /dɑl/
dowry *n* /ˈdaʊri/
dressing gown *n BRE* /ˈdrɛsɪŋ gaʊn/
dutifully *adv* /ˈdutɪfli/
endanger *v* /ɪnˈdeɪndʒər/
enormity *n* /ɪˈnɔrməti/
ever-encroaching *adj* /ˈɛvər ɪnˈkroʊtʃɪŋ/
fall *n BRE* /fɔl/
frisson *n* /friˈsɔn/
gambit *n* /ˈgæmbət/
garden *n BRE* /ˈgɑrdn/
grandeur *n* /ˈgrændʒər/
headhunting *n* /ˈhɛdhʌntɪŋ/
indifferent *adj* /ɪnˈdɪfrənt/
inedible *adj* /ɪnˈɛdəbl/
interpret *v* /ɪnˈtɜrprət/
intriguing *adj* /ɪnˈtrigɪŋ/
isolated *adj* /ˈaɪsəˌleɪtəd/
jaded *adj* /ˈdʒeɪdəd/
kin *n* /kɪn/
knot *n* /nɑt/
license number *n, coll* /ˈlaɪsns ˈnʌmbər/
lift *n BRE* /lɪft/
llama *n* /ˈlɑmə/
log off *v* /lɑg ˈɔf/
low-key *adj* /ˌloʊ ˈki/
motorway *n BRE* /ˈmoʊtər weɪ/
on second thought *idiom* /ɑn ˈsɛkənd θɔt/
outgoing *adj* /ˈaʊtˌgoʊɪŋ/
pants *n* /pænts/
pavement *n BRE* /ˈpeɪvmənt/
pin *n* /pɪn/
pinpoint accuracy *idiom* /ˈpɪnpɔɪnt ˈækyərəsi/
polygamy *n* /pəˈlɪgəmi/
postcode *n BRE* /ˈpoʊstkoʊd/
rake *v* /reɪk/
random *adj* /ˈrændəm/
renounce *v* /rɪˈnaʊns/
robustly *adv* /roʊˈbʌstli/

routine procedure *idiom* /ruˈtin prəˈsidʒər/
rubbish *n BRE* /ˈrʌbɪʃ/
rude *adj* /rud/
rural *adj* /ˈrʊrəl/
spear *n* /spɪr/
speed bump *n* /spid bʌmp/
spouse *n* /spaʊs/
stalk *v* /stɔk/
stamping ground *n* /ˈstæmpɪŋ graʊnd/
stereotype *n* /ˈstɛriəˌtaɪp/
stumble across *idiom* /ˈstʌmbl əˈkrɔs/
swearing *n* /ˈswɛrɪŋ/
tap *n BRE* /tæp/
tick *v* /tɪk/
toll *n* /toʊl/
transaction *n* /trænˈzækʃn/
tribe *n* /traɪb/
trousers *n BRE* /ˈtraʊzərz/
unfold *v* /ʌnˈfoʊld/
urban *adj* /ˈɜrbən/
venture forth *idiom* /ˈvɛntʃər ˈfɔrθ/
wild boar *n* /waɪld ˈbɔr/
windscreen *n BRE* /ˈwɪndskrin/
witness *n* /ˈwɪtnəs/
zip code *n* /ˈzɪp koʊd/

 ## UNIT 6

aerial *adj* /ˈɛriəl/
bombardment *n* /bɑmˈbɑrdmənt/
affliction *n* /əˈflɪkʃn/
aftermath *n* /ˈæftərˌmæθ/
allocate *v* /ˈæləˌkeɪt/
anarchist *n* /ˈænərkɪst/
armored tank *n* /ˈɑrmərd tæŋk/
at the stroke of *idiom* /æt ðə stroʊk əv/
automatically *adv* /ˌɔtəˈmætɪkli/
baffling *adj* /ˈbæflɪŋ/
barbed wire *n* /ˌbɑrbd ˈwaɪər/
be due to (something) *idiom* /bi du tə (…)/
bleak *adj* /blik/
break out *v* /ˈbreɪk aʊt/
bury *v* /ˈbɛri/
carol *n* /ˈkærəl/
casualty *n* /ˈkæʒəlti/
charge *n* /tʃɑrdʒ/
civil *adj* /ˈsɪvl/
civilian *n* /səˈvɪlyən/
clot *v* /klɑt/
coin *v* /kɔɪn/
come about *idiom* /kʌm əˈbaʊt/
comeback *n* /ˈkʌmbæk/
commander *n* /kəˈmændər/
course *n* /kɔrs/
cutback *n* /ˈkʌtbæk/
debate *n* /dɪˈbeɪt/
depot *n* /ˈdipoʊ/
despair *n* /dɪˈspɛr/
devastating *adj* /ˈdɛvəˌsteɪtɪŋ/
digestive *adj* /daɪˈdʒɛstɪv/
digestive disorder *n* /dɪˈdʒɛstɪv dɪsˈɔrdər/

disfigure *v* /dɪsˈfɪgyər/
donor *n* /ˈdoʊnər/
draft *n* /dræft/
dress code *n* /drɛs koʊd/
dump *v* /dʌmp/
ease *v* /iz/
election *n* /ɪˈlɛkʃn/
emancipation *n* /ɪˌmænsəˈpeɪʃn/
familiar *adj* /fəˈmɪlyər/
fire *v* /ˈfaɪər/
fly in the face of *idiom* /flaɪ ɪn ðə feɪs əv/
forces *n pl* /ˈfɔrsəz/
full of yourself *idiom* /fʊl əv yərˈsɛlf/
funds *n pl* /fʌndz/
graft *n* /græft/
grave *n* /greɪv/
gruesome *adj* /ˈgrusəm/
happy medium *idiom* /ˌhæpi ˈmidiəm/
hideous *adj* /ˈhɪdiəs/
invalid *n* /ɪnˈvæləd/
knockoff *n* /ˈnɑkɔf/
liberate *v* /ˈlɪbəˌreɪt/
literally *adv* /ˈlɪtərəli/
maim *v* /meɪm/
masculine *adj* /ˈmæskyələn/
medic *n* /ˈmɛdɪk/
merger *n* /ˈmɜrdʒər/
mutilate *v* /ˈmyutlˌeɪt/
no longer *idiom* /noʊ ˈlɔŋgər/
not have a clue *idiom* /nɑt həv ə klu/
organ transplant *n* /ˈɔrgən ˈtrænsplænt/
outbreak *n* /ˈaʊtbreɪk/
overlook *v* /ˌoʊvərˈlʊk/
pacifist *n* /ˈpæsəfɪst/
pay the price *idiom* /peɪ ðə praɪs/
peculiar *adj* /pɪˈkyulyər/
persist *v* /pərˈsɪst/
plastic surgery *n* /ˌplæstɪk ˈsɜrdʒəri/
plight *n* /plaɪt/
proximity *n* /prɑkˈsɪməti/
restructure *v* /ˌriˈstrʌktʃər/
rifle *n* /ˈraɪfl/
sacrifice *v* /ˈsækrəˌfaɪs/
savour *v* /ˈseɪvər/
screen *v* /skrin/
sentry duty *n* /ˈsɛntri ˈduti/
shake-up *n* /ˈʃeɪk ʌp/
skin *n* /skɪn/
slip-up *n* /ˈslɪp ʌp/
sophisticated *adj* /səˈfɪstəkeɪtəd/
subdue *v* /səbˈdu/
supreme *adj* /səˈprim/
technical glitch *n* /ˌtɛknɪkl ˈglɪtʃ/
transfusion *n* /trænsˈfyuʒn/
traumatized *adj* /ˈtrɔmətaɪzd/
trench *n* /trɛntʃ/
truce *n* /trus/
twitch *n* /twɪtʃ/
unassuming *adj* /ˌʌnəˈsumɪŋ/
update *v* /ˈʌpdeɪt/
uplifting *adj* /ˌʌpˈlɪftɪŋ/
vein *n* /veɪn/
veteran *n* /ˈvɛtərən/
vital *adj* /ˈvaɪtl/

wage *v* /weɪdʒ/
war *n* /wɔr/
wounded *adj* /'wundəd/
wrangle over *v* /'ræŋgl 'oʊvər/

UNIT 7

a blessing in disguise *idiom* /ə
  'blɛsɪŋ ɪn dɪs'gaɪz/
a change of heart *n, coll* /ə
  tʃeɪndʒ əv hart/
appetite *n* /'æpə,taɪt/
As if! *idiom* /æz ɪf/
ask (somebody) out *idiom* /æsk
  (…) aʊt/
at ease *n* /æt iz/
back off *idiom* /bæk ɔf/
beaming *adj* /bimɪŋ/
blow off *v* /'bloʊ ɔf/
born loser *idiom* /bɔrn 'luzər/
break off *v* /breɪk ɔf/
bring it on *v* /brɪŋ ɪt 'an/
broad *adj* /brɔd/
call off *v* /kɔl ɔf/
capitalism *n* /'kæpətl,ɪzəm/
cast *n* /kæst/
catch on *v* /kætʃ an/
chatter *n* /'tʃætər/
cheer (somebody) on *v* /tʃɪr an/
come out with *v* /kʌm aʊt wɪð/
consciously *adv* /'kanʃəsli/
cordon off *v* /'kɔrdn af/
critical *adj* /'krɪtɪkl/
crow's feet *idiom* /'kroʊz fit/
dawn on *v* /dɔn an/
deceptive *adj* /dɪ'sɛptɪv/
distract *v* /dɪ'strækt/
doom and gloom *idiom* /dum
  ænd glum/
drag on *v* /dræg an/
dream on *v* /drim an/
dump *n* /dʌmp/
easy come, easy go *idiom* /'izi
  kʌm 'izi goʊ/
enormity *n* /ɪ'nɔrməti/
fence off *v* /fɛns af/
firm *n* /fərm/
get a move on *v, coll* /gɛt ə 'muv
  an/
get over *v* /gɛt 'oʊvər/
gloomy *adj* /'glumi/
go off *v* /goʊ af/
grimace *n* /'grɪməs/
hang on *v* /hæŋ an/
hard on yourself *idiom* /hard an
  yər'sɛlf/
harshly *adv* /harʃli/
in the back of (somebody's)
  mind *idiom* /ɪn ðə bæk əv (…)
  maɪnd/
incessantly *adv* /ɪn'sɛsntli/
intense *adj* /ɪn'tɛns/
judge *v* /dʒʌdʒ/
Keep your chin up! *idiom* /kip
  yər tʃɪn ʌp/
lay (somebody) off *v* /'leɪ (…) af/
lighten up *v* /'laɪtn ʌp/
log off *v* /'lag af/

mouth *n* /maʊθ/
muscle *n* /'mʌsl/
nagging *adj* /'nægɪŋ/
negotiation *n* /nɪ,goʊʃi'eɪʃn/
nod off *v* /nad af/
not the end of the world *idiom*
  /nat ðə ɛnd əv ðə wərld/
nothing ventured, nothing
  gained *idiom* /'nʌθɪŋ 'vɛntʃərd
  'nʌθɪŋ geɪnd/
nuisance *n* /'nusns/
on the whole *idiom* /an ðə hoʊl/
partition (something) off *v*
  /par'tɪʃn (…) af/
precious *adj* /'prɛʃəs/
previous *adj* /'priviəs/
put off *v* /pʊt af/
road work *n* /'roʊd wərk/
savagely *adv* /'sævɪdʒli/
scare (something/somebody)
  off *v* /sker (…) af/
seal off *v* /sil af/
see (somebody) off *v* /si (…) af/
show off *v* /'ʃoʊ af/
signal *v* /'sɪgnəl/
sing (somebody's) praises *idiom*
  /sɪŋ (…) preɪzəz/
smirk *n* /smərk/
sneak up (on) *v* /snik ʌp (an)/
startle *v* /'startl/
submission *n* /səb'mɪʃn/
subtly *adv* /'sʌtli/
Those were the days! *idiom* /ðoʊz
  wər ðə deɪz/
turn into *v* /tərn 'ɪntə/
turn out *v* /tərn aʊt/
untangle *v* /,ʌn'tæŋgl/
verging *adv* /vərdʒɪŋ/
wear off *v* /wɛr af/

UNIT 8

a sec *idiom* /ə sɛk/
air traffic controller *n* /,ɛr træfɪk
  kən'troʊlər/
allergy *n* /'ælərdʒi/
applaud *v* /ə'plɔd/
at play *idiom* /æt pleɪ/
bar *v* /bar/
bare *adj* /bɛr/
berry *n* /'bɛri/
bet *v* /bɛt/
boardroom *n* /'bɔrdrum/
bombshell *n* /'bamʃɛl/
bond *n* /band/
breadwinner *n* /'brɛd,wɪnər/
build up *v* /'bɪld ʌp/
buoy *n* /bɔɪ/
by the same token *idiom* /baɪ ðə
  seɪm 'toʊkən/
cabin *n* /'kæbən/
career path *n* /kə'rɪr pæθ/
carve *v* /karv/
chicken pox *n* /'tʃɪkənpaks/
chilled *adj* /tʃɪld/
coarse *adj* /kɔrs/
coincide *v* /,koʊɪn'saɪd/
come across *v* /kʌm ə'krɔs/

convulsive laughter *n, coll*
  /kən'vʌlsɪv 'læftər/
crucial *adj* /kruʃl/
current *adj* /'kərənt/
decade *n* /'dɛkeɪd/
diminish *v* /dɪ'mɪnɪʃ/
dock *v* /dak/
draft *n* /dræft/
draught *adj* /dræft/
empathetic *adj* /,ɛmpə'θɛtɪk/
exquisitely *adv* /ɪk'skwɪzətli/
grand *adj* /grænd/
hands-on *adj* /,hændz 'an/
haul *n* /hɔl/
heir *n* /ɛr/
hilarity *n* /hɪ'lɛrəti/
hoarse *adj* /hɔrs/
hulking *adj* /'hʌlkɪŋ/
humiliation *n* /hyu,mɪli'eɪʃn/
hysterical *adj* /hɪ'stɛrɪkl/
job center *n* /'dʒabsɛntər/
learning curve *n* /'lərnɪŋ kərv/
lost in admiration *idiom* /lɒst ɪn
  ,ædmə'reɪʃn/
marble *n* /'marbl/
march *v* /martʃ/
matter *n* /'mætər/
minutes *n* /'mɪnəts/
multitasking *n* /,mʌlti'tæskɪŋ/
nurture *v* /'nərtʃər/
old-fashioned *adj* /,oʊld 'fæʃnd/
pace *n* /peɪs/
peer pressure *n* /pɪr 'prɛʃər/
prejudice *n* /'prɛdʒədəs/
pull your weight *idiom* /pʊl yər
  weɪt/
put yourself in (somebody's)
  shoes *idiom* /pʊt yər'sɛlf ɪn
  (…) ʃuz/
rash *adj* /ræʃ/
scorpion *n* /'skɔrpiən/
scathing about (something) *v*
  /'skeɪðɪŋ ə'baʊt (…)/
scrap *v* /skræp/
shortcut *n* /'ʃɔrtkʌt/
sigh *v* /saɪ/
squirrel *n* /'skwərəl/
statistics *n* /stə'tɪstɪks/
stony silence *n, coll* /'stoʊni
  'saɪləns/
stud *n* /stʌd/
survey *v* /sər'veɪ/
suspiciously *adv* /sə'spɪʃəsli/
take (something) into account *idiom*
  /teɪk (…) 'ɪntə ə'kaʊnt/
taken aback *idiom* /'teɪkən
  ə'bæk/
the opposite sex *idiom* /ðə
  'apəzət sɛks/
toddler *n* /'tadlər/
turbulent *adj* /'tərbyələnt/
ultrasound *n* /'ʌltrə,saʊnd/
unfazed *adj* /ʌn'feɪzd/
vale *n* /veɪl/
veil *n* /veɪl/
via *prep* /'viə/
voyeuristic *adj* /,vɔɪə'rɪstɪk/
wail *v* /weɪl/
weak *adj* /wik/

whirl *v* /wərl/
wind *n* /wɪnd/
wrist *n* /rɪst/
yearn for *v* /yərn fɔr/

UNIT 9

balcony *n* /'bælkəni/
barley *n* /'barli/
beam *v* /bim/
blast from the past *idiom* /'blæst
  frəm ðə pæst/
broad daylight *n, coll* /brɔd
  'deɪlaɪt/
bush *n* /bʊʃ/
caged *adj* /keɪdʒd/
cast *v* /kæst/
chase *v* /tʃeɪs/
compulsive *adj* /kəm'pʌlsɪv/
content *adj* /kən'tɛnt/
corn *n* /kɔrn/
deed *n* /did/
desperate *adj* /'dɛsprət/
destiny *n* /'dɛstəni/
devour *v* /dɪ'vaʊər/
dough *n* /doʊ/
enigma *n* /ɪ'nɪgmə/
epic *v* /'ɛpɪk/
equilibrium *n* /,ikwə'lɪbriəm/
eyes on the prize *idiom* /'aɪz an
  ðə praɪz/
fair and square *idiom* /fɛr ænd
  skwɛr/
flinch *v* /flɪntʃ/
fold *v* /foʊld/
go haywire *idiom* /goʊ
  'heɪ,waɪər/
goose *n* /gus/
gross *adj* /groʊs/
guard *n* /gard/
howl *v* /haʊl/
impetuosity *n* /ɪm,pɛtʃu'asəti/
indie *adj* /'ɪndi/
kinship *n* /'kɪnʃɪp/
loch *n* /lak/
long for *v* /lɔŋ fɔr/
loose *adj* /lus/
lose it *idiom* /luz ɪt/
make sense of *idiom* /meɪk sɛns
  əv/
meet and greet *idiom* /mit ænd
  grit/
misty *adj* /'mɪsti/
mood *n* /mud/
name and shame *idiom* /neɪm
  ænd ʃeɪm/
nearest and dearest *idiom*
  /'nɪrəst ænd 'dɪrəst/
obsessive-compulsive disorder
  noun /əb'sɛsɪv kəm'pʌlsɪv
  dɪs'ɔrdər/
outing *n* /'aʊtɪŋ/
palm *n* /pam/
primeval *adj* /praɪ'mivl/
quirky *adj* /'kwərki/
radiate *v* /'reɪdi,eɪt/
retreat *v* /rɪ'trit/
risky *adj* /'rɪski/

road trip *n* /roʊd trɪp/
roar *v* /rɔr/
run amok *idiom* /rʌn əˈmʌk/
run riot *idiom* /rʌn ˈraɪət/
run wild *idiom* /rʌn waɪld /
scrawl *v* /skrɔl/
self-conscious *adj* /ˌsɛlf ˈkɑnʃəs/
self-harm *v* /sɛlf-hɑrm/
shiver *n* /ˈʃɪvər/
shop until you drop *idiom* /ʃɑp ən'tɪl yu drɑp/
silhouette *n* /ˌsɪluˈɛt/
skid *v* /skɪd/
slump *n* /slʌmp/
sour *adj* /saʊər/
spark *n* /spɑrk/
submarine *n* /ˌsʌbməˈrin/
tactile *adj* /ˈtæktl/
tolerable *adj* /ˈtɑlərəbl/
tomboy *n* /ˈtɑmbɔɪ/
tone-deaf *adj* /ˌtoʊn ˈdɛf/
trance *n* /træns/
trap *v* /træp/
upcoming *adj* /ˈʌpˌkʌmɪŋ/
use it or lose it *idiom* /yuz ɪt ɔr luz ɪt/
vocation *n* /voʊˈkeɪʃn/
vow *n* /vaʊ/
valley *n* /ˈvæli/
ward *n* /wɔrd/
wheat *n* /wit/

UNIT 10

absurd *adj* /əbˈsərd/
allege *v* /əˈlɛdʒ/
alleviate *v* /əˈliviˌeɪt/
altitude *n* /ˈæltəˌtud/
ankle *n* /ˈæŋkl/
antibiotic *n* /ˌæntibaɪˈɑtɪk/
armpit *n* /ˈɑrmpɪt/
artery *n* /ˈɑrtəri/
assume *v* /əˈsum/
attempt *v* /əˈtɛmpt/
beg *v* /bɛg/
blink *v* /blɪŋk/
blond *n* /blɑnd/
bone *n* /boʊn/
brunette *n* /bruˈnɛt/
bulletin *n* /ˈbʊlətɪn/
burst *n* /bərst/
calf *n* /kæf/
capsule *n* /ˈkæpsl/
cheek *n* /tʃik/
chest *n* /tʃɛst/
chin *n* /tʃɪn/
clinic *n* /ˈklɪnɪk/
consequence *n* /ˈkɑnsəˌkwɛns/
consultation *n* /ˌkɑnslˈteɪʃn/
correspondent *n* /ˌkɔrəˈspɑndənt/
cramps *n pl* /kræmpz/
cure *n* /kyʊr/
cylinder *n* /ˈsɪləndər/
dark horse *n, coll* /dɑrk hɔrs/
deception *n* /dɪˈsɛpʃn/
diameter *n* /daɪˈæmətər/

dig down *v* /dɪg daʊn/
drug trial *n* /drʌg ˈtraɪəl/
elbow *n* /ˈɛlboʊ/
ethics *n* /ˈɛθɪks/
eyebrow *n* /ˈaɪbraʊ/
eyelash *n* /ˈaɪlæʃ/
fist *n* /fɪst/
fitfully *adv* /ˈfɪtfəli/
forbid *v* /fərˈbɪd/
forehead *n* /ˈfɔrhɛd/
fork *n* /fɔrk/
fraud *n* /frɔd/
growl *v* /graʊl/
harness *v* /ˈhɑrnəs/
havoc *n* /ˈhævək/
heel *n* /hil/
hide and seek *idiom* /ˌhaɪd n ˈsik/
hiding *n* /ˈhaɪdɪŋ/
hip *n* /hɪp/
humble *adj* /ˈhʌmbl/
hurricane *n* /ˈhərəˌkeɪn/
infection *n* /ɪnˈfɛkʃn/
inject *v* /ɪnˈdʒɛkt/
intestine *n* /ɪnˈtɛstən/
intrigued *adj* /ɪnˈtrigd/
jaw *n* /dʒɔ/
joint *n* /dʒɔɪnt/
kidney *n* /ˈkɪdni/
knee *n* /ni/
knuckle *n* /ˈnʌkl/
label *v* /ˈleɪbl/
leaflet *n* /ˈliflət/
lip *n* /lɪp/
liver *n* /ˈlɪvər/
local anesthetic *n, coll* /ˈloʊkl ˌænəsˈθɛtɪk/
lungs *n* /lʌŋz/
malfunction *v* /ˌmælˈfʌŋkʃn/
manifest *v* /ˈmænəˌfɛst/
medal *n* /ˈmɛdl/
mess up *v* /mɛs ʌp/
morphine *n* /ˈmɔrfin/
nail *n* /neɪl/
nausea *n* /ˈnɔziə/
neck *n* /nɛk/
news anchor *n* /nuz ˈæŋkər/
nod off *idiom* /nɑd ɑf/
northwards *adv* /ˈnɔrθwərdz/
op *n, coll* /ɑp/
opposition *n* /ˌɑpəˈzɪʃn/
pain relief *n* /peɪn rɪˈlif/
painkiller *n* /ˈpeɪnkɪlər/
paraglider *n* /ˈpærəˌglaɪdər/
Parkinson's disease *n* /ˈpɑrkənsnz dɪˌziz/
placebo *n* /pləˈsiboʊ/
play a role *idiom* /pleɪ ə roʊl/
policy *n* /ˈpɑləsi/
prescribe *v* /prɪˈskraɪb/
profound *adj* /prəˈfaʊnd/
psychosomatic *adj* /ˌsaɪkoʊsəˈmætɪk/
redhead *n* /ˈrɛdhɛd/
restrict *v* /rɪˈstrɪkt/
rib *n* /rɪb/
running order *n* /ˈrʌnɪŋ ˈɔrdər/
sedative *n* /ˈsɛdətɪv/
shin *n* /ʃɪn/
shoulder *n* /ˈʃoʊldər/

snag *n* /snæg/
spacious *adj* /ˈspeɪʃəs/
spread *v* /sprɛd/
stimulant *n* /ˈstɪmyələnt/
sue *v* /su/
supplement *n* /ˈsʌpləmənt/
suspicious *adj* /səˈspɪʃəs/
swallow *v* /ˈswɑloʊ/
tablet *n* /ˈtæblət/
tap into *v* /tæp ˈɪntə/
taste buds *n pl* /ˈteɪst bʌdz/
temple *n* /ˈtɛmpl/
thigh *n* /θaɪ/
thumb *n* /θʌm/
time trial *n* /taɪm ˈtraɪəl/
toe *n* /toʊ/
treatment *n* /ˈtritmənt/
unconscious *adj* /ʌnˈkɑnʃəs/
velodrome *n* /ˈvɛləˌdroʊm/
waist *n* /weɪst/
wobble *v* /ˈwɑbl/
wreak *v* /rik/

UNIT 11

aforementioned *adj* /əˈfɔrˌmɛnʃənd/
analyst *n* /ˈænəlɪst/
antiquated *adj* /ˈæntɪˌkweɪtəd/
appalling *adj* /əˈpɔlɪŋ/
aside *adv* /əˈsaɪd/
asphyxia *n* /əˈsfɪksiə/
bastion *n* /ˈbæstiən/
bear *n* /bɛr/
biased *adj* /ˈbaɪəst/
boast *v* /boʊst/
boiler *n* /ˈbɔɪlər/
break down *v* /ˈbreɪk daʊn/
catastrophically *adv* /ˌkætəˈstrɑfɪkli/
count on *idiom* /kaʊnt ɑn/
crease *n* /kris/
crooked *adj* /ˈkrʊkəd/
cycle *n* /ˈsaɪkl/
dial *n* /ˈdaɪəl/
dawn *n* /dɔn/
differentiate *v* /ˌdɪfəˈrɛnʃiˌeɪt/
disposable income *n, coll* /dɪˈspoʊzəbl ˈɪŋkʌm/
document *n* /ˈdɑkyəmənt/
domesticated *adj* /dəˈmɛstəˌkeɪtəd/
edit *v* /ˈɛdət/
excessive *adj* /ɪkˈsɛsɪv/
explode *v* /ɪkˈsploʊd/
fad *n* /fæd/
faulty *adj* /ˈfɔlti/
flawed *adj* /flɔd/
flesh *n* /flɛʃ/
focus group *n* /ˈfoʊkəs grup/
frivolous *adj* /ˈfrɪvələs/
fundamentally *adv* /ˌfʌndəˈmɛntəli/
handy *adj* /ˈhændi/
humorous *adj* /ˈhyumərəs/
immaculate *adj* /ɪˈmækyələt/

impartial *adj* /ɪmˈpɑrʃl/
impeccable *adj* /ɪmˈpɛkəbl/
incurable *adj* /ɪnˈkyʊrəbl/
intolerant *adj* /ɪnˈtɑlərənt/
laden with *adj* /ˈleɪdn wɪð/
mediocre *adj* /ˌmidiˈoʊkər/
minority *n* /məˈnɔrəti/
miraculous *adj* /məˈrækyələs/
notification *n* /ˌnoʊtəfəˈkeɪʃn/
objective *adj* /əbˈdʒɛktɪv/
outfit *n* /ˈaʊtfɪt/
overwhelming *adj* /ˌoʊvərˈwɛlmɪŋ/
perplexed *adj* /pərˈplɛkst/
petty *adj* /ˈpɛti/
plateau *n* /plæˈtoʊ/
playoff *n* /ˈpleɪɔf/
plumber *n* /ˈplʌmər/
posh *adj* /pɑʃ/
predecessor *n* /ˈprɛdəˌsɛsər/
pursuit *n* /pərˈsut/
rampant *adj* /ˈræmpənt/
random *adj* /ˈrændəm/
revolutionize *v* /ˌrɛvəˈluʃəˌnaɪz/
ridiculous *adj* /rɪˈdɪkyələs/
run into trouble *idiom* /rʌn ˈɪntə ˈtrʌbl/
second-rate *adj* /ˌsɛkənd ˈreɪt/
sheer *adj* /ʃɪr/
simplicity *n* /sɪmˈplɪsəti/
sketch *n* /skɛtʃ/
slot *n* /slɑt/
sport *v* /spɔrt/
stick *v* /stɪk/
stock prices *n* /stɑk praɪsəz/
strategist *n* /ˈstrætədʒɪst/
succumb to *v* /səˈkʌm tə/
tame *adj* /teɪm/
tension *n* /ˈtɛnʃn/
thirst *n* /θərst/
trivial *adj* /ˈtrɪviəl/
unjust *adj* /ˌʌnˈdʒʌst/
urgent *adj* /ˈərdʒənt/
virtue *n* /ˈvərtʃu/
white goods *n* /ˈwaɪt gʊdz/

UNIT 12

advent *n* /ˈædvɛnt/
all-consuming *adj* /ɔl kənˈsumɪŋ/
atmosphere *n* /ˈætməsˌfɪr/
bite off more than you can chew *idiom* /baɪt ɑf mɔr ðæn yu kən tʃu/
bland *adj* /blænd/
breathless *adj* /ˈbrɛθləs/
breeze *n* /briz/
build-up *n* /ˈbɪld ʌp/
buzz *v* /bʌz/
capture *v* /ˈkæptʃər/
closure *n* /ˈkloʊʒər/
cockpit *n* /ˈkɑkpɪt/
composed *adj* /kəmˈpoʊzd/
conceivable *adj* /kənˈsivəbl/
contract *v* /kənˈtrækt/
crew *n* /kru/
daring *adj* /ˈdɛrɪŋ/
deranged *adj* /dɪˈreɪndʒd/

diet *n* /ˈdaɪət/
discharge *v* /dɪsˈtʃɑrdʒ/
disengage *v* /ˌdɪsɪnˈgeɪdʒ/
drape *v* /dreɪp/
draw a line under *idiom* /drɔ ə
 laɪn ˈʌndər/
emergency procedure *n*
 /ɪˈmɔrdʒənsi prəˈsidʒər/
emotional wreck *n* /ɪˈmoʊʃənl
 rɛk/
enormously *adv* /ɪˈnɔrməsli/
epidemic *n* /ˌɛpəˈdɛmɪk/
etch *v* /ɛtʃ/
expanse *n* /ɪkˈspæns/
exposure *n* /ɪkˈspoʊʒər/
fasten *v* /ˈfæsn/
fire the imagination *idiom*
 /ˈfaɪər ðə ˌɪmædʒɪˈneɪʃn/
flight attendant *n* /ˈflaɪt
 əˈtɛndənt/
food for thought *idiom* /fud fər
 θɔt/
forbidding *adj* /fərˈbɪdɪŋ/
fragile *adj* /ˈfrædʒl/
free fall *n* /ˌfri ˈfɔl/
fuel *v* /ˈfyuəl/
fussy *adj* /ˈfʌsi/
grilling *n* /ˈgrɪlɪŋ/
grinding *adj* /ˈgraɪndɪŋ/
half-baked *adj* /ˌhæf ˈbeɪkt/
hindsight *n* /ˈhaɪndsaɪt/
in a flash *idiom* /ɪn ə flæʃ/
in retrospect *idiom* /ɪn
 ˈrɛtrəˌspɛkt/
influential *adj* /ˌɪnfluˈɛnʃl/
insert *v* /ɪnˈsərt/
latter *adj* /ˈlætər/
league *n* /lig/
legacy *n* /ˈlɛgəsi/
lunar *adj* /ˈlunər/
manned *adj* /mænd/
mask *n* /mæsk/
molasses *n* /məˈlæsəz/
obsessed with (somebody/some-
 thing) *v* /əbˈsɛst wɪð (…)/
on-board *adj* /ɑn bɔrd/
orbit *n* /ˈɔrbət/
ordeal *n* /ɔrˈdil/
overdo *v* /ˌoʊvərˈdu/
overshadow *v* /ˌoʊvərˈʃædoʊ/
penniless *adj* /ˈpɛniləs/
perspective *n* /pərˈspɛktɪv/
priorities *n* /praɪˈɔrətɪz/
privacy *n* /ˈpraɪvəsi/
proceed *v* /prəˈsid/
pull through *v* /pʊl θru/
punctual *adj* /ˈpʌŋktʃuəl/
rapid *adj* /ˈræpəd/
reel *v* /ril/
refund *v* /riˈfʌnd/
relief *n* /rɪˈlif/
restrain *v* /rɪˈstreɪn/
run-up *n* /ˈrʌn ʌp/
scale *n* /skeɪl/
shady *adj* /ˈʃeɪdi/
shudder *v* /ˈʃʌdər/
sit bolt upright *idiom* /sɪt boʊlt
 ˈʌpraɪt/
sour note *n, coll* /ˈsaʊər noʊt/

spark *v* /spɑrk/
sponsor *v* /ˈspɑnsər/
stagger *v* /ˈstægər/
stall *v* /stɔl/
starving *v* /ˈstɑrvɪŋ/
sticky *adj* /ˈstɪki/
stranded *adj* /ˈstrændəd/
subdued *adj* /səbˈdud/
summit *n* /ˈsʌmət/
take off *v* /ˈteɪk ɑf/
tube *n* /tub/
turnaround *n* /ˈtərnəˌraʊnd/
turning point *idiom* /ˈtərnɪŋ
 pɔɪnt/
unfold *v* /ʌnˈfoʊld/
vastness *n* /væstnəs/
viral *adj* /ˈvaɪrəl/
wrestle *v* /ˈrɛsl/

Pairwork Activities Student A

UNIT 3 *p. 24*

VOCABULARY AND SPEAKING

Describing trends: What's in a name?

Choose one of the names. Give a presentation to your partner on changes in the name's popularity.

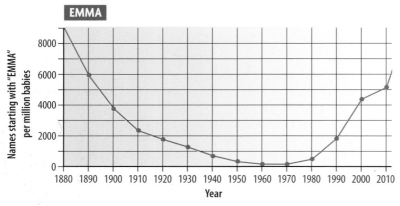

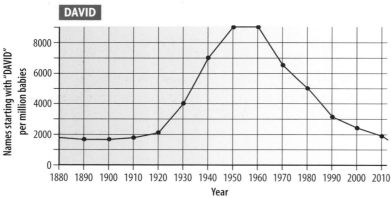

Listen to your partner's presentation. Write the name and draw the graph.

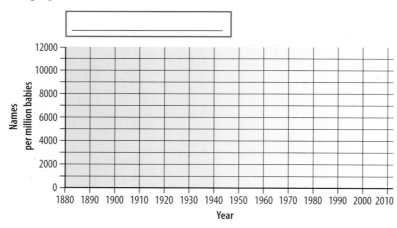

UNIT 4 *p. 29*

SPEAKING

Test your memory!

Take turns asking the questions while your partner answers with their book closed. Can you correct any of their statements without looking at the pictures?

Ask **Student B** questions about **the woman** who took part in the scam, and then answer **Student B**'s questions about the men.

1 What height and build was the woman?
2 What color hair did she have? Was it natural or dyed? How long was it?
3 Can you describe her coat? How long was her skirt?
4 What kind of gloves was she wearing? What color was her bag?
5 Was she wearing black or brown shoes?

Look at the pictures on pages 28–29 again. How accurate were your descriptions of the people?

> **What height and build was the woman?**

> **She must have been about … and I'd say …**

> **What color shirt was the man in the suit wearing?**

> **I'm pretty sure he was wearing a …**

In the **Jeweler's**

VOCABULARY

Idiomatic collocations

Look at the dictionary extracts to check their meanings and make notes on them. Write an example sentence of your own.

> **fine line** difficult to see or describe **SYN** subtle: *There's **a fine line** between love and hate* (= it is easy for one to become the other).
>
> **gray area** *noun* an area of a subject or situation that is not clear or does not fit into a particular group and is therefore difficult to define or deal with: *Exactly what can be called an offensive weapon is still a gray area.*
>
> **get/have itchy feet** (*informal*) to want to travel or move to a different place; to want to do something different
>
> **a level playing field** a situation in which everyone has the same opportunities
>
> **a long shot** an attempt or a guess that is not likely to be successful but is worth trying: *It's a long shot, but it just might work.*
>
> **a raw deal** the fact of somebody being treated unfairly: *Older workers often get a raw deal.*
>
> **the/a slippery slope** a course of action that is difficult to stop once it has begun, and can lead to serious problems or disaster
>
> **wake-up call** *noun* an event that makes people realize that there is a problem that they need to do something about: *These riots should be a wake-up call for the government.*

SPEAKING

The Unbelievable Truth

Prepare a short (2–3 minute) lecture about **FOOD** .

Apart from three truths, the rest of the lecture must be complete untruths invented by you. They can be obviously and ridiculously untrue, or very plausible.

You could include **three** of the following as facts – you can research more information about them if you're able to. You could also change details of some of the other facts to make them false, or invent your own false facts.

> - Chicken contains 266% more fat than it did 40 years ago.
> - All carrots used to be purple.
> - Honey will never go bad. It has been shown to last 3,000 years.
> - Peanuts can be used to make dynamite.
> - Almost half of the world's food is thrown away every year.
> - The amount of antibiotics used in meat production is four times the amount used to treat humans.
> - Two bananas will provide you with enough energy for a 90-minute workout.
> - Coconut water can be used as a substitute for human blood plasma in emergencies.

Work with **Student B** and take turns giving your lecture, using your notes. Your partner can challenge when they think that a statement is true. If they are correct, they receive a point. If they are wrong, you receive a point. At the end of your lecture, you receive a point for every truth that wasn't spotted.

Tell your partner what those truths were.

Pairwork Activities Student B

 UNIT 3 *p. 24*

VOCABULARY AND SPEAKING

Describing trends: What's in a name?

Choose one of the names. Give a presentation to your partner on changes in the name's popularity.

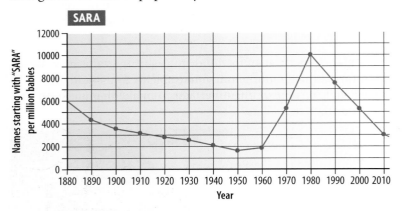

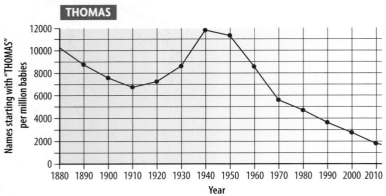

Listen to your partner's presentation. Write the name and draw the graph.

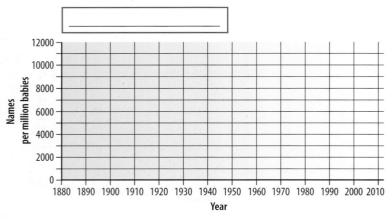

 UNIT 4 *p. 29*

SPEAKING

Test your memory!

Take turns asking the questions while your partner answers with their book closed. Can you correct any of their statements without looking at the pictures?

Answer **Student A**'s questions about the woman who took part in the scam, and then ask **Student A** questions about **the men**.

1 What color shirt was the man in the suit wearing? Did he have a tie?

2 Can you describe the other man's build? What color was his tie?

3 Did the man in the suit part his hair on the side or in the middle?

4 Did either of them wear glasses? Did either of them have a beard or mustache?

5 What color shoes were they both wearing?

Look at the pictures on pages 28–29 again. How accurate were your descriptions of the people?

VOCABULARY

Idiomatic collocations

Look at the dictionary extracts to check their meanings and make notes on them. Write an example sentence of your own.

> **a ˌforegone conˈclusion** if you say that something is a **foregone conclusion**, you mean that it is a result that is certain to happen
>
> **a/your last reˈsort** the person or thing you rely on when everything else has failed: *I've tried everyone else and now you're my last resort.*
>
> **ˌmixed ˈblessing** *noun* [usually sing.] something that has advantages and disadvantages
>
> **on ˈsecond thought** used to say that you have changed your opinion: *I'll wait here. No, on second thoughts, I'll come with you.*
>
> **ˌsaving ˈgrace** *noun* [usually sing.] the one good quality that a person or thing has that prevents them or it from being completely bad
>
> **a ˌsore ˈspot** a subject that makes you feel angry or upset when it is mentioned: *It's a sore spot with Sue's parents that she has thousands of dollars of credit-card debt.*
>
> **ˌwishful ˈthinking** *noun* [U] the belief that something that you want to happen is happening or will happen, although this is actually not true or very unlikely: *I have a feeling that Alex likes me, but that might just be wishful thinking.*
>
> **get/have cold ˈfeet** (*informal*) to suddenly become nervous about doing something that you had planned to do: *He was going to ask her, but he got cold feet and said nothing.*

SPEAKING

The Unbelievable Truth

Prepare a short (2–3 minute) lecture about **SLEEP**.

Apart from three truths, the rest of the lecture must be complete untruths invented by you. They can be obviously and ridiculously untrue, or very plausible.

You could include **three** of the following as facts – you can research more information about them if you're able to. You could also change details of some of the other facts to make them false, or invent your own false facts.

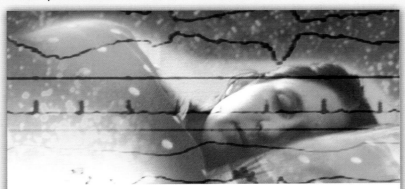

- Some studies suggest women need up to an hour's extra sleep a night compared to men, and not getting it may be one reason women are much more susceptible to depression than men.
- The extra hour of sleep received when clocks are turned back at the end of daylight savings in Canada has been found to coincide with a fall in the number of road accidents.
- As a group, 18- to 24-year-olds deprived of sleep suffer more from impaired performance than older adults.
- The record for the longest period without sleep is 11 days.
- Some deaf people make sign language in their sleep.
- Only one half of a dolphin's brain goes to sleep at a time.
- Cats sleep for 70% of their lives. With humans, it's around 30%.

Work with **Student A** and take turns giving your lecture, using your notes. Your partner can challenge when they think that a statement is true. If they are correct, they receive a point. If they are wrong, you receive a point. At the end of your lecture, you receive a point for every truth that wasn't spotted.

Tell your partner what those truths were.

Extra Materials

UNIT 2 *p. 13*

READING AND LISTENING

Pygmalion – how does it end?

Liza makes great progress, and Higgins wins his bet! She goes to a high society gathering, where she is taken for a princess. Higgins continues to treat Liza with contempt, but too late realizes that he is in fact very fond of her. She leaves him to marry Freddy.

In the movie version, *My Fair Lady*, the ending is different. In what way, do you think?

UNIT 4 *p. 27*

STARTER

1   Real. Rubber Duck is a "floating sculpture" by the Dutch artist Florentijn Hofman.
2   Real but staged. The workers didn't really have lunch like this. They just sat there for the photo.
3   Altered.
4   Real. It shows the Rainbow Mountains in China, where layers of different-colored rock have come to the surface.
5   Real. The beach, only meters from the runway on the island of St. Maarten, is a popular spot for planewatchers.
6   Staged. Two girls, ages 9 and 16, faked the photos by sticking pictures of fairies on pins in the ground. The photos were taken for real around the world.
7   Altered. It was widely circulated on the Internet as real, and was claimed to be a winner of the National Geographic Photo Contest. The magazine went public to deny it.
8   Real. This was disputed, but there's video evidence of the lightning strike at the time of the Pope's resignation.
9   Real. This is the maned wolf.
10 Real. The sailor really did grab the nurse and kiss her when the end of WWII was announced. The nurse slapped him afterwards.
11 Real. The couple put the camera on timer for a selfie and were upstaged by an inquisitive squirrel.
12 Real. It's Andre Agassi and Roger Federer playing on a helipad converted into a tennis court on top of the Burj al Arab in Dubai, over 695 feet above the ground.

UNIT 5 *p. 37*

STARTER

A		B
9	Beware: avalanches	Canada
2	No swearing	the US
1	Riding whales not allowed	Japan
6	Speeding endangers cassowaries	Australia
8	Street-food sellers not permitted	South Africa
10	Watch out for llamas	Bolivia
4	Caution: old-people crossing	the UK
5	Steep hill ends in crocodile river	South Africa
11	Ski-lift instruction	France
7	Speed bumps on road ahead	Jamaica
3	Road toll paid by license-number recognition	the US
12	Chewing betel nut is forbidden	Papua New Guinea

UNIT 5 *p. 42*

SPEAKING

A quiz to test your ability to learn a foreign language

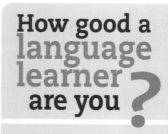

How good a language learner are you?

1 How many foreign languages can you greet someone in?

2 Learn these Samoan words (Samoa is an island in the South Pacific).

> **toalua** husband
> **tamaloa** man
> **tamaitiiti** child
> **loomatua** old woman
> **taulealea** youth

How did you find this task?
a   easy and interesting
b   very difficult
c   hard because a lot of the words were similar
d   so boring I didn't bother to try

3 Here is a new language:

> ek kum chuchu the train is coming
> ek namas chuchu the train is very big
> nek kum niva chuchu the train isn't coming
> ek chuchu it's a train

How would you say "It's not a train"?
a nek chuchu niva
b ek niva chuchu
c nek niva chuchu
d don't know

4 Fill in the blank with one of the words from below.

> Shakucomespiteare isos wonone ovofef tehe
> wororolid's grematerest's wririterners. Hehe wasis
> _____ onin Staratarafoorrd-inon-Aravont.

a borotone
b born
c shororit
d don't know

5 Read this list of words. Then, without looking, write down as many as you can remember.

pin	gadget	identity	arrogant
luxury	carefully	website	museum
knot	daffodil	anxious	interpret

6 In one minute write down all the things you could do with a cabbage, apart from cooking and eating it.

7 In one minute write down all the reasons you can think of why it might be useful to learn Eskimo.

8 What do the following words mean in Samoan? (**Don't look!**)

> loomatua tamaitiiti tamaloa toalua taulealea

UNIT 8 *p. 66*

LISTENING AND SPEAKING

Gender-neutral parenting

Read how Storm's mother reacted to criticism of her and her husband's ideas. Answer the questions.

> ## Canadian mother raising "genderless" baby defends her decision
> **Storm Witterick**
>
> Kathy Witterick, the mother of Storm, the Canadian baby being raised with only a few people knowing his or her sex, defended her choice.
>
> "The strong, lightning-fast, vitriolic response was a shock," said Kathy. "The idea that the whole world must know our baby's sex strikes me as unhealthy and voyeuristic."
>
> When Storm came into the world, Kathy (38) and husband David (39) sent out this email, "We decided not to share Storm's sex for now – a tribute to freedom and choice in place of limitation."
>
> While child development experts applaud efforts to raise children free of the constraints of gender stereotypes, they say these parents have embarked on a psychological experiment that could be "potentially disastrous."

1 What shocked her so much?
2 Do you think it is "unhealthy and voyeuristic" to want to know the sex of a baby?
3 What does she mean by a "tribute to freedom and choice in place of limitation"?
4 What do the experts applaud? What do they deplore?

 UNIT 9 *p. 72*

VOCABULARY AND PRONUNCIATION

The Night I Heard Caruso Sing

"I wrote the song after driving my dad up to Scotland in the mid-80s to revisit his old haunts. As we stood on the edge of Holy Loch, a nuclear submarine surfaced in front of us. It was a startling moment.

The song is about the redemptive power of music – not just Caruso – to make sense of life, to offer succor and wonder, even when life itself may seem frightening and unknowable." **Ben Watt**

UNIT 12 *p. 93*

STARTER

Turning points

In chronological order:

Russian Revolution

The Revolution in 1917 ended the reign of the Tsars and created the communist Soviet Union. This was the beginning of the division of the globe into communist and non-communist blocs, which came to its height in the Cold War, after World War II.

Women's vote

There were some minor instances of women receiving the vote in small communities prior to 1918. Women were also allowed to vote in post-revolutionary Russia in 1917, but the first real wave of countries giving women the vote came in 1918, after World War I. The struggle to get the vote was the beginning of what developed into the feminist movement.

Alexander Fleming

Fleming discovered penicillin, the first antibiotic, in 1928, but stopped work on it because it was too difficult to produce large enough quantities that would keep for very long. Its introduction on a mass scale in 1944 saved thousands of lives in World War II, and the subsequent development of other antibiotics revolutionized medicine.

Atomic bomb

The first successful test detonation was on July 16, 1945, in the New Mexico desert. The world woke up to the reality and horror of the atomic bomb after it was dropped on Hiroshima on August 6, 1945. Nuclear weapons have proliferated, and can be argued to have acted as a deterrent to the escalation of conflicts, but their shadow will always hang over humanity.

Founding of the UN

Preparations for the formation of the United Nations began in April 1945, but it wasn't founded until October of that year. The influence of the UN has often been seen as disappointing, but is a profound symbol of progress on the international stage.

Beatlemania

Although the craze for rock and roll began in the 1950s with Elvis Presley, fan hysteria for the Beatles in the early 60s was on a much wider, global scale. British Beatlemania began in late 1963 and spread across the Atlantic in 1964. The Beatles were greeted at JFK International Airport in New York by thousands of screaming women. Older generations disapproved of this wild and uncontrollable behavior, and the concept of the rebellious teenager was established.

First picture of Earth from lunar orbit

Apollo 8 took men out of Earth's orbit for the first time in December 1968, and the pictures taken of the Earth from over 200,000 miles away changed the way its inhabitants saw themselves and their environment.

The invention of the cell phone

In the early 1970s, Martin Cooper led a team of Motorola engineers that developed the first handheld cell phone. On April 3, 1973, he made the very first cell phone call in public, which was to Dr. Joel S. Engel, head of Bell Labs and a major competitor. The first cell phones were the size of a brick, weighed about 2 pounds, and cost $3,995.

Fall of the Berlin Wall

The Berlin Wall came down on November 9, 1989. The wall had been the ultimate symbol of the Cold War, and when Germany was reunited in 1990, it was seen as the end of communism in Europe. The collapse of the Soviet Union followed, and the dynamics of global politics changed forever.

9/11

The terrorist attack on the World Trade Center in New York City began early on September 11, 2001, when hijacked airliners were flown into the twin towers. The event traumatized all who witnessed it, and the US government's subsequent "war on terror" led to the invasion of Afghanistan and Iraq. Air passengers are reminded of this event whenever they go through airport security.

UNIT 12 *p. 101*

THE LAST WORD

1   a *I have known oceans of danger.*
    b *I have no notions of danger.*

2   a *It's important to give children an aim.*
    b *It's important to give children a name.*

3   a *I told the mail carrier I only accept addressed mail.*
    b *I told the mail carrier I only accept a dressed male.*

4   a *We discussed the subject of youth in Asia.*
    b *We discussed the subject of euthanasia.*

5   a *Don't tell me that's tough!*
    b *Don't tell me that stuff!*

Irregular Verbs

Base form	Simple Past	Past participle	Base form	Simple Past	Past participle
be	was/were	been	leave	left	left
beat	beat	beaten	lend	lent	lent
become	became	become	let	let	let
begin	began	begun	lie	lay	lain
bend	bent	bent	light	lighted/lit	lighted/lit
bite	bit	bitten	lose	lost	lost
blow	blew	blown	make	made	made
break	broke	broken	mean	meant	meant
bring	brought	brought	meet	met	met
build	built	built	must	had to	had to
buy	bought	bought	pay	paid	paid
can	could	been able	put	put	put
catch	caught	caught	read /rid/	read /rɛd/	read /rɛd/
choose	chose	chosen	ride	rode	ridden
come	came	come	ring	rang	rung
cost	cost	cost	rise	rose	risen
cut	cut	cut	run	ran	run
dig	dug	dug	say	said	said
do	did	done	see	saw	seen
draw	drew	drawn	sell	sold	sold
dream	dreamed/dreamt	dreamed/dreamt	send	sent	sent
drink	drank	drunk	set	set	set
drive	drove	driven	shake	shook	shaken
eat	ate	eaten	shine	shone	shone
fall	fell	fallen	shoot	shot	shot
feed	fed	fed	show	showed	shown
feel	felt	felt	shut	shut	shut
fight	fought	fought	sing	sang	sung
find	found	found	sink	sank	sunk
fit	fit	fit	sit	sat	sat
fly	flew	flown	sleep	slept	slept
forget	forgot	forgotten	slide	slid	slid
forgive	forgave	forgiven	speak	spoke	spoken
freeze	froze	frozen	spend	spent	spent
get	got	gotten	spread	spread	spread
give	gave	given	stand	stood	stood
go	went	been/gone	steal	stole	stolen
grow	grew	grown	stick	stuck	stuck
hang	hung	hung	swim	swam	swum
have	had	had	take	took	taken
hear	heard	heard	teach	taught	taught
hide	hid	hidden	tear	tore	torn
hit	hit	hit	tell	told	told
hold	held	held	think	thought	thought
hurt	hurt	hurt	throw	threw	thrown
keep	kept	kept	understand	understood	understood
kneel	knelt	knelt	wake	woke	woken
know	knew	known	wear	wore	worn
lay	laid	laid	win	won	won
lead	led	led	write	wrote	written

Phonetic Symbols

Consonants

1	/p/	as in	pen	/pɛn/
2	/b/	as in	big	/bɪg/
3	/t/	as in	tea	/ti/
4	/d/	as in	do	/du/
5	/k/	as in	cat	/kæt/
6	/g/	as in	go	/goʊ/
7	/f/	as in	four	/fɔr/
8	/v/	as in	very	/ˈvɛri/
9	/s/	as in	son	/sʌn/
10	/z/	as in	zoo	/zu/
11	/l/	as in	live	/lɪv/
12	/m/	as in	my	/maɪ/
13	/n/	as in	near	/nɪr/
14	/h/	as in	happy	/ˈhæpi/
15	/r/	as in	red	/rɛd/
16	/y/	as in	yes	/yɛs/
17	/w/	as in	want	/wɑnt/
18	/θ/	as in	thanks	/θæŋks/
19	/ð/	as in	the	/ðə/
20	/ʃ/	as in	she	/ʃi/
21	/ʒ/	as in	television	/ˈtɛləˌvɪʒn/
22	/tʃ/	as in	child	/tʃaɪld/
23	/dʒ/	as in	German	/ˈdʒɜrmən/
24	/ŋ/	as in	English	/ˈɪŋglɪʃ/

Vowels

25	/i/	as in	see	/si/
26	/ɪ/	as in	his	/hɪz/
27	/ɪr/	as in	near	/nɪr/
28	/ɛ/	as in	ten	/tɛn/
29	/ɛr/	as in	hair	/hɛr/
30	/æ/	as in	stamp	/stæmp/
31	/ɑ/	as in	hot	/hɑt/
32	/ɑr/	as in	car	/kɑr/
33	/ɔ/	as in	saw	/sɔ/
34	/ɔr/	as in	more	/mɔr/
35	/ʊ/	as in	book	/bʊk/
36	/ʊr/	as in	tour	/tʊr/
37	/u/	as in	you	/yu/
38	/ʌ/	as in	sun	/sʌn/
39	/ə/	as in	about	/əˈbaʊt/
40	/ər/	as in	bird	/bərd/

Diphthongs (two vowels together)

41	/eɪ/	as in	name	/neɪm/
42	/oʊ/	as in	no	/noʊ/
43	/aɪ/	as in	my	/maɪ/
44	/aʊ/	as in	how	/haʊ/
45	/ɔɪ/	as in	boy	/bɔɪ/

OXFORD
UNIVERSITY PRESS

198 Madison Avenue
New York, NY 10016 USA

Great Clarendon Street, Oxford, OX2 6DP,
United Kingdom

Oxford University Press is a department of the
University of Oxford. It furthers the University's
objective of excellence in research, scholarship,
and education by publishing worldwide. Oxford
is a registered trade mark of Oxford University
Press in the UK and in certain other countries

© Oxford University Press 2016

The moral rights of the author have been asserted

First published in 2016

2020 2019 2018 2017 2016

10 9 8 7 6 5 4 3 2 1

ISBN: 978 0 19 472658 0
STUDENT BOOK (PACK COMPONENT)

ISBN: 978 0 19 472657 3
STUDENT BOOK WITH OXFORD ONLINE SKILLS
PROGRAM (PACK)

ISBN: 978 0 19 472676 4
OXFORD ONLINE SKILLS PROGRAM (PACK
COMPONENT)

ISBN: 978 0 19 472672 6
STUDENT BOOK ACCESS CARD (PACK COMPONENT)

Printed in China

This book is printed on paper from certified
and well-managed sources.

ACKNOWLEDGEMENTS

The publisher is grateful to those who have given permission to reproduce the
following extracts and adaptations of copyright material: p.4 Adapted extract
from Top.10 Things that Make Humans Special by Charles Q. Choi,
www.livescience.com, 22 August 2011. Copyrighted 2014. Live Science.
112309:914DS. Reproduced with permission of Wright's Media; p.11
Front cover from Pride and Prejudice (Oxford World Classics) by Jane
Austen, Oxford University Press, 2008. Reproduced by permission of
Oxford University Press; p.11 Front cover from Jemima J by Jane Green
(Penguin Books, 1998). Reproduced by permission from Penguin Books
Ltd; p.11 Extracts from Jemima J by Jane Green (Penguin Books, 1998).
Reproduced by permission of David Higham Associates Ltd; p.11 Front
cover from James And The Giant Peach by Roald Dahl (Puffin Books,
2007). Reproduced with permission from Penguin Books Ltd; p.11 Extract
from James And The Giant Peach by Roald Dahl (Puffin Books, 2007).
Reproduced by permission of David Higham Associates Ltd; p.11 Front
cover and extract from The Other Boleyn Girl by Philippa Gregory, Harper,
2011. © 2001 Philippa Gregory. Reprinted by permission of HarperCollins
Publishers Ltd; p.11 Extract from Psycho by Robert Bloch, Robert Hale Ltd.
© 1959 The Estate of the Late Robert Bloch. Reproduced by permission.
p.11 Front cover from America's Queen: The Life of Jacqueline Onassis by
Sarah Bradford (Penguin Books, 2000, 2013). Reproduced with permission
from Penguin Books Ltd; p.11 Extract from America's Queen: The Life
of Jacqueline Onassis by Sarah Bradford, (Penguin Books, 2000, 2013),
Copyright © Sarah Bradford, 2000. Used by permission of Penguin Books
Ltd and Viking Penguin, a division of Penguin Group (USA) LLC; p.11
Extract from Before I Go to Sleep by S.J. Watson (HarperCollins Publishers
Ltd, 2011); pp.12–13 Extract from Pygmalion by George Bernard Shaw,
first published in Everybody's Magazine, 1914. Reproduced by permission
of The Society of Authors, on behalf of the Bernard Shaw Estate; p.16
Definitions from Oxford Advanced American Dictionary for learners
of English. © Oxford University Press 2011. Reprinted by permission;
pp.22–23 Adapted extract from The Bearable Lightness of Giving by
Mike Colman, Courier Mail, 25 May 2012. Reproduced by permission of

Copyright Agency; p.24 Graph "New Cars against Age of Customer" from
Demand Curves by Dent Research, www.hsdent.com. Copyright © 2011
Dent Research. Reproduced by permission; p.24 Graph "Happiness Scale"
from We're happiest at 74: It's all downhill till 40, then life gets better, say
scientists by Fiona Macrae, Daily Mail, 23 February 2010. Reproduced by
permission of Solo Syndication; p.24 Graph "Favorite color by age group"
from Colour Assignment: Preferences – favorite color by Joe Hallock,
www.joehallock.com. Reproduced by permission of Joe Hallock; p.24
NameVoyager Graphs Tracking US Popularity of Names Over Time, from
BabyNameWizard.com. Copyright 2014 by CMI Marketing, Inc. Reprinted
with permission; pp.38–39 Adapted extract from Tribe Swap by Donal
MacIntyre, The Mail on Sunday, 29 April 2007. Reproduced by permission
of Solo Syndication; pp.46–47 Adapted extract from First world war: 15
legacies still with us today by The Guardian, Süddeutsche Zeitung, El
País, La Stampa, Gazeta Wyborcza and Le Monde, www.theguardian.
com, 15 January 2014. Copyright Guardian News and Media Ltd 2014;
pp.62–63 Adapted extract from Female pilots: a slow take-off by Emine
Saner, www.theguardian.com, 13 January 2014. Copyright Guardian
News and Media Ltd 2014; pp.62–63 Adapted extract from Desperate
husbands by Hugo Carey, The Sunday Times, 26 July 2009. Reproduced
by permission of News Syndication; p.66 Adapted extract from Canadian
Mother Raising 'Genderless' Baby, Storm, Defends Her Family's Decision
By Linsey Davis and Susan Donaldson James, www.abcnews.com, 30 May
2011. Reproduced by permission of ABC News; pp.73 and 169 The Night
I Heard Caruso Sing Words and Music by Ben Watt © 1988, Reproduced
by permission of Sony/ATV Music Publishing (UK) Ltd, London W1F 9LD;
p.74–75 Extracts from Wild Harmonies (originally Variations Sauvages,
© Editions Robert Laffont –Paris 2003) by Hélène Grimaud, translated
by Ellen Hinsey, copyright © 2006 by Penguin Group (USA), Inc. Used by
permission of Editions Albin Michel and Riverhead Books, an imprint
of Penguin Group (USA) Ltd; p.88–89 Extract from Are our household
appliances getting too complicated? by Tom Meltzer, www.theguardian.
com, 27 February 2013. Copyright Guardian News and Media Ltd 2013;
p.99 Extract from Experience: running a marathon nearly killed me
David Byrom, The Guardian, 22 March 2014. Copyright Guardian News
and Media Ltd 2014; p.100 Extract from Experience: Our plane was
hijacked" by Nancy Traversy, www.theguardian.com, 5 October 2013.
Copyright Guardian News and Media Ltd 2013; p.92 Extract from The
Fun They Had by Isaac Asimov, published in 50 Short Science Fiction
Tales edited by Isaac Asimov and Groff Conklin (Scribner Publishing,
1997). Reproduced by permission of Asimov Holdings LLC; p.106 Graph
"What is the primary way you watch TV?" and adapted graph "To what
broad age group do you belong?" from Analysis of Primary TV Watching
Habits, May 2014 Insight Report. Data reprinted with permission from
CivicScience, Inc. © 2014; p.107 Graph "Desire for spice peaks at midlife",
www.npd.com. Reproduced by permission of The NPD Group; pp.125–126
Adapted extract from The Zebra Story by Gareth Davies, 16 January 2014.
Reproduced by permission of Gareth Davies; p.127 Extracts from For all
mankind by Boffin Media, first broadcast on BBC Radio 4, 19 December
2012. Reproduced by permission of Boffin Media; p.127 Extract from Oh
What a Lovely War by Joan Littlewood and the Theatre Workshop (1967).
Reproduced by kind permission of the Estate of Joan Littlewood and The
Sayle Literary Agency. Sources: www.atlanticphilanthropies.org, www.
theguardian.com, www.xcmag.com Audio script; p.35 extract from 'The
Unbelievable Truth ' is licensed courtesy of Random Entertainment
Ltd; p.50 'The Christmas Truce, 1914 – Oh what a lovely war! Interview'
reproduced by permission of Richard Carrington; p.73 'The night I heard
Caruso sing' recorded by 'Everything but the girl' is licensed courtesy
of Warner Music UK Ltd; p.94 extract from 'For all Mankind' is licensed
courtesy of Boffin Media Ltd. Extracts from p.58 'Smile', p.86 'The
Internet of things', p.82 'Down to earth with a bump', and p.42 'Found in
translation' are licensed courtesy of BBC Worldwide Ltd.

Illustrations by: Cliparea/Woodoo Art p.83; Ian Baker pp.7, 40, 59 (Ben is
gaining…and He drove off…), 68, 76; Fausto Bianchi/Beehive Illustration
p.113; Peter Bull Art Studio pp.24,164 (graphs), 166 (graphs); Gill Button
pp.14, 16, 25, 44, 65, 67, 91, 101 (Invention, shower); Otto Dettmer p.20;
Mark Duffin pp.35 (grenade etc), 101 (potato clock); Rudolf Farkas/Beehive
Illustration p.50; Martina Farrow p.14; Martin Hargreaves/Illustration
Ltd pp.8-9; Martin Sanders pp.37, 38, 86; Phil Schramm/Meiklejohn
Illustration pp.88–89, 90; Louise Weir pp.28–29, 164, 166.

We would also like to thank the following for permission to reproduce the following
photographs: Cover: Paul Harizan/Getty Images(2); Global: InnaFelker/
shutterstock; p.3 Login/shutterstock, Stephen Alvarez/Getty Images; p.4
skynesher/istockphotp; p.5 Vibrant Image Studio/shutterstock, Shunyu
Fan/Getty Images, Cyril Ruoso/ Minden Pictures/Getty Images,
AxiomPhotographic.com, RIEGER Bertrand/Getty Images, PjrStudio/Alamy
Stock Photo, OUP/Dennis Kitchen Studio, Inc, Blend Images - Jacqueline
Veissid/Getty Images, Purepix/Alamy Stock Photo; p.6 Paramount/The
Kobal Collection; p.8 Robert Adrian Hillman/shutterstock; pp.8–9 Irina
Tischenko/123rf.com; p.10 iconogenic/Getty Images; p.11 yukipon/
shutterstock, Front cover from JAMES AND THE GIANT PEACH by Roald
Dahl (Puffin Books, 2007). Reproduced with permission from Penguin
Books Ltd., Front cover from JEMIMA J by Jane Green (Penguin Books,
1998). Reproduced by permission from Penguin Books Ltd., Front cover
from PRIDE AND PREJUDICE (Oxford World Classics) by Jane Austen,
Oxford University Press, 2008. Reproduced by permission of Oxford
University Press, PSYCHO by Robert Bloch, Robert Hale Ltd. © 1959 The
Estate of the Late Robert Bloch. Reproduced by permission., Film I Vast/
Filmgate Films/Millennium Films/Scott Free Productios/Studiocanal/The
Kobal Collection, Front cover and extract from THE OTHER BOLEYN GIRL
by Philippa Gregory, Harper, 2011. © 2001 Philippa Gregory. Reprinted by
permission of HarperCollins Publishers Ltd., Front cover from AMERICA'S
QUEEN: THE LIFE OF JACQUELINE ONASSIS by Sarah Bradford (Penguin
Books, 2000, 2013). Reproduced with permission from Penguin Books Ltd.;
p.12 Sasha/Hulton Archive/Getty Images, Geraint Lewis/Alamy Stock
Photo; pp.12-13 Hrisi093/shutterstock; p.13 geraint Lewis/Alamy Stock
Photo, Diana Mower/shutterstock; p.15 Front cover from JEMIMA J by Jane
Green (PenguinBooks, 1998). Reproduced by permission from Penguin
Books Ltd.; p.17 Edwin Verin/shutterstock, Devid Camerlynck/
shutterstock, alexsvirid/shutterstock, Fer Gregory/shutterstock; p.18
iLoveCoffeeDesign/shutterstock, Nigel Sutherland/cartoonstock.com; p.19
Pavel Vakhrushev/shutterstock, Lalo De Almeida/Contrasto/Eyevine; p.22
Photo Shane O'Neill. Courtesy of The Atlantic Philanthropies; pp.22–23
OUP/Shutterstock/rSnapshotPhotos; p.23 Courtesy of The Atlantic
Philanthropies, Treatment Action Campaign, South Africa. Photo Audra
Melton/The Atlantic Philanthropies, Injury Prevention Partners - Vietnam.
Photo Audra Melton/The Atlantic Philanthropies, Cardiovascular Centre at
Hue Central Hospital - Vietnam Le Nhan Phuong/The Atlantic
Philanthropies, Courtesy of PublicAffairs; p.26 Andrey_Popov/
shutterstock, Mike Baldwin/cartoonstock.com; p.27 Mark Ralston/AFP/
Getty Images, Bettmann/Corbis, Blend Images/Alamy Stock, Imaginechina/
Corbis, Eric Draper/Getty Images, SSPL/Getty Images, David Jenkins/Getty
Images, US Air Force Photo/Alamy Stock Photo, Filippo Monteforte/AFP/
Getty Images, Tierfotoagentur/Alamy Stock Photo, Alfred Eisenstaedt/The
LIFE Picture Collection/Getty Images, Melissa and Jackson Brandts/Getty
Images, David Cannon for Dubai Duty Free via Getty Images; p.30 Rich

Legg/Getty Images, Charles Barsotti/Conde Nast/The Cartoon Bank; p.31
Mike Baldwin/cartoonstock.com; p.32 Imagno/Getty Images, Hulton
Archive/Getty Images, Vitaly Korovin/shutterstock, Kjpargeter/
shutterstock, LiliGraphie/shutterstock, Scisetti Alfio/shutterstock, Cover
of THE MEMOIRS OF SHERLOCK HOLMES Oxford World's Classics, (2009)
by Arthur Conan Doyle and edited by Christopher Roden, isbn:
9780199555482, OUP(2), Transcendental Graphics/Getty Images; p.33
SSPL/Getty Images, Lukiyanova Natalia/frenta/shutterstock, glaz/
shutterstock, Buyenlarge/Getty Images, OUP; p.34 Bettmann/Corbis, Dave
Carpenter/cartoonstock.com; p.35 Russell Kord/Alamy Stock Photo,
Photograph By David Yeo, Camera Press London; p.36 Copyright of the
photo provided: © Ron Mueck. Courtesy the artist, _Anthony d'Offay and
Hauser & Wirth.Ron Mueck, Seated Woman, 1999. Modern Art Museum of
Fort Worth, Texas; p.37 Aflo Co., Ltd./Alamy Stock Photo; pp.38,39
©Tigress Productions Limited. From the television series 'Edge of
Existence' and 'The Curious Tribe'; p.39 145/Alan Copson/Ocean/Corbis;
p.40 Fran/cartoonstock.com; p.41 Blend Images/Superstock; p.42 Courtesy
of L. Grissell(2), Finished Camel/Alamy Stock Photo; p.43 Clive Brunskill/
Getty Images, Anne-Christine Poujoulat/AFP/Getty Images, Jonathan
Larsen/Diadem Images/Alamy Stock Photo, Jetta Productions/Getty
Images; p.44 4x6/istockphoto, Rtimages/shutterstock; p.45 Pictorial Press
Ltd/Alamy Stock Photo, Bettmann/Corbis, gary warnimont/Alamy Stock
Photo, Corbis(2), GL Archive/Alamy Stock Photo, David Turnley/Corbis;
p.46 pio3/shutterstock, Olivier Le Moal/shutterstock, Jag_cz/shutterstock,
Lt. J W Brooke/ IWM via Getty Images, © Imperial War Museums (Q
24047); pp.46-47 Mansell/Getty Images, Willi Rolfes/ NiS/Minden Pictures/
Corbis; p.47 Popperfoto/Getty Images(2), Museum of London/Heritage
Images/Getty Images, Florilegius/Alamy Stock Photo, Boyer/Roger Viollet/
Getty Images; p.48 Yulia Mayorova/shutterstock, Fabrizio Bensch/Reuters/
Corbis; p.49 The National Archives/SSPL/Getty Images; p.50 DmyTo/
shutterstock.com, pio3/shutterstock; p.51 Mike Gruhn/cartoonstock.com;
p.52 Stockbyte/Getty Images; p.53 Kenneth Johansson/Corbis, David
Livingston/Getty Images, culliganphoto/Alamy Stock Photo; p.54 Sergey
Galushko/Alamy Stock Photo, Stockbyte/Getty Images; p.55 Imgorthand/
Getty Images, Alberto Incrocci/Getty Images, Dave Allen Photography/
shutterstock, Franz Pritz/Getty Images, Halfpoint/shutterstock; p.57 OUP/
Gareth Boden; p.58 Steve Bloom Images/Alamy Stock Photo, Jon Kopaloff/
FilmMagic/Getty Images, LUCAS CRANACH THE ELDER (1472-1553),
portrait of Georg Spalatin,1537. Oil on red beech, 4.6 × 22.5cm. Staatliche
Kunsthalle, Karlsruhe/AKG London, THE LAUGHING CAVALIER, 1624 (oil
on canvas), Hals, Frans (1582/3-1666)/© Wallace Collection, London,
UK/Bridgeman Images, Paul Burns/Getty Images, SELF PORTRAIT IN A
TURBAN WITH HER CHILD, 1786 (panel), Vigee-Lebrun, Elisabeth Louise
(1755-1842)/Louvre, Paris, France/Bridgeman Images, Courtesy Everett
Collection/REX Shutterstock, Stephane Cardinale/People Avenue/Corbis,
THE CHESHIRE CAT/British Library, London, UK/© British Library Board. All
Rights Reserved/Bridgeman Images; p.59 Ward Sutton The New Yorker
Collection/The Cartoon Bank, Peter Arno/Conde Nast/The Cartoon Bank;
p.60 Juniors Bildarchiv GmbH/Alamy Stock Photo; p.61 Popperfoto/Getty
Images, Ziggy Kaluzny/Getty Images, Jiji Press/AFP/Getty Images, Gen
Nishino/Getty Images, Peter Cade/Getty Images, Petro Feketa/Alamy Stock
Photo; p.62 The Sunday Times/News Syndication, Nick Morrish/BA; p.63
Excentro/shutterstock, By kind permission of Yvonne Pope Sintes, Barrie
Harwood Photography/Alamy Stock Photo, Mimadeo/shutterstock; p.64
Universal/ The Kobal Collection; p.66 Barcroft Media(2), Steve Russell/
Toronto Star via Getty Images; p.69 Alex Staroseltsev/shutterstock, Mary
Steinbacher/Getty Images, M. Eric Honeycutt/Getty Images, Peter Beavis/
Getty Images, quavondo/Getty Images, Robert Deutschman/Getty Images,
Ghislain & Marie David de Lossy/Getty Images; p.70 By kind permission of
Icon Books, Ian Shaw/Alamy Stock Photo, Sarahbean/shutterstock,
CREATISTA/shutterstock, Blue Jean Images/Superstock, ian west/Alamy
Stock Photo; p.71 Enka Parmur/shutterstock, vicgmyr/shutterstock,
Rebbeck_Images/istockphoto; p.72 Westend61/Corbis, Michael Ochs
Archives/Getty Images, Mondadori Portfolio via Getty Images; p.73 Joel
Rogers/Corbis, Jose Luis Roca/AFP/Getty Images; p.74 Franck CRUSIAUX/
Gamma-Rapho via Getty Images; p.75 Pierre Perrin/Zoko/Sygma/Corbis,
By permission of Keynote Artist Management photo ® Thorge Huter,
Courtesy of Penguin Group USA; p.76 Oliver Benn/Alamy Stock Photo; p.77
hulya-erkisi/Getty Images, BSIP/UIG/Getty Images, Nancy Kedersha/
Science Photo Library, Puwadol Jaturawutthichai/shutterstock, Thomas
Northcut/Getty Images, maga/shutterstock, Cultura/Judith Wagner
Fotografie/Getty Images, age fotostock/Alamy Stock Photo; p.78 piotr_pabijan/shutterstock; pp.78-79
Eddie Keogh/Reuters/Corbis; p.79 Cordelia Molloy/Science Photo Library,
Jezper/shutterstock; p.80 Ariel Skelley/Getty Images; p.81 piotr_pabijan/
shutterstock, Caters News Agency Ltd, imageBROKER/Alamy Stock Photo,
Image Source Salsa/Alamy Stock Photo, Action Press/REX Shutterstock,
Photri Images/Alamy Stock Photo; p.82 Jim Wileman(2), Theo Allofs/
Corbis, Vit Kovalcik/shutterstock; p.84 OUP/Gareth Boden; p.85 Andrey
Alyukhin/123rf.com, Jean/Jean/EMPICS Entertainment/Banksy images by
permission of Pest Control, Angel Jimenez de Luis/Getty Images,
Imaginechina/REX Shutterstock, Manuel Alvarez Alonso/Getty Images;
p.90 Mike Baldwin/cartoonstock.com; p.92 LOVEgraphic/shutterstock,
solarseven/shutterstock, Victor Tongdee/shutterstock, Algol/shutterstock;
p.93 NASA, INTERFOTO/Alamy Stock Photo, World History Archive/Alamy
Stock Photo, Arthur Buckley/NY Daily News Archive via Getty Images,
Heritage Image Partnership Ltd/Alamy Stock Photo, Lionel Cironneau/AP/
Press Association Images, Everett Collection/REX Shutterstock, Chris
Collins/Corbis, SI1 WENN Photos/Newscom, Peter Purdy/BIPs/Getty
Images; p.94 Chris Howes/Wild Places Photography/Alamy Stock Photo,
NASA Photo/Alamy Stock Photo, Suppakij1017/shutterstock; p.95
konradlew/istockphoto, Cultura Science/Jason Persoff Stormdoctor/Getty
Images, marilyn barbone/shutterstock; p.96 Space Frontiers/Getty Images,
NASA; p.97 Jerome Favre/Bloomberg via Getty Images, By Permission of
Little, Brown and Company. Malcolm Gladwell, THE TIPPING POINT: HOW
LITTLE THINGS CAN MAKE A BIG DIFFERENCE ISBN: 9780349113463, By
permission of Hush Puppies - a division of Wolverine Worldwide Europe
(2); p.98 Oli Scarff/Getty Images; p.99 Ron Dale/shutterstock, Andy Rain/
epa/Corbis, Guardian News & Media Ltd 2013; p.100 AD Hunter/
shutterstock, Guardian News & Media Ltd 2013; p.103 Sabphoto/
shutterstock; p.104 Olha Rohulya/shutterstock, eran yardeni/Alamy Stock
Photo, Peter Dedeurwaerder/shutterstock; p.105 Andrew Bret Wallis/Getty
Images; p.107 Robin Beckham/BEEPstock/Alamy Stock Photo, Simon
Potter/Getty Images, Image Source/Getty Images, Nattika/shutterstock,
rangizzz/shutterstock; p.109 FotografiaBasica/Getty Images; p.111 Danita
Delimont/Alamy Stock Photo, Bobby Bradley/Getty Images, Steve
Debenport/Getty Images; p.112 Tanya Constantine/Getty Images,
Vincenzo Lombardo/Getty Images; p.114 Radius Images/Alamy Stock
Photo, Ian Dagnall/Alamy Stock Photo, Sashatigar/shutterstock,
Ungureanu Alexandra/shutterstock, Moneca/shutterstock; p.115 Tetra
Images/Getty Images; p.116 Tomohiro Ohsumi/Bloomberg via Getty
Images(2); p.117 Alexander Fleming (1881-1955). British microbiologist./
Photo © Tarker/Bridgeman Images, Advertising Archives; p.165 Gang Liu/
shutterstock, Robyn Mackenzie/shutterstock; p.167 Mariia Masich/
shutterstock, Hannah Gal/Science Photo Library; p.168 Warner Bros/The
Kobal Collection; p.169 Steve Russell/Toronto Star via Getty Images, David
Corio/Redferns/Getty Images.